D0952883

THE ECSTASY OF SURRENDER

THE ECSTASY OF SURRENDER

12 SURPRISING WAYS LETTING GO CAN EMPOWER YOUR LIFE

JUDITH ORLOFF, M.D.

HARMONY
BOOKS · NEW YORK

Published in the United States by Harmony Books, an imprint of the
Crown Publishing Group, a division of Random House LLC,
a Penguin Random House Company, New York.
www.crownpublishing.com

Harmony Books is a registered trademark and the Circle colophon is a
trademark of Random House LLC.

Library of Congress Cataloging-in-Publication Data
Orloff, Judith.
The ecstasy of surrender : 12 surprising ways letting go can empower your life /
Judith Orloff, M.D.
    pages cm
1. Autonomy (Psychology) 2. Dependency (Psychology) 3. Stress management.
I. Title.
BF575.D34O75 2014
158.1—dc23   2013037087

ISBN 978-0-307-33820-4
eBook ISBN 978-0-8041-3707-2

Printed in the United States of America

Illustrations by Jane Whitney
Jacket design by Jess Morphew
Jacket art: © *Claudia McKinney/Phatpuppyart.com*

10 9 8 7 6 5 4 3 2 1

First Edition

FOR MY SPIRITUAL TEACHER

Grace is ever present. All that is necessary is that you surrender to it.

—RAMANA MAHARSHI

CONTENTS

Part Three

RELATIONSHIPS, LOVE, AND SENSUALITY

Part Four

MORTALITY AND IMMORTALITY:
CYCLES OF LIGHT

Part Five

EMBRACING ECSTASY

MY INITIATION INTO SURRENDER

MY LIFE HAS NEVER BEEN CONVENTIONAL. I'VE NEVER FIT INTO the mainstream. I've gotten used to being the exception to the rule—the one to whom things happen that don't happen to most people. As a child I had visions nobody could see. I could sense energy no one else could feel: it radiated around everything, from friends to the moon to a lonely discarded tin can. I am and always have been more at home in the dream world than awake. Because I am an empath, my body is highly sensitive in ways that confound what science defines as "normal."

I've gotten used to not reacting "like I'm supposed to." I get tired of people trying to fit me into some box that has nothing to do with who I am. I've gotten over trying to pass as "normal." I'd rather just be my creative, quirky self. Perhaps you can relate to my feelings because each of us is unique, beautiful, lovable, and surprising, spontaneously unfolding moment to moment.

That's why I was excited about writing a book on surrender. Writing is my passion, an alive, ever-changing meditation. I can happily spend years writing a book, so I asked myself, "What do I most want to write about? What do I most want to learn?" It has never interested me to just recount what I know. Instead, I write about what I yearn to discover. And my attraction was to the concept of surrender: the ability to be fluid, to bend like a willow in the wind during life's climaxes and lows. I want to be increasingly able not to clench, obsess, overthink, overcontrol, fight with my life, or let my stubborn streak obstruct my spiritual expansion.

I long to uncover the secrets of the universe—not just with my mind but with my heart, soul, and intuition. I want to fly. I want to soar. Who says we don't have wings? I don't care whether anyone says it's impossible.

So, with these priorities, I began writing this book. Surrender: it sounded good and it felt really right. I was ready to practice letting go more deeply. However, I didn't fully understand what I was signing up for which I found out included both losses and gains. In the process, life asked me to jump off a lot of ledges and have faith that all would be well. Why did this happen? Stable parts of my world started shifting in unexpected ways that required me to change. I've had to let go of a lot. For instance, I sold my condo where I wrote all my other books because of unrelenting noise and lengthy construction. I've exchanged a permanent address for a nomadic lifestyle and a post office box for now. During the move, I chose to give away most of my possessions to make a fresh start. That was just for openers. Then I had to let go of a love who left me; a therapist; many outmoded views about intimacy, including my erotic inhibitions; my obsessive attachment to certain men; and the desire for others to approve of my boyfriends, my intuitive explorations, or anything else. Throughout all this, I surrendered my ego again and again, trusting that a higher compassionate force was guiding me.

Why surrender? What's the advantage of going beyond your comfort zone? Whether you surrender a little or a lot, you'll experience more passion and power. As I did, you can also undergo a rebirth in areas where you may feel bored or stuck. This flux of letting go, not knowing but moving forward anyway is a vibrant process of refining your body and soul. I experienced this, not without fear—but not without hope, either. I've surrendered as the opposites of fear and joy often pulled at me simultaneously. But I was also melting into the dazzling beauty that was impelling my life. My intuition brought me here. I trust it more than anything. So I allowed myself to be led by my inner voice and by the mystery.

On this journey, I've discovered there's a strange and wonderful ecstasy that comes from surrendering. It creeps up on you. Then one day you look at yourself and you are shining. You may not know exactly how you arrived here but you're different, and it is a blessing.

By surrendering I've become healthier, braver, more intuitive, more flowing and fun, younger, more untamed, and more spiritually pliant. I've shed layers of fear and limitations that kept me locked in a life that was no longer large enough for me.

I tell you all this, the revelatory and the challenging parts, to prepare you for the greatest adventure you may ever go on. If you're like me—someone who wants to become everything you were meant to be and more—surrender is a doorway in. I offer myself as your guide. In this book, I want to share with you what I've learned about surrender. I want to trust you with my secrets. I can't predict what will happen to you or what you will have to let go of but I do know the result will be pure and good and right, and it will exceed your highest expectations. If you're game, I'll stay there beside you with love.

Hang on and ride the wild dragon of surrender to freedom.

You lose your grip, and then you slip
Into the masterpiece.
—LEONARD COHEN

....

AN INTRODUCTION TO LETTING GO:

PREPARING TO SURRENDER, TRUST, AND

FLOURISH

I HAVE A CONFESSION TO MAKE: I LOST CONTROL TODAY—BUT IN the most wonderful way. Before work, before the holy hours of seeing patients, before writing these pages, I just danced. During this secret time before the day began, my body moved to Bob Dylan's "Sad-Eyed Lady of the Lowlands." Spontaneous movements, nothing planned, nothing known or predictable. Venus rising in the predawn summer sky. Morning waves breaking at a distance: the Pacific Ocean, in its light and darkness, my companion for so long now. I did not hold back. I did not resist, argue, distrust, or overthink. I simply let go. This is the ecstasy of surrender.

In this book, I invite you to explore the sublime state of surrender: how to increasingly achieve it each day to improve the quality of your life, reduce stress, and have much more fun by lifting the curse of being overly serious. You'll learn to surrender in a world that relentlessly conspires to interrupt flow with instant messaging, texting, and emails at every turn. You'll also discover how to conquer fears and other resistances that stop you from letting go or keep you stuck in reverse. In Sanskrit, surrender is *samprada*—to give completely or deliver wholly over. I'm defining it as the grace of letting go at the right moment—the ability to accept what is, to exhale, and to flow downstream with the cycles of life instead of battling them, obsessively attaching to people and outcomes, and anxiously brooding.

I'm intrigued with the idea of surrender not as defeat or loss, as it is frequently thought of, but as a positive, intuitive way of living, a power that grows as you develop trust in the moment as well as in change and the unknown. Contrary to common stereotypes that equate surrender with weakness, I'm presenting it as a way to gain mastery of your life, not give up power. Surrender doesn't mean always saying yes to everything—this can be dangerous and unwise—but it does mean going fully with a decision even if it makes you withdraw from someone or say no to anger or fear. Nor does surrender mean being a pushover or allowing yourself to be taken advantage of. Quite the opposite. By knowing when to assert yourself and when to let go, you're actually taking back control of your life. Plus you get more of your needs met by being a smarter communicator. Throughout the book I'll show you how to put this liberating approach into action so you can flourish.

Though surrender may seem counterintuitive to making your goals happen, it can actually be the magical factor that facilitates this and relieves gridlock in relationships, work, and every other area, especially when it seems as though things couldn't get any worse. Life becomes easier when you're able to let go. Burdens will lift or lessen. Without wanting to, we may become overly defensive or controlling and hold our hearts back way too much. But surrender frees you from these cages so it'll feel safer to love. It also offers release when you're tired, stressed, overwhelmed or just want to close your eyes and not think about anything for a while. I'm fascinated by how hard it is for most of us to let go. Surrender is essential to delight in, say, the bliss of orgasm or a belly laugh, or to drift off to sleep. But we also need to learn how surrender is necessary to experience the subtler ecstasies in the rest of life.

The new take on surrender I'm proposing involves expanding your consciousness about how best to approach the world and yourself so that you can live more effortlessly and joyfully. We're all taught the virtues of being in control so surrendering may take getting used to. Unless we had extraordinary parents or teachers, most

of us didn't learn the merits of letting go. There are so many clench-
ings that happen to us each day and throughout a lifetime that we end
up shouldering chronic tension. It's difficult to be powerful and tense
at the same time. To lighten your load, surrendering involves reprogramming old habits and being willing to let go of the drama.

As with any new relationship, begin gradually to establish trust
and feel safe. See how surrender feels, note the advantages, and remember to appreciate the enjoyment, even ecstasy, often linked with
the release. Start by drinking a glass of water very slowly, savoring
every drop. Take a deep breath when you're caught in traffic (a necessity in Los Angeles, where many people would drive from their living
room to the kitchen if possible) or when your computer malfunctions.
With the pressure off, notice if you start hitting green lights more
frequently or if technological snafus resolve more quickly. Surrender
is especially useful in what astrologers call "Mercury-in-retrograde
phases," when everything backfires or goes wrong. As you start to
gain trust in the act of surrendering, challenge yourself with other
levels we'll discuss too. For instance: How can surrender benefit you
when you're arguing with your spouse? When your kids leave for
college? During periods when finances are hard? When you're overly
possessive or clingy with a partner who needs space? Or when you
can't lose weight despite dieting? In each situation you'll see where
surrender fits in and ways it can bring breakthroughs.

Try stretching past the border of your resistance, toward the degrees of trust you've never experienced, the serenity you've never allowed in. Then reach further. The practice of letting go will empower
you to get through difficult periods and also to celebrate joy because
both require a surrender. Ironically, surrendering to joy—really rel-
ishing it—may be the most unfamiliar act of all.

I'll address surrender step by step, offering a range of strategies
to put into action. For instance, the art of knowing when to *do* and
when *not* to do is a unifying theme of this book. Surrender doesn't
mean being passive or impotent. It means leaving no stone unturned
in manifesting your goals or solving a dilemma—but not letting the
death grip of over-efforting or being too obsessive sabotage you or
stop magic from intervening. As you'll see, sometimes it's better to

"be the mountain," to let things come to you. You'll learn to discern the correct balance between trying to make things happen and letting go, between doing all the work yourself and delegating responsibility. And, at the right moment, even surrendering the outcome itself can optimize the chance of achieving a goal as well as impart a merciful knowing that all is well even if that goal doesn't materialize. Of course, no one likes losing a friend or a partner or being uemployed, but you'll be able to accept these changes with more equanimity, without torturing yourself. As compassion grows, surrender becomes easier because you'll become gentler with your own journey and less tight-fisted with others. Still, what most tests my heart are those times when, despite the intensity of my desires, something is just not meant to be. Then and always, the basis of surrender is "to bloom right where we're planted," as St. Francis de Sales wrote. We must do our best to accept both satisfactions and letdowns in the spirit of growth.

What I adore about surrender is that it helps me attune to the natural rhythm of things. This is invaluable, for example, when I feel a project isn't moving "fast enough," when I'm without a lover but am longing for that connection, or when I'm working too hard or I'm creatively stuck and require a "reset" day to go inward and "sharpen the ax," as Abraham Lincoln said. Each instance trains me to honor proper timing and self-care, to stop worrying, and to enjoy what's good today. Getting to this state can be easier at some times, harder at others but it's where I want to be and what I continually strive for.

My passion for writing this book comes from witnessing the transformative effects of surrender on my patients' health and mood as well as on my own. I'm an assistant clinical professor of psychiatry at UCLA and have had a private practice for more than twenty years. In that time I've seen a vast array of people benefit: overbearing spouses, hyperstressed parents, insomniac money managers, love addicts, and out-of-work actors. Surrender is a secret to health and beauty. It makes you feel good and look good instead of becoming tight, tense, obsessive, and burned out by adrenaline and cortisol, stress hormones that cause you to age faster, die sooner, and develop a greater risk of heart disease, cancer, and inflammation. In contrast, the relaxation of surrender boosts your brain's endorphins—euphoric, opiate-like painkillers—and serotonin, which is a natural antidepressant. Think of how staggeringly different people of the same age can look and act. Our ability to be flexible with life plays a large role in this. As a psychiatrist, I've seen the repercussions when patients don't surrender—how their career dreams self-destruct when they push too hard, how they fight their children to the point of alienating them, how clenching around conflict can aggravate depression and pain. I understand and strongly empathize with people who are cornered in these dead-end places where nobody wants to wind up, but my message of hope to you is that there is a better way to be.

This book is so crucial to me because I work in a mainstream medical system that typically worships the intellect, equates statistics with reality, and views surrender as counterintuitive since it means giving up the fight or failing. This can apply to everything from how you communicate with your opinionated mother to how you deal with job stress or make health care decisions. Plus many doctors have a truly phobic, if unconscious, fear of death—they dread our final surrender because they're unable to sense that there's anything other than this material world, and they compensate by being overly controlled and technical. This compromises patient care and the compassion we medical practitioners must provide. During my psychiatric training, I was taught to help patients take control of their lives. This is essential but the counterbalancing advantages of letting go weren't equally emphasized. Though I have nothing but awe for the wonders of modern science and take enormous pride in being a physician, I intend to keep expanding the paradigm of conventional medical thinking, which has been my mission for the past two decades.

My basic job as a psychiatrist is to help patients deal with their problems so that they can lead happier lives. However, my approach combines mainstream medicine with the complementary fields of intuitive and energy medicine as well as spirituality to show how surrender can foster well-being and reduce suffering. Using this blended wisdom, I've been privileged to assist my patients in achieving balance during periods of both abundance and loss. My role isn't to fix their discomfort or to protect them. Rather, it's to use my intuition along with traditional psychiatric skills to catalyze each person's inner resources, helping him or her navigate life's passages with more ease, instinct, and love. The trick to this—a skill we all must learn—is to surrender to what each day brings, just as a surfer both navigates and yields to a great wave. You don't want to go too slow and resist the wave, nor do you want to go too fast or push because both lead only to pain and confusion. I teach patients to ride the momentum, to stay centered with open eyes and open hearts.

A key to surrender is that it comes from your intuition, not just the linear mind. The more surrendered you are, the more intuitive and open to a deeper flow of knowledge you will be. As you'll see in upcoming chapters, intuition lets you tap your inner genius, giving you access to solutions outside the bounds of ordinary reason and letting you travel in realms where time does not exist. Creative people know this well. The legendary musician, composer, and producer Quincy Jones says in my book *Positive Energy*: "Jazz people really trust intuition. They have to. They live off it. They exist because of it." My patients in the arts are quite familiar with surrendering to intuition—it's central to the creative process. However, with many of my analytical attorney patients who are always poised for the next clever chess move, it's often a huge operation to get them out of their heads, though it can be done. You can't think your way to surrender.

I'll teach you to access intuition, the inner voice that tells you the uncensored truth about things and provides flashes of insight both while you are awake and in your dreams. Intuition doesn't cater to what you want to hear, nor is it politically correct. It simply offers information; you can choose to act on it or not. When you slow down enough to listen, you can connect to your intuition which means listening to your gut instincts and your body's signals when you need to make a decision. It's heeding the goose bumps that convey what feels right and what feels off. It's watching for signs and synchronicities, those moments of perfect timing when you're shown a direction or when a situation suddenly falls into place. Most important, though, intuition lets you sense the vast domain of your heart and draw on that sustenance. You'll tap that intuition by remaining receptive and playful, not mentally straining to figure something out. I invite you to stay open. People with closed minds cannot experience expanded states of consciousness.

When working with patients, I always tune in to intuition, then weigh my intellect's input. First I ask myself, "How does this person or the decisions he or she is facing feel in my gut?" I'm also aware of any sensations and knowings that register about the issues a patient raises. Then I ask, "What does my mind think about the situation?" Especially thrilling are electric instants when intuition compels my mind to ask a particular question rather than pursuing a different line of reasoning simply because it seems logical to do so. The beauty of an intuition-propelled intellect is that the insights I'm moved toward are rich and alive compared to those I get from a purely rational assessment which can feel more constricted and superficial. I love what Albert Einstein said: "We must take care to not make the intellect our god. . . . It cannot lead; it can only serve."

The linear mind may be an astute analyzer and sparring partner, but it can't do what intuition and the heart can. It can't *feel* anything or expand beyond logic. It can't fully know love, compassion, or unrestrained creative flow. It cannot experience a spiritual connection resonant in every fiber. Nor can it intuit that death is not an end. Our mind's tendency is to clench, to calculate, to protect, to fear the unknown and what's "unproven."

A profound influence on my work with surrender has been my Daoist teacher with whom I've studied for over twenty years. Our practice entails cultivating the power of the heart, intuition, and meditation to hear inner stillness. It emphasizes harmonizing as the basis of surrender: with nature, with yourself, and with others. Especially during conflict, most people expect you to butt heads. But the strength of harmonizing is that it puts you in sync with people. By getting on their wavelength, you can intuitively size them up, then make informed, centered choices on how to proceed. It's similar to the ancient martial arts discipline of jujitsu which uses the art of softness and yielding (rather than brute force) to neutralize an opponent. I'll describe how harmonizing is the ultimate success strategy because you own the moment in a disarming way.

In this book, I'll ask you to think of surrender in specific terms so that you can pinpoint what it feels like in a range of circumstances from noisy neighbors to delayed flights, getting along with family, and excelling in your career. Over the years I've discovered there are four main types of surrender: intellectual, emotional, physical/sensual, and spiritual. As we go on, I'll discuss practical ways to apply these different facets of letting go. They'll work together to enhance your complete experience of letting go.

- *Intellectual surrender.* Your mind needs to understand the benefits of letting go so that it doesn't fight you. Give it some good reasons, such as "You'll feel relieved when you stop obsessing about that man" or "If you keep pressuring your boss about a promotion, he'll resent it." You want your intellect on your side.

- *Emotional surrender.* You'll allow yourself to feel and observe (not spew) your emotions instead of tightening around fear and worry or only partially allowing pleasure in. As you let go on an emotional level, you'll be able to release resentments and pass through difficulties more smoothly.

- *Physical/sensual surrender.* Breathing fully counteracts stiffness and buildup of stress or chronic pain, especially if you're glued to a computer all day. Regular movement such as stretching, yoga, walking, or aerobics expels tension and loosens you up. Also, this surrender includes exploring sexuality as well as the primal sensuality of nature, weather, and the elements. Gazing at the moon, a body of water, or a shooting star helps you realize that a natural universe surrounds you, instilling wonder and tranquility.

- *Spiritual surrender.* This involves opening to a compassionate force, a great kindness larger than your smaller "I-me-mine" identities (such as "I'm a good wife" or "I'm a hard worker"). This could be God, Goddess, nature, love, or something nameless. Through this connection, you begin to trust that something beautiful exists beyond the mundane. The sensation of having a hole in your gut can only be filled by spirit—no person, job, food, or drug can heal it. *Surrender isn't about giving up or giving in; it's about giving over.* You're not alone—never have been. Knowing this allows you to become more comfortable with uncertainty and makes letting go easier.

We'll also identify what inhibits you from surrendering so that you can remove these obstacles. Frequent fears include losing control or the upper hand, getting hurt, feeling vulnerable, not getting what you want, or lacking faith in a spiritual force that can assist you during turmoil. As you'll see, the answers may involve reprogramming negative, untrue conditioning from family such as "You can't trust anyone" or "Only wealthy people are successful." You'll also examine your resistance to joy in many areas. What stops you from madly loving someone? Being sexy? Applying for a daring job? Taking dance classes? Wearing a bathing suit? Each chapter of this book illustrates how surrender informs issues such as money, love, play, work, your body, and your health. *Lifting fear facilitates surrender so you can create a life of joy and grace.*

In my role as a physician, I've also seen that fear of death is a factor that contributes to my patients' reluctance to let go. They may not even be aware of this fear but when it is left unaddressed, it constricts their capacity to fully surrender to all aspects of life. I want to help you candidly address and make peace with your fear of death too. Only then will you know the solace that we are more than our bodies, that our spirits endure.

Talk about anxiety relief! I appreciate the Buddhist teaching of impermanence—that change is constant and nothing material lasts forever, yet there is still a "groundless ground." In other words, an invisible spiritual matrix exists everywhere at all times and it ensures that you'll always be supported. To Buddhists, everything we do is in preparation for our moment of death—the luminous appointment we all must keep, our ultimate surrender. This is meant not to be morbid but to be hopeful.

Most people in our culture are in denial about death and fear it. I've seen my physician colleagues, lovely, intelligent people, stop looking in the eyes of the dying and resort to icy technicalities when talking to a terminal patient's relatives. Even with my own mother's oncologist, who was also her close friend, I had to broach her need for hospice care when it was clear she was soon to pass. He said, "It's just too painful to admit. I feel like a failure that I couldn't keep Maxine alive and cure her cancer." Accepting the surrender of death crystallizes the here-and-now importance of love. (No one has ever told me on his or her deathbed, "I wish I'd worked more" or "If only I had more money or a larger stock portfolio.") Acknowledging death lets you live fully in every moment and love every person as if each encounter were your last. Then there won't always be a part of us holding back with our intimates, with our work, or with ourselves.

Each of us becomes ready to surrender for different reasons and the accompanying change is sometimes painful. Just as a seed starts in the darkness and then splits apart to become something larger and more alive, surrender impels our consciousness to grow—a worthy struggle that reaps amazing results. Often patients enter psychotherapy with me after undergoing the trial-by-fire version of surrender, their egos so beaten down that they've finally reached the point of saying, "I can't take it anymore—I have to change." A marketing executive, battling drugs at forty, said, "Lying unconscious and alone in an emergency room after a massive cocaine overdose forced me to surrender to getting sober. I knew it was surrender or die." A highly independent college professor who felt powerful by being "in control" told me, "My wife getting diagnosed with Alzheimer's disease let me realize that asking for help isn't a sign of weakness." A workaholic computer consultant said, "I took on so many clients that I started getting constant, excruciating back pain. This forced me to lighten up and say no to doing too much."

Crises can be a fierce motivator and surrender is invaluable when life is overwhelming or you're so upset it's hard to make it through the day. To my patients in this state I say, "Come sit next to me. Let's start over again. In each new moment there is a new beginning." I'm also dedicated to helping them—and *you*—benefit from miraculous but less dramatic everyday surrenders. Changing jobs, beginning a new relationship, and simply remembering to exhale before a meeting are all chances to let go and surrender to new adventures.

Some surrenders are critical to your immediate sanity if a situation is out of your hands. One patient who feared flying but had to do it monthly for work could really get freaked out on a plane, especially during turbulence. She'd keep telling herself, "I'm thirty thousand feet off the ground in a small metal capsule. Nothing's supporting us except thin air. This is nuts. If humans were meant to fly, God would've given us wings. We're going down." Then she'd break out in a cold sweat. That's where our work together could intervene. She had to surrender to the fact that for *everyone* it's an act of faith to get on a plane. True, she wasn't the pilot, but she could control one thing: her attitude. So instead of fixating on her anxieties, she surrendered by shifting her attention to positive thoughts, including faith in the pilot's skill. First she focused on the statistic that flying is actually a thousand times safer than driving in a car. That helped. Second, she lost herself in reading instead of obsessing over being confined in a plane. These strategies, along with breathing exercises and praying, enabled her to be less tense when she flew.

Over the years, my own surrenders have been many. I keep learning to trust the process, including facing my resistances and fears, as I melt more deeply into letting go. Particularly freeing has been my surrender to always feeling different from everyone else, like a sister from another planet. When I was a girl I never understood why I could accurately predict unnerving events such as earthquakes or the unexpected suicide of my parents' friend, or how I could feel someone's pain in my own body. I came from a lineage of physicians, including my parents, who were all rigorous scientific thinkers. My ongoing fascination for what is unseen, mysterious, and inexplicable seemed to clash with that. I lacked support for my childhood intuitions (they upset Mother and Dad so I was forbidden to mention them) or the subtle sensitivity of my constitution which is much like a wire without insulation. "You need a thicker skin," grown-ups told me over and over again. Today, my outsider spirit—I identify with rebels and misfits on the fringe—feels gratifying and real. These are my people, my tribe. I'm happiest in a jean skirt with turquoise toenails, watching the sun set with friends in the Santa Monica beach parking lot by the Ferris wheel. But in my early life I was desperately torn between wanting to fit in at those endless country club dinners that my Armani-clad parents herded me to and knowing I never would. Some people are born with the gene to make small talk but not me. Then as now, I have no idea how to do it. I'm still a bit unsocialized in conventional terms—I'm not wild about dressing up or going to cocktail parties. All this and more is me: the me I continue to discover and surrender to, and who I pray my loved ones will keep embracing as I evolve.

Some surrenders happen quickly. They immediately feel right and it's easy to let go. More often, though, I've observed that there are three common stages. As you practice the different surrenders in each chapter, keep a journal of the stages you go through, to log your progress. Be aware that resistance, a form of fear, is natural and to be expected. So don't be put off or discouraged by this aspect of yourself. It's simply one stage of the process that we all go through.

- *Stage 1: Resistance.* Initially, a part of you doesn't want to let go. Fears such as "I'll get hurt if I fall in love again," "I'll be a failure if I don't get promoted" or "Why start a diet? I'll never lose weight" stop you. Discuss your resistances with a friend or therapist to help you release them.

- *Stage 2: Acceptance.* Next, you become practical and use common sense to see the situation clearly. For instance, you realize, "My behavior isn't working so I'm willing to risk trying something new" or "I've done as much as I can for now. Pushing isn't helping. It's better to back off."

- *Stage 3: Letting go.* This may be a partial or full surrender. You don't have to feel completely ready. A little willingness is enough. Take it slow. Let go of a fear or counterproductive reaction just for a minute, an hour, a day. See how it feels to stop pushing. Do things differently. The benefits will motivate you to continue.

Be aware of these stages as you explore each topic in the book, from success to money and love. Above all, be patient with yourself, even if surrendering doesn't come immediately. You will get the hang of it. Don't let resistance stop you!

In praise of embracing surrender in daily life, I've divided my book into six parts. I'll describe how surrender can improve your relationships, health, and communication skills. I'll examine some tender, highly charged areas including sex and death, where, as I've noted, many of us get trapped in unenlightened mind-sets. You'll learn to view all of these in new, affirming ways so that you'll feel more at ease as you practice surrender. I'll clarify what forces *not* to surrender to such as fear and impatience. I'll also share my personal journey with each area, including my resistances and victories, because I want to use my life to lift yours, to make your path to letting go easier.

Every chapter has specific tools for surrender and quizzes to guide you with simple how-to exercises that give results. But this book doesn't have to be read in any particular order—you can go straight to the topic that's most relevant to you.

In "An Introduction to Letting Go," you'll learn what stops you and how you can surrender anything that prevents your happiness.

Part One, "Power and Money," describes how true power is intimately related to surrender. From this perspective, you'll redefine the meaning of success and prosperity, going beyond just the kind based on material accumulation or outer achievements. It involves surrendering to the power of a heart-based and intuitive intelligence to establish a "new normal." This lets us break the trance of the primitive "reptilian brain" which is programmed for survival through dominating others, aggression, and staying on top of the food chain.

You'll also take a self-assessment test to determine your relationship with power and letting go. This will establish a baseline of where you're at now so that you can record your progress as you apply surrender to different topics in this book. Furthermore, I'll help you see beyond the material seduction of money to tap its spirit of abundance. This entails viewing money as a conduit for the power of good and discarding the cockeyed notion of equating self-worth with net worth.

In Part Two, "Reading People and Communication," I'll teach

you the art of reading people, not just with your mind but also with the secret weapon of intuition. In my work, reading people gives me particular joy since deeper forms of relating let us get down to the business of loving one another. I'll describe methods to tune in to someone's voice, body language, priorities, and thinking. Reading people can stop you from getting drawn into drama. It lets you be more empathic and a better communicator. Then we'll discuss types of difficult people, including the anger addict, the gossip, and the narcissist, and how to successfully deal with them.

Part Three, "Relationships, Love, and Sensuality," will help you explore surrendering to the divinity of the body and sexual pleasure, even if you may feel out of contact with those aspects of yourself now. I'll share simple, comfortable techniques for opening sensuality (including stretching and touch) that you can try on your own or with a partner. I'll also discuss the vulnerable area of intimacy. When is it right to surrender to another? What if you're afraid of losing yourself in a lover? What is a soul mate, a soul friend, or déjà vu? How can you be attracted to someone and stay centered? What if your body is telling you yes about someone but your intuition is saying no? Why are you drawn to unavailable people? You'll see how karma, intuition, and common sense converge to reveal an inspired path for when and how to surrender to those with whom we feel kindred. We'll also return to the ancients' appreciation of nature, the elements, and animals as teachers and healers to rekindle your sensuality and your bond to sentient life forces. Nothing, absolutely nothing, happens in the universe by mistake. Aligning yourself with the flow of nature ensures that you'll be headed in the right direction.

Part Four, "Mortality and Immortality: Cycles of Light," describes the surrenders involved in the mysteries of illness, aging, death, and thereafter. We've been duped by society's fear-based attitudes. To surrender, it's essential to let go of fear, which is a form of resistance. You'll learn the Daoist practice of harmonizing with illness to heal instead of making "dis-ease" the enemy. You'll experience the radiance and passion of aging instead of feeling remorse or shame. You'll realize that death as an end is an illusion so you can examine other possibilities.

Part Five, "Embracing Ecstasy," conveys that the great reward of surrender is that you can celebrate joy as it continues to blossom throughout your life. The more you can surrender, the more joy you'll experience.

Writing this book has been a devotional for me, a prayer about deeply trusting the time I'm allotted and shedding my inhibitions and fear. For years I've been edging closer to surrender but now my longing for this state, for the tenderness of bowing to the deities of flow, has grown so compelling that everything else seems contingent on it—my relationships, my work, my embrace of goodness and the heart.

I want my life to be on fire. I want to inhabit the moment as much as I can and have a great time just being Judith. I want to trust intuition, instant by instant so that I can sense perfect timing—when to move ahead and when to wait. This is so appealing because it places me in the center of passion, attuning to what feels most true. Sometimes, I know I can be stubborn, willful, and impatient. Seeing this in me, my Daoist teacher has said, "You can be like a child in the backseat who keeps asking, 'Are we there yet?'" I know how small and frantic it feels to come from these spots. As much as anyone, I don't like it when I am denied what I want or when things go slower than my timetable. And I have strong appetites. I'm not just an angel. I am fascinated by all of life, light and dark. My interests have a wide range. In every experience, however, I'm an indefatigable explorer of better ways to live that are more in sync with intuition than with willfulness, fear, or desire. I specialize in pondering the imponderable to arrive at solutions that appeal to common sense by heeding the larger voices calling. I can't tolerate stagnating in old behaviors that are not spurring the evolution of my own growth as well as collective consciousness. Thus, being an apprentice of surrender has intense attraction for me. It offers me an opportunity to refine myself so that I'm not perpetrating my own suffering by oppressively clinging to things.

I am drawn to ecstasy and choose it as a friend rather than seeing it as a mysterious fluke that no one can replicate. Ecstasy is so enticing and rare because it comes from letting go, from trusting. I'm not talking about some blissed-out state that blinds you to discernment. Rather, it's the sweet clarity of surrender, the pleasure of connecting intimately to friends, family, lovers, work, the earth, and a primal current of knowledge untainted by fear. It's a revery for the moment—a realization that the person in front of you *is* your spiritual experience and you are his or hers! As I've said, nothing in this universe happens by mistake. Surrendering to the integrity of life's flow—really trusting it—is my ongoing practice and it can be yours too. Don't take my recommendations on blind faith. Try the strategies I'm suggesting. Evaluate the results. Allow this book to draw you into your own experience of surrender and your own capacity for ecstasy.

Part One

POWER AND MONEY

Be willing to surrender what you are for what you could become.
—MAHATMA GANDHI

....

1

THE FIRST SURRENDER

REDEFINING TRUE SUCCESS, POWER, AND

HAPPINESS

ARE YOU LONGING FOR YOUR LIFE TO BE EASIER AND MORE effortless? Would you like to stop pushing, micromanaging, and forcing things so you can relax? What if you could enjoy what you have instead of always lusting for more? What if you could live in "the zone," propelled by powerful currents toward the right people and opportunities? What if you could stop worrying about money? Let me take you to the magical place where the river flows. Something good is coming. Prepare to experience the ecstasy of surrender.

This chapter is a love letter to the powers of intention, intuition, and staying close to your essence in practical ways with practical real-world results. It's the perfect platform to make things happen in your life from work to love to finances. You'll excel without ever losing a sense of soul. Here I present a new step-by-step model of how to achieve true success and power with more ease and contentment. My approach is twofold. First, it's about devising action plans, staying positive, and using the grit of determination but without trying so hard that you burn out or sabotage yourself. You'll also keep releasing fear, a virus of the mind which can spread to many areas and restrict your success. Second, my approach involves surrendering to the mysterious, tender forces of goodness that are greater than your will to succeed. Allowing yourself to be guided by them makes the difference between feeling frustrated that success is "taking too long" and being carried on the wings of a great wind toward your destiny. Then, with these combined tactics which may seem antithetical but aren't, nothing can stop incredible experiences from coming your way.

Both as a physician and in a very intimate sense, I've seen that our attitudes about success and power can make or break our ability to surrender to flow on all levels. Why? What you and I believe—that success comes from integrity versus winning at any cost, from trusting your gut rather than succumbing to public opinion, from compassionate communication versus revenge, arrogance, or resentment—determines how we get along with ourselves and others.

Like many of us, I lead a busy life. I want to accomplish a lot. That's why surrender is so important to me. I'm tenacious in pursuing my goals but I don't want to clog the flow of success by micromanaging or inserting my will into places where grace belongs. I feel successful when goals are progressing or at least when I know I've given them my all. I've come to appreciate that surrender is never about being perfect. It's about doing your best and remaining authentic. Being perfect is impossible. It's just a futile attempt to control what can't be controlled. As a recovering workaholic, admittedly I still have a lot I want to achieve in my life, from writing to helping patients to teaching. There are also practical, noble daily successes, from working out to paying bills to making a dent in my to-do list of chores. I take pride in my accomplishments, large and small, no matter how mundane. I also realize that success doesn't have to involve many goals—what matters is the clarity and heart we bring to a task.

However, for me, success can never be about just what I "do." It's also when I can laugh, love, and really surrender to feeling happy about the tiniest things. It's reveling in winter thunderstorms, warm fires, night-blooming jasmine, and shooting stars. It's having a peaceful mind and some blessed downtime rather than knotting myself in frustration, especially when things fall apart. I don't always succeed at this, but I am learning. If we can't find even an inkling of happiness inside, on both steep and easy paths, we won't be able to enjoy the aspect of success that I'm suggesting which is independent of accomplishments. But this enjoyment is possible and I'll show you how to get there.

I'm a stickler about using time well. Life is precious. It goes by fast. Your time is the most valuable gift you can give to a goal or to a person. Thus, I intend to worship every moment and seek happiness wherever I go. Whether I'm presenting a keynote address or waiting in line in the post office, it's in the doing that the ecstasy comes. My advice is to call off your search for happiness. As Willa Cather writes, "What if Life itself were the sweetheart?" Happiness is here, now, present in every moment, if you allow it. Don't miss that gift. I even try to be happy when I'm miserable (it's possible to feel both at once!) by remembering the treasure of simply being alive. You can make happiness what you want it to be. Surrendering to what is, instead of bearing down or freaking out, is a fundamental secret to being happy that I want to share with you.

MASTERING THE ART OF EFFORTLESSNESS

Though surrender is typically considered counterintuitive to success—it's wrongly associated with weakness and defeat—I am here to tell you that it can make you more powerful. Surrender is all about winning. It gives you the maximum result with the minimum effort. Surrender lets you turn away from old ways of doing things so that you can regroup and grow stronger. In both your career and your relationships, it can benefit you when done at the right time and in the right way. Otherwise you can jinx success by over-efforting and being too intense. For grace to enter your life, you must make room for forces beyond your control.

Recently I gave a talk about how surrender furthers success at a TEDx (Technology, Energy, Design) conference for three hundred movers and shakers in business and health care. Following my talk I was honored to be interviewed by a group of middle school student journalists reporting on the conference. They asked me, "How is surrender helpful for kids and teenagers?" My response: "If you're lucky enough to learn how to surrender fear and worry early on, you'll be much more successful. Many kids are full of anxiety and feel pressured on all sides by assumptions and assignments from parents and teachers. You don't want to worry your way through school. Nor do you want to succumb to all the pressure. You're at a perfect age to practice surrendering stress and unrealistic expectations so you can be more open, relaxed, and able to enjoy the incredible life that is ahead of you." By their smiles I could see they liked that answer. It made sense to them.

Surrender opens you to states of grace where blessings of success are bestowed. You can't will grace to appear in your life but you can invite and welcome it in with a more surrendered outlook. Let the information I'm presenting about the proper role of taking action versus surrendering control enable you to excel in all areas. Striking this balance while also allowing grace to do its work lets you experience the art of effortlessness. In one sense, this entire book is about power: how to claim it, how to use it with both heart and intelligence, and how it can be misused or corrupted. And that's why we begin here.

In this chapter, you'll learn to reevaluate success and power in terms of what really matters. This takes courage and a willingness to radically question the status quo. Once you've identified affirming, durable beliefs about these topics, you'll have something priceless to keep surrendering to as you melt rigid, frigid, and fearful places within. What a relief it will be to dissolve all of that pent-up tension. This ongoing process is about purification and awakening as well as saving ourselves and our wild, precious world.

SURRENDERING TO A NEW PARADIGM: THE DANCE BETWEEN DESTINY AND WILL

A mogul who rises to the top by hurting people has a crippled heart and is an abuser, not a success, no one to admire. True success isn't using power just for power's sake to pump your ego or your profits up. It is never causing intentional harm for personal gain, no matter how much money or status you accumulate. I love that Google's intention statement as a small start-up company was "Don't be evil," an admirable code of conduct that urges all its employees to act honorably and treat others with respect. We all know that the saying "Nice guys finish last" equates niceness with weakness. For me, the factor that decides whether you finish first or last isn't about "being nice." It's about finding a smarter model for success where you're able to be nice but also know how to mindfully use power to reach your goal.

We need a new conversation around what it means to be successful and powerful to dispel dysfunctional stereotypes that keep us from soaring. We must break the rules of our psychotically materialistic society to find a more heartful way to live that yields concrete, everyday gains. We must reject the cult of greed which equates success with people who make an excess of money, whatever the tactics, and tells us that we have to become tightwads or fear-based about finances to feel safe in an unsafe world.

I've consistently seen with patients and in myself that resisting or stiffening during challenging times only increases stress and saps power, creating what I call a bunker mentality. Everything becomes about defensiveness, worry, and fear, not love. Similarly, people get more severely injured in accidents when they tense up. If you fight pain or adversity, the spasm of discomfort tightens. But when you relax, suffering lessens. This applies just as much to daily life. One patient got so uptight about money in the bad economy, she alienated her only daughter by refusing to help pay for her modest wedding on Santa Monica beach, though she could've afforded it. Another patient, a young, gifted actor just beginning his career, felt so inadequate around other "successful" performers, he'd freeze during auditions so his talent couldn't shine. Both patients undermined their own success by surrendering to fear, an automatic reaction they didn't know how to resist. In psychotherapy, I taught them to say no to fear and yes to the more loving, powerful parts of themselves, a conscious choice to move toward the positive. Similarly, I want to show you how flowing with challenges, rather than clenching onto fears and outmoded beliefs, enables you to solve problems more creatively. It's miraculous how much your energy and focus clear when you shift from holding back to letting go.

As part of this new conversation, I'd like you to factor intuition into your equation for success. This inner voice that tells you the truth about things is the antidote to fear and an overanxious mind. It's a creative ally that helps you hold a clearer, bolder vision of how to succeed, even when you're at an apparent dead end. In over two decades of practicing medicine in Los Angeles, I've seen it all when it comes to people trying to make it big in their careers—but what's often missing is intuition. I've watched my patients strive, hope, scheme, dream, get crushed, or triumph. But, prior to working with me, they were mostly driven by willpower, not their inner voice; this often threw off their choices. There's more to success than just determination or even passion.

That's where destiny comes in. It's the reason we came this way and it's what can make us whole. We can't control everything, as much as we may try. However, as I discovered in my life, the curveball is that destiny might not fit the scenario that you had in mind. As the Yiddish expression goes, "Man plans. God laughs." To align with and fulfill your destiny, listening to intuition is key in the new paradigm of power. You can't just think yourself there. Here, success is determined by your willingness to surrender to unexpected possibilities.

Let me tell you how intuition helped me find my true calling. In my early twenties, I'd dropped out of college to live with my artist boyfriend in an old converted brick Laundromat in Venice Beach. To help support us, I worked in the bedding department in the May Company, a job I enjoyed and which instilled in me a love for luxurious sheets and towels. During my time off, I volunteered in a parapsychology lab at UCLA with Dr. Thelma Moss, my mentor, and began to embrace my intuition after having been so frightened by it since childhood. Then one night I had a startling dream. In it, I was told, "You're going to become an MD, a psychiatrist, to have the credentials to legitimize intuition in medicine." In the dream this seemed perfectly reasonable, though when I awoke I felt like someone was playing a practical joke. Me, a psychiatrist? I am the daughter of two physicians and it might have seemed logical that I'd follow in their footsteps, but I'd never shown the slightest interest, nor had my parents pushed that since I was terrible in science. Besides, I'd been around physicians all my life. They were nice enough but, honestly, a bit boring, though there were exceptions, including my parents. I'd always been more creative and gravitated to eccentric artists and outsiders. I didn't know what career I'd choose, but going through fourteen years of medical training was definitely not my plan. In fact, after I took a career aptitude test in high school, the psychologist, whose brown hair was pinched in the scariest, tightest bun I'd ever seen, warned, "Never go into the helping professions! You're better off in the arts." It wasn't surprising. Back then, the thought of listening to someone else's problems had no appeal at all.

Still, since I was starting to trust my intuition, I decided to give my dream a chance, as absurd as it seemed to every logical fiber in my being. So I made an agreement with myself. I'd enroll in one course in Santa Monica City College just to see how it went. To my amazement, though I'd been out of school a few years and hadn't missed it, I lit up in this geography class. We studied the moon's cycles, the earth's strata, and how the wind formed—natural forces I'd always felt inexplicably connected to. And so my learning cycle began. One class became two, and then I continued on to complete fourteen years of medical training. This dream led me to my true calling.

About success, my point is that sometimes all you have to do is open up a crack to your intuition's guidance, whether you think it's doable or not. That's enough. I didn't need to completely surrender to the idea that I'd be a doctor. I didn't even have to believe that it was possible. However, what I did do was take a tiny step forward to allow for the possibility. Initially, my logical self kept insisting, "This is ridiculous." True, on one level it was. But logic doesn't know everything. Thank goodness I didn't allow it to jam the works of my destiny unfolding. I was riding an invisible wave that felt wonderful and right. I just tried to let go and trust it.

Personally and as a physician, I've come to view success in very simple terms. Bottom line, it means fulfilling your destiny without resisting that intuitive flow or letting logic talk you out of it. If you fight the flow or ignore your inner voice, success might not find you. This doesn't mean that you don't pursue your dreams. Go wild trying to manifest them. But, when you've done all you can, you must let go and surrender to what is meant to be. Otherwise, you just end up torturing yourself and getting nowhere, a painful scenario I've observed with numerous patients who kept clutching a dream that wasn't viable. I guarantee that if a job, a relationship, or wealth is meant for you, it will find you in Timbuktu. Still, the choice is yours to accept or decline. However, if something isn't your destiny, it just won't happen no matter how frustrating that feels or how hard you work for it. To paraphrase a Rolling Stones song, you can't always get what you want, but you get what you need. In the end, destiny is what happened or didn't happen in your life. Even so, to boost your chances of success, intuition puts you in synch with what's meant to be so that you can go for it!

Success is looking for you as much as you're looking for it, but you must recognize each other to click. The art of manifesting goals involves both effort and surrender. To achieve that balance, whether you're searching for passionate work or wanting a project to move ahead, practice the following exercise.

DISCOVERING YOUR DESTINY: A SURRENDERED PERSON'S GUIDE TO SUCCESS

With any goal, first set your intention such as "I'd like a higher-paying job" or "I want to change careers." Second, listen to your intuition to see if this goal feels right. If it does, do everything to make it happen. Then let go of the results as you let destiny and your angels work their magic. If your goal hasn't manifested yet, or there's a detour, get quiet for a few minutes and tune into the situation. Here's how:

- Make sure there are no interruptions.
- Sit upright in a comfortable position.
- Close your eyes. Take a few deep, slow breaths to relax.
- If thoughts come, picture them as clouds floating in the sky. Do not attach. Keep refocusing on your breath.
- Then listen to your intuition. In your gut, does the goal still feel right? If so, do you sense it is better to go slower? Be more

assertive? Wait? Explore other options? Notice any images, "aha" moments, helpful phrases, or knowings that come through.

Continue following your intuition's lead. If you have success, great. If a block persists, listen to any fresh insights your intuition offers. If a goal doesn't happen, know you did your best. It's natural to feel disappointed or angry. Still, focus on being grateful for the other blessings you've been given. Remember, when one door closes, another opens. Letting go of what's not working makes space for new possibilities. If your intuition suggests an idea you'd never thought of before, explore it. See if there is energy there. If so, go with the flow of where it takes you.

LIVING YOUR OWN LIFE, FINDING YOUR PURPOSE

Many patients come to me asking, "What is my purpose? How can I find it?" I tell them that we have many purposes in life—for instance, being a good friend or parent, rocking in our career, caring for elderly family members, overcoming fear, developing spirituality and heart. *I want to emphasize that it's not necessarily better to do "big" things— sometimes this is not what we're meant to do.* I will never tire of saying that small acts of love have enormous power. What is most crucial is that we bring our best to every situation. Our greatest purpose is to live life as it comes, be good people, help others when we can, and aim for a higher, more heartfelt level of existence.

Everyone has a unique calling whether it's running a country or managing an office, teaching kids or raising kids. One of my workshop participants sells yoyos on the streets of Manhattan, a vocation that brings her much joy, makes children giggle, and helps hardworking New Yorkers take a play break. One academic year I supervised Ann, an astute, sensitive UCLA medical student who's also a U.S. naval officer, an unusual combination. I was struck by the clarity Ann has about her own destiny, though it's not what one would've predicted from her conservative Lebanese background. She felt drawn to work with injured American military personnel in combat zones, an inspiring calling. Or I think of my Daoist teacher, who came to Los Angeles from Malaysia over twenty years ago to open a Chinese restaurant but ended up devoting his life to teaching spirituality. He says, "Success that comes to us naturally is most meaningful. What we strive for is less important"—a traditionally Daoist viewpoint that reveres the organic flow of things. In your life, focus on finding what's right for you.

From my viewpoint, one career choice is not better than another if it's your true path. At the start you never know how you can grow or what good you can achieve in the position you're in. With some patients I've seen that what they strive for is not what they're meant to do. Consulting your intuition will reveal the right path, not just some great idea or grandiose notion that has no relation to the trajectory of your spirit. Maybe you're happy with your career, and if so, that's wonderful. But if you aren't, let intuition lead you to your own brilliance.

Steve Jobs, the creator of Apple Computers, said in a rousing 2005 speech to Stanford University graduates, "Your time is limited so don't waste it living someone else's life. . . . Don't let the noise of others' opinions drown out your own inner voice. And most important, have the courage to follow your heart and intuition. They somehow already know what you truly want to become. Everything else is secondary." Jobs brought a messianic intensity to transforming our world's technology. Yes, he was intelligent, but his intuition took him into realms of genius. I hope his devotion to intuition inspires you, as it does me. In all your endeavors, let your inner voice spur you to find success and satisfaction.

Society has it backward. The surrender I'm asking of you is to realize that true success is about living from the inside out so you can be privy to intuitive wisdom and feel genuine contentment. Take some time to absorb the importance of this basic principle. It isn't just a theory, but a transformational shift in consciousness.

To discover your own truth about success and power—not anyone else's—I urge you to question what your parents, peers, or the world says. Examine ideas you've never examined before. There's what you're supposed to think, and there's what you really think when you look hard inside for what matters. Enlist both your intellect and your intuitive intelligence to see a wider view of what power means.

What has helped me do this in my life is that ever since I came out of the womb, for better or worse, I've always questioned authority. The corporate culture's "this is just the way it's done" attitude has always made me squirm in revolt. I question things not to be contrary but to find what genuinely feels right in my gut. When I was growing up, my physician mother kept telling people, "Judith's first word was 'no.'" She was both proud and rueful about raising a daughter who had such a mind of her own and didn't like being told what to do. I appreciate my rebel side which still gets excited by Alice Cooper and purple hair—but now I have more empathy for the challenges it posed for Mother when I didn't listen and then crossed all of her lines. As my confidence has grown and I've become more certain of my identity, I've mellowed a bit. I've also learned the satisfaction of reaching a middle ground with others while also staying true to myself and not dimming my fire.

Here's why it's so important for you to reevaluate power and success. When you believe you're a failure if you don't make a certain income, look a certain way, get a certain job, or have a certain type of house, you'll be missing out on magnificent qualities in yourself that signal true power. Plus, you'll be surrendering to negative, inaccurate visions about who you are that don't serve you. There's so much more to you and to us than that small way of thinking.

To wake up to a new paradigm of success and live it, you don't have to be old or sick or in crisis, though unfortunately many people require these radical incentives for their beliefs to change. There's nothing like facing your mortality or experiencing depression to quickly crystallize priorities so that you can surrender to new ways of living. However, at this very moment, if you're open, your perspective about power and success can start to shift without any crisis at all. You'll see how popular opinions about these issues are often fear-based and programmed by a part of your brain that is biologically obsessed with survival rather than awakening. Just because a majority agrees on something doesn't make it so.

STOP COMPARING YOURSELF TO OTHERS

As part of this new paradigm of success, it's also essential to surrender the habit of comparing ourselves to others, a skill you'll keep improving throughout this book. I realize that comparing is a natural tendency we all have. Sometimes it's neutral, for instance when you're simply evaluating similarities and differences. In addition, comparisons can be productive—say, when healthy competition prompts you to excel or if you're inspired to emulate those you admire. However, comparing hurts success when you become jealous or if you judge yourself as better or less than others. Interestingly, without comparisons jealousy couldn't exist. One patient argued, "Judith, comparing is part of human nature." I agree, but it's a part that needs to evolve. The type of success I'm advocating is based on a philosophy of abundance, not fear, jealousy, or scarcity. I'm not just dreaming of some distant utopian world. Your view of success can change in the here and now if you want it to.

What makes the habit of comparing so addictive? Society condones it, nearly everyone does it, your insecurities fuel it, and the habit is hard to break. Expect to encounter resistance to surrendering comparisons in many areas, including your body image, job, or bank account. Typically, you'll make progress and then slide back a little, but increasingly you'll feel the relief of succeeding without putting yourself above or below another. I don't care how much money people make or how "perfect" their life seems. Bottom line is, we're all on equal ground—an indisputable truth from where I stand. In a spiritual sense, comparing yourself to someone else is comparing apples and oranges. Why? Your life is uniquely designed for your growth. Every situation you encounter can help you become a stronger, more successful, and surrendered person. For all of us, living this takes practice. The following exercise offers strategies to assist you.

SURRENDER COMPARISONS, BUILD SELF-ESTEEM

Select one person to whom you compare yourself—perhaps a successful colleague or relative with the Midas touch, a coworker who received a promotion, or a skinny friend. Make this person your test case before you go on to others.

- *Turn around your attitude.* Shift your mind-set to focus on what you do have and what you're grateful for in life, not what you're lacking.

- *Give to others what you most desire for yourself.* Enlist this secret to success: If you want to be appreciated, appreciate others. If you want your work to be valued, value others' work. If you want love, give love. If you want a successful career, help another's career to flourish. What goes around comes around when you surrender comparisons.

- *Learn from a rival's positive points.* Get your mind off what you think you lack so you can learn from someone who has the success you desire. Yoko Ono said that if you transform jealousy to admiration, what you admire will become part of your life.

- *Wish a rival well.* This may be hard or even feel impossible, but try. It helps you let go of jealousy and attract more success.

Surrendering comparisons lets you put your eyes back on your own self and your own success—where they belong—instead of wasting energy obsessing over other people's good fortune or beating yourself up. Even if you don't completely mean what you say during this exercise, I advise that you "fake it until you make it," as twelve-step programs suggest. Often, just having the right intention and choosing the higher ground (even if you're not totally there yet) precedes an attitude change. You act "as if" until the new behavior becomes part of you. When your heart is in the right place, you'll become what you want to be. Praise yourself for all the baby steps you make in the direction of self-compassion and gratitude for your life.

WHAT DO TRUE SUCCESS AND POWER MEAN?

....

Try not to become a man of success but rather try to become a man of value.
—ALBERT EINSTEIN

Success has many facets. As a psychiatrist, I respect that each person has different values and needs. Marriage might mean success for one, misery for another. A six-figure income can represent success from doing a fulfilling job, or it can ruin someone by subsidizing a drug addiction. Beauty can mean a blessing for some, a descent into the horrors of anorexia for others. I've had the privilege of seeing my patients' raw, uncut realities—behind the flawless makeup and the mansions, behind the smiles that go on everywhere except with their spouses and children at home. I know well never to judge people's happiness simply by how they appear to the world.

Because of this, I want you to identify what success specifically means to *you*. I have a wide definition of success, and your job is just one part of it. I'm defining success as coming from both outer and inner sources. Outer success alone is flimsy when it's not matched by the sense of worth you feel inside. Success involves *doing* as well as *being*. It's about becoming integrated and whole.

I want you to view success as an undertaking driven by a healthy conscience and by a desire to improve yourself and be of service to others, no matter what your job is. Success is when you give your all, then let go of the results. Whether or not you land the job, the relationship, or any other goal, each outcome offers an elegant lesson in surrender. My Daoist teacher says, "If you have never met failure, you have never succeeded." As painful as it feels, sometimes you try your best but don't succeed. Though failure can be a blow to your ego and heart, learning to deal with it successfully, without getting hopeless or cynical, is a sign of a truly powerful person. Thus, success is the art of wielding power with humility and a sense of the sacred so that your ego won't be seduced by it—this applies to your family, work, or anywhere else. Otherwise the cost to your soul and to others is too high. Success can lead to a thriving career but it also must reflect how you deal with all aspects of living. Instead of simply getting what you want, it's the quality of who you are as a person along the way that matters.

What is power? How can you constructively harness it? *Power is strength*. In the world, it's your ability to get things done, to affect people, to create positive change, to achieve a quality of life; sometimes it's simply having a hand to hold. It's the awareness that if something isn't working in your life, you can make a change. However, your power comes from drawing on inner spiritual forces too. It's an elegant balance, to be in the world but not of it, to be able to tell the difference between light and shadow powers and then choose which to follow.

Success involves your ability to tap and surrender to the different sources of power, both material and spiritual, and use them for good. It's a path to contentment instead of constant frenetic striving. That's what this book is focused on and can help you attain.

I am not underestimating the value of external power. It can have enormous advantages. Consider Bill Gates using his wealth to fight AIDS, Oprah using her celebrity to promote literacy, and brave filmmakers such as Steven Spielberg who combine passion and clout to go against the Hollywood machine to make brilliant movies. Professional degrees carry weight too. In my life, I am forever grateful for my medical degree and all the doors it has opened for my work with intuition. It's the luxury of the well-off to pooh-pooh material-world power and to proclaim that inner power is all you need. A friend who's a Los Angeles County social worker and has seen it all says, "Tell that to a homeless woman who just wants food, clothing, and shelter to survive."

Power has different levels. As we'll discuss, it's as much about finances as it is about how you view your body, your relationships, your work, aging, and also death. To claim your full power, the kind that strengthens with time, you must address all of these in a surrendered way, not holding on too tightly to anything. But you must also reach further than the physical world to tap what's deep within you. If you don't, you'll wrongly perceive that the money, the position, and the degree are the only successes that matter, the only markers that can make you feel powerful. This is an illusion of our linear mind which is notoriously blind to its own limitations.

Here's a practical example of how surrendering assists you in manifesting the success and power you desire. When I first met my patient Big Al, an endearing hulk of a tattooed country musician from Mississippi, he was derailing his fledgling career by trying too hard. At twenty-two, Big Al was obsessed with climbing the Billboard charts and being a star. Anything less was a failure to him. He wasn't pretentious or an egomaniac. He was just impatient, immature, and more than a little macho. To make matters worse, Big Al mainly measured success by the number of seats he filled in a venue, not by the real enthusiasm of those who did show up, a critical indicator for building word-of-mouth support. Given these attitudes about success, you can understand his dismay at having sparse turnouts as his band toured every bar and county fair from Atlanta to Los Angeles. Still, he could really play guitar. Record labels had begun to call though each time he came close to a deal it would fall apart. Despite these letdowns, Big Al not only kept going but he became totally crazed about landing a contract. He told me, "I wouldn't take no for an answer. I kept calling and calling. I made record executives nervous. They started avoiding me but I couldn't give it a rest. Finally I burned myself out. I kept worrying. I didn't sleep. Exhausted, I had to take a break."

That's what led Big Al to me. I felt for this driven, charming young man who would sing me snatches of Loretta Lynn songs during our sessions. I know about wanting something so much that you sabotage yourself with all that pushing—and the physical and emotional fatigue that results. I know the frustration of a project taking what seems like too long to manifest. I also know what it's like to arrive for book signings with only a handful of people in the audience, a rite of passage for most new authors that can either build self-confidence and a surrendered approach to success or break you. Putting oneself out in public is not for the weak of heart. However, Big Al had fallen into a common trap: the death grip of his ambition was strangling the possibility of achieving it.

Big Al was a perfect example of how wanting something too

much can weaken your power. I told him, "Being assertive is fine but continually trying to force people to do what you want is a form of insanity—you repeat the same actions with the same negative results." Big Al had bottomed out doing things his way and was ready to surrender. Still, as we worked together, the chest-thumping macho voice in his head that bellowed, "You're not a real man if you're not in control" required lots of reassurance and reeducation. He needed to come to see that surrendering at the right times is sexy, smart, and powerful, not a betrayal of some masculine ethic.

My job as a psychotherapist gets easier when a patient comes in this beaten down by self-defeating behavior. With Big Al, timing was on my side. I made the most of his readiness by offering him tools that I'll share with you. These included meditating to calm his inner slave driver and connecting with a sense of spirit larger than himself while listening to his intuition about ways to succeed. What in our therapy worked best for Big Al? He told me, "Getting a better attitude and permission to lighten up so I could enjoy the ride wherever it took me, whether I got a Grammy or not." All of this took several months to sink in but the tool I offered that was of immediate use was reciting the Serenity Prayer. Big Al took a copy on the road with him and silently repeated it before each show and whenever he got too pushy or had anxious thoughts, especially in the middle of the night when his mind wouldn't turn off. The prayer goes: "God, grant me the serenity to accept the things I cannot change, the courage to change the things I can, and the wisdom to know the difference."

In your own life, the Serenity Prayer is a way to reclaim your power when you're worried, uncertain, or overzealous. I think of it as a "flare prayer." It's quick, to the point, and effective. This prayer illuminates the graceful dance between the personal and the spiritual: when to act, when to let go. It speaks to our power and our limitations; we're freed from having to be superhuman. To remind myself to surrender, I keep it taped on my refrigerator door. As a regular practice, I suggest you say this prayer. Then you can make discerning use of your time and resources. Let it be a staple in your quest for success.

As is true for many of us, Big Al didn't knowingly torpedo his career. He just got swept up in a frenzy to control with nothing to counter it. These days, Big Al is more accepting of and grateful for his life. He uses the Serenity Prayer with the other strategies I prescribed when his old ideas about success intrude. Today his career is heating up and he's having more fun. Big Al is hopeful but not fixated. He's experiencing his true power.

Even if you feel out of contact with your power now, I'll help you find it. As a first step, whether you're feeling strong today or discouraged by setbacks, these are attitudes to cultivate and emulate in others.

THREE ESSENTIAL KEYS TO SUCCESS

1. Be proud of who you are, not just what you have.

2. Appreciate the value of the love you offer to yourself and others.

3. Embody the good and do good in the unique sphere of your life. No act is too small to be meaningful.

SURRENDERING TO HAPPINESS: DO YOU FEEL THE FORCE?

Success isn't just about achievements; it's about loving life and allowing happiness in. Bliss is real when you can let go enough to feel the force. Your attitudes matter. Success isn't either outer or inner. However, the sequence of what you focus on is critical. First focus on the kind of person you want to be, then on outer accomplishments. If you focus on externals first, you'll be addicted to those sources of success, a house of cards that easily collapses. *You'll confuse who you are with what you have.* I'm proposing a different kind of life. Though success naturally reflects pride in, say, your job, your paycheck, and family, it can't only rely on these. In my medical practice, I've frequently seen that when celebrities' careers crash, they feel like nothing without an adoring public. I try to soften this agonizing fall from grace by offering new, more surrendered coping skills. I've also treated patients who have all that money can buy but feel too unhappy to enjoy it. One Fortune 500 CEO candidly told me, "I've met ill and handicapped children who're happier than I am." Contrary to media hype, having money doesn't make you a secure or content person. In fact, research shows that money frequently brings more problems to the wealthy than it solves. Also, it's easy to believe that something outside— meeting Mr. or Ms. Right, or winning the lottery—will bring lasting happiness. But to be happy, you must be willing to release this belief. An outer fix alone, no matter how uplifting, can't sustain happiness because you'll always be wanting more.

Neuroscience supports this. Studies show that we have a biologically determined set point for happiness just as we do for weight, a default setting we quickly return to whether we encounter good fortune (including money and fame) or hardship. However, the secret to shifting the set point—compared to simply having transient blips of happiness if something goes well—is to embrace a different kind of success within. Research reveals that biotech workers who regularly practiced mindfulness meditation (a technique where you focus on feelings of lovingkindness, gratitude, and the present moment) had increased activity in the brain's "happiness center" and felt healthier, more optimistic, and less stressed. Months later, follow-up studies showed that these workers had the same amount of boosted activity in that brain region, even if they'd stopped meditating, suggesting that their emotional set point had been raised.

Therefore, to stay happy, remember that a positive inner focus shapes outer successes. Otherwise you'll be stuck on the hamster wheel of constant striving without any lasting gratification. Once you've reached a goal, you're immediately racing on to the next. I've been there. Surrendering to happiness means being grateful for what you have achieved, even if it's just getting out of bed in the morning during trying times. Gratitude is an ecstatic feeling, a way to allow contentment in. Try it for a second, a minute, then more. Savor how this feels. As is true for many of my patients, contentment may take some getting used to—focusing on discontent is much more familiar—but you deserve to feel that good. Surrendering to happiness also means letting everyday life delight you, giving thanks for the love that is around you, for your body, for your breath. I know how depleting the "If only I could succeed with ___ I'd be happy" mentality can be. I've been caught in it more than once in my life! However, I want you to understand that this mind-set is an illusion. It leads to nothing but a craving for more.

As you go on to discover new levels of power in yourself, let this sink in: *Material success, as financially comfortable as it can make you, as pleasant as it can be, isn't required for happiness. It won't make you any happier than you would be otherwise in the long run.* So part of success is being smart enough to know what *can* make you happy and going after that as your base. If you are king or queen of the world but feel joyless, what's the point?

THE HABITS OF SURRENDERED PEOPLE: HOW SURRENDERED ARE YOU?

Since being able to surrender at the right moments strengthens your power, it's essential to examine how you can let go more easily and when overcontrol works against you. As in shamanic practice, you must be trained in how to use power well. You'll learn to approach true success with awareness.

In my medical practice, I've identified specific habits of surrendered people that dramatically enhance their health and allow them to excel in many aspects of their lives. I help my patients develop these habits as part of psychotherapy. To find out how surrendered you are on a range of topics that we'll address here and in future chapters, including work, play, and aging, take the following questionnaire. It's a way for you to refine your beliefs and identify where you get hooked by sabotaging ones. This self-assessment tool will let you evaluate success and power by a new set of standards. Answer "mostly true" or "mostly untrue" to each question. Approach the questions in the spirit of curiosity and growth. The purpose is to get a baseline score, then watch it improve as you apply the techniques in this book. This will clarify which areas are flowing in a successful direction and which ones aren't.

THE SURRENDER TEST

	Mostly true	Mostly untrue
1. I recognize I cannot control everything.	_____	_____
2. After I've done what's possible to make things happen or change a situation, I can let go and accept life without fighting it.	_____	_____
3. I don't try to force things when a door is shut.	_____	_____
4. I am comfortable with uncertainty.	_____	_____
5. I remember to exhale during stress.	_____	_____
6. I'm able to give and receive love.	_____	_____
7. I can feel powerful without dominating others or telling family and friends what to do.	_____	_____
8. I don't withhold attention or love or keep people dangling to feel in control.	_____	_____
9. I feel successful apart from my job or net worth.	_____	_____
10. I see my body as sacred and don't obsess on weight or wrinkles.	_____	_____
11. I can accept the aging process and feel good about myself.	_____	_____
12. I don't compare myself to others.	_____	_____
13. I can let go and enjoy lovemaking.	_____	_____
14. I feel sensually connected to nature.	_____	_____
15. I practice physical movement to keep my body flexible and healthy.	_____	_____
16. If I'm ill, I practice self-compassion and surrender to the healing process instead of beating myself up.	_____	_____
17. I'm in touch with a sense of spirituality larger than my will.	_____	_____

	Mostly true	Mostly untrue
18. I listen to my intuition to help make decisions, especially when I don't know the answer or face obstacles.	_____	_____
19. I'm open to new ideas and can let go of ones I once held to be true.	_____	_____
20. I can embrace happiness.	_____	_____
21. I allow myself to experience loss and grief without bottling up my feelings.	_____	_____
22. I don't fear death.	_____	_____
23. I'm not attached to "being right" and can admit when I'm wrong.	_____	_____
24. I can be spontaneous and playful.	_____	_____
25. I can welcome silence, stillness, and meditation.	_____	_____

How to Interpret This Test

To calculate your score, total the number of "mostly true" responses. A score of 20 to 25 suggests that you're experiencing a very high level of surrender in your life. A score of 15 to 19 suggests a high level. A score of 6 to 14 suggests a moderate level. A score of 5 or below indicates a minimal level. A score of zero indicates that it's difficult for you to release excessive control but surrender is closer than you think as you begin to practice it more.

Whether your "surrender score" is high or low, be kind to yourself in areas where you may be clutching tightly to unproductive habits and behaviors. Pay special attention to any emotionally charged responses to questions where you dig in your heels, perhaps too much, about why you can't surrender. For instance, "I'm finally finished with my degree but I'll never get a job" or "I won't forgive my boss for not giving me a promotion. It is so unfair." Be gentle with your resistance, rigidity, or fear of letting go. Don't judge yourself. It's all fine. At this stage, simply notice where you're at as nondefensively as possible. While reading on, just keep an open mind for new, more surrendered approaches to an issue that can result in greater success.

The information you uncover from this test can benefit you in important ways. You'll have better insight into how you're conditioned to respond so you're not condemned to repeating negative patterns where you clutch instead of let go. You'll begin to clear your fears and resentments so they don't block you. You won't have to obsessively control everyone and everything to feel comfortable or safe. You'll be loving without always watching your back so that you don't get hurt. These are just a few of the good things that await you.

Now that you know where you stand, you can start to develop the habits of a surrendered person by practicing the strategies in this book. What matters most is your willingness to increasingly let go and move with the flow. The goal is to become more relaxed and fluid, less tightly strung. At this point, no worries if you don't know how or if you're feeling frustrated, stuck, or caught in what the Swiss psychiatrist Carl Jung called "the devilish, skillfully twined knot that locks and seals you." This is all about to change. Now is your opportunity to remove what binds your power and to become more outrageously successful than ever before.

SURRENDER AFFIRMATION FOR SUCCESS

I am ready to enjoy the contentment and relaxation that comes from true success. I acknowledge that I am so much more than just my job or my bank account. I want to release the notion that status, riches, or acclaim are the solutions to happiness. I love and respect myself always.

There is no power on earth like unconditional love.
—WARREN BUFFETT

2

THE SECOND SURRENDER

FOUR VITAL INSIGHTS INTO POWER AND

LETTING GO

I HAVE MANY AMAZING STORIES TO TELL YOU ABOUT THE RELA-
tionship between power and surrender in daily life. I want to help
you discover a vision of lasting success beyond one-upsmanship,
social status, and income. What excites me more than those limited
standards of self-worth is how surrender can revolutionize success
when you let go to an intelligence greater than the self with all its
advantages. Pairing this with clear thinking and a good heart is an
unstoppable combination.

I'd like to highlight four vital insights that will give you immediate access to new levels of power in various areas including your job,
finances, and relationships. You'll benefit whether you're negotiating
a raise, planning a career move, or simply seeking abundance in your
life. Do you realize how much more power you'll have when you're
not overly attached to the results? Your power will keep increasing
as you let yourself surrender using the strategies I'm suggesting. The
infinite kind of power I'm talking about boggles the linear mind, but
your intuitive self feels more at home with truths that go further
than logic. This power is fluid, cellular, a force that keeps growing
within. Accessing it requires a light touch and a willingness to get

out of your own way so it can flow. You are a vessel for this power, never the master of it.

Here's where my system differs from old-school beliefs. When power becomes just about ego, its potential shrivels; it becomes a relic of what it could be. Clenching only depletes power and cuts you off from the source. The answer is to respect the strengths of the ego but also become larger than it. That's why I'm so drawn to kneel in prayer during my meditations, grateful for even the smallest hints that a greater power has to offer. You can't insist on this power but you can rely on the generosity of its flow if you stay true to the best in yourself.

Many people have it backward. They go after power in the world to define themselves, to feel significant, rather than first connecting to an inner, heartful power base, a much stronger position. Realizing that your will alone is not the last word on power opens you to other sources to connect to and gives you an edge. Try this chapter's methods even if they seem unfamiliar to you or run counter to everything you've heard people say. We'll start with conventional paradigms of power, their strengths and weaknesses. You need to know this, especially if you live or work in situations that operate by these rules. Then you can rally your skills within that system and also clearly recognize age-old power games so you're not sucked into them. In addition, I'll offer you solutions to generate success in other, more expansive ways that surpass this antiquated paradigm. You'll consider: Why do I want power? What blocks it or scares me about surrendering to it? Am I addicted to it? Where do I give it away? How can I reclaim it?

External power is catnip for the ego and control freaks. Too many people lack insight and compassion about how to use their influence well; this makes power dangerous. To achieve a well-rounded balance of power, you'll learn to choose what types (light or shadow) you want to surrender to. The following insights will accelerate your success in using specific tools for surrender.

THE FIRST INSIGHT:
BREAK THE TRANCE OF THE REPTILIAN BRAIN: WHY POWER IS SO SEDUCTIVE

....

The reptilian complex in the human brain is in some sense performing dinosaur functions still.
—CARL SAGAN

Power is so seductive because it appeals to our most ancient, hardwired impulse for survival located in the reptilian brain. Think of this structure at the base of your brain right above the spinal cord as your primal self. Its biological directive is simple: to keep us alive. How? By controlling vital functions such as breathing, heart rate, and blood pressure. Also it gives us the drive to get ahead and assert ourselves with others and in our environment to protect us from threats. In fact, this part of our anatomy is so tenacious it can even keep operating when people are pronounced brain-dead and other organs have long since yielded to the inevitable. Though our reptilian drive plays an indispensable role in our lives, we may not realize how heavily it programs us, too often trumping more enlightened responses. The difficulty is that it reacts to perceived threats, even non-life-threatening ones, as if we were being attacked by a tiger in the jungle—not a smart or sensitive way to deal with troublesome people or situations. Surrender is a dirty word to the reptilian brain; it equates it only with extinction.

I'm going to show you a better way to be. This part of our brain is not all of who we are, but when it remains unconscious, it can distort our self-image, work, relationships, sexuality, and ambitions for success. We often see raw reptilian power in daily life: the maniac who cuts you off in traffic, the heartless conglomerate that takes over your company, the "might makes right" rationale for endless wars. Also, it's evident in kids gleefully transfixed by bloody video games in which they annihilate foes with savage gusto. I observe a surprising amount of reptilian drive while shopping at Whole Foods among the mellow, health-conscious crowd. One day a friend—a Hungarian pistol in her late seventies—nearly ran over me with a shopping cart. She wasn't just in a hurry. She wanted to assert that she owned that aisle; she was marking her territory. And we all know to watch out for those supermommies in their yoga outfits and SUVs, lest we take our lives in our hands by getting in their way as they barrel though their busy days. Many of us lack enough self-knowledge to resist obeying our reptilian impulses. Thus we surrender to them and they possess us, frequently to our detriment.

Whether simply aggressive or ruthless, the reptilian brain is fixated on:

- Survival of the fittest.

- Rising to the top of the pecking order.

- A kill-or-be-killed instinct.

- Hunting, conquering, and domination.

- A marking of territory to defend against intruders (including behaviors ranging from putting your arm around your spouse if someone flirts with him or her to gang turf wars).

How the reptilian brain influences us as men and women is complex, tempered by many factors ranging from our parents' values to our own degree of enlightenment. But here I'm addressing only basic biological tendencies for both sexes. I'm not stereotyping by gender or minimizing how male/female roles have evolved in many cultures today. On the most primitive level, here are some biological tendencies to consider.

In men, reptilian power is the sense of taking charge and the testosterone rush a man gets from being a muscle-flexing hunter-gatherer who kills the food, reproduces, and protects his family. Research has documented that this also has an erotic effect via increased testosterone. It makes a man feel potent so he wants to procreate: a clever incentive for enhancing survival. Even now, don't society's conventional criteria for success mean having a "good job," advancing up the pecking order, and being the breadwinner for the family? If the provider is unable to do this, he and others may consider him a failure.

Though this drive motivates a woman's ambition in the workplace, it's closely linked to procreation. It impels a woman to find the strongest mate—both protector and companion—to bear offspring with. Hence the sometimes crazy-making sexual pull of the biological clock. (Of course, female warriors have always existed and mothers are fierce defenders of their young.) A woman's reptilian drive can also make her automatically react to a male's position of power, whether he's the head of a tribe or a mega-millionaire, by responding to him sexually. The female brain's primitive pairing of erotic desire with a successful mate partially explains why, throughout history, many women have been attracted to rich and powerful men. As a psychiatrist and a woman, I tell you: this isn't an instinct you want to have guide your romantic life. Why? It doesn't factor in a partner's loving heart and sensitivity so you might end up with a "successful" narcissistic control freak. As you'll see in Chapter 8, in which I discuss sexuality, there are much healthier triggers for attraction you can surrender to.

How does this information make you more powerful today? The upside for both sexes is that your reptilian brain motivates you to succeed in your career, rigorously compete, and provide for and protect your family. However, the downside—and it's a gigantic one—is that it's clueless about the worth of other kinds of power since it turns everything into a question of fear and survival. Although our brains have evolved higher centers for emotions (limbic lobe) and reasoning (cerebral cortex), when it comes to primal power, the reptilian brain often keeps us locked in a trance.

From a reptilian paradigm, here are some common beliefs that can limit you if you're controlled by them:

- Success will always depend on being stronger, bigger, better, and richer than others.

- Being in control and making conquests are valued over sensitivity (reptiles are cold-blooded and emotionless; some snakes abandon their young after birth).

- With a predator-in-the-jungle mind-set, you will reveal only the minimum of information necessary to gain leverage over people, and never show weakness. Many attorneys as well as Wall Street and Hollywood power brokers are known for operating like this.

- To feel attractive, you'll need to be young and tall with washboard abs and thick hair if you're a man, or young with a symmetrical face and a curvy figure if you're a woman. These biological markers of a reproductively desirable mate then determine what we judge as "handsome" or "beautiful." (Angels, however, might define our beauty quite differently!)

Think about it: is this the reality you want to dictate your views of success? Not me. I cringe at such a grim prospect. Why? *Because in our world, that paradigm values the love of power over the power of love.* Relationships, even with your spouse, can be reduced to power struggles and mind games. As Henry Kissinger said, "Power is the ultimate aphrodisiac." Power becomes the intoxicating addiction that we surrender to, more than other goals or intimacies, though many people aren't aware enough to realize or admit it because that behavior is so automatic and so often condoned by others.

Here's a diagram of the brain that shows the relationship of its different lobes: reptilian (brain stem), limbic, and cerebral cortex. As you access your full power, it's helpful to visualize the geographical shift in your brain that you will make.

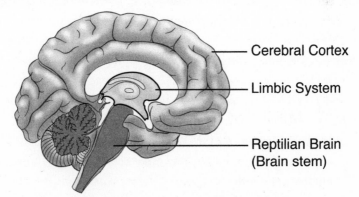

[Figure 1.] Reptilian Brain, Limbic System, and Cerebral Cortex Diagram

Surrendering the Addiction to Power: Using Your Reptilian Brain Plus More

Let's capitalize on the assets of our reptilian brain by channeling those assets positively, and also reaching beyond them to claim a fuller spectrum of powers. No one wants to be controlled by a Stone Age brain in a modern world that begs for us to be more compassionate in order to survive in a way that truly sustains us. Once we can recognize our reptilian impulses we can choose other options. We won't have to become the limited person musician Leonard Cohen sang about: "you who must leave everything that you cannot control. It begins with your family, but soon it comes around to your soul." Our hearts are larger and more generous than our genetic or psychological programming. Our spirits know a different kind of power, a greater power. That is what I will help you surrender to.

Of course, as a psychiatrist, I appreciate that changing our perspective in this way can be like turning the *Titanic*. However, life sometimes assists you in opening your mind and surrendering to fresh ways of thinking. Listen to how Gerald Levin, formerly CEO of Time Warner, found a new paradigm of success and power to live by. What motivated him to change? He told me:

> Business had always been about leverage and negotiation. I had to get one up on you to kill the competition. I held my cards close to my vest. I would only divulge what served my purpose, not yours. In the old power paradigm, if I showed weakness, I wouldn't be effective. So I'd better be superman in board meetings. When I was diagnosed with prostate cancer, the company said, "Tell no one." I went into surgery under an assumed name. Employees thought I was on vacation. The fear was that as CEO, if I showed vulnerability, the company would get attacked by a foe. It's a Neanderthal mentality.
>
> I was at the top of my corporate game when my son, a teacher in the Bronx, got murdered. The AOL–Time Warner merger that I had created was in trouble. To cope, I shut down my feelings. I didn't know who I was or where I was going. Then I fell in love with my wife, Laurie. She had a healing center which was based on collaboration and

spiritual values, a radically different paradigm than corporations. So eventually, after leaving Time Warner, I started working there.

What role did surrender play in his transformation? He told me:

Surrender meant giving up the illusion that I alone control my environment and my destiny. Nor did I carry the impossible burden of having all the answers. Since death, loss, and change are inevitable, I had to craft my identity around something deeper that would last longer than the trappings of external power. Once I could "surrender" to the sense of being connected to a greater spirituality, I used my experience in our healing work to serve others. Now I'm on a spiritual journey, one that I intend to savor every step of the way.

From Gerald Levin's candor, we can learn about power as it is conventionally seen, and power as it could be. The lessons aren't just about corporations. They apply to psychological dynamics with your supervisor, employees, or coworkers that can affect your success. Even if you don't change jobs, how you approach people can evolve. Understanding the rules and drawbacks of traditional power, you'll be able to succeed in any system. Whether you work in a diner or at the Pentagon, you can utilize the principles of surrender to better your situation. Here are some strategies to practice.

SURRENDER TO NEW KINDS OF POWER

- *Practice intellectual surrender.* The key to this surrender is making your mind feel safe enough to soften resistance to new ideas by supplying good reasons to do so. Here's how. First, reassure it: "I'm extending my power base, becoming more a master of my own fate. I'm not giving up anything or ignoring my survival instincts." Next, remind yourself what will improve in your life by seeing power in larger terms. For instance, "If I don't have to control everything, my stress hormones will decrease so I can relax. When I'm less uptight, I'll have more energy and confidence. I'll live longer, have better sex and relationships." You're giving your intellect a say in the decision to update your perspective and let go of knee-jerk reactions. Now you can experiment with other ways to be.

- *Surrender old behaviors and shift out of the reptilian power mode.* The quickest way to release old behaviors is to try new ones. List three habits you'd like to let go of. For instance:

    1. I yell at people who cut in front of me in line.
    2. I have to be right or have the last word to feel powerful.
    3. I'm afraid to share information with coworkers because they'll get ahead of me.

    Then, just once, do the opposite. For instance, if a guy cuts in front of you in line at the market, it's natural to feel upset, but choose to respond from a calmer place. Smile at him (genuinely, not sarcastically) and graciously let him and every one of his six children in. Or admit to your mother-in-law that you're wrong and, of course, she's right. Or, as a gesture of camaraderie, share information with a diligent coworker (not the office rip-off artist), simply to be helpful. Afterward, notice others' reactions. When you refuse to engage in typical power plays, I predict you'll see a lot of faces lighting up. People will get happier around you, give you unexpected hugs, even reciprocate your kindness. You'll be more appreciated and trusted. When you help someone else, you always help yourself. This feels wonderful and also attracts more success to you. If you like the results of this approach, keep using it.

- *Surrender ineffective communication styles.* Reptilian types take pride in being rulers of their domain. The art of communicating with them is to support what they do well, then clearly express your own needs. For instance, genuinely commend a macho boss about how much time and effort he or she is putting into the business, saying, "You've made terrific changes in our department." Then wait for the right opening to mention a pet project you have in mind that will enhance profits. Applaud your husband on his success with a business deal, then discuss spending more quality time together. The worst thing you can say to someone operating in the reptilian paradigm is "You let me down" or "I'm sorry you're having difficulty with ___." In their eyes, you're questioning their prowess in the world. They feel uncomfortable admitting that there's room for improvement. Naturally, no one likes being criticized, but people in this mode will shut down, deny, or go on the attack when their warrior-selves are challenged. Therefore, frame everything with respect to their values. This isn't simply ego-stroking. It's honoring what's meaningful to them.

Surrendering to new kinds of power lets you approach the reptilian mind-set more discerningly. You're opening the heart, which in turn allows you to start feeling the ease, even ecstasy of surrender. I realize that this doesn't have the super-intense adrenaline surge of the reptilian "I'll get you back" aggression that some people live for, but it is one of the most peaceful, luscious, restorative sensations I know. It's crucial to get used to feeling that good—which, paradoxically, is difficult for many of us. Surrendering, in this sense, means weaning ourselves off an addiction to adrenaline power surges and embracing the consciously sought pleasure of higher ground solutions. No one's perfect. Just give it your best. Doing this is emotional evolution.

THE SECOND INSIGHT:
BEYOND THE ALPHA DOG AND QUEEN BEE: SURRENDER
TO YOUR SPIRITUAL POWER

....

Love conquers all things; let us surrender to Love.
—VIRGIL

Alpha dogs and queen bees (alpha females) are those in positions of power whom others follow and defer to. They savor control, making the rules, and leading. It's often hard for them to grasp how surrendering to forces larger than the will, such as spirituality, can be more powerful than pure effort.

Humans and other animals are driven by the alpha force. Packs of wolves and dogs have an alpha male and female that eat and mate first; chimpanzees bow when their alphas pass. Alphas assert authority with eye contact, what's called "the stare." They'll never be the first ones to avert their eyes. Think of showdowns in politics or high-stakes business negotiations where locking eyes is a way to assert dominance. Bees have an alpha too: the queen bee, a hive's supreme mother. Armies of worker bees pamper and protect her.

Being an alpha can bring out the best or worst in us. A Stanford Business School study found that alphas are bold risk takers and leaders. On the down side, they tend to be self-centered, lack compassion, and consider compromise a weakness. The study also showed that power affects how people eat! When participants were offered a plate of cookies, those in power positions took the extra cookie, chewed with their mouths open, and scattered crumbs—a rather unattractive picture!

Alphas are experts at wielding "hard power" (a foreign policy term)—taking a macho stance by "steeling up" to succeed. Problem is, many alphas stay "steeled up" and guarded at other times too. In contrast, "soft power" utilizes diplomacy, collaboration, compromise, and intuition to win people's hearts. The soft powers aren't less powerful than the hard ones—you just have to know when to use them and how they can complement each other.

Why do we become an alpha dog or queen bee? Our temperament, education, and upbringing contribute. I was raised by two physician parents so some alpha power feels natural to me. Though I'm basically quiet and contemplative, I learned to emulate their take-charge authority. I saw how my parents could handle emergencies, make quick decisions, and save people's lives. I also inherited the alpha perseverance necessary to get through medical school. Growing up, I've had extra-strong alpha female role models; my father was more mellow. Nothing could stop my mother or her sister, my aunt. In fact, at Mother's request, the saying on her gravestone is "Never say never. Say maybe." So, for me, seeing strong women like this and loving women like this forever molded my view of power.

I appreciate how being an alpha can help you succeed. But it's also crucial to enlist soft power to make more love, not war, in your life. Understanding your biology lets you do this.

Harness the Neurochemicals of Power

Biology plays a significant role in becoming an alpha. For both men and women, specific neurochemicals support specific kinds of power. However, you can decide which neurochemicals you want to surrender to. It's not a passive process, as many think. Below is a primer on how some basic neurochemicals motivate you. Knowing this lets you choose what sort of power you're after and what kind of person you want to be.

Alpha or Hard Power

Hard power is fueled by a cocktail of potent neurochemicals that provide a rush. Alphas thrive on and can become addicted to this high.

- *Adrenaline: the fight-or-flight hormone.* Alphas go for the adrenaline rush which comes from the challenge of the fight, whether it's negotiating a deal or conquering adversaries. Being the victorious tiger in the jungle is the goal.

- *Testosterone: the sex and power hormone.* Alpha males are high on testosterone. This hormone is linked to a strong sex drive, a love of the hunt, risk taking, status, and competition, whether it means winning at games, romance, arguments, or war. When an alpha male entrepreneur I know built a phallus-shaped building in Hollywood, his friend, also an alpha male, built another one across the street! Success sends testosterone skyrocketing, while failure, including when a man's favorite sports team loses, diminishes it. Biologically, that's why alphas are addicted to success. However, it's circular: aggression and violence increase testosterone, and in turn, testosterone may boost the tendency for aggression and violence. Men with low testosterone (the hormone wanes with age as estrogen levels rise) are more motivated to cooperate than compete. Women's testosterone levels also increase during competition, but the act of winning or losing doesn't alter the levels. It's the game, not the outcome, that matters most for women.

- *Dopamine: the pleasure hormone.* Alphas crave activities that stimulate dopamine: sports, competition, even action movies. Dopamine is linked to addiction and the brain's pleasure center. Cocaine, nicotine, sex, food, and power are so addictive because they increase dopamine.

Soft Power

Soft power is fueled by neurochemicals that calm you and open your beautiful heart. You can increase them by releasing tension via exercise, meditation, or connecting with spirituality and compassion. These neurochemicals balance the hard powers and make them more effective. Otherwise you'd just be pushing or maneuvering to gain control. My Daoist teacher says, "Strive to relax as well as to achieve." Though soft power feels divine and can be addictive in a healthy way, alphas need to get used to tapping in to its benefits since it lacks the same aggressive rush of hard power.

- *Endorphins: the feel-good hormones.* These are your brain's natural, opiate-like painkillers, which bring you well-being, even euphoria, after exercise (the "runner's high") or during meditation and other relaxing activities. Though alphas love the endorphin spike from competitive sports, they aren't as instinctively attracted to the power of meditation or spiritually oriented activities.

- *Oxytocin: the love or cuddle hormone.* Women produce more oxytocin than men. It spikes during orgasm, birth, and nursing, and spurs women to bond with friends, causing a warm, fuzzy "wash of love" effect. This instills a sense of loving power that comes from connection, something alpha men often appreciate more with age and also as they learn to balance hard and soft power.

- *Serotonin: the happiness hormone.* This mood regulator alleviates depression and anxiety and makes you more successful and happier. With insufficient serotonin, you lose power, get depressed, feel tired, and are less motivated to succeed. Stress, workaholism, and excessive effort decrease serotonin. Exercise, meditation, spiritual practice, high-protein foods, and a positive attitude increase serotonin, as does chocolate!

The Power of Spiritual Surrender: Get Out of Your Mind and into Your Heart

I appreciate the potency of hard power with its energizing neurochemicals and seek to embody it in a balanced way myself. But I also appreciate that to succeed, we must embrace softer power—it is an essential, blissful part of who we are both neurochemically and spiritually. It's only considered soft in a conventional sense because accessing it involves being receptive, relaxed, and willing to be guided by forces other than effort and control. This is where the concept of spiritual surrender comes in. You do it again and again, not just once or twice. Gradually you can let down your guard more, trust, and let go. Spiritual surrender is central to the new paradigm of success because it ensures that a loving heart will inform all of your ambitions.

Spirituality, as I'm defining it, is a quest for meaning that goes beyond the linear mind and what's material to surrender to a vaster force of compassion. It comes from the noble, lifelong work of opening the heart, which links us to something larger. Doing this affects the way we interact, the way we love, the way we forgive. Spirituality shines light into the darkness, our negative parts and also parts of us we can't see. How do you awaken spirituality? As I'll show you, by connecting to the transcendent, a higher power of your own, whether it's God, Goddess, angels, a beneficent intelligence, nature, love, or something nameless. I'll share various techniques to help you connect, including meditation, contemplation, communing with nature, and prayer. The poet Rumi wrote, "Give your life to the one who already owns your breath and your moments. If you don't . . . you'll be foolishly ignoring your dignity and your purpose." Sure, you can try to go it alone without partnering with spirit, but as I've seen with patients, eventually it gets pretty tiring lifting every brick yourself. Why? You're using only personal power which is puny in comparison.

Sometimes it's hard for my alpha patients to grasp that spiritual power is an infinite source of good ideas and grace, unlike their finite ability to control. But once they give connecting to spiritual power a chance, they discover its real-world advantages. If you are an alpha, I hope you can do that too. Try to stay open. Narrow-mindedness will keep you from experiencing expanded consciousness. Your higher power is more perceptive than your intellect can ever be. Try getting used to that idea.

No matter how intelligent or talented you are, spirituality can only make you better. I'm not talking about spiritual make-believe where everything is sweetness and light. In the new paradigm of power, you'll consult it in every decision, from sealing a million-dollar deal to resolving conflicts with your kids. It's not just an extra thing to do—it's a strategic alliance that enables you to find creative, caring solutions, especially when your best effort isn't helping.

As an ongoing approach to life, try surrendering to a higher power to assist you, even if you don't understand it or fully believe. Then wait, watch, and breathe. In this letting-go state, your energy goes to where it can do the most good, a secret to conjuring power without effort. If you can back off enough to listen, spirit will show you a flow you can go with.

The best way I know to experience (not just think about) spirituality is to get in the habit of surrendering more and more to the unconditional love in your heart. This works beautifully with your spiritual beliefs, traditionally religious or not. You get there by first getting quiet within yourself, an enormously spiritual act that you need to keep developing. It makes me smile when one of my super-achiever alpha patients who has come to value this says about himself: "I'm just a guy trying to learn how to sit still and quiet my mind." Truly, he has his values straight! Stillness is the doorway to the heart, and to heaven. What is heart? In everyday terms, you can see it in the adoring way your puppy looks at you or in children's innocence. The heart is understanding that goes beyond fear or what makes you feel safe, and it allows you to be authentic around people: it's big love, not stingy love or love with strings. Nelson Mandela, Gandhi, and the Dalai Lama are models for the heart from whom we can learn. I agree with Buddhist teacher Stephen Levine when he says that the goal of spiritual practice is to "keep your heart open in hell."

Why am I calling the heart a power? Because once it becomes your focus, you'll always succeed in the most important way by ensuring your priorities are intact. Can you become an external success without the heart? Probably. Can you be truly great or happy? No. Coming from the heart doesn't make you sentimental, naive, or weak. Rather, when coupled with common sense, gut instinct, and hard power, it lets you be strong enough to be humble and secure enough to uphold the right priorities in your successes.

To me, heart is the most attractive quality in anyone. Take Fifi, who runs the dry cleaner's in my medical building. Her heart is so big she makes everything around her beautiful. Her tiny office in the parking garage is a refuge for receptionists, parking attendants, security guards—and me. There's always a crowd in there, laughing, talking, sharing. Fifi is kind and funny, and she has a warm glow around her that we lucky people can bask in. Her loving presence goes beyond words. Before seeing patients I frequently stop to visit and feel the love, an opportunity I am grateful for.

Recently I was asked in an interview for a health magazine, "What practice can't you live without?" It's the three-minute heart meditation I'm about to describe. I practice this meditation several times a day and recommend it to my patients, whether they are alphas or not, and in all my books. If I'm pushing too hard, it helps me let go. If I'm frustrated or overwhelmed, it centers me. If I'm confused, it provides clarity. When you reach further than your mind and let go to the limitless reach of the spirit, the answer is waiting. To contact your heart, utilize the following meditation.

SURRENDER TO SPIRIT WITH THIS THREE-MINUTE HEART MEDITATION

Identify a situation when control isn't working. Take a break from trying to make it happen. Instead, spend just three minutes meditating on the heart and surrendering to a power greater than your will. This meditation is meant to be a quick surrender; you can meditate longer at another time. Doing this once or throughout the day feels good, even ecstatic. Let in the well-being.

Relax in a quiet place. Stop checking your messages. Find a spot where you won't be interrupted. Shut your office door, go into your bedroom, or take a walk. Then sit upright in a comfortable position. Keep your back straight—a signal to yourself to stay awake. Close your eyes, a way to get closer to what's sacred in yourself. Become still. If thoughts intrude, let them pass by like clouds in the sky. Take a few long, deep breaths to release tension from your body and relax your jaw. When thoughts arise, keep returning to the rhythm of your breath.

Focus on your heart. Next, rest your palm above your heart in the middle of the chest, the energy center for compassion, what's called "the little sun." Notice what you feel. Relax into the sensations. Don't hold back. See what you experience. It may be warmth, clarity, comfort, a melting of tension, joy, ecstasy. Don't question or analyze. Allow it to happen.

Surrender a problem to spirit. While focusing on the heart, inwardly ask your higher power for assistance. You can be very specific. For instance, "Please help relieve our financial stress so we don't lose our home" or "Please help me find a more inspiring career." It's powerful to admit you don't know everything, that you are humble enough to ask for assistance. Don't attempt to figure it out. Try to release any attachment to an outcome. Simply say, "Thy will, not mine, be done." One patient lifts her arms over her head and says, "Here is the problem. Take over!" My Daoist teacher tells us to say, "I am complete, surrendered, accepting the flow." There is nothing else to do. Simply let go. See what happens.

After practicing this meditation, stay aware of new insights or changes in your outer circumstances. Enlisting the heart invites in the right kind of power. As the writer Goethe said, "Be bold— and mighty forces will come to your aid." Alphas appreciate mighty forces, and this is another way to find them. In my medical practice, I minister to the heart, increasingly letting go and trusting it, and urge my patients to do the same in their lives. This is not just magical thinking—it's saying, "I alone can't solve this problem." Surrendering control reduces stress hormones and boosts endorphins as well as allows the ingenuity of spirit in. My patients have shared these results with me. One reported, "I tried getting pregnant for three years, but a few months after letting go of worrying and stressing, it happened." Another realized, "I had to stop making a romantic relationship into something it wasn't for a better one to come along." Another stopped trying to convince her alcoholic friend and coworker to get sober. As hard as that was, she let him reach bottom; then he sought treatment himself, and she was right there for support. This meditation works because you're relaxing your grip on "making things happen" to provide more oxygen. But it's not that simple. The mystery of the heart has its own ways to intervene if you can open to its clarity and direction.

Over a lifetime, there are countless surrenders to the heart, and to spirit. Little by little it becomes easier and deeper. The meditation I shared may seem deceptively simple, but you are actually shifting worlds. If necessary, schedule regular times to breathe and connect. Try not to let the busyness of life intrude. This meditation never grows old, nor can you fully master it: the power of your heart just keeps expanding. As Rilke wrote in *Letters to a Young Poet*, "Go into yourself and see how deep the place is from which your life flows."

THE THIRD INSIGHT:
WIELD LIGHT POWERS, NOT SHADOW POWERS

You're gonna have to serve somebody.
—BOB DYLAN

Power in its most basic form is undifferentiated energy. How you use it is up to you. There are light and shadow powers. I want to help you choose the direction in which to surrender so you don't inadvertently serve forces or people that don't ultimately serve you. What's the difference between these powers? Light powers are fed by the heart. They include compassion, collaboration, hope, integrity, humility, and concern for a higher good. Shadow powers are fed by fear and are incredibly magnetic if you are susceptible. These include manipulation, greed, selfishness, revenge, and cutthroat tactics to get what you want.

We all have a shadow side. It's not just "them." It's you. It's me. It's us. Being human, we're all capable of kindness and cruelty. This is true whether you're Mother Teresa or a serial killer. Dark energy is real and addictive, and it must be respected. I've felt its enticing draw in erotic moments and in some power situations. The chilling part is that it can feel so tantalizing it makes you glaze over and forget your priorities. (Remember in *Lord of the Rings* when the innocent hobbit Frodo was seduced by the dark ring of power.) You go unconscious, would give anything to keep that rush going, and are lost—unless you yank yourself out of its clutches before it consumes you. No kidding— this is potent stuff, not just fluffy New Age speculation. However, to ensure that we don't surrender to the shadow and become the kind of people we loathe, we must take command of our shadow side so that it doesn't unconsciously run us. We must identify and bravely, with conviction, say no again and again to the less-than-admirable or seducible aspects of ourselves or the behavior of others. This means that we may have to turn down some "irresistible" relationships and opportunities, as frustrating as that is, so we can succeed without forfeiting our souls.

The old paradigm of power supports doing what's necessary to win. Many people who buy into this paradigm operate by shadow ethics, though they don't see it that way. They believe that certain behaviors are acceptable because, as a slick, "successful" attorney I know says, "it's just how the 'real world' works." In the new paradigm of power, however, the bottom line is that either you're adding to the light or you're detracting from it. Every action counts though some breaches are bigger than others. Not that we don't make mistakes or fumble or forget, but we pick ourselves up and keep moving toward an illuminated path, even if the entire world seems to be in shadow.

You may be afraid to claim your power since you associate it with your shadow side, a dynamic that's often unconscious. For example, you might fear abusing power at work or in relationships since you did so in the past or watched your parents abuse it. Or, wary of rejection, you're reluctant to ask for what you want or boldly present your ideas. Sometimes people try to repress their shadow sides by becoming overly nice, overly "spiritual," or saccharine. This never works and is a setup for their darkness to finally erupt as depression, anger, or violence. For myself and certain patients, this fear stems from feeling unsafe to express power. I've seen this in healers and teachers who're frightened of publicly revealing their talents. Some even experience stage fright. When I first started speaking to audiences about intuition, I got in touch with a fear that I'd be physically harmed. Intellectually I realized this was irrational, but the feeling arose from a different place. Like other healers I've known, I've experienced a viscerally felt collective memory for periods such as the Salem witch hunts, when "seers" were persecuted or burned at the stake. But I've realized it's safe to have a voice now. My patients have experienced the same relief from this insight too.

Know Yourself: Don't Surrender to Your Shadow Side

I'd like you to honestly examine your relationship to power and how to best use it in your life. Be gentle with yourself. Take ownership of your shadow side so that you don't act it out or keep attracting people who will act it out for you. If you're deceptive, you'll attract deception. If you're forthright, you'll attract honesty in others. Of course, we all get caught by ego, insecurities, ambition, and excessive control. There is no shame in this but don't get stuck there. First, go through the following list to identify your motivations, even if they're hard to admit. Then you can begin to surrender those that no longer suit you.

WHY DO I WANT POWER AND SUCCESS?

ON THE LIGHT SIDE

To feel proud of myself and my accomplishments.

To gain confidence and mastery in my job or relationships.

To be acknowledged and respected.

To provide for myself and my family.

To be emotionally strong for myself and supportive of others.

To positively affect others and the world.

ON THE SHADOW SIDE

To feel superior over people.

To pump up my ego and brag about myself.

To manipulate and control others so that they do what I want.

To be rich, famous, or get ahead, no matter what it takes.

To have people say yes to me.

To strike back at others if they "deserve" it.

Evaluate which attitudes most frequently guide your life and cultivate the positive ones. You might relate to some attitudes on the light side and some on the shadow side or you might alternate depending on how much you want something. Strong desires can make you susceptible to the shadow. That's natural. But by identifying your shadow side, you can then investigate and surrender the insecurities or vulnerabilities that hook you into it. For instance, one patient honestly discovered, "I need to act superior with others because I feel poorly about myself." Another found out, "My father punished me when I 'deserved' it. That's why I do that to my employees when they make mistakes." One businessman admitted, "My mother was so manipulative I couldn't bear to let anyone control me again. So I became controlling." My patients' tender admissions were the first step to self-knowledge and dealing with power differently. Similarly, explore what motivates your shadow side so that you can heal the wound. There is always a wound behind shadow motivations.

Happy, secure people aren't lusting after power and control to override their insecurities. Little by little, your goal is to make the tipping point go toward the light and to catch shadow motives quickly so they don't control you.

Selling Out Your Power: The Price You Pay to Win

The shadow is the consummate trickster and can be treacherously compelling. It knows just how to entice by offering what you most long for—say, riches, sex, beauty, or acclaim—then rationalizing ways you have to compromise yourself to get it. As Abraham Lincoln said, "If you want to test a man's character, give him power." But some choices aren't as blatant: marrying for money instead of love, forgetting old friends when you become successful or hiring a shady partner to play the "bad cop" to help you advance your career. If you're ever faced with these kinds of compromises, I urge you to reconsider the price you will pay and walk away from the temptation. *All that glitters is definitely not gold.*

A Faustian bargain is a classic pact with the devil. In Goethe's masterpiece *Faust*, a physician and scholar who becomes dissatisfied exchanges his soul for unlimited worldly knowledge, power, sexual charisma, and pleasures—an archetypal human struggle that's worth examining in ourselves. Aided by the demon Mephistopheles, he seduces an innocent girl who is nearly destroyed by his deceptions and desires. Of course, as payment Faust must endure the damnation of eternal hell where the devil delights in his torment.

Though most of us don't intentionally make such a pact or set out to be deceptive, I've watched intelligent and otherwise "nice" people delude themselves. It's possible to sell your soul through unconsciousness too. As the Buddha says, "Suffering comes from both ignorance and denial." One patient bragged, "I know how to get away with having emotional affairs so my wife never finds out." Another patient, a quarterback, convinced himself, "It's okay to shoot steroids to compete." Also, people compartmentalize—for instance, they'll rationalize, "I'm an ethical person even if I go for the jugular with a competitor. Playing hardball is expected." This reasoning lets them feel good about themselves since, in their denial, they figure, "I give to charity and I'm loving with my kids and my dog." But this kind of reasoning chills me to the bone. They don't recognize the glaring incongruence that who they are matters everywhere.

At a time in my life when I was undergoing financial pressure, I had a dream that warned me about a Faustian bargain I was entering into by seeing too many patients and wearing myself out. In the dream, I sold my treasured jade Quan Yin pendant for a high price (Quan Yin is the goddess of compassion in Daoism). Quickly I realized I'd made a terrible mistake by selling something that was priceless to me. I was overcome with dread and remorse. So I immediately found the buyer and returned his money, and he returned my Quan Yin. What a feeling of relief! When I awoke, I asked myself, "Why am I selling myself out?" I realized that my fatigue from being overscheduled was making me lose the joy of seeing patients, and my compassion. Without knowing it, financial fear had gotten the best of me. In truth, I was okay enough moneywise to weather this stressful period without selling out the love of my work or the quality of my patient care. Staying close to my essence—by listening to intuition via dreams and my gut—stops me from betraying what's most important to me. Thanks to the dream, I got a better hold on my fear and went back to a schedule that felt comfortable.

We all have different susceptibilities for seduction. Think about yours. Is it in the area of money? Sex? Recognition? Relationships? Youth? Beauty? Gerald Levin told me, "At my job, people told me yes all the time. I could get on a private plane to go anywhere. You begin to wrongly believe how indispensable you are."

In the real world we can make all kinds of Faustian bargains but your options are simple: you surrender to either the light or the shadow. Each choice affects you differently. It's folly to think that you're ever getting away with something. Since the shadow is so adept at tantalizing us with fame, fortune, and glamour, I understand how much sexier its power can seem compared to doing the right thing. But the shadow can never deliver satisfaction that sticks because you'll always be wanting more. It promises so much but only creates suffering. It can and will take you down. Each step you take toward the shadow, on purpose or not, darkens your heart, and as time passes, gradually an emptiness will enter and your light will dim. Trust me: you do not want that. It's a consequence more severe than forgoing any goal, no matter how intensely you desire it.

Listen to what I've seen happen to patients whose choices have turned against them in this way. On an intuitive level, I can sense an eerie vacantness, a rigid plastic quality sealing them off from their life force. It feels like they are slowly fading. I've watched these people age in the saddest way: sparkless, lost, with a strange and overly effusive laugh that's devoid of joy. They might even say they're happy since they don't know anything different. But after leaving positions of power, they wonder why so-called friends have stopped calling, or why their marriages seem passionless (even though they've hardly put time into them). A friend who's a sex therapist tells me that a number of her male patients who run corporations seek out a dominatrix. It's only by becoming submissive that they can get sexually aroused. In my practice, I've sat across from outwardly successful men and women who'd had panic attacks, mysterious pain, impotency, loss of libido, or a feeling that "nothing matters," as though they'd rather die than show this side of themselves to the world. Some were once altruistic but sacrificed their integrity for fame and fortune, a scenario that occurs frequently if you're unclear about power.

Even so, in psychotherapy I can guide these patients toward new choices and help them surrender to truly sustaining power sources, such as by practicing unconditional kindness and learning the value of the heart in themselves and the world—changes you can make too. This, along with meditation and deepening their spirituality, reverses some of the damage and lets them enjoy the success of being good human beings. But in your life, if the shadow courts you, don't let it get that far. Though sticking to the higher ground may seem like the harder choice, it is your hope for happiness and freedom.

Keep Your Power, Surrender Low Self-Esteem: Three Common Manipulators and Shadow Techniques They Use

To stay powerful you must remain centered and confident. You can do this by recognizing some classic shadow techniques which I discuss below. Whether it's a business partner or a relative, their endgame is to gain the upper hand while you squirm. Some people do this consciously, others unconsciously. These confusion tactics work only if you're unaware of them or have low self-esteem. They're intended to throw you off balance which then puts the other person in control. In fact, just saying, "I'm confused about your comment" places you in a weaker, defensive position.

Throughout the ages everyone, from courtesans to politicians, has successfully employed these techniques. Athletes know about them. When a player is about to kick a field goal, the opposing coach will purposely call a time-out to throw off that player's concentration. The idea is that once you wobble, you're less powerful. So stay alert and you won't be disempowered.

In the following exercise, you'll identify three manipulators and learn counterstrategies to their mind games. This surrender focuses on strengthening your self-esteem. You must release the notion that *anyone* can steal your power and know you'll be able to stand up to those who try. You must protect your light in practical ways and recognize what kinds of people not to surrender to.

Manipulator #1: The Flatterer—Tells You What You Want to Hear and Plays to Your Fantasies

Flatterers and flirts tell you you're beautiful, smart, or talented, listen to your every word, then reel you in to gain control. Flatterers get a charge out of having power over you and putting you in a dependent position. They adore seeing themselves as your knight in shining armor but there's no follow-through. Just as snake charmers entice a cobra by playing a beautiful song on the flute, flatterers tell you what you want to hear—but they don't give you what you need. They play on people's vulnerabilities or vanity. A charming television producer once told me, "I'm thrilled about your project. I'll take good care of it and you." He'd said the perfect thing and seemed sincere and likeable, so I signed with him. But over time this man's behavior didn't match his words. He'd say one thing and do another, and he rarely gave me a straight answer or progress reports. Finally I ended our relationship and moved on. Of course, it's wonderful to be appreciated but these kinds of hollow compliments are just words, not reliable support.

Surrender low self-esteem. Recognize your need to be flattered and validated. Begin to surrender this need by focusing on people's actions rather than their words.

How to get your power back. Realize not all attention is positive. Identify areas where you might be vulnerable to flattery or the need to be understood. Is it in romance? Business? Creativity? Physical appearance? Then stay aware. If someone's compliments are backed by actions, terrific. If not, bring this up so he or she has a chance to correct course. However, if a person doesn't change, consider letting go of the relationship or at least lowering your expectations.

Manipulator #2: The Intermittent Reinforcer—Sporadically Gives You Attention to Keep You Enticed

This is a crafty way of charming you into a relationship. Here, someone intermittently gives you love or attention, then withdraws it. Slot machines use this technique of paying irregularly to keep gamblers glued to the machine. You never know when you'll win, but you believe that a payoff will eventually come. There's nothing like throwing you a morsel of high-quality affection or mind-blowing lovemaking to keep you seduced. They are intimate one day, elusive the next, leaving you wanting more. They believe that if you know what to expect, their spell will be broken. Abusers use this technique, alternating pleasure, pain, and calculated absences to hook you in. If they were constantly mean, it would be much easier to break free.

Surrender low self-esteem. Don't be satisfied with sporadic crumbs of attention or love. See if the person is capable of more when you bring it to his or her attention. While sometimes these manipulators will say exactly what you want to hear, rarely do they follow through.

If they can't back their words with dependable actions, say no to this behavior.

How to get your power back. Set clear limits that this treatment is unacceptable. State your needs in a kind but firm tone, then offer solutions. For instance, with a spouse: "I'll feel safer in our relationship if you are more consistently caring. Let's plan a date night each Saturday." Or with a buyer who seems interested in your product but hasn't fully committed: "Let's meet to pin down a financial approach that works." Making concrete suggestions to alter this intermittent reinforcement pattern can shift the dynamics of a relationship. If it doesn't, you accept these limitations or let the relationship go.

Manipulator #3: The Dangler—Uses Temptation to Gain Control

These manipulators are similar to intermittent reinforcers but specialize in getting you hooked in by dangling a specific carrot in front of you, something you want that they have. This goes further than simply giving you sporadic attention. To get under your skin, they create expectations, then send mixed signals by playing hard to get or disappearing indefinitely, and they offer no reinforcement at all. For instance, you have a fantastic meeting with a potential client, then can't reach her. Or an intriguing man you're dating says he wants to get closer but keeps canceling your plans and doesn't reschedule for weeks. Nearly every teen knows what it's like to be left swirling in that disempowering conundrum: "Why didn't he or she text or call? I thought we connected. Did I do something wrong?" They feel powerful while you're simply confused, scrambling while trying to figure them out.

Surrender low self-esteem. Don't tolerate people who disappear after they make a connection to you. Especially if you had parents who withdrew emotionally, take care not to keep repeating the pattern of chasing others to win their love.

How to get your power back. Notice the craving for love or success this manipulation triggers in you but take a breath to become centered. Tell yourself, "I am a wonderful person. I deserve to be around others who respect and appreciate me, not game players." Once, maybe twice, you can let these people know of your interest in them. Do not pursue someone who doesn't reciprocate.

By recognizing these shadow techniques, you won't be deceived by a wolf in sheep's clothing. Knowledge is power. It prevents your innocence and goodwill from being pummeled. A patient recently told me, "I always want to expect the best from people." That's admirable, but you also must see through these manipulations and put your time and energy to more productive use.

THE FOURTH INSIGHT:
LEARN WHEN TO PRACTICE POWER VERSUS POWERLESSNESS

There's an art to learning when to make an effort and when to let go.

Sometimes you have the power to make things happen. Sometimes you don't. No amount of brainstorming, convincing, or cajoling will further your cause; forcing things only increases inertia and distress. In these instances, the new paradigm of power offers a savvier approach than simply aggressive strategies to bulldoze an impasse. Here it means recognizing that you are powerless at the moment to logically solve a problem or move a goal forward, and then tuning in to intuition for inspired input. This along with the heart meditation will put you back on track. *Powerlessness is not failure.* It means seeking success by listening to your inner wisdom to determine your next step.

Intuition tells you the truth about a situation, not just what you want to hear. It comes through in quick transmissions, unlike the laborious A + B reasoning of analyzing. Larger voices are calling you. Be ready to receive their messages by listening to quieter inner truths. You have a boundless intelligence within that you can't access unless you are still. It lifts you beyond suffering to find answers that uniquely make sense for your spirit. At times, particularly when you've reached a block, it's more powerful not to think about something for a while than to ruminate. Intuition attunes you to the movement of flow which the linear mind can't do. Complementing logic, it'll tell you when something feels right and if the momentum exists to proceed. You need to know this so you're not futilely swimming upstream or partnered with the wrong people. Intuition makes you more powerful because it stops you from wasting your time on a plan that won't work while enlarging your vision about what is meant to be.

With all your projects and aspirations, watch for the following intuitions to determine if you're heading in a positive direction.

INTUITIVE SIGNS YOU'RE IN THE FLOW WITH A GOAL

- You feel excited, energized, and happy.

- You're not constantly encountering roadblocks and struggle.

- Synchronicities—moments of perfect timing—assist you in reaching your goal.

- You're making progress and can overcome obstacles.

- It feels right in your gut.

INTUITIVE SIGNS YOU'VE REACHED A PLACE OF POWERLESSNESS

- You're pushing hard but nothing is happening.

- The more you try, the worse things get.

- You're turning people off with your pushing.

- Your gut tells you to back off; you're tired of the struggle.

- You feel chronically sick or drained.

These reliable signs will guide you in the right direction. However, as I've seen in my own life, sometimes anxiety or being too attached to a goal can stop me from listening. This is especially true if I perceive that people aren't following through with what they're "supposed" to be doing. Recently, a beloved creative project had a deadline looming. My partners hadn't yet turned in the work we needed to go forward. Worse, they'd become elusive, busy, telling me, "We're doing the best we can." I feared the project would fall apart, that they'd let me down. My anxiety began getting the best of me. So I cranked up the pressure on them, a tactic that failed miserably. It only made them more defensive and feel as if I didn't believe in them. These people had always been trustworthy before. I didn't want to blow it. That's when I knew I had to surrender or else sabotage myself with pushing. For the moment, I was powerless to make things happen or to control other people's behavior. I had done what I could to express my needs. Now I needed to let go of the results and rein in my anxiety. So, over the next few weeks, I did a lot of breathing, meditating, reciting of the Serenity Prayer, and talking to friends and God. I stopped being demanding. Instead, I expressed appreciation for my partners. I'm pleased to report that surrender was the best medicine in this situation. My partners warmed up to me again and turned in the necessary work on time.

In all situations it's important to be aware of flow. Though success thrives on work and perseverance, when you're in the flow without expectations sometimes opportunities just arrive that feel intuitively right. Watch for these situations, even if they're different from what you've imagined. At such times, simply try to get out of your own way by not overthinking. Surrender as the blessing unfolds. This is what happened to actress Roma Downey, who didn't specifically seek her role on the television show *Touched by an Angel*, but there it was. Roma, angelic herself, told me:

I was just a woman looking for a job. I wasn't on any kind of a mission. This role was offered to me. I didn't get any other job. I got a job playing an angel. I felt privileged to be that voice for twenty-five million people. Every week there was a message, and at some point I'd reveal myself as an angel and deliver the message: that there was a loving God and that everyone is loved. Before that scene, I used to pray that I could get out of the way and let the message come through. Soon, it became obvious to me, Della Reese, and the cast that we were all conduits for this message. Della said, "If we've been called to do this, we have to set our egos aside and let grace move through us." She taught me about surrendering to the power of love which was such a gift. For nearly a decade, playing an angel on this show let me move into my heart.

However, when flow is absent and you're spinning your wheels, intuition can show the way. Here, the intellectual surrender is realizing that you're unable to solve a problem by analyzing or exerting your will, and that's okay. The spiritual surrender is accepting your own powerlessness to effect change at that time. Both of these surrenders prepare you to receive intuitive guidance.

My patient Doug, a Caltech-educated engineer, had been out of work for months. He'd done everything logical to find a job: scoured the papers and the Internet, asked friends for leads, gone on interviews. Still, to his dismay, nothing came through. Doug told me, "I can't stop worrying. My savings are dwindling." In earlier sessions, he'd resisted pursuing intuition. Doug had a good heart, but he was a pragmatist, valued facts and figures, and rejected anything he considered "woo-woo." Nevertheless, at this point, since nothing else was working, he'd reached a state of powerlessness. Nerve-racking as it was for him to be in this position, the great thing (from my perspective) was that he was finally ready to try something new. So, in a session, I took him through the following intuitive problem-solving technique which I also recommend to you. The idea is to formulate a question, then tune in to an answer that has been beyond your reach.

SURRENDER TO YOUR INTUITION: MAKE SPACE FOR GRACE

1. *Choose a question.* For instance: "How can I find a job? Meet my soul mate? Support a friend? Resolve this conflict?" Address only one issue at a time to get the clearest answer. Record your question in a journal.

2. *Take a few deep breaths.* Slowly inhale and exhale. Focus on the sensations of breathing. This will calm and center you.

3. *Tune in.* In this quiet state, inwardly ask your question. Then simply stay open. Don't try to figure out the answer. Mental effort blocks intuition. Just notice any images, impressions, gut feelings, or "aha" knowings that come. For instance, you may get a strong sense not to give up on a project or a person suddenly comes to mind who can help. Your gut is a valuable intuitive indicator. Discomfort such

as nausea, a knot, or queasiness warns you to be cautious. But when your gut is comfortable, it's a positive sign to move ahead. Notice if any decision tightens or relaxes it. Record your intuitive response.

4. *Act on your intuition.* Follow the intuitive advice and notice the results. Did your life improve? Did the issue get solved? Are you in a better place? Positive results will reinforce you in regularly surrendering to intuition.

As was true with Doug, the answers you get may be direct and simple. In our therapy session, when Doug tuned in, he received one intuition that was sufficient: a snapshot-like flash of the cover of a local throwaway newspaper. He hadn't looked in it before because he'd considered it "too small" and "not prestigious enough." The intuition piqued his curiosity since it seemed to come out of nowhere. Partly to humor me and partly out of desperation, Doug picked up a copy. To his amazement, a classified listing appealed to him. He applied for and got the job which he's had for the last year.

Intuition is a power tool for everyday life. Don't wait for a crisis to use it. Whether you feel powerful or powerless, intuition can lend insight to all situations. The key is to let go of expectations and let your mind be as blank as possible. Then, just receive. Your intellect is astute but intuition is inventive in other ways. Try surrendering to it both when you're stuck and when you're not. Allow yourself to be surprised by what it tells you. It'll loosen you up so that you don't become one of those horribly uptight people who always need to be in control. You deserve to have more fun than that.

In this chapter, I've discussed four insights into power that you can keep applying and surrendering to in your life. The purpose of understanding power is to propel you to the light. There are many murky areas to avoid. I know how easy it is to get sucked into them. However, with the knowledge I've presented, you also have the tools to pull yourself out. Expect challenges on the path to awakening. Surely, you'll be tempted by ego, desire, and Lord knows what else but if you persist in surrendering to the right values and the heart, you'll be fine.

Consider: How much are we really in control anyway? Is success shaped mainly by destiny or drive? I believe it's both. I've seen patients who've worked hard for years on a project, yet despite effort and desire, it wasn't meant to be. Others seem to succeed effortlessly or at least with less struggle. Whenever I bemoan to my best friend, Berenice, a psychotherapist at eighty-five, why I haven't found my soul mate yet, she claims it's my karma, my path. I protest, "Shouldn't I go out to more parties? Isn't it just about me leading so much of a solitary life immersed in my writing so much of the time?" Berenice doesn't think so. I'm not as sure. I do need to go out more. But I suspect that she may be mostly right. I've gone out. I've met men but I haven't found someone right. Berenice says, "When you're supposed to find him, you will." Though my heart is full of longing, this is the surrender I strive for.

What I do know is that we can't control everything, although some people like to think they can. Why is control so important to them? It provides the illusion of security, of being immune to threat. Buddhists teach the precept of impermanence, that life is in constant motion, that nothing is forever, including our stay here. It's important to remember this. There's an honesty to admitting powerlessness in situations beyond your control. That's why powerlessness is so awesome. It allows you to surrender at critical moments instead of scrambling to control what you can't. As you explore power and success, appreciate your assets but don't get too impressed with yourself. I'm moved by what Martha Beck says: "Real power is unspectacular, a simple setting aside of fear that allows the free flow of love. But it changes everything." Do this and you really have a chance at something good.

SURRENDER AFFIRMATION FOR HUMBLE POWER

Go placidly amid the noise and the haste . . .
Enjoy your achievements . . .
Keep interested in your own career, however humble . . .
. . . everywhere life is full of heroism.

—MAX ERHMAN, "DESIDERATA"

Have you too gone crazy
for power,
for things?
—MARY OLIVER
. . . .

3

THE THIRD SURRENDER

MANIFESTING THE HEART OF MONEY: SEEING

BEYOND MATERIAL SEDUCTION AND FEAR

THE HOTTEST, MOST HIGHLY CHARGED TOPICS I ENCOUNTER
with patients are money and sex. Both strike such intimate chords
involving trust that research has ranked them as the issues couples
most frequently argue about. Money can bring out your most fearful self or your largest heart. Which one you surrender to changes
everything. You're about to learn how to make peace with money and
tap its highest good. How do you do this? By finding effective ways to
surrender fear, stinginess, and other resistances to abundance so that
money can flow more freely into your life.

In this chapter, you'll see the powerful relationship between
money and surrender. Money can trigger wildly polarizing feelings,
including anxiety and self-loathing if people don't have enough, or
grandiosity and arrogance if they have a lot. I've observed how my
patients' attitudes about money can dramatically help or harm their
health. For instance, when one patient, a poetry-loving librarian,
stopped comparing his income with what his brother, a stockbroker,
earned, both his shame about money and his acid reflux ceased. And
when another patient who owns a chain of car dealerships stopped
throwing tantrums when employees didn't jump to instantly meet

his needs, his blood pressure dropped along with the tension in his company. The result? Morale increased and so did sales.

Imagine conquering your worry about finances, especially during tough times. Imagine not being chronically stressed out or ashamed about how much you make. I'll show you how surrendering to the right attitudes about money can add years to your life by removing the onslaught of stress hormones that batter your immunity and serenity. Money is a universal form of power. The tricky part is learning to mindfully harness that power without letting it harness you. *Money itself is neutral. Your attitudes and what you do with it determines the effect it has.*

This chapter's focus isn't on how to get rich quick and buy a fancy house or car, or on financial advice. Rather, it's about developing a positive, surrendered relationship with money so that, wealthy or not, you'll be happy. I am adamant about keeping my patients focused on knowing they're not just their bank account. Otherwise, their view of money can become so distorted they feel like a disgrace if they don't earn some magic number. It's an easy trap to get caught in but it's my job to rescue them from it. If not, they won't be able to appreciate their amazing selves, regardless of cash flow—which would be a real tragedy.

I refuse to accept that money defines you; in my gut, that feels soulless and blind to the wonder of our true character and spirit. With patients, I always emphasize that being broke or severely financially limited—which may be a temporary situation—isn't the same as being poor, which I'm defining as an emotionally impoverished state of mind, regardless of how much money you have. Being poor is when you can't recognize your blessings and nothing is ever enough, a kind of curse. As much as some patients protest, "Judith, you're not being practical in a society that's all about money," I keep refocusing them on building new and empowered views about finances that will never fail them. This doesn't mean you can't be rich and successful. You just don't have to be greedy, conniving, or harm others or the earth to do it. Remember, it's not money that is the root of all evil but the love of money—the obsession with it—that causes harm, an offshoot of Jesus' teachings.

Greed is toxic. Placing money over relationships or using it to control people can cause serious damage. I agree with filmmaker Tom Shadyac who says that "greed is a form of mental illness." I've seen it take heartbreaking tolls on families. I've watched siblings fighting bitterly over an inheritance at their mother's deathbed, parents bribing their children to attend business school so they can become millionaires, and wealthy relatives who won't give a penny to help an ill family member.

My attitudes about money have been shaped by my upbringing. I was raised in an upper-middle-class home. Both Mother and Dad, who loved being physicians, worked long hours in their medical practices for forty years. On Saturdays, Mother often took me with her in her beloved pink convertible Cadillac on house calls. My parents were practical about money, generous, not materialistic. I learned to save for a rainy day, to donate to charity, and to spend money on what I enjoyed if I could afford it. We were fortunate to always have enough money, never enduring the torment of hunger or the fear that we couldn't pay the rent. Then and now, I'm truly grateful for financial security.

Still, my mother sent some confusing messages about others' wealth and fame. Despite her sensible financial views, she was also enchanted by the rich and famous. She got energized by the charisma and charm of movie stars and loved spending time with them. "They're so alive and doing so many interesting things," she'd say. Growing up, I met many of my mother's celebrity patients. Once, as a teenager, she took me to the hospital to deliver her homemade chicken soup to Mick Jagger! Of course I was thrilled—but, disconcertingly, she seemed to make celebrities into superpeople who were bestowed with special graces that we mere mortals lacked. This fueled my insecurities around not measuring up, though of course that wasn't her intention.

On top of that, my parents belonged to a ritzy country club with ritzy people where I felt like an alien. Mother adored wearing mink coats over her designer clothes and holding court at luncheons with glamorous guests. I would just sit there quietly, overshadowed by her gregariousness, not to mention her terrifyingly ample bosom which she'd proudly display in low-cut outfits. For years Mother and I fought about my clothes. "You'd be so beautiful if you just dressed more elegantly," she'd tell me—a crushing remark that made me feel I wasn't beautiful at all. But instead of succumbing to her ferocious opinions about how I should dress and behave, I rebelled by living in jeans and T-shirts, by writing poetry, by loving the song of the creek and the moon, by walking barefoot instead of in high heels. I've always been more inner than outer-focused. For years, I rebelled to protect my spirit from being squelched by Mother's mainstream vision of who I should be. Though our battles weren't usually focused on money, they dealt with related issues of image and the proper way to behave. In a positive way, I believe, these disputes influenced my disinterest in materialism and instilled a reverence for an inner life.

There was nothing fundamentally wrong with Mother being starstruck and having some wealthy friends, except that I watched her painful struggle with self-esteem, even in her later years. She told me, "Being around important people makes me feel important"—a poignant admission. The tragedy was that Mother always believed a part of herself was lacking, despite her generous heart and amazing talents as a physician. I saw her suffering, which ultimately motivated me to love myself more and not make my worth contingent on the fickleness of glamour, wealth, or anything else. These were profound lessons about what not to surrender to.

Prepare to examine your relationship to money. I'll help you surrender unproductive attitudes that prevent abundance. In this chapter, you'll discover: Can money really make you happy? When is earning it more stressful than it's worth? What is your money type? How can it help or hinder you? Are you a denier? A procrastinator? A spending addict? How can you become comfortable talking about money and ask for what you deserve? You'll also surrender to intuition—your inner genius—so you won't overthink financial decisions or miss out on "aha" solutions. Abundance is free-flowing, a joyous momentum you must intuitively sense and trust to succeed.

MONEY: A PATH TO SURRENDERING TO YOUR HEART

I listen carefully when people talk about money. Often they focus on the amount they have, whether it's sufficient or not, how it can take care of their health, primary needs, and families. Some people's eyes are lit up by ambition or the allure of power and prestige. Some talk passionately about giving. Others brag about possessions. I've met wealthy people who're humble, grateful, and generous, while others are condescending tightwads. I like to track the way we think about money, how it can improve or ruin lives.

However, what I'm most intrigued by is how to utilize money (no matter how much you have) as a path to awaken and surrender to the heart rather than solely as a vehicle for comfort or material gain, as valuable as these are. This elevates the purpose of money, a game-changing shift of consciousness that aligns you with a flow toward abundance on many levels rather than just things. You can move mountains more easily when the energy of love propels your goals. As we'll discuss, awakening means understanding what money can and can't do, not through the lens of society's clichéd assumptions, but with clarity and kindness. Then you must prepare to surrender your illusions, as ingrained as they may be. *Money without heart goes bad quickly.* I've seen it lead to arrogance that turns people ugly or to conspicuous consumption or gambling addiction. It can also become an excuse to torture yourself if, say, you have to take a salary cut, an awful feeling. That's why it's critical to bring heart into all financial issues, including what you invest in and practicing self-compassion during rough periods.

Research has shown that happy people look for opportunity where others see only crisis. Therefore, I'd like you to view money issues as opportunities to become stronger and more loving rather than a victim, including when nothing feels fair. Even if you've never thought of money this way, give it a try—then watch the results. My Daoist teacher says, "The light is in the heart. Open the heart and that light will surface." Here, this means finding the place where money and heart intersect, then tapping that vital energy to affirm life.

THREE STRATEGIES TO TRANSFORM YOUR RELATIONSHIP WITH MONEY: SURRENDERING FEAR AND ILLUSION

Strategy 1: Examine Your Expectations About Money

Ask yourself what your expectations of money are. Are they realistic or not? I'll help you find out. Your beliefs can make you feel powerful or powerless.

Keep in mind that money is only one ingredient in personal prosperity. Certainly it can bring freedom and relieve stress when your basic survival needs are met, and these are true gifts. Also, money provides numerous lifestyle advantages by providing disposable income. For my patients, these include travel, having a nice car, and being able to buy organic food for their family. My friend Michael Crichton, the late author, told me, "The best thing fame and fortune brings is more opportunities." Marlon Brando said, "The principal benefit acting has afforded me is the money to pay for my psychoanalysis." Personally, I thank my lucky stars for the luxury of time it offers to write my books and take the breaks I desperately need to replenish myself.

Still, despite these undeniable perks, I want to discuss where money doesn't live up to its hype so that you don't look to it for the wrong reasons. As beneficial as money is, it won't solve all your problems or cure feelings of inferiority, nor will it magically turn you into a nice, content, or grateful person. *It cannot save you from yourself or your pain.* I've treated patients with the means to vacation in paradise but they end up constantly arguing with their spouses when they could've been having the time of their lives. They are unable to enjoy or be thankful for what they have. Warren Buffett, one of the richest people in the world, observes about the wealthy: "Money just amplifies their traits. If they were jerks before they had money, they simply become jerks with a lot of money." However, if you were loving to begin with, chances are you'd be loving with wealth too. The following summary will let you have realistic expectations about money and surrender ones that are not.

FIVE THINGS MONEY CAN DO

- *Meet your basic needs.* Having food, clothing, shelter, enough to live on and pay everyday bills relieves suffering and offers stability.

- *Offer a higher quality of life and a safety net*—an education, medical benefits, material comfort, and treats such as travel, movies, and healthful food.

- *Give you free time.* You can relax, play, exercise, create, or enjoy your kids instead of always working to pay bills.

- *Provide access to people, influence, and opportunity.* Money can help open doors, give you veto power, and increase your influence so that more people pay attention to you and your cause. It can also fund your dreams such as a new business so that you don't have to stay in a job you don't love.

- *Help others and reward someone's quality work.* Charitable giving relieves suffering. Money used for humanitarian purposes can, for example, abolish poverty, open schools, and find cures for disease. In addition, generous salaries, tips, and bonuses are ways of saying thank you to someone for a job well done. Also, it can help you empower other people to do their good work.

FIVE THINGS MONEY CAN'T DO

- *Make you happy if you're not happy inside.* Research indicates that wealth doesn't ensure happiness and that it can impair one's capacity to enjoy small pleasures.

- *Make you more important or deserving than anyone else.* Money doesn't place one person above another. In fact, research reveals it can make people ruder and less empathic.

- *Buy true friends or love.* In surveys, employees who are friends of their bosses say they're reluctant to be honest for fear of losing their paychecks. In all relationships, money is often a barrier to honesty and unconditional love if one person is financially beholden to another. Plus, wealthy people who lose their wealth often lose their "friends" too.

- *Be a substitute for self-esteem.* Money can boost self-esteem, but it's only one of many reasons to feel good about yourself. True confidence must also come from within to complement external sources. Otherwise it won't last.

- *Fill the hole of loneliness, loss, or lack of spiritual connection.* Money can't keep you warm at night, be a substitute for love, or provide the inner resources to heal. Spiritual attainment is not for sale. Money can't provide a link to a loving intelligence greater than yourself. You must develop it.

Surrendering the expectation that money alone can make you happy (especially if you're not content otherwise) is one key to feeling fulfilled. As tempting as it may be to believe such magical thinking, it's just not going to happen, no matter what the media or your boss or your mother says. Accepting this will spare you years of frustration spent looking for happiness in the wrong places. Remember misguided King Midas who could turn anything to gold, a wish granted by the gods. But when he touched his daughter and she turned to gold, he withdrew his wish, and thereafter appreciated what really counted in his life.

Money sometimes creates problems. In fact, trust fund babies, misers, and lottery winners are notoriously miserable. Take one winner who won a $315 million jackpot. Five years later he blamed the lottery money for his granddaughter's fatal drug overdose, his divorce, his inability to trust, and hundreds of lawsuits filed against him. He said, "Nearly all my friends have wanted to borrow money. Once they did we couldn't be friends anymore." Though each person who gets instant wealth deals with it differently, there are some very real issues that arise that can complicate life.

For much of human history, we never used money. Communities worked together to provide for one another with gifts, bartered goods, and shared valubles to sustain the group. Societies can exist, be happy, and flourish without money or owning things. Today, I am inspired by the Native American potlatch ritual in which leaders give away valubles to their tribe to spread abundance to all. However, once money became a norm, communities began to dissolve and were less interdependent.

Most people are misinformed about happiness. I agree that being able to put food on the table and pay your rent, along with the other benefits of money I've cited, can make you happier. Nevertheless, scientific studies spell out what can make us happy or not. They report that a meager 10 percent of happiness comes from external factors such as social status or wealth. Actually, people are proven to be happier when they stop trying to outdo the Joneses. Another 50 percent comes from your genetic makeup and a whopping 40 percent from inner changes you can make, such as becoming more grateful, compassionate, and meditative. Understanding this will clarify your relationship with money and help you let go of notions that don't make sense.

Here's a longer-term perspective to consider. Money is not a lasting currency of the spirit. It's a human invention, temporal. We can use it well now but when we leave here, and we all will, money can't come with us. At that point, we must surrender it and all material attachments. Still, what we do with money and how we treat ourselves during financial stress can add or detract from our light and the light around us. The light is our essence, the heaven in ourselves that travels with us through time and space. It brightens as our hearts grow. Nothing is more important. We are caretakers for our light. When all else falls away, this is who we are.

Strategy 2: Surrender Your Illusions About Money

Why is money so seductive? Because of the intense fantasies we project onto it: happiness, "being somebody," admiration, a charmed life, no suffering or loneliness. A common illusion is that money always brings less stress. Sure, sometimes it can when it meets our basic expenses and allows us time to relax. But often I've seen with patients and friends how making money is more stressful than it's worth. Their income goes up but so do expenses. One patient in advertising bought a bigger house but had to work longer hours to pay the mortgage. As a result, he didn't get to see his spouse and kids as much, was often exhausted, and had less downtime to unwind. He ended up getting an ulcer! I want you to stay aware of this trap and avoid it.

What fuels our illusions about money is that on a deeper, often unconscious level, money functions as a narcotic to numb fears of not being "enough" or of feeling impotent when you realize that you can't control everything. Also, when we don't fully grasp that a spiritual reality, which imbues us with true power, exists now and in every moment, material wealth takes on inflated clout. It's not surprising that money evokes such magical thinking. Many people are attracted to the rich and famous or lust after wealth. Whether they're aware of it or not, many expect wealth to fix a part of themselves they feel is lacking, but this never works.

I've seen how fantasies about money can drive people to buy expensive clothes they can't afford in order to impress others and maintain an image. Or befriend people they may not even like. Or work in jobs that feed their power drive but not their hearts. Gordon Gekko, the ruthless broker in the film *Wall Street*, said, "It's not about the money. It's about the game, the game between people." The power rush is about winning the game to command respect and feel in control.

Money can bewitch us because it plays on a primal need to be taken care of and a fear of not having enough, two biologically compelling motivators. For these reasons, some of my patients, both men and women, frankly admit they'd prefer a rich mate. Remember, I'm in Los Angeles! Of course, they'd say they want a caring partner too. However, money comes first. My patient Nicole, a hardworking beautician who wasn't a spendthrift, told me, "I'm tired of financial stress." Nicole thought money would solve all her problems—a difficult fantasy to dispel, though I tried, because she was burned out from struggling. She needed a quick fix. She wanted to be saved. So

Nicole married the wealthiest man she met, who seemed like a good person, and found a way to love him. I'm a therapist and my role isn't to judge what will make my patients happy, though I'll discuss the potential pitfalls of a choice and urge them to find mates with deeper credentials than cash.

As with Nicole, even though I intuitively foresaw conflict, if someone is determined to go down a path, I'm there to help them. Yes, part of Nicole's fantasy did come true—her finances were covered. But she hadn't expected her Prince Charming to use money to control her with golden chains. I've seen many wealthy husbands and wives who'll gladly give their spouse a credit card. But then they use the card to track where the spouse goes, whom they're with, and what they purchase. Or, they threaten their spouse's allowance if the spouse doesn't defer to their needs. So, like Nicole, my patients end up in a horrifying scenario in which they become the dependent spouse who must be compliant, trapped in a relationship where they're controlled by money.

Nicole had to experience this reality for herself before she could begin to surrender her illusions about money. Clearly, it wasn't the panacea she had hoped for. I was glad that she stayed in psychotherapy instead of running. From our work, she learned to honestly communicate with her husband about her feelings that he controlled her with money. But it wasn't easy. Fear constrained her. She was afraid he'd leave her, that she'd be broke and lonely again. But since her marriage felt intolerable, and she'd reached bottom with it, she was willing to fight for a healthier relationship or start over alone if necessary. Beaten down, ripe for surrender, she was ready to release her fear and claim her power. Fortunately, her husband was willing to address his need for excessive control with money and other issues. He changed because he truly loved her. This surrender on both their parts made a more authentic, caring marriage possible.

Sometimes surrendering illusions about money means accepting the harsh reality of a bad economy. Not long ago, as part of a television news show about coping with layoffs, I had the honor of working for several months with a group of women who were profiled on the program. They were known as the "Victorville Twelve." They'd lost their jobs at the same credit union in Victorville, California. These twelve inspiring women sat in my living room, sharing their tears about very real financial worries and frustrating job searches. Previously they'd prided themselves on being self-sufficient. But now, as fate would have it, this massive layoff united them. To survive, they formed what they named the "sisterhood of support." They told me that acknowledging that they couldn't control employers or the economy let them accept their situation more calmly. But being there for one another was what got them through, sometimes a moment at a time. Our sessions helped these women surrender to hope, not fear. They learned to lean into change, lean into friends for support, lean into forces larger than themselves and surrender to that power. Trusting intuition also helped them come to this place. Though their minds told them, "It's weak to be dependent," I asked them to listen to what their gut said. In every case, their gut confirmed the rightness of connecting.

It's heroic surrendering to a life you hadn't hoped for, yet still trusting that circumstances will improve. Eventually, some women got jobs, others returned to school, and a few retired. Now, a few years later, they share their children's weddings, the birth of grandkids, graduations, and potluck dinners. Economic hardship spurred these women to emotionally surrender to a new form of loving. They probably wouldn't have been motivated to stretch their hearts like this, but losing their jobs with few other prospects rocked their world. They could've been heartless to themselves in numerous unforgiving ways, but together they were determined not to feed the scary voices in their heads and to stay positive. A need for surrender often arises from crisis. The recession brought out a deeply caring side of these women and an appreciation for interdependence, dispelling the illusion that to be strong they had to cope with financial duress alone.

The gift of surrendering illusions surrounding money is that you'll approach finances more clearly and compassionately, with less angst, especially if you don't have a choice or if there's disappointment involved. The purpose of this isn't to deprive you of anything but to harmonize with what is and to find enterprising solutions.

When money becomes less about things, appearances, or pumping up puny egos, it can promote healing in you and everything you touch. Feelings of happiness, even ecstasy, come when illusions recede and you use money in service to the heart whatever situation you face. The following affirmations will help you surrender fear and build gratitude, even if you're not there yet. Repeat them once or more each day and let the change begin.

SURRENDER YOUR ILLUSIONS ABOUT MONEY WITH THESE AFFIRMATIONS

I am grateful for all the benefits of money.
I am grateful to be able to give and receive.
I am more than my job or my bank account.
I surrender the illusion that money alone can make me happy.
I surrender the illusion that money defines my self-worth.
I am a valuable person who deserves abundance.

Strategy 3: Recognize Money as a Mirror

Money mirrors how we feel about ourselves. It's like a Rorschach test, where people project meaning onto amorphous inkblots. You might see a murderess in a blot, while I see an angel. Similarly, we imbue money with meaning. It can reflect back everything from pride in your work and generosity to the more contracted states of shame, guilt, and failure. For instance, one patient who invested much of his savings in a start-up design business that failed became so full of self-blame he felt like "a total loser." As with this man, when money mirrors such painful feelings, the solution is of course to regroup financially. But it also involves using what you see to heal hurt places and soften the blow of loss. Learning to be loving with yourself, rather than punishing, is a magnificent surrender that financial stress can catalyze.

It takes guts to look into the mirror of money and discover what it reveals, both your best qualities and those in need of healing. Ask yourself, "What do I see? Is it appreciation for what I have, or fear of not having enough? Is it gratitude for my job, or shame about my salary? Is it humility, or arrogance? Charity, or greed?" In the end, whether you're rich or not, you want to look at money and say, "I feel good about myself. I've done my best to support myself, my family, and repay debts. I've helped the needy. I've used it to relax and have fun. I've gone for my dreams, though sometimes I've failed. When I've made mistakes or misused money I've tried to right those wrongs." The purpose of this self-evaluation is to see where you're at now, then bring more heart into how you view money. One of the bravest things we can do is to be willing to see ourselves clearly and surrender our shortcomings.

Money also mirrors our priorities. Gloria Steinem astutely observed, "We can tell our values by looking at our checkbook stubs." Therefore, in the spirit of awakening, study your checkbook or credit card statements. Then notice what your expenditures reveal about you, positive or not. When I reviewed mine I saw how many charges I had for healthful food, books, and music, all passions of mine that reflect priorities I'm proud of. However, most of my spending went toward maintaining my office, computers, paying repair people, and other daily practicalities. Rarely did I spend on new clothes, makeup, or nice things for my home. What this mirrored back was the monastic, sometimes lonely (though internally rich) existence I lead writing much of the year, living in sweat pants and Spirit Animal hoodies. Lost in the time warp of creating or waiting to create, I don't get out much to shop or give myself other simple treats that are also necessary for balance. Examining what I spent money on made me more aware of areas where I neglect myself so I could be sweeter to myself in these ways.

Surrender Shame, Build Compassion

Of all the challenging emotions money mirrors, shame can often have the most sting. Shame, a specific form of fear, comes from feeling defective. It is a sense of humiliation and worthlessness that makes the soul cower. Shame stops you from asking for what you deserve to be paid or even from discussing money at all. It can drive you to keep up appearances since your real self doesn't feel worthy. Financial shame arises from comparisons. Your coworker gets a bonus, but you don't, so you feel like a loser who wasn't deserving enough to merit one. You can't afford a vacation, but a friend is renting an Italian villa with his family; you are envious, but even more devastating, you are ashamed that you aren't a good enough provider to give that to your family too. True, it's hard to stay centered when someone gets what you want and deserve. It's instinctive to compare, but we must not get stuck there or let the shame of not being "enough" overtake us.

My patient Julie and her husband, Rob, both computer programmers, had to downsize from owning a home to renting an apartment to keep their physically handicapped child in a special school. Julie told me, "We live in a crazy city where everything goes up but our incomes." Julie and Rob would do anything for their son, and made the difficult choice to downsize with dignity. Still, even knowing they did the right thing, they both wrestled with feelings of humiliation about not being "good enough parents and providers," a heartache that lurked beneath their efforts to be upbeat. Losing one's home strikes to the core of primal insecurities about failing to care for family. We all know how destabilizing even a voluntary move can be; this isn't even a fraction of the stress Julie and Rob were suffering.

Shame is not your friend. It disconnects you from your power by inflaming self-doubts and harsh self-perceptions. The last thing you want to do is go with its flow. Shame is an emotion that is starving for your heart. Its antidote is compassion. To restore your power, shame must be addressed in a mindful way, using love to counter your feelings of not measuring up in the arena of money. Since love and self-compassion are stronger than shame, they'll help you surrender this feeling more easily. Love tips the scale in your favor.

I showed Julie and Rob how to reframe their choice. We focused on the courage they showed when confronting real financial limitation, and on their devotion to their son. These truths needed to be their guiding light, not shame. Also, there can be a grace to living with less. We discussed making the new apartment warm and inviting instead of judging it as "a sad step down." Even though shame had grabbed them in the gut and didn't want to let go, the perspective I suggested gradually allowed Julie and Rob to surrender to the move with more tranquility. In our work, I helped them rally a defense against shame with compassion, a shift that takes practice. But they badly wanted this change, and went for it. What a relief they felt as shame began to disappear. I was pleased to watch Julie and Rob grow closer during stress instead of breaking apart, as I've seen many families do. Still, it's always a choice which emotion we surrender to. As a therapist, I've seen time and again how hard it is for beautiful people to see what's beautiful in themselves. But that's where I come in. Once Julie and Rob could appreciate the loving parents they were, shame could only retreat. There is a kind of domestic heroism that too often goes unacknowledged. What they achieved reminded me that, in all situations, the power we have is our own attitude.

Why Is It So Hard to Discuss Money?

Shame takes many forms. In 1983, when I first opened my medical practice, I was ashamed and embarrassed to discuss my fee with patients. Would my patients think I was asking for too much? Too little? Was I a skilled enough therapist to even get a fee? A part of me felt like a sham, a pretender. I hadn't yet fully grown into my physician's identity. As I became more confident in being a doctor, I became more at ease discussing money issues with patients.

It takes practice to talk about money. To surrender shame about being paid what I was worth, I had to face my insecurities and realize it was okay to be fairly compensated for my work. Also, I needed to see there's nothing "unspiritual" about making a living. Similarly, I urge you to examine areas where you feel undeserving of compensation or abundance. Secrecy only empowers shame.

To confront shame about money, write your feelings in a journal using this format: "I'm ashamed to discuss money because ___." Pinpoint the causes of shame, such as "I'm being rude," "I'm not good enough," "I'll be rejected," or "They'll think I'm greedy." Admitting these feelings is a healthy start. Then, in baby steps, begin to practice discussing money and requesting what you want. For instance, before a job interview or asking your boss for a raise, rehearse what you're going to say with a supportive person. (My patients do this with me!) Then you can get used to expressing your financial needs with greater conviction.

When you look into the mirror of money, consider how you can use what you see to grow wiser and more loving. Surrendering shame, worry, or other negative emotions frees you from your small, fear-based self so that you can inhabit a more spacious part of your being. This exercise can help you do this.

SURRENDER SHAME ABOUT MONEY WITH A LOVINGKINDNESS VISUALIZATION

- *Sit quietly and breathe.* Gently close your eyes. For a few minutes, take a few slow, deep breaths to expel stress. Mindful breathing allows the body to unclench and surrender more easily.

- *Name a financial shame or worry you'd like to release.* For instance, being unemployed, having to borrow to pay bills, or perhaps lack of generosity. To avoid getting overwhelmed, choose only one shame to focus on.

- *Visualize shame lifting.* Just for today, imagine a life without this shame. Imagine feeling comfortable in your own skin, able to accept things just as they are without worry. Allow that comfort in. No arguing, no resistance. Then repeat this mantra: "I am not my shame. I am larger." Feel the pleasure of that expansion. You can also inwardly request to connect with a sense of spirit greater than the shame—it could simply be love—and ask, "Please take this shame away from me." Stay open and innocent. Let the burden of shame lift. Keep breathing it away. Allow yourself to feel good about who you are. Say, "May I be free of shame. May I be free of worry. May I surrender to peace."

This visualization sets a tone for change and healing. But to uncover the root of shame it's also crucial to review your upbringing. Is shame about money generational? Did you learn it from family, teachers, or friends? Also, truly surrendering shame means looking further than this world. There is an intangible loving force that can help lift your burden of shame if you reach out, let go, and trust.

WHAT IS YOUR MONEY TYPE? SURRENDERING UNHEALTHY PATTERNS

To identify your style of relating to money, I want to present some common money types, with their pluses and minuses. Think of this as your financial personality. It reflects the basic way you manage money, the attitude to which you revert under financial stress. Each type is influenced by upbringing, role models, and temperament. If your parents were stingy or generous, chances are you're similar— but change is possible. I've seen many patients remain stuck in an unhealthy money type for years and wonder why they're still in debt or denial. To prevent this, you'll pinpoint what about your type works or doesn't so you're not always struggling. I'd like you to focus on the qualities you want to strengthen and those you want to surrender. The key to financial success is to release emotional habits that are holding you back such as worry or procrastination. Then you can generate the good fortune you deserve.

To determine your money type, review the descriptions below. Ask yourself, "Am I a worrier? A gambler? A smart saver? A miser? Do I trust my intuition with money or second-guess my hunches? Since opposites often attract, you may choose a partner who's a different type. This can have a balancing effect as long as you're both willing to compromise, say, on risk taking versus safer investments. Though you may contain aspects of other types, pick the one you most resonate with. Evaluate your financial habits with kindness, in the spirit of becoming more self-aware. Don't make this an excuse to beat yourself up. The goal is to develop a successful approach to money and get pleasure from what you spend on.

Money Type 1: The Worrier

Worriers can be thrifty, astute problem solvers, and will avoid errors because of their diligence with finances. They're responsible, stay on top of things, and don't slip into denial about money. Worry can motivate them to solve problems and be prepared. During hard economic times, with careers in jeopardy, many people will relate to this type. Of course, legitimate financial concerns arise that require solutions, but worry takes concern into the realm of suffering.

The downside is that worry increases stress hormones, decreases immunity, and impairs health and sleep. Plus, worriers can turn every purchase into a fingernail biting experience. Worriers are experts at asking, "What if?" They torment themselves with fears such as "I'll never be able to pay my bills" or "I can't spend on a new car—what if the stock market plunges again?" They project worry into the future and create scenarios of impending doom that, in extreme cases, can paralyze their decisions. I have one patient who worries that if he doesn't worry about money, bad things will happen—this is a form of superstition. Thus, worriers have difficulty enjoying their money since they're constantly afraid of scarcity and fuel poverty consciousness. It's important for them to focus on surrendering worry so that they don't sabotage abundance with their panicked relationship to finances.

To find out if this is your money type, take the following quiz.

QUIZ: AM I A WORRIER?

- Do I worry about money every day?

- Do I make financial problems larger, not smaller?

- Do I have difficulty falling asleep because I'm worried about money?

- Do I worry about money even during comfortable times?

- Do I find I can't stop worrying, even though I try?

- When one financial worry is solved do I immediately go on to another?

If you answered yes to all six questions, worry plays a very large role in your financial life. Four or five yeses indicate a large role. Two or three yeses indicate a moderate role. One yes indicates a low level. Zero indicates that this is not your primary money type.

The art of surrendering worry is to stay focused in the present moment rather than making up worst-case scenarios to freak yourself out, and take action where you can such as slowly paying off a debt. My Daoist teacher says, "Worrying doesn't change anything." Whether you worry about money chronically or occasionally, it's an attempt to control the future. What's hard for worriers to accept is that despite their valiant efforts to be financially secure, they can't control everything. To worry less and relax more, practice this exercise.

SURRENDER WORRY, BE IN THE NOW

1. *Use deep belly breathing to let go.* Worry makes your body tense. Breathing lets you physically surrender tension. If you're worried, place one hand on your chest, the other on your belly. Then slowly inhale through your nose to a count of eight. Simultaneously, feel your belly expand (not your chest, as in regular breathing). The hand on your belly should rise higher than the other one. Hold your breath for a few seconds. Then slowly exhale through your mouth to a count of eight. Repeat this exercise at least three times at each sitting, several times each day, to surrender worries. In yoga, this practice is thought to facilitate the greatest flow of life force throughout the body.

2. *Be in the now.* When worried thoughts project you into the future, bring yourself back to the now. Tell yourself, "Today, I'll do what I can to improve my finances, and that will be enough." Focus on self-compassion and appreciating the baby steps you take to move forward. To release money worries also say the Serenity Prayer I presented in Chapter 1 as frequently as needed. One way to know you have surrendered is that for periods of time, you may even forget to worry!

Money Type 2: The Procrastinator

This money type notoriously avoids dealing with finances. They live from paycheck to paycheck and wait until the last minute to address bills. Their motto is "I'll put it off until later." They don't worry about long-term savings, cutting expenses, or future planning. For the short term, the feel-good benefit of denial is that stress is reduced as thoughts of financial pressure disappear. But reality will catch up with them when bills mount and creditors start calling. Then panic and guilt about not fulfilling responsibilities set in. Procrastinators have a fear of imperfection, which unconsciously causes them to put decisions off, a self-defeating mentality. Other motivators include anxiety about not having enough money (paying bills makes them confront this—that's why they avoid it), fear of failure, lack of focus, boredom, an unrealistic sense of time, and low energy. Just like an ostrich, they prefer to hide from financial responsibilities until circumstances force them to take action.

To find out if this is your money type, take the following quiz.

QUIZ: AM I A PROCRASTINATOR?

- Do I put off financial decisions?

- Are my bills piling up?

- Do I have difficulty making decisions about money?

- Do I keep ignoring my credit card debt?

- Do I glaze over when paying bills?

- Are my taxes or other bills always past due so I accrue penalty charges?

If you answered yes to all six questions, procrastination or denial play a very large role in your financial life. Four or five yeses indicate a large role. Two or three yeses indicate a moderate role. One yes indicates a low level. Zero indicates that this is not your primary money type.

As a psychiatrist, I know how much diligence it takes to surrender denial. This is something procrastinators have to want to do. Then, gradually, they can train themselves to address money at a comfortable pace so they don't automatically escape into denial when overwhelmed. The secret to letting go of procrastination is finding the sweet spot between accepting financial responsibility and taking time out from stress to unwind. Then finances become about balance and self-awareness rather than dealing with the consequences of living with blinders on. The following exercise will assist you in this.

SURRENDER PROCRASTINATION AND DENIAL, SET SMALL GOALS

- *Be willing to change.* A willingness to admit and release old habits is a wonderful start. Tell yourself, "I can learn to manage money in a time-effective way."

- *Start with one small doable goal.* Break large complicated tasks into smaller pieces. Complete one task, no matter how small. For instance, start by paying the phone bill instead of taking on your entire bank statement. Then you can go on to another task. Do not exceed four tasks in one day.

- *Stay focused and minimize distractions.* Check email, Facebook, or voice mail only twice a day instead of every ten minutes. Find a quiet room where you can concentrate. Resist the urge to take a break or do something else.

- *Set a deadline.* Tell yourself, "I will finish paying four bills in an hour." Then you won't be tempted to put them off.

- *Affirm your success.* Tell yourself what a good job you did. If perfectionist thoughts come in, such as "I should have done more," say, "Thank you for sharing," and praise yourself again.

- *Relax and have fun.* Reward yourself for the positive steps you take forward. Don't be tempted to deal with more financial issues today and risk getting overwhelmed. Tomorrow you can return to this exercise and set further small goals. This approach enables you to experience success, build up to larger goals, and melt the denial behind procrastination.

Money Type 3: The Spending Addict

Spending addicts prefer the thrill of spending to the security of saving money. Compared to successful risk takers, who make calculated risks with a clear financial plan, this type spends on impulse whether they can afford it or not. Spending becomes a drug, a way to self-medicate low self-esteem, hurt, and disappointments by futilely trying to fill an emotional hole with material things—a temporary fix at best. (They may be cross-addicted to alcohol, sex, food, or other substances too.) But nothing is ever enough. Hard-core spending addicts can't stop spending despite the negative fallout, a compulsion many gamblers and shopaholics know. They max out credit cards, borrow to pay for essentials, or risk their life savings. Then they lie to cover their tracks.

Spending addicts tend to make money and lose it quickly. They are not afraid to risk, nor are they worriers; they have the chutzpah to go for high stakes, and sometimes they win. However, they're addicted to the adrenaline rush of risk taking and making a quick buck. Compulsive gamblers are an extreme version of spending addicts. Research shows that these gamblers have lower baseline levels of adrenaline in daily life compared to those who gamble casually. Biologically, they may crave the thrill of gambling to raise their adrenaline levels. What makes gambling hard to surrender is that when they attempt to stop their habit, their adrenaline dips and they experience withdrawal, becoming restless and irritable.

All spending addicts live on the edge; chaos and drama surround their finances. There are degrees of spending addiction, ranging from periodic shopping sprees to losing their kids' college fund at the blackjack table. Either way, the craving to buy or bet or overspend is unhealthy to surrender to.

To find out if this is your money type, take the following quiz.

QUIZ: AM I A SPENDING ADDICT?

- Do I have difficulty controlling my spending?
- Do I get a thrill from spending money or gambling?

- Do I overspend to escape worry, anger, or loneliness?

- Am I a compulsive shopper, unable to pass up "bargains" I can't afford?

- Are my debts affecting my serenity and reputation?

- Do I have a bad credit record?

If you answered yes to all six questions, addictive spending plays a very large role in your financial life. Four or five yeses indicate a large role. Two or three yeses indicate a moderate role. One yes indicates a low level. Zero indicates that this is not your primary money type.

A spending addiction is primarily an emotional and spiritual issue, not a financial one. Treatments include counseling, twelve-step programs such as Gamblers or Debtors Anonymous, and learning money management skills. Healing comes from learning to address and let go of painful emotions without trying to numb them with spending. In addition, twelve-step programs teach that self-knowledge and willpower alone aren't sufficient to cure a spending addiction. Surrendering the will by enlisting the help of a higher power is also necessary for recovery. Admitting your powerlessness to deal with money in a healthy way and that all your best efforts to control spending failed are the first steps to this surrender. In addition, practice this exercise.

SURRENDER YOUR SPENDING ADDICTION, CONNECT TO A HIGHER POWER

- *Admit the problem.* Being honest about an inability to control your spending is the first step to healing.

- *Identify what's upsetting you before you spend.* For instance, "I don't feel appreciated at work" or "I'm angry that my boyfriend cancelled our dinner."

- *Ask for the spending urge to be lifted.* When an intense craving to spend hits, stop and take a breath. Even though every cell in you is screaming "To feel better, I need that $500 purse or that

Mercedes," try something different. Inwardly say, "I'm power-less over my urge to spend. I surrender it to you. Please lift it from me." Repeat this request as often as you like. Then relax, keep breathing, and feel the cravings lessen with this spiritual surrender.

Money Type 4: The Saver, Miser, or Hoarder

These types are practical, good at planning for the future and saving for a rainy day. If their incomes allow it, they regularly contribute to a retirement fund, avoid credit card debt, and don't spend their principal unless necessary. They think clearly about money and stick to purchases within their means. They value financial security, bargain hunting, and coupon clipping, but they're not cheapskates—many also include tithing in their budget. Smart saving requires thought and commitment.

Nevertheless, there's a difference between being financially responsible and being obsessive. Savers who go overboard can become penny pinchers or greedy misers. It's hard for them to enjoy their money, take vacations, or spend on themselves and others. Misers cheat themselves of joy by clinging to money, afraid of deprivation or destitution. These people are not having fun or prospering. While savers have positive impulses to conserve funds, being miserly is the dark side of savers. Feeling loss of control in their lives, they become overly controlling with their finances. But no bank balance will ever be sufficient to relieve their anxieties or make them feel safe in the world.

To find out if this is your money type, take the following quiz.

QUIZ: AM I A SAVER?

- Am I diligent at saving money but don't hoard?
- Do I prefer conservative investments to risk taking?
- Can I enjoy spending money on things I can afford?
- Do I try not to spend more than I make?

- Am I against greed?

- Do I give to charitable causes?

If you answered yes to all six questions, being a saver plays a very large role in your finances. Four or five yeses indicate a moderate role. Two or three yeses indicate you are a saver but may have penny-pinching habits that could use some loosening up. One yes indicates that you may have miserly tendencies. Zero indicates that this is not your primary money type.

The most extreme, unhealthy version of a saver is a hoarder. This is someone who collects possessions, including things like magazines, notes, or newspapers, and can't get rid of them. Lately, hoarding has been brought into public awareness with television programs that shockingly show people's homes so crammed with stuff that the inhabitants can barely move.

When savers turn into misers or hoarders it may suggest obsessive-compulsive disorder which makes them clutch money and things to ward off anxiety, the opposite of surrender. Freud attributed this behavior to disrupted toilet training—misers and hoarders become anal retentive to feel in control. They're emotionally and financially withholding; it's too anxiety provoking to let go. Trauma also can play a role. A patient's father-in-law, a Holocaust survivor, earned a fine income but used to collect old clothes on the streets to store in his home. He didn't allow himself pleasure from money and was stingy with relatives. When his cherished granddaughter, a conscientious college student, asked for a car loan, he charged her interest! Misers don't consider how clinging to capital constricts abundance. They can't surrender control and be generous because they fear scarcity. To avoid becoming a mean, miserly Scrooge or a hoarder, try the following exercise. Whether you're a wise saver or a bit of a tightwad, it'll help you practice joyful giving.

SURRENDER STINGINESS, PRACTICE ANONYMOUS GIVING

Spread abundance by anonymously leaving small amounts of money for people to find. At the location of your choosing, leave $1 to $5 there—but don't get found out. It can be anywhere—a hallway in your doctor's building, a bathroom in a public place, a potted plant. Someone will find it and feel lucky. Then they'll believe anything is possible. Experience the happiness of this as you let stinginess go. Be a self-appointed money gnome who spreads abundance in the world.

Money Type 5: The Intuitive Spender

This money type is comfortable using intuition in financial decisions. They are not captives of an overcontrolling mind. At their best, intuitive spenders balance logic with gut instincts in money management, hiring, and investments. This gives them an edge: they have access to multiple forms of information rather than living only in their heads. If they don't know what to do, they leave time for intuition to work on the problem. *Science* magazine reports that shoppers made better decisions when they slept on it and enlisted the wisdom of their unconscious. Whether intuition tells this money type to spend or not, they don't talk themselves out of the advice. Furthermore, they won't make potentially profitable choices if the situation feels wrong. Intuitive entrepreneurs invest in people so they factor in the chemistry of the team. Steve Jobs, founder of Apple, said about hiring people, "In the end, it's based on your gut." Intuitive spenders "listen for the goose bumps" and follow their gut about financial decisions. Famous for this is hotel magnate Conrad Hilton who was known for "Connie's hunches." However, intuitive spenders get into trouble when they simply go on impulse and disregard logic. Also, they can misread a financial situation if they can't distinguish intuition from wishful thinking or fear.

To find out if this is your money type, take the following quiz.

QUIZ: AM I AN INTUITIVE SPENDER?

- Do I check in with my gut about finances?

- Do I look beyond logic for answers?

- If a decision feels right do I act on it or if it doesn't can I let it go?

- Do I trust my gut when it says "beware" of an investment?

- Will I take a reasonable financial risk based on intuition?

- Do I consult my intuition about how to creatively make money and where to invest or donate?

If you answered yes to all six questions, you trust intuition and it plays a very large role in your spending habits. Four or five yeses indicate a large role. Two or three yeses indicate a moderate role. One yes indicates a low level. Zero indicates that this is not your primary money type.

Some intuitive spenders have had to learn to trust their gut. One of my patients ignored an intuition that warned, "Don't buy a car," since logic argued, "Why not? I can squeeze it into my budget." Soon after the purchase, he faced unexpected medical expenses which he then couldn't afford. In addition, a sense of buyer's remorse can indicate an unheeded intuition. Another patient bought a gorgeous couch when her gut said no and ended up getting back pain from it, though it'd felt comfortable in the store. And one patient who was anxious about purchasing a home had a strong inner voice say, "Sign the papers. It'll be fine"—and it was. These experiences helped my patients trust their intuition more in future money matters.

Smart intuitive spenders also have good common sense. If they suspect their accountant of doctoring the books, they don't depend on intuition to prove their case—they get an auditor. But if they're about to spend on something that doesn't feel right, then intuition provides clarity. Intuitive spenders can be brilliant money managers if they're clear about what messages they're surrendering to. The key is to let go of overthinking or fear and trust authentic intuitions. Here are some guidelines to follow.

SURRENDER TO INTUITION, ACT ON ITS ADVICE

- *Tune in to your inner wisdom.* When making a spending decision, inwardly ask yourself, "Is this the right choice?" Then take a few quiet moments to notice how your gut feels about it. Is it queasy? In knots? Relaxed? How about your body? Does it feel energized? Or does this expenditure feel more like a headache than an asset? Also listen to flashes of insight or "aha" moments about whether or not to move ahead.

- *Trust these reliable intuitions.* Authentic intuitions convey information neutrally and unemotionally—they're simply data. Or they have a compassionate, affirming tone and feel right or wrong in your gut. Often they convey a detached sensation, like you're in a theater watching a movie. Do not trust messages with a high emotional charge or intense desire attached to them. These are usually fears or wishful thinking.

- *Let go and take action.* Follow what your intuition says without resisting it or arguing. Then notice the results. Successes build on one another, allowing you to keep surrendering to your intuition.

I'd like you to use the five money types I've outlined as a platform for growth, even if you're not currently the type you want to be. Whatever type you identify with, it's always essential to balance giving versus saving or taking some chances on your dreams versus letting fear paralyze you. By knowing your money type and being willing to surrender negative patterns, you'll be in a stronger financial position.

Generosity is intimately related to abundance. It releases bound-up energy and lets your heart (along with intelligent planning) guide money matters. Give to causes you resonate with. Recently I donated funds toward buying a hundred-foot Buddha for an impoverished, remote mountain village in Thailand. Helping their community build a sacred site vital to them made me happy (as did the photos I received of smiling people praying there). When you give financially, even a little, it releases uptightness about money in many ways. It's saying to the universe, "I won't hold back. I will share what I can. I want to be open and fluid and full of goodwill." My advice is, go for it! Giving from your heart attracts prosperity.

In this chapter, I've presented a perspective about money based on surrendering to the wisdom of our intellect, intuition, and spirit. For optimal financial results, use them all—but remember, *gratitude* for what we have is what makes us content. Money will bring out the best or worst in us. With the tools I've offered, your better self can win. Don't ever feel alone in the quest to stay true to your highest financial integrity. You'll always have a friend over here cheering you on if, inevitably, your ideals waver. I agree with my entrepreneur friend who says, "I want to be a billionaire of karma." Regardless of how much money you have, let it make your life and the world a better place. In the words of the Buddha: "Neither fire nor wind, birth nor death can erase our good deeds." Abundance is a state of mind more than a reflection of wealth.

Still, each of us has different money karma. Over the years, I've watched how some patients seem to effortlessly turn everything into gold, while others work feverishly and save but can't seem to amass wealth. Why this happens sometimes goes beyond all the best financial strategizing: it has to do with what is fated. The course of people's lives differs depending on their soul's needs. (As I keep saying, earning more isn't always better.) This is where surrender is liberating. If you're not destined to be well-off, though you've made noble attempts, try to make peace with that, tough as it may be in our materialistic world. Don't get down on yourself. *You haven't done anything wrong.* The point always is to make the most of what you've got, be generous when you can, and create love around you. Release. Let go. Be thankful for little things. The reward of surrender, in finances and all else, is to experience the bliss of bowing to what is.

Once, on a meditation retreat, my Daoist teacher warned me against making huge amounts of money. His remark puzzled me: I'd never had that desire, nor was there any such possibility. Then, synchronistically, totally out of the blue, a hot advertising agency approached me with a really lucrative offer to endorse a product! Of course, my interest was piqued; I seriously considered it. But ultimately, I had to turn the offer down, though saying no to that kind of money wasn't easy. The offer didn't feel right in my gut because I would've been endorsing something I didn't believe in. Doing so would've cost me far more than the money was worth. In my case, my body would've predictably rebelled as it had so often before when I'd been going down the wrong path. Literally, I would've been sick to my stomach, or worse. My teacher's admonition made me aware of how wealth and the complexities that accompany it, could distract me from the quiet simplicity of life and vibrant health I require to flourish. I want to honor the sacrament of my life and do my best not to deviate from the heart that guides me. But, when I'm tempted or falter, I want to quickly pick myself up and head toward love, always love. Everything about money—having it and not having it—can catalyze this kind of surrender in all of us if we allow it to.

SURRENDER AFFIRMATION FOR ABUNDANCE

I'm committed to being loving with myself about money. If I'm going through a hard time, I will not beat myself up. If times are good, I will enjoy my blessings and help others with what I have. I am committed to abundance on every level.

Part Two

READING PEOPLE AND COMMUNICATION

Break on through to the other side.
—THE DOORS
....

4

THE FOURTH SURRENDER

LEARNING THE ART OF READING PEOPLE

LET ME TELL YOU THE SECRET OF HOW TO READ PEOPLE. IT'S A powerful yet practical skill that must be used responsibly and with humility. To do this, I'll show you how to lose your mind a little and surrender in a good way!

Logic alone won't tell you the whole story about anybody. You must also surrender to other vital forms of information so that you can learn to read the important nonverbal cues that people give off. You'll be letting go of any limits that prevent you from perceiving in deeper ways. By surrendering to new forms of knowing, you're saying to the universe, "I am open to understanding others in order to cultivate the best in our relationship and to compassionately resolve conflicts." Then, with an open mind and heart, you'll be able to shrewdly scan the subtleties of human behavior—whether you're dealing with your boss or your spouse—to grasp people's conscious and unconscious state of mind.

What you're about to discover may introduce you to abilities that you don't even know you have. Once you can read people without your intellect tripping you up, your relationships will never be the same. I realize how ingrained the concept of "the mind knows all" is in our hyperintellectualized world and in conventional medicine. But

I want to help you surrender this dogma so you don't cheat yourself out of seeing the whole person. To do this, you must also be willing to surrender any preconceptions or emotional baggage such as old resentments or ego clashes that stop you from seeing someone clearly. The point is to receive information neutrally without distorting it. Then, when you let go of who you think people are and can truly read them, you can forge a useful and wondrous mutual connection. The purpose is to communicate better and to empathize with where people are coming from, even if you disagree with them. It is never to control or manipulate. When you can read people, you can reach them, especially if nothing you're saying is getting through or if someone seems impossible to deal with. This skill provides X-ray vision into touchy situations, whether a family member feels misunderstood or you suspect a competitor of pulling a fast one. It can also tune you in to the desires of loved ones so that you can bring them joy.

My job as a psychiatrist is to read people—not just what they say but who they are. Interpreting verbal and nonverbal cues, I want to see past their masks into the real person, the one who may be hiding, scared, or trying to look important but who is afraid inside of not mattering. These are simply resistances that arise when people become rigid or defensive. I want to know what holds people back and what takes them to the stars. Because I specialize in difficult situations such as reuniting estranged families, resolving workplace feuds, and healing betrayals, teaching my patients to read others helps them strategically respond rather than just react. But some patients aren't exactly sure why they've come to me, only that they feel cut off or lost. In our work, I help them find that answer.

In medical school I was taught to read the body's signs of illness—the yellow skin of jaundice, the protruding eyes of hyperthyroidism, the swollen calves of heart failure. However, the way I read people today incorporates the skills I learned in medical school and then goes beyond them. As much as I respect and enjoy the fact-finding, analytic mind my training emphasized, we must tap other kinds of intelligence. Doing this is an enormously satisfying form of creativity when you can go with it. Material reality doesn't always impress me or convey the depths of human nature. To see further, the techniques

I use and will teach you include decoding body language, emotions, and energy, and using remote viewing. You'll learn to utilize what I call "super-senses" to look further than where you usually put your attention, helping you access life-changing intuitive insights. What captivates me is peering into my patients' hearts and souls so I can truly help them.

Reading people lets you find the best in everyone, no matter how difficult or annoying they seem. Take forty-year-old Ken, a middle school teacher who'd come in for headaches and stress. In our first session, my head began to hurt too as he started to instruct me on "what a therapist should do." It wasn't easy for me to like him. I realized that being controlling was his defense against insecurity and feeling out of control. I also knew that once I had a better sense of Ken's vulnerabilities, more compassion would follow.

What enabled me to go further was my intuition. Over the years, I've trained myself to use intellectual and intuitive listening simultaneously. Thus, as I sat with Ken, I inwardly had a sudden flash. I saw a lonely boy escaping from his parents' violent fights into science fiction novels. This image felt clear and right. It gave my heart a quick way to connect with him. Still, since he hadn't yet mentioned domestic violence, I didn't raise the subject until trust developed between us. However, I did ask him, "What do you like to read?" Immediately Ken's face lit up and he described his love of Robert Heinlein's sci-fi novels. This naturally prompted him to describe the role reading had in his childhood. My intuition provided the perfect icebreaker to begin establishing rapport with a good man who'd become supercontrolling in order to cope with a chaotic home.

In this chapter, I invite you to explore different methods of reading people, including intuition. These all require surrendering pure logic so that you can also receive alternative, nonlinear forms of input. FBI profilers are trained to do this too—they access "expert intuition," a speedy way of deciphering many levels of information, from words and gestures to microexpressions. You'll discover how these ace profilers, known as "truth wizards," assemble their hunches to uncover information. I'll show you how to apply these detective skills in your life too. Have fun: think of practicing these techniques as an adventure in exploring and letting go to new forms of awareness that can improve your relationships. Allow your mind to be blown a little—it's a good thing.

However, reading people involves more than information gathering. It lets us glimpse the mystery of the human experience. Layers of static disappear to reveal clarity. For me, it's poetic and sensual and it allows me to feel the rhythms that propel people, whether they are aware of these influences or not. It's flowing with others in the most radical way: how their bodies move, the sparkle in their eyes, the music of their voices, how they breathe. Whether someone breathes shallowly or fully speaks volumes about that person's capacity for surrender and joy. The reason I delight in knowing all this is because connection means everything to me; I'm not interested in just skimming the outer regions of the psyche. I marvel at not having to hold back, at being able to surrender to a form of seeing I don't presume to fully understand but connect with profoundly.

SURRENDER TO THE POWER OF LOGIC AND BEYOND

To read people accurately you must surrender biases, some walls must come down. Most people operate at a low level of sensitivity compared to their potential since they rely on the intellect to interpret reality. As brilliant as the intellect is, you have to be willing to let go of old, limiting ideas and accept that:

1. Logic doesn't have all the answers.
2. Words only present part of the story.
3. You are more than your linear mind.

Your intellect may resist intuition since it dismisses data outside of its own ability to track the world. But to access other kinds of input, you must learn to go further than "local awareness," which is defined by what we can see, hear, and touch. Then you can open to what the new scientific paradigm terms "nonlocal awareness," which is more intuitively based and can perceive beyond the material world. Surrendering in this sense first means mentally getting out of your own way, to hear intuition by stilling the mind. What's interesting is that when the mind is still, you automatically slip into nonlocal consciousness. *The only thing that stands between you and intuition is the incessant chatter in your brain.* Learning to let go of this chatter is forever life-changing. When I first began incorporating intuition into patient care, I made a deal with myself: I'd keep my mind open a crack to scrutinize if intuition was valid. I was tentative and slow in surrendering my resistance, but a crack was all I needed. Once you can start to do this, the intuitive experiences speak for themselves.

In the seminars I present on intuition to skeptical physician groups, I always say, "Try these methods. Notice the results with patients. If they help you to be a better doctor, keep using them." (Also, to avoid arousing an audience's resistance, I never use "psychic," an antique term that conjures only fortune-tellers and charlatans.) With my patients, I'm totally results-oriented. I have no use for techniques that don't work. If you're skeptical or on the fence about intuition, simply be willing to consider the advantages of trying something new. Then you decide. The point is to know what the intellect excels at and accept where it can't go. To overcome intellectual resistance, here's a simple surrender request you can make.

A SURRENDER REQUEST FOR SKEPTICS

Let me be willing to experiment.

Let me be willing to open my mind.

I want to release my closed-mindedness.

I want to release my rigidity.

I want to be receptive to what I haven't yet discovered.

As you learn to read people, take your time. Think of it as building up muscles that were inactive before. The intellect loves factual evidence—this tempers all of its arguments. So reassure it; tell it, "I won't be convinced of anything until I see proof." When your intellect recognizes the worth of these techniques, it'll feel safer loosening its grip as you venture outside its comfort zone.

HOW TO IGNITE YOUR SUPER-SENSES

People who read others well are trained to read the invisible and fine-tune their senses, including the sixth sense. They pick up on verbal contradictions and signs of anger or unease, signals others typically miss. During this process always ask yourself, "What motivates this person in this moment?" Empathy means putting yourself in someone else's shoes, and this is what you'll do in a successful reading. The idea is to gather information with every perceptual ability you possess, but not to overidentify with anyone. I'll show you how to be caring but objective.

During readings, the first step is to become as neutral as possible. This makes you objective. As odd as it may seem, reading people is not personal. Try to simply receive information without filtering it through your personal beliefs or emotional reactions. While tuning in, you may like the person you see, or not. However, your job is to observe, not to judge—not to approve or disapprove. Otherwise the reading becomes all about your values and feelings, defeating your purpose. Most people, when they look at others, see only themselves! However, when you're neutral, your assessments are more exact. Reading people isn't about you—it's about who they are, what motivates them.

To release judgment, it's useful to consider this perspective: everyone contains the best and worst of human nature. We all have the potential in our DNA to be a saint, a sinner, and everything in between. It's not just "the bad guys" who have the capacity for deceit, anger, or drama. The difference is that you are in control of which parts of yourself you come from. Try to have compassion for others' faults rather than condemning or vilifying them. As the Haggadah says, "May I open my heart to all broken things." To perceive people accurately, you must surrender judging them.

Before you do a reading, here's an exercise I suggest that you use to become neutral and still the noise in your mind.

SURRENDER MENTAL CHATTER AND JUDGMENT

Take a few deep breaths. Bring your awareness completely to the present moment, not the past or the future—this keeps the reading fresh. Picture your mind as a clean, empty slate. Temporarily set aside your problems, to-do lists, judgments, or preconceptions. (You can always return to them later!) If these or other thoughts pop up, visualize them passing by like clouds in the sky without becoming attached to them. Do the same for self-doubts such as "I'm not intuitive. I can't do this." Just let them go by focusing on breathing, not on your thoughts or fears. This distracts the mind's chatter, lulling it to sleep so it's not in the front of your consciousness. While reading people, simply note what you perceive. Do not analyze it until later. Surrendering mental chatter even for a few moments can be bliss. It's a free-floating empty space where anything is possible.

While practicing the following four techniques, keep training yourself to be neutral. You will improve at this. These techniques provide different pieces of the puzzle to understand others. One may appeal to you more than another, but experiment with each. They can be mixed and matched. The idea is to scan everything from people's body language to their emotional energy. Don't get bogged down in excessive detail. Just notice what "hits" stand out most. Even one is revealing. Keep a journal of your observations so you can refer to them. Then use what you discover to see through people's defenses and raise the bar of communicating with everyone.

FOUR TECHNIQUES TO READ PEOPLE

The First Technique: Observe Body Language Cues

If you meet a woman at a conference who you think might be right for a job in your company, how can reading her help you decide? Or you're talking to someone at a coffeehouse and wonder, should you ask him or her out? Research has shown that words account for only 7 percent of how we communicate whereas our body language accounts for 55 percent and voice tone accounts for 30 percent. FBI profilers also say that microexpressions, tone, and gaze can expose deception.

Here, the surrender to focus on is letting go of trying too hard to read body language cues. Don't get overly intense or analytical. Stay relaxed and fluid. Be comfortable, sit back, and simply observe. You're training yourself to develop a more detailed eye for the world. Note what you pick up without straining. If you're not getting cues or are unsure about the ones you observe, don't force things to fit. Wait until the signs are clearer. Too much effort blocks the process because you're trying to push something that can't be pushed. After the reading, you can analyze what signs ring true and let them guide your interactions.

CHECKLIST OF BODY LANGUAGE CUES

PAY ATTENTION TO APPEARANCE

This offers general information about personality, body image, and priorities. When reading others, notice the following: Are they wearing a power suit and well-shined shoes, indicating ambition? Jeans and a T-shirt, indicating comfort with being casual? A tight top showing cleavage, a seductive choice? A pendant such as a cross or Buddha, indicating spiritual values? Are they decked in expensive jewelry, suggesting materialism or the need to impress? Is there never a hair out of place, a sign of perfectionism? Or are they unkempt, indicating lack of self-care? Also notice if they are stick-thin, average weight, or obese, suggesting their eating, exercise, and health habits, from anorexia to food addiction.

NOTICE POSTURE

When reading people's posture, ask yourself: Do they hold their head high, suggesting they're confident? Think of a dancer or yoga practitioner. (Paris Hilton says, "Always act like you're wearing an invisible crown.") Or do they walk indecisively or cower, a sign of low self-esteem? Do they swagger with a puffed-out chest, a sign of a big ego? Do they have a playful bounce in their step, indicating energy and enthusiasm? Is their posture slumped with their neck jutted forward, suggesting long hours at a computer and/or no exercise and stretching regime? Is their posture rigid, shoulders scrunched up to their ears, revealing tension? Or are their shoulders and body relaxed, signs of being comfortable in their own skin?

WATCH FOR PHYSICAL MOVEMENTS

Leaning and Distance

Observe where people lean. Generally, we lean toward those we like and away from those we don't. A person who moves closer to you can be signaling seductiveness, indicating a romantic interest or a desire to convince you of something. Depending on your relationship with them, it can feel nice or like a boundary violation. In contrast, when people face away from you while talking, it conveys "I'm not interested." Celebrities in public can have quirky body language. One habit that amuses me is that women, especially, often greet one another by putting their cheeks together, puckering, then kissing in the air, as if trying to protect their makeup or hair. Also, observe how far people stand from you. Moving too close or talking in your face can indicate aggression, self-obsession, or poor boundaries—when you inch backward, such people often inch forward, disregarding your needs. Other intrusive gestures include patting your butt or backslapping.

Crossed Arms and Legs

This pose suggests defensiveness, anger, or self-protection. Notice the direction in which people cross their legs. While seated, they tend to point the toes of the top leg toward someone with whom they're at ease—and point away from others they don't like. Men and women who sit with their legs wide open give off sexual signals. Foot tapping or restless legs are signs of anxiety.

Finger Pointing

This can indicate blaming, criticism, anger, or telling someone what to do.

Hiding One's Hands

When people place their hands in their laps or pockets or put them behind their back, it suggests that they are hiding something. They may be telling you one thing but you're not getting the whole story. Cracking their knuckles is a sign of tension.

Standing with Legs Shoulder Width Apart

This position signals dominance and determination. When asserting a point in a discussion, this traditional stance of power communicates, "I'm standing my ground."

Lip Biting or Cuticle Picking

When people bite or lick their lips or pick their cuticles, they are trying to soothe themselves under pressure or in an awkward situation.

Brushing Hair off the Face

This movement, along with hair tossing, can signal anxiety, flirtation, or a combination of both. It calls attention to one's face and neck and is often a sign that a person is attracted to someone, especially when it's done by women.

Signs of Lying

There are no foolproof clues, but these gestures make FBI profilers suspicious. Men tend to stroke their neck, which is calming, lowering their heart rate. For women, touching the suprasternal notch at the top of the chest, indicates discomfort and protecting themselves. Also, scratching one's nose can be a sign of deception: lying often increases adrenaline, which causes capillaries to expand, making a person's nose itch. In addition, during an interrogation, if a suspect moves away from the interviewer (a "nonverbal torso lean"), this suggests dishonesty or avoidance.

INTERPRET FACIAL EXPRESSION

Reading faces is an ancient system of evaluating character. It reflects our temperament, mood, and approach to life. As part of reading people's faces, notice the following: Is their face serious? Intense? Sad? Smiling? Pouting? Childlike? Cruel? Peaceful? Are they blushing, indicating embarrassment? Or do they have tears of sadness or joy? Emotions can become etched on our faces. Deep frown lines suggest worry or overthinking. Crow's feet are the smile lines, signs of joy. Pursed lips signal anger, contempt, or bitterness. A clenched jaw and teeth grinding are signs of tension. FBI profilers say that microexpressions of fear, anger, or a sinister smile that doesn't match the content of a person's speech suggests deceit.

TRACK EYE CONTACT

The eyes are the windows into the soul. When you're observing people, ask yourself whether they make confident eye contact, or whether their eyes drift, suggesting distraction, disinterest, or avoidance. (FBI profilers associate poor eye contact with lying.) Do they lock eyes without wavering, signaling dominance? This intimidation tactic is used in police work. (Predators never take their eyes off their victim. In combat, weaker animals break the gaze.) Are their eyes intrusively probing, indicating poor boundaries or the need to control? Or do they keep a respectful distance yet still connect well with you? Are their eyes shifty, suggesting manipulation or deceit? Mischievous? Kind? Or perhaps amorous, sneaking glimpses of your body, a sign of attraction? Tired people may have dark circles around the eyes. Glassy, red eyes indicate crying or allergies. Furthermore, under stress our eyelids twitch and we blink more often. The normal blink rate is six to eight times per minute. Blinking patterns can reveal how calm or uptight one is. When two people are discussing a topic of mutual interest, on average they make eye contact between 30 and 60 percent of the time.

BE AWARE OF SCENT

We have a thousand different kinds of smell receptors and can detect more than ten thousand odors. Our scent can reveal personal habits. Do you smell cigarettes, cigars, alcohol? Can you detect body odor or bad breath, suggesting poor self-care or a medical disorder? Is their perfume or cologne overwhelming communicating "Notice me," a desire to be attractive (even dominate), or an insensitivity to how others are affected. Are you drawn to their smell, a primal attraction? Is their fragrance appealing? Pheromones are hormones of attraction that subliminally function as an aphrodisiac.

NOTICE BREATHING PATTERNS

How fast or slow we breathe can be informative. People who are rushing around or stuck in their heads thinking or worrying forget to breathe deeply. They tend to hold their breath; you can barely see their chest moving. This suggests tightness, tension, or the need to overcontrol. Hyperventilating or rapid breathing is associated with anxiety, anger, extreme emotion, or illness. FBI profilers say that a quick exhale can signal lying or nervousness. Relaxed breathing, where the chest is visibly expanding and contracting slowly, indicates lack of tension, a surrendered relationship with life, and a healthy connection to the body.

ACTION STEP: APPLY WHAT YOU HAVE LEARNED ABOUT BODY LANGUAGE

Using the checklist of signs I've presented, you can practice reading body language cues wherever you go. Get in the habit of people watching. I suggest starting with strangers—that way you'll more easily remain neutral. Go to a mall, a supermarket, or a park. Notice how others look and move. It's fascinating. Watch the way they hold their bodies as they eat lunch, cash a check, talk to their families, or just wander around. But don't stare obviously—that makes anyone uncomfortable.

Here's how I use this information about body language to uncover patients' hidden feelings. Take Angie, who said she felt fine about her divorce while folding her arms and clinging to her body for dear life, signaling unspoken fears. Or Jack, who swore he'd quit cigarettes though I smelled smoke on his clothes, announcing the truth. Or Izzy, a high-strung computer programmer, who said his mother "could do no wrong," but cracked his knuckles whenever he talked about her, indicating repressed conflict about her. At the right time, I gently give patients feedback on their body language to help them discover what it reveals about themselves. Because these physical gestures are often subconscious and automatic, people seldom realize what they are communicating.

In every area of your life, these skills are advantageous, from offering you an edge at business meetings to providing empathy for those close to you. For example, if a coworker is sitting on his hands while sharing the details of a project, you might tactfully inquire about information he may have omitted. Or if your sister is biting her lip while discussing her teenage son's unapologetic rudeness, this sign of anxiety suggests that you be especially sweet with her. Consider yourself an explorer in the world, honing your powers of observation. Again, surrender entails letting go of stereotypes and simply following the lead of what people's bodies tell you.

The Second Technique: Listen to Your Intuition

You can tune in to someone beyond their body language and words. Intuition is what your gut feels, not what your head says. It's non-verbal information you perceive via images, "aha" moments, and body knowings, rather than logic. If you want to understand someone, what counts the most is who the person is, not his or her outer trappings. Intuition lets you see further than the obvious to reveal a richer story.

When tuning in, be careful of projecting onto others what para-psychology researchers call "intellectual overlay." It's when your mind distorts the accuracy of a reading by trying to make it fit expected assumptions. This won't do you any good if you want to hear intuition. For instance, once I had an intuitive hit that a patient was having a passionate affair with someone named Sam. I asked her about this mysterious fellow she'd failed to mention in our sessions and her face lit up with a grin. "You're close," she said. "Sam is my new Chihuahua puppy!" We both got a good laugh out of my misreading of the situation. Without realizing it, I had assumed Sam was a man, an example of intellectual overlay that reminded me how assumptions can sneak in. Or imagine your mother says about a guy she'd like you to date, "Everyone adores Harold. I adore him. You will too." This statement could cloud your reading of Harold. Without neutrality, you'd be seeing Harold through your mother's eyes; you might even end up marrying the man of her dreams instead of your own! Realize that intuition is not a popularity vote. It has nothing to do with other people's opinions or peer pressure.

Here, the surrender to focus on is letting go of preconceptions. Intuition happens quickly, so stay aware. The goal is not to think about others or yourself. How can you let go enough to achieve this? As I do with patients, make the person you're reading the only one in your universe for that time. Put your attention only on her, her voice, her needs, the intuitive messages you receive when you're with her. This surrendering of self-preoccupation feels like a delightful relief—my personal issues recede and I'm just focused on my patient. It's similar to the instinctive surrendering of self that happens when you're caught up in watching a film or lost in a song. You become absorbed in someone else's story rather than your own. A light touch and a sense of play will let you enjoy the experience. Tuning in involves being receptive, not control. You're not reaching for information but you'll be shown things. Train yourself to stay aware of the following intuitions.

CHECKLIST OF INTUITIVE CUES

HONOR YOUR GUT FEELINGS

Listen to what your gut says, especially during first meetings. The visceral reaction that occurs before you have a chance to think relays whether you're at ease or not. Science associates these feelings with a "brain" in the gut called the enteric nervous system, a network of neurons that process information. Gut feelings occur quickly, an internal truth meter. Suzy Welch, former editor of the *Harvard Business Review*, says, "My gut is my relationship radar. It tells me if someone is a phony so I don't invest in their business." On the other hand, when patients say, "My gut told me that a decision was wrong but I did it anyway," they always regret that choice.

People can make your gut feel good or sick. Ask yourself, "What is my gut's reaction to others? Is it in knots? Do I suddenly feel nauseated or acidic? Does my gut relax about certain people? Do I get a sense of trust or does something feel off? Be careful not to talk yourself out of these intuitions. If you're unsure about your gut's take on a relationship, simply go slow until you get a clearer read.

FEEL GOOSE BUMPS

Goose bumps are marvelous intuitive tingles that convey that we resonate with people who move or inspire us, or who are saying something that strikes a chord. Goose bumps also happen when you experience déjà vu, a recognition that you've known someone before, though you've actually never met. Don't worry if you don't get goose bumps around people—they indicate a special connection—but gravitate toward those people with whom you do. Negative goose bumps, however, are warnings of danger or deception, a response to fear. The hairs on your neck stand on end in a bad way, communicating, "Beware. Stay away." When you get goose bumps, either positive or negative, use this "tingle factor" to inform your relationships.

PAY ATTENTION TO FLASHES OF INSIGHT

In conversations, you may get an "aha" moment about people, an insight that comes in a flash. Stay alert, otherwise you might miss it. We tend to go on to the next thought so rapidly that these critical insights can get lost. So if your spouse is furious and you get a sudden picture of her as a frightened child, this is your cue to make that child in her feel safe and understood. Or if a business colleague isn't budging on a point in a negotiation and you get a flash that tells you, "Let him think about it overnight rather than pushing," follow that guidance. See.if this breathing room allows things to shift. These flashes provide extra insight into people. To gain confidence in them, practice following their instructions. Then notice if your life improves.

WATCH FOR INTUITIVE EMPATHY

Sometimes you can feel people's physical symptoms and emotions in your body, which is an intense form of empathy. For instance, you arrive in a great mood for lunch with a friend, but you leave with a headache, exhausted, though the conversation wasn't stressful. Or you notice you're happier just being around a certain co-worker. In both cases, you may be absorbing the feelings of others. So when you're reading people, notice, "Does my back hurt when it didn't before? Am I depressed or upset after an uneventful meeting?" To determine if this is empathy, get feedback. For example, ask your friend, "Do you happen to be tired or have a headache?" If yes, then you'll know it's her. When it's inappropriate to inquire directly, notice if you feel better after people leave. Empathy often subsides when you're not in their presence.

Your intuition about people will get stronger with practice. To avoid errors, I pay special attention to what gets in the way of tuning in. I'd like you to notice these factors in yourself too. The main hazards are (1) wanting something so much you can't remain neutral, (2) being too emotionally invested in a situation to see it clearly, and (3) projecting your own fears and expectations onto others. In these situations, I try to honestly admit what's holding me back. When strong passions obscure my vision about love, work, or anything else, I do my best to detach from these feelings by refocusing on my breath and practicing this chapter's exercise on surrendering mental chatter. This helps distract my mind so I can find a neutral space from which to tune in. At those times when I don't succeed, I accept my limitation and wing it on logic or common sense until I'm clearer. In addition, I try to be vigilant about withdrawing my projections. For instance, if I say, "You are envious," but really I'm the envious one, I need to address the causes of my envy before I can accurately read you. What excites me about the process of developing intuition is that we must be self-aware and open to our own growth. Then we'll be able to remove blocks that distort perception.

The Third Technique: Sense Emotional Energy

Emotions are a stunning expression of our energy, the "vibe" we give off. We register these with intuition. Some people feel good to be around; they improve your mood and vitality. Others are draining; you instinctively want to get away. This "subtle energy" can be felt inches or feet from the body, though it's invisible. Indigenous cultures honor this energy as life force. In Chinese medicine it's called *chi*, a vitality that's essential to health. Though the molecular structure of subtle energy isn't fully defined, scientists have measured increased photon emissions and electromagnetic readings among healers who emit it during their work.

Emotional energy is contagious. It can make the difference between a toxic relationship and a healthy one. It's crucial to get a clear
read on this aspect of anyone with whom you plan to regularly interact. Then you can decide whether a relationship is feasible based
on your energetic compatibility. In my medical practice and life, this
chemistry is a deal breaker. Experience has taught me that it's point-
less to work with a patient or form a friendship if such basic rapport
isn't there. When the energy feels right, you don't have to force a
fit. Forcing anything is simply the mind's attempt to interfere with
flow. Of course, we all have quirks, anxieties, and fears but energy ce-
ments your bond with others and motivates you to work through the
rough spots. Nevertheless, healthy relationships have a momentum
that carries them, a surrender that feels more natural when you're
both in synch.

When reading emotions, realize that what others say or how they
appear may not match their energy. You must let go of the notion that
what you see is what you always get. As a psychiatrist, I've observed
how people go to great lengths, purposely or not, to appear in certain
ways—to impress, to say the right thing, or to sell you on something—
but this "self" isn't aligned with their true emotions. Consider these
examples: Your spouse apologizes for blowing up but her hostility
still lingers. A man you just met tries to charm you, but you don't feel
much heart there. A friend seems cheerful but you sense that she's
hurting inside. Realize that just because people smile, it doesn't mean
they're happy, and just because people are reserved, it doesn't mean
they're not ecstatic. Ultimately, the energy transmitted by someone's
smile and presence tells the truth about where that person is at. So be
smart enough to correlate people's energy with their emotions. Most
people aren't being intentionally misleading; often they don't know
what they feel or project. They might tell you one thing—and believe
it—but you'll learn to decode their emotions.

Here, the surrender to focus on is saying yes to the messages your
body sends. Your mind may want to talk you out of your body's wisdom. Don't allow it to. Reading energy lets you attune to how you
relate to people, whom you feel comfortable around and whom you

don't. To avoid bad relationships and regrets, you must let go of trying to convince yourself of anything the body's intuition doesn't affirm. To help with this surrender, here's what to do. When identifying how you energetically respond to others, always ask, "How does my body feel? Does my energy go up or down?" Then follow your body's lead rather than resisting it. In practical terms, this means you want to marry someone who increases your energy, not drains it, regardless of how perfect he or she looks on paper. You want to sit beside a co-worker who's positive, not negative. You want to choose friends you resonate with so that you can nurture one another. Then notice the positive difference in your life. To experience the pleasure of compatible relationships, use the following tips.

STRATEGIES TO READ EMOTIONAL ENERGY

SENSE PEOPLE'S PRESENCE

This is the overall energy we emit, and it's not necessarily congruent with words or behavior. It's the emotional atmosphere surrounding us, like a rain cloud or the sun. For instance, we may give off an aura of mystery, joy, or sadness. To compare extremes, think of the Dalai Lama's light, compassionate presence versus Charles Manson's deranged darkness. Presence is also associated with charisma, a personal magnetism that you're drawn to. Warning: charisma doesn't always contain heart. Charisma without heart can't be trusted. It's a dangerous combination present in many con artists and seducers.

As you read people, notice: Does their overall energy feel warm? Calming? Uplifting? Invigorating like a breath of fresh air? Or is it draining? Cold? Detached? Angry? Jarring? Depressed? Do they have a friendly presence that attracts you? Or are you getting the willies, making you back off. Also see if people look anchored in their bodies, indicating that their feet are firmly planted on the ground. Or are they floating outside themselves, which may indicate flakiness and distractability?

WATCH PEOPLE'S EYES

We can make love or hate with our eyes. Our eyes transmit power-ful energies in what the Sufi poet Rumi calls "the glance." Just as the brain has an electromagnetic signal extending beyond the body, studies indicate that the eyes project this too. In fact, research reveals that people can sense when they're being stared at, even when no one is in sight—an experience reported by police officers, soldiers, and hunters. Indigenous cultures respect the energy of the eyes. Some believe that the "evil eye" is a gaze that inflicts injury or bad luck on its target. Also, science has documented "the look of love": joining eyes with a loved one (or even a dog) triggers a bio-chemical response, releasing oxytocin, the warm and fuzzy "love hormone." The more oxytocin your brain has, the more trusting and peaceful you'll feel.

Take time to observe people's eyes. Are they caring? Sexy? Tranquil? Mean? Angry? The way others look at you can make you feel adored or afraid. Also determine: Is there someone at home in their eyes, indicating a capacity for intimacy? Or do they seem to be guarded or hiding? Certain people's eyes can be hypnotic. Avoid looking deeply into eyes you distrust or sense may be dangerous. The less you engage negative people, the less they'll focus on you. On the other hand, feel free to fall into the eyes of people you cher-ish. Enjoy all that beautiful energy!

NOTICE THE FEEL OF A HANDSHAKE, HUG, AND TOUCH

We share emotional energy through physical contact, much like an electrical current. Ask yourself whether a handshake or hug feels warm, comfortable, and confident, or whether it is offputting, making you want to withdraw. Are people's hands clammy, signal-ing anxiety, or limp, suggesting being noncommittal and timid? Is their grip too strong, even crushing your fingers, indicating aggres-sion or overcontrol? Along with physical cues, the energy of touch reveals people's emotions. Some hugs and handshakes impart kind-ness, joy, and calm, whereas others feel clingy, draining, even hostile. Therefore, spend time with people whose energy you like. Be wary of those whose energy you don't like, so you're not depleted. Avoid physical contact (including making love) with anyone whose energy doesn't feel good.

LISTEN FOR PEOPLE'S TONE OF VOICE AND LAUGH

The tone and volume of our voice can tell much about our emotions. Sound frequencies create vibrations. Some frequencies we hear. Below an audible range, sound can be felt (think of a bass's vibration). When reading people, notice how their tone of voice affects you. Words ride the energy of tone, its warmth and coldness. Ask yourself: Does their tone feel soothing? Or is it abrasive, snippy, or whiny? Are they soft talkers or mumblers whom you can barely hear, signs of meekness or low self-esteem? Or do they talk too loud or too much, signs of anxiety, narcissism, or insensitivity? Are they fast talkers, trying to sell you something? Or boring you to death with a slow monotone, suggesting depression and no spontaneity? Be aware of sighing, which relays sadness or frustration. Also, a pinched voice suggests emotional repression, overcontrol, or a thyroid disorder. Always observe how much people laugh, a sign of lightheartedness. Does their laugh sound genuine? Fake? Childlike? Joyous? Or are they overly serious, rarely laughing? In addition, FBI profilers interpret a quivering voice and sudden change in pitch as potential signs of deception.

SENSE PEOPLE'S HEART ENERGY

The most important aspect of energy to read is whether people exude a sense of heart. This is the lovingkindness in us, our capacity for empathy, giving, and connection. When heart is present, you'll feel the warmth of unconditional love emanating from others, which makes you feel safe and at ease. It's the unspoken sense of being accepted, not judged. No one can fake this. Our heart presence builds through our good intentions, deeds, and emotional work to overcome fear and negativity. The heart is the most positive quality anyone can have. It's healthy to be drawn to it.

Reading energy is a game-changer. It enables you to see past fantasies or desires to pinpoint someone's motivations by sensing invisible messages they give off. I was once attracted to a man, a successful financial manager who knew exactly what to say to touch my heart. Todd was from the country club set and much too conservative for my taste—I often fall for wild, creative men. Yet he was smart and boyishly playful, and he seemed to "see" me and respect my sensitivities. We could discuss anything from politics to the nature of the universe, and he'd speak to me in an appreciative low tone of voice I melted around (I'm very responsive to sound). Still, from the start, when I looked into Todd's eyes, I had the oddest feeling—there was no "there" there. His eyes seemed cold, vacant, even a touch mean. However, for better or worse, I was drawn to him, which doesn't happen to me every day. I really wanted to surrender to my romantic feelings for Todd, to explain away the niggling truth his eyes conveyed, though I knew I ignored this red flag at my own peril. But, as the desiring mind can do when it wants something, it downplayed intuition. I rationalized, "You're just too picky. Todd is wonderful. It's crazy to let his eyes stop me." My friends also told me this, and I agreed. So, for a year, I stayed in the relationship. But in the end, this man's eyes revealed his true colors.

The problem was that Todd was a supersmooth operator and my raging hormones were blinding me. Also, I was naive. I confused his seductive energy with heartfelt caring and was horribly susceptible to the charisma he wielded so well. It was a perfect storm of forces I didn't have a handle on. I needed to sort them through before I could read him from a neutral place which at that time was light-years away. A policy of mine is to study what makes me weak or strong, so that I can learn from it. If something knocks me off my center, I want to know why and not repeat the situation. To break Todd's spell, I had to grasp that what excited him most was not to love me but to have power over me. I just couldn't grasp how he or anyone could feel that way. He'd reel me in with gorgeous intimacy, then be unavailable. Or he'd be incredibly sensitive, then incredibly cold. I kept racking my brain, "What could he possibly be getting from this?" Slowly I came to understand that he got off on the rush of being in control. For him, it was an aphrodisiac. I didn't operate like this, nor had that been a dynamic in my past relationships. But, thanks to Todd, I can recognize it now. In retrospect, I'm grateful to have learned this lesson about power versus love from a perfect teacher. Also, I realized that once again, I'd talked myself out of intuition in favor of passion. I'd surrendered to the wrong thing, to what I wanted, rather than what I saw. However, being human, I sometimes have to keep making the same mistakes until I finally learn. Today, I value the energy of the eyes more than ever. It communicates someone's essence.

In your life, get used to reading people's emotions. Factor what you sense into your total assessment. Maybe just a single red flag will appear, and you're not sure what to do. In that case, take your time. Watch how people treat you. Notice if their words back up their behavior. The purpose of reading energy is to become more empathic by sensing the nuances of different personalities. Stay alert to the signals energy sends so that you can see the whole person.

The Fourth Technique: Remote Viewing

Remote viewing is a form of intuitive reading in which you tune in to a person or situation at a distance to accumulate nonlocal information about them. Studies at the Stanford Research Institute have shown that college students without previous remote viewing experience could quickly learn this technique with accurate results. The U.S. government has invested over $20 million in formerly top-secret remote viewing programs to aid in espionage and military applications. In fact, one viewer was awarded the Legion of Merit for determining "150 essential elements of information . . . unavailable from any other source."

Starting in the late 1980s, I was honored to work as a remote viewer for a decade at the Mobius Society, headed by my friend and mentor Stephan Schwartz. We used remote viewing in police investigations to locate buried ships at sea, to make financial forecasts, and to research causes of illness (adventures I described in *Second Sight*). Once I participated in a murder case, though I soon found that I wasn't cut out for delving into the terrible darkness of a killer's psyche. The perversions, pain, and gruesome violence that inhabited his head were way too vivid for my sensitive makeup. Though other remote reviewers in our group could handle it, I just couldn't get neutral. Learning the discipline of remote viewing was a pivotal step in developing my intuition. It trained me to quiet my mind, proactively tune in from an objective space (rather then just getting spontaneous intuitions) and apply what I discovered to solve problems. I felt exhilarated, like a child playing in realms of consciousness that science alone couldn't enter. I'd always sensed that this freedom was possible, but at Mobius I was finding it. It took a few years for my intuition to mature enough so that I felt competent in remote viewing. Then, I began incorporating this method with psychotherapy.

In my practice, remote viewing is time-saving and practical. It lets me read new patients (prior to setting an appointment) to see if we're a good therapeutic match or else refer them to a practitioner who's a better fit. I view this as a fact-finding mission. I'm also provided with extra insights when our work is stuck or if I'm not grasping a person's perspective. As part of therapy, I teach patients to apply remote viewing to their own lives and professions. I've shown film directors how to use it to choose winning projects, demonstrated to business owners how it can help them hire the sharpest employees, and helped parents use it to gain insight into their children. Used in conjunction with logic, it's a pragmatic action tool that gives my patients more data to make informed decisions.

To address privacy issues involving remote viewing, one strategy is to inwardly request permission to do the reading and only proceed if you intuit a yes. However, my experience is that if people don't want to be viewed, I simply don't receive information, either about a specific aspect of their lives or about anything. It feels as if they're not letting me enter, much like in science fiction films when there's an impenetrable force field. If I try to push when there isn't an opening, it doesn't do any good. Literally, there's no flow to go with. So, out of respect, I just stop.

While developing remote viewing skills, I needed to surrender in some fundamental ways that challenged the dogma of my medical training. First, the scientist in me had to stop resisting forms of knowing that weren't acknowledged by conventional medicine. One of the most confounding notions to by-the-book academicians was that it was possible to read strangers at a distance without ever having met them. But, in my practice, this was something I did every day with remote viewing! To deviate from the rigors of my medical training and reengage intuition, which I'd shelved in deference to science, was a massive shift. I had to get used to it. This is where surrender came in. I had to give myself permission to gradually be less rigid despite the loud protests of my linear mind. It wasn't a battle of wills—it just meant leaving more space for alternatives. At my own pace, I discovered I could integrate traditional medicine with intuition without sacrificing anything. For me it was never about choosing one or the other, an either-or. I was on a learning curve about how they could collaborate. Today I'm much less inhibited about doing what's still deemed impossible. In fact, it gives me a thrill! But fortunately, science is also catching up. A recent Cornell University study, "Feeling the Future," documented the ability to sense the future. Though these findings have surely startled some conservative thinkers, they're a remarkable advance in our understanding of consciousness.

To do a clear remote viewing, I also had to surrender my need to be politically correct when I picked up controversial or bizarre information. This meant gradually letting go of my fear about what others might think. In the beginning, whenever I'd receive anything that felt embarrassing or irrelevant, I'd withhold it from Stephan. I didn't want to look bad, be wrong, or rock the boat. For example, one time I picked up that a well-respected, law-and-order judge was sexually promiscuous. On another case I saw a "normal" soccer mom conversing with a deranged-looking rubber ducky. As things turned out, the judge proved to be a swinger and the soccer mom had suffered psychotic breaks that only her family knew about. Intuitions I feared were "too weird" often were the most right on. Thus, it was from censoring that I learned not to censor. Airbrushing the information that comes from remote viewing undermines its worth.

Also, I had to surrender the idea that I was infallible. Inevitably, I would sometimes be wrong. For instance, once I incorrectly predicted that an investment group would financially succeed on a project to improve air quality. My strong desire that the project work out precluded me from seeing that it wouldn't. Another time, I predicted that a fellow remote viewer's surgery would go poorly, but it went perfectly; my fear of losing him made me misread the situation. In both cases, I couldn't get neutral. My emotional blind spots threw my intuition off. Also, during remote viewings, I had to realize that although I could tune in, I might be shown only certain pieces of information—I couldn't necessarily see everything. All this was part of the discovery process. I came to grasp that my misses were as valuable as the hits. Making mistakes shows me where I hold back or misinterpret information, so my readings can improve.

To use remote viewing, focus on surrendering your need to always be accurate or "look good" so that you can fully engage this technique. No one can be right all the time. Trying to do so chokes intuition. At the start of a reading, tell yourself, "I want to trust where this remote viewing takes me." Then keep letting go to the instinctual rhythms of sensing rather than thinking. Allow your awareness to expand past the borders of your resistance. Learn from your blunders and your hits. While exploring remote viewing, notice what your surrenders are. Perhaps they're similar to mine, or different. Be patient with yourself. There's a mounting sense of competence and joy from going with the flow of intuition.

Remote viewing is not a supernatural ability. We all can do it if we can quiet the voice that has a million good reasons why we can't. In the spirit of experimentation, tell that voice, "Thank you for sharing." Then see for yourself by practicing the following exercise.

HOW TO DO REMOTE VIEWING

Take a few minutes to do this before meeting people to get a sense of them or afterward to fill in the pieces. When tuning in, first you want to link your consciousness to the person by becoming at one with him or her. Once linked, you will receive intuitive information.

1. *Close your eyes and breathe.* Take a few deep breaths to relax your body. Slowly still your mind and clear mental clutter. If thoughts intrude, picture them as clouds passing in the sky. Keep returning to the breath as much as necessary.

2. *Shift your awareness.* In a quiet state, shift your focus from your daily concerns and the sights, smells, and sounds of your environment. Remain as neutral and still as possible.

3. *Focus on a person's name.* Hold a name lightly in your mind, never straining. A first name is adequate. It doesn't matter how many people share the same name. Every person has a unique identity on an intuitive level. In a focused state, you'll naturally tune in to your target. Names have a specific energy you can sense. As you tune in to the name, ask yourself, "Does the energy feel peaceful? Afraid? Giving? Frazzled? In pain?" Remember, do not judge or get emotionally involved. Simply let yourself connect with that basic energy, a form of deep empathy. This allows you to link up with someone's essence. Try to blend with them, no resistance. Once this occurs, you'll be shown information. Intuitions will come. Remain as neutral and free of assumptions as possible.

4. *Stay open.* Notice any images, impressions, body sensations, emotions, or "aha" moments that come to you. Whether you have one or many, you'll be given exactly what you need.

5. *Don't analyze.* Simply receive the intuitions. Note them all. You can see how they apply later.

6. *Come back to yourself.* Take a few breaths again to detach from whomever you are reading. Completely break the connection. You don't want to carry someone around with you. Bring your attention back to your body. For a few seconds, rub your palms together, creating friction. Then gently place them over your face while deeply

inhaling. This reconnects you with your own essence. It's a beautiful way to separate from someone and return to yourself.

Immediately record your impressions in a journal so you don't forget them. As I've discussed, the most accurate intuitions are either neutral—simply conveying information—or compassionate. They may feel strangely impersonal and unemotional, as if you're just an observer. Also evaluate how well the reading matches how a person appears. If there are discrepancies, weigh these in your assessment. Perhaps you're considering embarking on a project with a coworker. She has some compelling ideas, and you want to go ahead, but you get a flash in your remote viewing that she's an alcoholic. What to do? Be cautious. Don't jump into anything or let your mind talk you out of your intuition. Spend a little more time with the coworker. Notice her drinking habits. See if alcohol is a problem. What's useful about remote viewing is that you can correlate your reading with a person's behavior. On the other hand, if your head says, "She doesn't fit the profile of what I thought I wanted," but your remote viewing conveys that she'll be an asset, it's well worth exploring.

The closer you are to someone, the harder that person may be to read. But it can be done. Before you tune in, practice the strategies I've presented for quieting your thoughts and staying neutral. Lao Tzu says, "To the mind that is still, the whole universe surrenders." If you want to understand why people behave as they do and change unhealthy patterns, such clarity allows you to find compassion.

In this chapter, I've discussed four distinct but complementary methods to read people. It's vital that you use them to help people. When your goal is simply personal gain or to get the upper hand, it creates bad karma, exploits others, and is a waste of power. Always stay pure in your intentions. If you do, practicing these methods will enable you to see yourself more clearly and understand what makes people tick. There's a healing impulse to seeing. The clarity you gain from reading others can benefit your life too.

I hope I've sparked your curiosity to explore realms of wisdom that exist beyond the obvious. One of my first memories is of lying in a crib, looking into the spaces between things. These have always attracted me more than material reality. As a little girl, it was my secret pleasure to melt into what's invisible, surrendering to a place I could not see but which felt more like home than what's solid. Growing up is complicated. Our minds learn so much about how to behave and perceive. I enjoyed the cerebral aspect of maturing, but this also seemed to be a distraction from other intuitive realms—probably because it felt as if I was being asked to forsake my invisible fascinations for only what the linear eye could see. You can understand why it means so much for me to develop all aspects of this sacred thing called vision.

SURRENDER AFFIRMATION FOR TRUSTING INTUITION

I am willing to accept that there is more to me than my linear mind. I am ready to surrender to my intuition so I can read people in new ways. I release all thoughts that tell me I can't do it. I want to embody poet Walt Whitman's words, "I am large—I contain multitudes."

Out beyond ideas of wrongdoing and rightdoing,
there is a field. I'll meet you there.
—RUMI

....

5

THE FIFTH SURRENDER

CULTIVATING IMPECCABLE

COMMUNICATION

COMMUNICATION IS POTENT MEDICINE. WHAT WE SAY AND HOW we say it can hurt or heal. Communication is ordinarily thought of as an exchange of verbal and nonverbal ideas and feelings. At its best, we feel seen and heard. At its worst, it can be denigrating and destructive. Surrendering nonproductive communication styles and embracing those that work for you will help you get the results you want in all your interactions.

Impeccable communication is all about surrender. It's knowing when to be assertive, when to let go. It means both expressing your feelings and having a willingness to release hurt and resentments that close your heart. It's about being fluid rather than rigid, controlling, or oppositional. It also utilizes your sixth-sense people-reading skills to reach people and not be drawn into drama. You'll learn to recognize that there's a flow to all interactions and decide which ones to surrender to or not. The company you keep is critical to your well-being. If a relationship is positive, go with it. If it's negative, you'll learn to set clear, loving boundaries. You don't have to apologize for expressing your needs. Enlist my favorite mantra: " 'No' is a complete sentence." Saying no takes practice but it's one of the most lifesaving words in my vocabulary.

This kind of communication is similar to navigating a river. Some directions feel good and flow; others do not. You can't force the currents to go your way. When you pressure people you'll just turn them off. In relationships, there's an energy you must attune to, make adjustments for, and trust.

I'll show you how to communicate even with impossible people and have grace under pressure using the Daoist practice of harmonizing with them to get results. Then you won't get flustered or be baited into yelling matches, playing endless blame games, or hammering a point to death in a disagreement—ego-based reactions that have nothing to do with intuition or emotional intelligence. My Buddhist friend Ann jokes with me: "If only people always reacted in the ways we wanted them to!" But they don't. Nor would it be nearly as interesting if they did. So it's time to retire the "if onlys" and deal with what is. Sensing the flow between people helps you know when to assert yourself and when to compromise or back off. You'll also be able to work around someone's resistance if you hit a wall, a priceless maneuver most people haven't learned. What I'm describing is tactically wise, but even more, it's an honoring of the life force that propels our interactions.

Impeccable communication means relating to others with compassion, flaws and all. This applies especially during arguments or when relationships are strained. Truth is, people can be annoying and disappointing, as we all sometimes are. None of us is perfect; most of us are doing the best we can. So keep searching for a part of someone that you can empathize with, even when it's a stretch. You may not always succeed, but keep trying. This doesn't make you a doormat or a victim. Rather, such compassion allows you to become the finest version of yourself, even as you set limits to bad behavior.

Over the years, I've watched patients turn difficult communications into open, loving ones by surrendering. For instance, Jill had to surrender her need to idealize men when her "perfect husband" began criticizing her. Rick had to work through and surrender his anger after he caught his partner in an act of infidelity. Ultimately these relationships succeeded because both parties were willing to try to resolve the conflict and surrender resentments rather than fan the flames of hurt, anger, or the need to "be right"—even if they were right. This enabled them to open their hearts to healing and change. It would've been easy for my patients to degenerate into finger-pointing and bickering but through psychotherapy and by using the strategies in this chapter, they didn't.

In my life, I strive for impeccable communication, especially when there's conflict. Recently a friend broke his hip roller-skating. He's always been active so being physically limited was a challenge for him. Cooped up, he became testy when I visited. Every time he would ask for advice, he'd pick a fight with me. I felt hurt, like I was getting my hand slapped whenever I offered assistance. As a doctor, I'm used to being authoritative and fixing things. I'm a can-do person. Still, I can sometimes get pushy and controlling. Had my friend just said, "Judith, I know that you're trying to help. I can handle this on my own," I would've gotten it. But he didn't. When I asked him to stop snapping at me, he simply got more obstinate. I aspired to be patient, but I was getting mad! For a while I loved this man but didn't like him very much.

I had to ask myself how surrender could improve our communication. I began by no longer giving him medical advice. Once I accepted that I was powerless over how he chose to deal with the injury, I stopped myself from making suggestions unless he reached out. I did my best to support him in the ways he said he needed. What helped me surrender my need to intervene was to empathize with his position—how incapacitated and in pain he felt. Also, he didn't want his competence questioned. It's much easier to be nice when you're well, something we often forget. My surrender also entailed accepting that even close relationships will go through rocky periods. Communication may be imperfect at those times, but if that's the best we can do, that's okay. Still, I had to set a boundary with his anger. I said, "You'll have to be nicer or you'll force me to leave." I was sure he didn't want this, and he began trying to control his temper. Thankfully, as he recovered, his anger diminished.

To preserve valuable relationships, sometimes you've got to fight a few dragons. My friend and I both came through this having learned more about ourselves and each other. He gained greater insight into dealing with his anger and I became less controlling. As a result, our friendship deepened.

Surrender can improve your communication in many kinds of challenging interactions. Here, I'll present five common types of difficult people and the strategies for approaching them from a surrendered, compassionate position. Then you won't go on the warpath or turn allies into enemies. For instance, when should you surrender your need to be right in order to restore love at home, or surrender resentments so that you can forgive? How do you avoid taking things personally? Or deal with a friend or spouse who's doing something you disagree with? What if you love someone but don't like them very much? How do you cope with an anger addict? A gossip? A guilt-tripper? A narcissist? In all these scenarios, you'll learn to keep your cool and set healthy boundaries.

REMOVING BARRIERS AND DRAMA: THE LAWS OF IMPECCABLE COMMUNICATION

I suggest that you follow some general laws of communication so that you're able to flow with difficult people and prevent blocks in your daily life. These will ensure that you're leading from a position of strength, not anger or desperation. You'll be flexible instead of just meeting conflict with an oppositional force. I adhere to these laws so that I can treat people with an attitude I'm proud of, instead of shrinking into the smallest parts of myself. Be aware that your ego will no doubt resist these principles since their aim is to create open channels of communication between people instead of stonewalling or defending, responses the ego is more accustomed to. These laws value "we" as well as "me," a necessary consideration when you're tuning in to flow. As you'll see, this approach works wonders in getting your needs met, sometimes against all odds, even with people you don't like. The result is that you become a master at diffusing negativity, not a pushover. Let's say you're deadlocked in an argument; nobody's giving in. Then what? Don't turn it into a battle for supremacy. Instead, give the first inch, an act of true strength.

Apologizing for your part in the conflict shows that you value the relationship more than your ego. This opens the door for others to admit their part too. It's people with real power who step up first to surrender their ego, promoting impeccable communication.

Ego is not all bad. It gives us a healthy sense of self and a useful sense of determination. There's a role for it, but just not here. Don't let your ego interfere with making breakthroughs in communication that aren't possible when ego is in charge. As you think about your relationships, I'd like you to begin considering these questions: "What beliefs or behavior would it be useful for me to surrender? Where do I cling to ego or the desire to control?" Since we all need reminders about these principles, I suggest that you post a copy of them on your refrigerator, in your office, or anywhere else where you can use this as a visual prompt.

THE LAWS OF IMPECCABLE COMMUNICATION

DO

1. Be calm, not emotionally reactive.

2. Avoid defensiveness—it makes you look weak.

3. Patiently hear people out without interrupting or needing to have the last word.

4. Empathize with where people are coming from, even if you disagree with them.

5. Pick your battles; apologize when necessary.

DON'T

1. Be drawn into drama.

2. React impulsively out of anxiety or anger (you may say something you'll regret).

3. Hold on to resentments or stay attached to being right.

4. Attempt to manage other people's lives or become their therapist.

5. Shame people, especially in front of others.

Get in the habit of applying these laws with both friends and foes. The dos involve surrender and discernment. They will move you closer to resolving conflict by helping you harmonize with another's position, even if you disagree. This sets a tone to resolve conflicts or set boundaries whereas antagonism just alienates. People can smell the toxic mix of judgment and blame a mile away. You'll never get your needs met if you're coming from this place or badgering someone. Once you can listen neutrally to an adversary's stance, you can decide what action to take. The don'ts involve defense, ego, and control. They create blockages, animosity, and inertia, but with mindfulness you'll get better at avoiding these emotional land mines. Nevertheless, if you get caught in them, as we all will, you can always change course. How you treat yourself and others—whether you like them or not—is part of the ongoing experiment in compassion that I'm championing in this book. In addition, enlist the following strategies for each challenging personality type in your life.

HOW TO COMMUNICATE WITH DIFFICULT PEOPLE

Difficult people can suck the oxygen out of the room if you let them. To successfully deal with them, you must be methodical. Many of us spend an inordinate amount of time and energy contending with these types at work and at home. It's a reflex to emotionally contract around them, which makes you feel powerless, irritated, hurt, or miserable—reactions that just wear you out. But they can't steal your happiness unless you let them.

Your attitude is important. Personally, I view difficult people as bodhisattvas, spiritual teachers who are meant to awaken us, though they aren't conscious of their role. But nobody said awakening is always pleasant or easy. Most difficult people aren't trying to harm you: they are just unconscious or self-absorbed. Very few are truly dark and have evil motives. I'll demonstrate what difficult people can teach you about surrender such as the attitudes you must release to triumph over them or the ability to set boundaries—and which of their behaviors you must not surrender to. Your tone of voice is important as well. I'll teach you how to set limits and firmly say no with love, instead of sounding snippy or blaming when someone "steps over the red line," which is my Buddhist friend Ann's term for a boundary violation. I'll show you why your tone of voice is important—a critical tone only inflames people, no matter how perfect your words are. Also, some people talk a lot but don't seem to say anything. To get the attention of chronic talkers or those on a rant, it helps to open your remark by lovingly saying their name: for instance, "Robert, I understand what you're saying. . . ." Hearing our name aloud instinctively makes us pause. Remember, we all can be difficult at times. Let this sobering fact curb your enthusiasm for chastising the shortcomings of others in word or tone. Do your best not to vilify people, even when they're obnoxious or unkind. Realize that anger addicts, guilt trippers, and the other types I'll discuss aren't happy people; they're insecure, wounded, and disconnected from their hearts. Don't forget this as you practice my techniques.

I get a charge out of thinking up disarming responses for difficult people, both to show them they didn't "get me" and also to reverse the tone of the interchange without their quite knowing what hit them. I think of it as creative boundary setting without being obvious about it. For instance, my gym doesn't allow cell phones. When I nicely asked a guy there to get off his, he sarcastically said, "Oh, I'm really sorry I'm disturbing you." But rather than being nasty back (though I was tempted), I paused for a split second to collect myself. That was enough for me to both summon restraint and try to switch gears. As a result, instead of giving what I got, I sweetly thanked him for his sensitivity, as if he were my hero. He must've thought his sarcasm sailed over my head because he quickly got into being appreciated and didn't use his cell phone around me again. I made a tactical decision. I was in the right, but I didn't push that or make him feel wrong. I wasn't looking for drama. I just wanted the guy to be quiet. He never would've stopped talking had I gotten into it with him on his level. Sometimes, to get your needs met, surrender comes down to not trying to force others to concede their error. However, your ego is unlikely to be in love with this approach. To soothe it, let your ego know it's right. That's what I had to do with mine. But also go further.

Next, I asked myself, "What will I gain from fighting with this fellow? I'll just be upset and he'll still be on his cell phone. It's not worth it." That's where reasoning out a situation can facilitate surrender. It's a choice. The challenge around bad behavior is to maintain your power and priorities while setting clear boundaries, no matter how annoying, negative, or full of themselves others can be.

Type 1: The Anger Addict

These types deal with conflict by accusing, attacking, humiliating, or criticizing. There's a spectrum to anger. It can range from a coworker's belittling tone to your fire-breathing spouse yelling, cursing, throwing things, or resorting to physical violence. Some anger addicts withhold love or use the silent treatment to punish you. These personalities usually behave the worst with those closest to them. I've had to hold on to my seat during many couples therapy sessions as one spouse spitefully calls the other a "rotten lover" or an "unfit mother." One wife got so angry she swore at her husband in three different languages! Such wounding words can fracture someone's self-esteem and poison the well of trust. They are nearly impossible to take back, even with an apology.

Unchecked anger addicts are dangerous and controlling. They inflict emotional damage by wearing down your self-esteem and they refuse to be held accountable for their actions. Some have hair-trigger tempers so you walk on eggshells around them. You don't feel safe expressing yourself because you live in fear of their eruptions. Anger can tyrannize relationships. One woman I treated had stopped having any male friends because she was afraid of her partner's unrelenting jealous anger. If she went to lunch with a male colleague from work, for instance, her partner would barrage her with cell phone messages during the meal. Initially, unable to set boundaries, she appeased him by giving in. My patient told me she didn't want to "create a war at home" by doing anything to provoke his wrath. Clearly we had our work cut out for us in therapy. She didn't want to leave her partner but she needed to be strong enough to assert healthier limits in the relationship.

Many anger addicts had rageaholic parents and unconsciously re-peat that pattern. Father Greg Boyle, a mix of tough guy and teddy bear, runs a therapeutic program for former gang members in the East Los Angeles barrio. Rehab at Homeboy Industries starts with removing their tattoos (sometimes covering nearly every inch of the face and body), a gang's emblem of anger. Father G, as he's affection-ately called, told me, "Anger is a language for people who haven't transformed their pain so they project it outward. We teach kids to release anger by assessing the damage it causes them by holding on to it such as getting arrested or losing their lady's love. They want to hurl rage at those who've done them wrong—the mother who put cigarettes out on their arms, the father who beat them—but they're just singeing themselves." Part of surrendering anger meant real-izing that their parents were sick and couldn't do better. The kids came to see that they weren't the cause of their parents' anger and that "they are exactly what God had in mind when God made them," as Father Greg so rightly puts it. This helped them surrender the past and move on.

Though your family situation may be less brutal, the common dy-namic with anger addicts is that they use anger to cope with feeling inadequate, hurt, or threatened. Anger is one of the hardest emotions to control due to its evolutionary value of defending against danger. When you're confronted with anger, your body instinctively tight-ens, the opposite of a surrendered state. It goes into fight-or-flight mode. Adrenaline floods your system. Your heart pumps faster. Your jaw and muscles clench. Your blood vessels constrict. Your gut tenses. In this hypercharged condition, you want to flee or attack.

Instead of running or retaliating, try my approach. First, take a breath to calm down. Tell yourself, "Do not respond with anger. That will just make things worse." If the person is being abusive, excuse yourself from the situation. If you can't escape—say, with a boss—try to stay centered and nonreactive so you don't feed the anger. Later, when you can address the anger more fully, admit your unedited re-actions to yourself or a supportive person. This prevents anger from building up. You can't start that process of surrendering anger until you've acknowledged the raw emotion. I've watched patients attempt to bypass this stage because they think it's "spiritually incorrect" to feel, "I want to kill that jerk for treating me this way." Not so. It's necessary to admit your honest reactions. There's no way of surrendering anger, let alone forgiving someone, without acknowledging where you're at. *However, this is not the place you want to communicate from if you want to be heard by an anger addict.* It's counterproductive to just blurt out everything you feel. Sometimes the surrender that's called for is to refrain from responding until you're clearer. When you're exposed to anger, here are some steps to calm your system and clear your head. Without this you're trapped in reactive behavior, which gets you nowhere at all.

HOW TO COMMUNICATE WITH ANGER ADDICTS

1. *Surrender your reactivity.* Pause when agitated. Take a few slow breaths to relax your body. Count to ten. Don't react impulsively or engage the anger even though your buttons are pushed. Reacting just makes you weak. Though you may be tempted to lash out, try not to give in to the impulse. No matter how vile people are, wait before you speak. They want to drag you down to their level but you don't want to go there. Keep breathing the anger out to quiet the fight-or-flight response; this lets you surrender reactivity. Focus on your breath, not the angry person. You may still feel upset but you'll be calm and in charge at the same time!

2. *Practice restraint of tongue, phone, and email.* Do not retaliate or respond at all until you are in a centered place. Otherwise you might communicate something you regret or can never take back.

3. *Blend, relax, and let go.* Resistance to pain or strong emotions intensifies them. In martial arts, you first take a breath to find your balance; then you can transform the opponent's energy. Try staying as neutral and relaxed as possible with someone's anger instead of resisting it. At this stage, don't argue or defend yourself. Rather, try to let the person's anger flow right through you. Visualize yourself as transparent so nothing clings to you. Keep breathing the person's anger out. When you hold your breath, the anger lodges

in your body. This approach to anger doesn't make you a victim or a doormat. Nor does it mean you won't stick up for yourself. It's a Zen tactic to neutralize anger so that it can't attach to you. Martial artists flow with their opponent's aggressive movements. Then they act from that attuned, surrendered stance.

4. *Acknowledge the other person's position.* To disarm angry people, you must weaken their defensiveness. Otherwise they'll dig in their heels and won't budge. Defensiveness stifles flow. Therefore, it's useful to acknowledge an anger addict's position, even if it offends you. From a centered place say, "I can see why you feel that way. We both have similar concerns. But I have a different way to approach the problem. Please hear me out." This keeps the flow of communication open and creates a tone for compromise.

5. *Set limits.* Now, state your case. Request a small, doable change that can meet your need. Then clarify how it will benefit the relationship. Tone is crucial. For instance, calmly but firmly say to an in-law who's yelling at you, "I love you but I shut down when you raise your voice. Let's work this out when we can hear each other better." Then you can discuss a solution. This doesn't mean you stay in abusive relationships. If people persist in dumping toxic anger, you must limit contact, define clear consequences such as "I can't see you if you keep criticizing me," or let the relationship go. When you can't leave, such as with an angry boss, practice harmonizing and letting the emotion pass through you. Also, you might try a reasonable approach, like "I did my best but let's discuss constructive ways to find a solution." You can also use "selective listening" and not take in all the details of an outburst. Focus on something uplifting instead.

6. *Empathize.* Ask yourself, "What pain or inadequacy is making this person so angry? Then take some quiet moments to intuit where the person's heart is hurting or closed. This doesn't excuse bad behavior but it will allow you to find compassion for the suffering behind it, even if you choose not to be around the person. Then it's easier to surrender resentments so they don't eat at you.

Gathering your power before you respond to anger takes awareness and restraint. Admittedly, it's hard to surrender the need to be right in favor of love and compromise. It's hard not to attack back when you feel attacked. But, little by little, surrendering these reflexive instincts is a more compassionate, evolved way to get your needs met and keep relationships viable if and when it's possible.

Type 2: The Passive-Aggressive Person

This is a close relative of the anger addict. These types express anger with a smile or exaggerated concern but always maintain their cool. As the name states, they exhibit a passive form of aggression. They are experts at sugarcoating hostility. They often use procrastination, bumbling inefficiency, and the exasperating excuse of "I forgot" to avoid commitments or let you down. These people are infuriating because of their seductive or innocent veneers. They appear eager to please but know exactly how to make you mad.

Passive-aggressive behavior ranges from simply irritating to manipulative and punishing. This is different from occasionally being absentminded, lazy, or busy. Passive aggression is repetitive and has a covert angry edge to it. For example, your spouse keeps forgetting your anniversary when you've repeatedly expressed how important celebrating it is. Your roommate brings home a gallon of ice cream when he'd agreed to honor your diet. A potential employer dodges your call, not wanting to personally reject you. Your friend is chronically late every time she's supposed to meet you. Or you ask a coworker for help and she says "no problem" but shows up after your deadline. Passive-aggressive people promise anything, then do exactly as they please. They hide anger beneath a compliant exterior. They don't give straight answers, instead offering vague responses such as "I'll get back to you." Then they don't follow through so you must keep reminding them. Sometimes their remarks can be hurtful, especially because they come at you sideways—you don't know what hit you. A patient was newly dating a hotshot marketing executive who told her, "I'll give you my private email," which made her feel special and valued. After weeks when he never sent it and she asked him about it he responded, "I've been so busy, it must've just slipped my mind." But then he still didn't send it. His lack of follow-through made her feel like she wasn't important enough for him to remember.

Why do people become passive-aggressive? They're typically raised in families where it's not safe to express anger—they're never taught to communicate it in a healthy manner. They adapt by channeling these feelings into other less obvious behaviors; this gives them a sense of power and control. They're masters at shirking responsibility by hurting you in ways that appear unintentional or unavoidable. Passive-aggressive people operate by stuffing anger, being accommodating, and then indirectly sticking it to you. When confronted, they'll drive you crazy with a variety of "the dog ate my homework"–type excuses, blame others, or yes you to death without changing. Since many are unaware of their anger, they feel misunderstood or that you're holding them to unfair standards.

HOW TO COMMUNICATE WITH PASSIVE AGGRESSIVE PEOPLE

1. *Surrender doubt and trust your gut reactions.* With these types you may question yourself since their anger is so masked. It's important to recognize the pattern. Their mixed messages will test your patience. So when you doubt yourself, take a breath and try to let the doubt go. Tell yourself, "I deserve to be treated more lovingly. I will trust my gut reaction when I feel jabbed." This affirmation helps you release doubt so you don't convince yourself you're imagining things. Then move forward to improve communication. You must surrender the idea that these people will ever change if you don't speak up. They aren't motivated to change unless someone calls them on their behavior. When it's not appropriate to be direct, such as with a boss who might retaliate or fire you, keep letting the zingers go by, accepting your powerlessness to change him or her.

2. *Address the behavior.* Focus on one issue at a time so that people don't feel attacked or overwhelmed. Let's say a friend is always late. In a calm, firm tone say to her, "I would greatly appreciate it

if you can be on time when we go out to dinner. I feel uncomfortable waiting in a restaurant alone." Then notice her reaction. She
might say, "You're right. I'm always running behind. I'll try to be
more organized." Then see if the lateness improves. If she is eva-
sive or makes excuses, request clarification about how to solve the
problem. If you can't get a straight answer, confront that too. Being
specific pins down passive-aggressive people. If nothing changes,
keep setting limits or stop making dinner plans. With a close friend
who continues to be late, it's always an option to accept and acclimate to his or her shortcoming when the pros of the relationship
outweigh the cons.

Type 3: The Narcissist

With narcissists, everything is all about them. They have an inflated
sense of self-importance and entitlement, crave attention, and require
endless praise. They love to toot their own horns. Narcissists can't
get enough of being treated like a VIP. Their favorite topic is themselves and they rarely ask about you unless it can benefit them. Some
narcissists are obnoxious egomaniacs. But others are charming, intelligent, and masterful seducers. If you're needy or vulnerable, they
love being your white knight, riding in to save the day. Narcissists are
highly intuitive and know how to play you like a fiddle so that you're
enamored of them. They are mainly interested in power and move in
for the kill with their charm. However, once your admiration stops
or you dare to disagree, they turn on you by becoming aloof, punishing, controlling, or passive-aggressive. Beneath the pretty clothes, the
charisma, and the smile lurks a cold heart. *Narcissists are dangerous
because they lack empathy and are incapable of unconditional love.* Despite their charm, they have cold, unresponsive hearts. There are always strings attached to getting their approval. You must compliment
them or build them up to stay in their good graces. Narcissists are
experts at compartmentalizing which explains why they're notorious
for cheating on their spouses. They lack the empathy to emotionally
connect or register the consequences of their choices. They always
take much more than they give.

These types have often been raised by narcissistic parents who wanted their children to be mini versions of themselves. They might've been treated as the golden child which fuels their sense of specialness and entitlement but they're never seen for who they are. In later life this leads to angry, abusive behavior when they're frustrated or feel criticized. (Disapproval crushes them.) Growing up with narcissistic parents is crazy-making. To the world, the parents may be celebrated, with cancer wards or museums named after them, but at home they're often withholding and punitive. Narcissists are frequently buffered by a circle of admirers who are kept around only because they agree with them. For these types, it's all about appearances and adulation.

Hard as it may be to grasp, full-blown narcissists rarely have insight into their behavior, nor do they regret how they treat you. One patient made lunch plans with a "famous author," a narcissist who unapologetically double-booked appointments. The author didn't hesitate about canceling lunch with her for someone "more important" an hour before their meeting. I always advise patients to expect such behavior from narcissists and I tell them, "Don't invite trouble by falling in love with one." As one patient says, "Around narcissists I feel sleazy weasel vibes," a sign to stay away. However, if you're already involved, setting consequences such as "I want a separation unless we get professional help" may motivate them to act. Still, even when narcissists want to change, I've found their growth in therapy to be minimal: they aren't self-reflective and they always think the problem is you. Nevertheless, sometimes when narcissists hit rock bottom from substance abuse and enter spiritually based twelve-step programs, they are able to surrender enough ego to begin to make change. Also, Freudian analysts claim to achieve steady progress with narcissists in daily psychoanalysis over many, many years.

I'll teach you to communicate with narcissists so you won't get seduced into annihilating relationships that are murder to get out of. I've worked with numerous patients, both men and women, who fell madly in love with narcissists, totally giving their hearts. In every case, their self-esteem got battered and they became exhausted or ill. Falling in love with a narcissist is like falling in love with a ghost.

There's no real warmth or ability to be there for you. However, they're master manipulators and love to toy with you. That makes them feel powerful. One patient told me, "I knew I should leave. But each time I tried, he'd woo me back, promising to change, saying *exactly* what I wanted to hear. He was so incredibly sincere and articulate. Plus we had two beautiful kids and I still loved him. But despite his promises, all he gave me were crumbs. His behavior was perfect for a few weeks but it didn't last. He never really changed. It took me a decade to be strong enough to leave. When I did, it freed me. I'll never go down that rabbit hole again."

Still, you may be in a situation where you choose not to leave a narcissist. Another patient told me, "In the slow job market, management is pushing employees to work harder and tolerate worse treatment. We don't have another job waiting in the wings. We're forced to put up with a demanding, narcissistic boss to keep food on the table." Of course, I sympathized. Whether you decide to stay with these difficult people or say goodbye to them, the next exercise will help you mindfully deal with them.

HOW TO COMMUNICATE WITH NARCISSISTS

1. *Surrender the belief that your love can change them.* Many caring people enter these relationships hoping that their compassion can reform a narcissist. The thinking is, "If they feel loved, they'll become the caring people they really are inside." Hear this: textbook narcissists don't play by these rules. They value control and power over love. Moreover, since they lack empathy, they're incapable of the give-and-take of intimacy. They sour love by making you jump through hoops to please them. A narcissist's lack of empathy is difficult to grasp. That's why many people resist this surrender. Sometimes it takes years of enduring a narcissist's abuse until what I'm describing rings true. Keep your expectations realistic. Enjoy a narcissist's good qualities but understand they're emotionally limited, despite being sophisticated in other areas. Surrendering the notion that your love can change a narcissist will spare you years of torment and struggle.

2. *Don't make your self-worth dependent on them.* Avoid the trap of always trying to please a narcissist. Guard your sensitivities. Seek out loving friends. Share your deepest feelings with those who will treasure them.

3. *Clarify how they will benefit.* To get your goals met with narcissists, frame your request in ways they can hear. Stating your emotional needs rarely works, nor does complaining or being assertive. For example, if you want a vacation, don't tell your boss that you're exhausted. Instead say, "Your business will benefit if I leave on these dates." As police interrogators understand, ego is the Achilles' heel of narcissists. They can be cajoled into confessions through flattery. Though such ego stroking is tedious, it will bring results.

Type 4: The Guilt Tripper

These types are world-class blamers, martyrs, and drama queens. They know how to make you feel bad about something by pressing your insecurity buttons. They use guilt to manipulate you into doing what they desire. They like to see you squirm and to throw you off your game. This gives them a sense of power and control.

Guilt can be conveyed with words, tone, or even a glance. Guilt-provoking needling ranges from "How can you splurge on such a state-of-the-art stereo system when people are starving?" to "I sacrificed everything for this marriage" to "When I'm dead and buried you won't have to worry about me anymore." One patient's parents made her feel guilty about "wasting time" reading comic books as a child. Later they told her, "Don't be lazy. Get moving. You're only as good as your last accomplishment." The implication was that my patient wasn't okay unless she was having continual successes in the outer world. No wonder she was stuck on the hamster wheel of overachievement and never learned to relax. My own mother didn't hesitate to lay Jewish guilt on thick. When she disapproved of my boyfriends she'd say, "You're going to give me a heart attack if you go out with him." Once she even opened a window and stood there hyperventilating to prove her point. It was all about "How can you do this to me?" Though her guilt tripping never deterred me from seeing someone (I was too rebellious), I was still dogged by a nagging dread that I really might be killing my mother.

Guilt trippers play dirty. To get their way, they exploit your desire to please them or be a good person. They often start sentences with, "If it wasn't for you . . ." or "Why don't you ever . . . ?" They'll talk about life being unfair and compare you with others who're doing it better. "Why can't you be more like Buster? He's so good to his wife and is such a hard worker." They also remind you of how much they always do for you. After you've been guilt tripped, you may feel two inches tall. So you may pick up the lunch check instead of splitting it, work overtime to prove you're not lazy, or listen endlessly to their woes to show how caring you are. Even though you know better, guilt has a sneaky way of insinuating itself into your insecurities.

Be aware that there's a difference between healthy remorse and guilt. Remorse is regretting how a situation turned out or how you behaved. Then you can acknowledge the mistake and make amends. You'll feel genuinely sorry but you don't stay stuck there. Guilt, however, is when you become attached to remorse and self-blame, a reverse form of ego where you keep focusing on an alleged lack or mistake. As a psychiatrist, I've seen how guilt can turn into an obsession, the antithesis of surrender. Of course, you want to be accountable for wrongdoing but you don't want to use it as an excuse to punish yourself. Try the following tactics to keep guilt in perspective.

HOW TO COMMUNICATE WITH GUILT TRIPPERS

1. *Surrender the notion that you have to be perfect.* Everyone makes mistakes. It's human. You don't have to be perfect or squeaky clean. If you hurt someone or made a mistake, accept that you can't change the past. But you can make amends when appropriate. Apologize for offending a relative, pay back money owed, or simply convey, "I wish I had been there for you more." If your guilt is self-inflicted— say, you're forced to file for bankruptcy—take a small constructive step such as paying your gas bill instead of feeding the guilt. Or cut yourself a break for bingeing on chocolate but then try to eat more

healthfully. Focusing on solutions instead of wallowing in guilt is a way to surrender to positive forces rather than succumbing to the pull of negativity. You're taking action instead of continuing to brood about what can't be changed. The best amends you can make are to be a more loving, responsible person in the future. When someone continues to guilt trip you, try to understand that he or she just can't do better, and use the techniques below. Guilt trippers tend to lose interest if you don't fall for their manipulations.

2. *Surrender guilt with tears.* One physical way to release guilt if you're fixated on a mistake you made or on not meeting someone's expectations is to cry. Do this when you're alone or with a supportive person. Tears release stress hormones and help you heal. As you cry, your body expels guilt and tension. This helps you let it all go. Don't fight the surrender of crying. Let tears cleanse stress from your body.

3. *Know your guilt buttons.* No one can make you feel guilty if you don't believe you've done something wrong. However, if you doubt yourself, guilt can creep in. One of my patients, a huge tough-guy bouncer from Brooklyn, was guilt-ridden every time his ninety-year-old mother said, "If you were a better son, you'd spend more time with me." In fact, he called and visited frequently. He said, "To Ma, nothing is ever enough." So his surrender was to accept that he was a good son and that he'd probably never please his mother completely. Accepting his powerlessness to completely please her quelled his guilt and brought him comfort.

4. *Set limits.* Start a conversation positively. In a matter-of-fact tone say, "I can see your point of view. But when you say _____, my feelings are hurt. I'd be grateful if you didn't keep repeating it." You might make some topics taboo, such as money, sex, or personal appearance. If guilt trippers respect your limits, great. If not, you might want to limit contact. With those you can't avoid, such as family, keep the conversation light, don't go for their bait, and try to gradually heal your insecurities so that you don't buy into their guilt trips.

Type 5: The Gossip

These busybodies delight in talking about others behind their backs, putting them down, and spreading catty rumors. They'll say, "Poor Jean looks like she's gained twenty pounds," or "Harry is having an affair," or "Lola went into rehab." They revel in other people's bad news to make themselves look better. Gossip also comes from anger and jealousy. These types don't typically gossip about happy things; they prefer to focus on flaws, tragedies, and betrayals. They long to capture your attention with insider information so that you like them. Gossipmongers lure you in by making it seem as if they're sharing the tidbit confidentially, which makes you feel special. They can be cloying and insincere. Gossip is a form of bonding that gets reinforced in high school. It gives these types a sense of power and self-esteem they don't know how to legitimately achieve. Having the dirt on classmates, teachers, or parents puts them in the "in-crowd." It would be the rare teenager who didn't want to hear all this. Gossiping spills over into adulthood. In the office or among friends and family, it may be difficult to resist listening to the latest titillating details.

Why is gossip so prevalent? Why are gossip magazines and soap operas so popular? In part, gossip is a mindless escape into other people's drama. It helps you forget about your problems and incessant mental chatter by focusing on somebody else. (I admit that I lose myself in *People* magazine on airplanes. I enjoy being mindless for a while. Most of us do.) Celebrities are prime prey for gossip—the public seems endlessly fascinated with their larger-than-life personas. What do people get from gossip? Some gossip just puts you "in the know." But negative gossip appeals by consoling your insecure side. You may figure, "If the rich and famous have it worse than I do, my problems don't seem so bad." If a stunning actress is anorexic or has cellulite it proves she's human, which can make you feel better about your body. Our insecure side likes seeing other people's flaws so we can feel more adequate.

We've all engaged in gossip. However, as we grow more aware, we realize that it mainly stems from insecurity or pettiness and won't attract positive, compassionate people. The inclination to talk about others is natural. In primordial times, knowing one another's business was part of being in community. But there's a difference between badmouthing people and simply sharing information that they don't mind being public. Gossip may be simply nosy, such as "Did you hear how much money he's making in his new job?" or it can involve salacious rumors that ruin relationships and reputations. The gossip uses information as ammunition to do harm. When someone gossips about you or a loved one, it can feel enraging, humiliating, and intrusive. Though your instinct is to attack, resist surrendering to that impulse. Take a step back. Wait to respond when you're calmer. Do some deep breathing, go for a walk, or meditate. Then enlist the following approach with these difficult people.

HOW TO COMMUNICATE WITH GOSSIPS

1. *Surrender the need to please everyone or control what people say.* It's your job to like yourself. That's where your focus must be—not on what people think. Your opinion of yourself matters most. If it's good, then gossip has less bite. Try to accept that not everyone will like you or approve of you. Parental voices can stand in the way of this surrender. When they say, "You have to be popular and liked by all," tell these voices, "Thank you for sharing," then exhale them out of your system. Say to yourself, "I accept that I can't please everyone or control everything." Notice how good this release feels. If people's gossip can't be addressed directly, tell yourself, "I'm powerless over their opinions or loose lips." Realizing there's nothing you can do will help mute the noise of other people's opinions. You'll be happy you didn't spend more time worrying about the crude remarks.

2. *Be direct.* If it's appropriate to confront someone, say in a calm, firm tone, "Your comments are inconsiderate and hurtful. How would you like people talking about you that way? Please stop saying these things about me." Calling people on the gossip will often stop them. When it doesn't, you can remind them once or twice, then try to let the comments and the relationship go.

3. *Change the subject.* If coworkers or friends are gossiping and you're uncomfortable about asking them to stop, change the subject so that you don't have to participate. If they try to get you to join in, don't. Refuse to take part in it. The gossipmongers will eventually get bored of trying to entice you and will move on.

4. *Censor yourself.* Be discerning. Don't share intimate information with gossipmongers. You will only be providing them with new material to spread rumors. Share your secrets only with trusted friends.

5. *Don't take gossip personally.* It's none of your business what other people think of you. This may be a hard place to get to, but you must in order to be free. Most people take everything personally. One friend even took it personally when a kid kicked the back of his seat in the movies. With gossip, even if it's meant personally, don't take it that way. Realize gossips aren't happy or secure. They blab about other people besides you. Do what you can to set limits with their comments. Then rise to a higher place and ignore them.

Communicating with difficult people will test your character as well as every surrender skill I've presented. Let your encounters with them make you more confident and free. They'll push emotional buttons you didn't even know you had but your job is not to get thrown off. You'll be tempted to fight back or get down on their level. But increasingly, you'll hold your ground. Think of this as warrior training. Remember, the secret to success is being yielding, not rigid (this isn't passivity; it's a strategic choice). Remain calm and assertive, not violent or combative. When someone is intimidating, you might feel shaky and unsure. But have faith in yourself and apply what I've taught you. Plus, a helpful prayer I use and recommend to patients before approaching difficult people is "Feet, don't fail me now." These words summon your strength and the assistance of the Beyond, whether you're walking into a difficult situation or away from one. It may seem like you're on your own, but truly, you never are. When you set a clear intention, are not reactive, and let your actions come from your heart, you'll be supported by the universe in mysterious and powerful ways.

In this chapter, I've discussed how to improve communication using the principles of surrender. Realize that people have minds of their own. Don't pressure others or they'll clam up. You'll drive yourself crazy trying to make them behave differently—and it rarely works. An ancient sage said, "Smiling is my favorite exercise." Smile at adversaries but also be strong. Greet everyone with a lightness of being and enormous patience.

It feels so much better to let go than to try to force the river. I'm ecstatic when I can walk around unpressured, neither on other people's backs nor on my own. Surrender lets me slow down and see past a momentary block to a greater breakthrough. Obstacles are a function of how we flow with energy. When our ego loosens its grip, even a little, rather than clenching or flailing around, the path opens, as do possibilities. In my life, I don't want to be stopped by my ego, my stubbornness, or my anger. I want to dance in joyful states beyond the claustrophobic bounds of my mind. One of my favorite mantras is "Nihil obstat," Latin for "No obstacles." When you surrender, nothing hinders you or stands in your way. Surrender returns you to the spirit of flow, the breath of all being. It's just waiting for you to embrace it.

SURRENDER AFFIRMATION FOR COMPASSIONATE COMMUNICATION

I'm ready to surrender all obstacles that prevent mutual understanding and compassion with people in my life. I'm ready to stop trying to control or pressure others. I'm ready to compromise and release my attachment to needing to be right. I am ready to enjoy harmonious and loving relationships.

Part Three

RELATIONSHIPS, LOVE, AND SENSUALITY

Love brought me that far by the hand . . .
Then just kept standing there, not letting go.
—SEAMUS HEANEY

....

6

THE SIXTH SURRENDER

HONORING SOUL MATES, SOUL FRIENDS, AND

ANIMAL COMPANIONS

INTIMATE RELATIONSHIPS BESTOW REMARKABLE GIFTS AND are compelling teachers of surrender. They keep challenging you to open your heart, to become a gutsier, more confident, more giving person. The impulse of intimacy is to transform us, to melt our fears and inflexibilities. It wants us to flow like water, to be sensual, joyous, and free. The right relationships fortify your resilience and fearlessness, empowering success in all aspects of your life. No matter what happens, you know you're not alone. You know someone's got your back. This is a great benefit of letting people care for you and of your caring for them. Being valued and adored makes you stronger. If you want relationships that truly do your soul good, I'll share with you how to surrender to the ecstasy of loving.

I believe in love. I want relationships where deep is calling to deep, the kind that are so strong you can feel the universe rush through them. In my life, I want to love as madly as possible and release any impediments within or without that stop me. It's both exciting and scary to let someone into your heart. The surrender of love is allowing yourself to be taken on a journey without knowing the destination. The power of real connection—to yourself, to others—speaks to the holiness that binds us together. Above all else, I value loving: the surrender that it continually asks of me, how impossible it seems at times, how ecstatic it feels when fear fades and I can soar with those I cherish to shining parts unknown.

I'm excited to share with you ways to surrender to love and overcome obstacles to intimacy. We'll focus on what I'm calling soul connections, those kindred spirits with whom we feel an especially strong bond, as if the relationship always was and will be. When a relationship echoes the eternal, there's an energy, a fatedness that brings you together. Meeting these soul mates, soul friends (known as *anam cara* in Celtic lore), and animal companions can feel more like a reunion than a first encounter. You recognize each other in a sixth-sense way. Even if this knowing takes a while to register, it crystallizes over time. Something in you resonates. Pieces fall into place. Of course, I value other kinds of caring relationships but here we'll explore finding and surrendering to those that live in the depths of our souls.

Maybe you already believe in these kinds of connections. If not, I want to reignite your faith. The rewards of surrendering to relationships of this caliber are many: the comforts of companionship, passion, trusting the person and yourself enough to keep surrendering to the healing power of love. You can be yourself without having to constantly be "on." Soul connections feel alive, even ecstatic. In contrast, the cost of letting fear or overthinking stop you is a shrinking of your heart, of possibility. Turning away from a soul connection is like turning away from a part of yourself. It's foolish, even harmful to discount these bonds. If you do, thereafter it can seem as if something's strangely missing. You feel an ache that can't be consoled.

When I treat patients who haven't pursued these relationships, they often miss the link between why they feel incomplete and why they haven't fully loved. As a psychiatrist, I consider it a great victory to support them in becoming confident enough to risk surrendering to love, maybe for the first time, whether with a romantic partner, a friend, or a kitten they rescued from a shelter. The important thing is to start to love someplace. From there, we begin by identifying where in their lives they've been frightened, have lost faith, or have shut down.

Let me tell you about my patient Sid, a dentist, who's wife left him for a twentysomething salsa teacher. "I never saw it coming," Sid said, wincing. I wasn't surprised that he'd entered therapy angry and disillusioned. He was consumed with doubts about his sexual attractiveness and his worth as a man—not an easy admission for anyone to make. As is frequently true of people in pain, his first response was to say about love, "Never again." Like a hurt animal, he just needed to hole up and lick his wounds. The last thing he wanted to do was surrender to another relationship. I respected that. At this point, it wasn't my role to disagree or to urge change. I knew it was healthiest to let Sid vent and grieve as he saw fit, a necessary phase of the wild emotional ride of recovering from the shock of betrayal.

Letting go, freely expressing hurt and anger, is where healing begins. Bottling up emotions is bad for us. The magic of therapy is that it keeps energy flowing so that pain won't stay stuck. I admired Sid for being willing to work through the hell he was in and having faith that there might be light on the other side. Our sessions became his safe place to mourn a decades-long marriage he thought had been solid, and to gradually rebuild his self-esteem. Mercifully, time heals if we cooperate by doing the required emotional heavy lifting. You can't rush healing. After six months, Sid had enough distance to decide, "I don't want to be one of those bitter people who become partly dead when they've been wronged. I'm tempted to try dating again." That was my opening. We began to discuss how to overcome his fears and choose a good relationship. Also, to help him find the right person, I taught him to develop intuition and listen for synchronicities and the feeling of déjà vu.

Some of the dates he had over the next year were real bummers, leaving him disheartened. But just when he was about to give up, a college friend he hadn't seen in years happened to invite him to a party. There he met Edna, a master gardener. On first look, she didn't appear to be his type. Still, he found himself talking to her. Imagine his surprise when he began feeling chills of recognition. Something about Edna made him grin foolishly. He found himself happy just looking at her and felt an immediate sense of deep ease.

Now they've been married for five years. Sid calls her his "real soul mate." They've had the usual ups and downs but they trust each other and feel safe enough to keep surrendering to the exciting journey they're on as a couple.

Sometimes letting go of the wrong relationship lets you find the right one. Pain can be the catalyst to go higher in your life. I love the Yiddish saying "There's no heart as whole as a broken heart." As was true of Sid, reopening your heart is always possible, even after great suffering.

In this chapter, we'll explore the fundamentals of soul connections: What is a soul mate? How can intuition and déjà vu help you find one? What stands in the way? For example, are you attracted to unavailable people, delusional relationships, or emotional affairs? Are you an empath who is afraid of becoming engulfed by a relationship? Do you confuse lust with love? What if your head says yes but your gut says no? What if a soul mate doesn't reciprocate your feelings? Do you hold on to someone even if it's not good for you? How do you let go, even when you don't want to? Maybe you're doing everything right but still can't find a partner. What then? I'll also illustrate the invaluable role of surrender when you're in a relationship. At what point do you compromise instead of asserting yourself? How can you communicate better by releasing ego, fear, rigidity, and expectations that your partner will be perfect? We'll go on to the wonder of soul friends, a sisterhood and brotherhood of kindred support. Then we'll celebrate the blessing of animal companions, our four-legged gurus of unconditional love.

Soul connections involve flow, trusting what intuitively moves you about someone. Despite the distractions and demands of our fast-paced world, I urge you to follow through on these connections. Don't talk yourself out of them. If you feel inexplicably drawn to the person beside you on the plane, young or old, strike up a conversation. Regrettably, we often explain away our intuition, thinking, "Oh, this is weird. I don't even know the person." If you react this way, it's too late. The opportunity is lost. Why not risk investigating relationships that feel right? Who says that everything has a pat, predictable explanation? Surrendering to the flow of relationships means recapturing spontaneity, letting the mystery have a hand in enchanting your life. Be playful. Take a chance. If it doesn't work out, so what? But if it does . . .

Soul connections don't happen every day. When you find one, be grateful. They are gifts. Accept them graciously. The love you've been wishing for is here.

ATTRACTING A SOUL MATE

. . . .

Your task is not to seek love but to find all the barriers
within yourself that you have built against love.

—RUMI

The term "soul mate," *amor platonicus*, was coined in the fifteenth century by Florentine scholar Marsilio Ficino, but the concept has appeared in many cultures since ancient times. The oldest record dates back five thousand years to the Egyptian legend of Osiris and Isis. Brother and sister, husband and wife, their eternal love lasted a lifetime and beyond. Plato's *Symposium*, a radical dialogue on the nature of eros, describes how the male and female were originally one person but Zeus feared their power and divided them. Afterward, each kept looking for its other half. Similarly, in Celtic lore, our souls begin as one being that gets broken apart. The search to reunite with our soul mate is a search for balance. In Yiddish, finding your *bashert* means finding your predestined partner, what's meant to be.

I'm defining a soul mate as a fated romantic relationship with someone to whom you feel a special affinity. You fall in love with and support each other's soul as well as each other's body. My spiritual teacher says to beware, as "your soul mate can turn into your cell mate" when there's not a mutual desire to grow. Support is the key concept here. You're each other's biggest fan and safe place to fall. You both can take each other further than either of you can go alone. The relationship is never denigrating, abusive, or based on narcissism or control. When you meet, something in you awakens, even rejoices. You can finally breathe. The wait is over—you're home again.

However, contrary to what you may think, a soul mate isn't

necessarily some ideal person who will make your life perfect or cure your loneliness. Nor do you always have to like each other or agree. But he or she will help you evolve. You'll learn from one another. There is no deadline for a soul mate. One can arrive when you're twenty or eighty, whenever the time is right. Sexual attraction is part of the bond, though this may vary in different phases of life. Some of these relationships are incredibly smooth, whereas most have more challenges. However, with soul mates, two are stronger than one. You make each other better.

A soul mate relationship requires continual lessons in surrender. If you cohabitate, you may see each other every day and every night, which keeps emotional issues in the forefront. This can get intense in ways that friend relationships might not because your ongoing exposure is compounded by the complexities of intimacy. Familiarity isn't always bliss! (This is also true if you have regular contact but live apart.) The good news is that the more you know someone the more you can love that person. The rest of the news is that the more you know someone the more he or she also can press your buttons. Soul mates are mirrors for each other, what's loving, smart, and adorable as well what's annoying, negative, and rigid. Thus, your relationship may experience tumultuous periods or you may have disagreements that require the two of you to expand your hearts and surrender your egos, in small and larger areas—for instance, the chick flick or testosterone-charged action film you see to please your spouse, the obligatory visit to your toxic in-laws, or larger arguments that require compromise on everything from parenting styles to work schedules to dealing with money. You surrender to these compromises in service to the "we" of love.

My spiritual teacher jokes with me, saying, "Don't ask for a relationship. It will bring problems. You just have to decide which sets of problems you want to get involved with." I know he's right. But, being both tenacious and a romantic, I believe that the challenges of intimacy are worth it, even if I risk the agony of heartbreak. A soul mate union invites you to open differently than you would alone, becoming flexible and letting go of behaviors that don't benefit you or the relationship. In some ways, for me, it's easier to be on my own, but moving beyond my comfort level lets me surrender in ways I long for. As fiery as it can get with a soul mate—good passionate and bad passionate—your mutual bond, the familiarity and instinctive trust, motivates you to resolve conflicts instead of bolting. Getting to the other side of an impasse, working out a problem, feels marvelous. As barriers dissolve, the space between two people opens; there's room for ecstasy.

I have gained much from Edgar Cayce's readings on soul mates. Cayce, perhaps the most famous American intuitive of the twentieth century, writes that soul mate relationships aren't created out of thin air, as the world frequently thinks, but have evolved over numerous incarnations. He says that we have many possible soul mates in our lives, not just one. Think of it: you have the potential of running into former spouses from previous eras at any time! When a woman asked Cayce if there was someone other than her fiancé who could make her happy, he replied, "You might have twenty-five or thirty such relationships if you choose to make it so." (Also, he says soul mates play different supportive roles in many parts of our lives such as colleague, teacher, and friend.) Still, Cayce suggested that instead of looking for a person simply to make us happy we'd be better off finding someone to facilitate our wholeness and spiritual growth. This was how he defined a soul mate—not as an "other half" who completes us.

Just as swans mate for life, some soul mates come together for a lifetime. Others are partners for shorter periods or primarily to bring children into the world. A reader once asked me, "With all your intuition, why haven't you found a lasting relationship?" Believe me, I've asked myself that more than once. However, I've come to understand that I've needed different soul mates throughout my life. Each taught me just the right lessons when I was ready. One long, cherished relationship could go no further because, heartbreakingly, my partner was not ready to work through the block. Others have ended when we went as far as we could go. We loved each other, learned what was needed, then parted amicably or stayed close friends. In all soul mate unions, you have issues from previous eras—karma—to work out. For me, finding a relationship that endures has taken a long time but I am still hopeful.

It's important to carefully choose our companions in all areas of life. People can help or hinder our well-being. As a psychiatrist, I appreciate how much we can understand ourselves through our relationships. Therefore, it is critical to find a partner who supports us in becoming our best selves.

I'm interested to track how my friends met their soul mates at varying ages, at different phases of their lives.

Stephan and Ronlyn. Stephan, in his sixties, met Ronlyn again after the death of his beloved wife of twenty years, also a soul mate. Mutual friends brought Ronlyn to a dinner party Stephan was giving. Incredibly, as a teenager Ronlyn used to babysit Stephan's young children. Today they are happily married.

Arielle and Brian. Arielle, at forty-four, had a dream in which she "saw" Brian, her future husband, though they hadn't actually met yet. A few weeks later, Brian showed up at a business conference they both attended. Instantly they recognized each other, married a few months later, and have been together for over a decade.

Berenice and Lou. At twenty-eight, Berenice met her husband, Lou, while on a date with someone else at a coffee shop in Manhattan. Though Berenice and her date were sitting with friends, her eyes locked with Lou's. He came over and asked for her number. Out of respect for her date, she didn't give it to him. But a week later, while she was having lunch at a museum, Lou was there! Berenice said, "It was fate. I knew I was going to marry him. We remained married for fourteen years. We had children and grew in many ways together." Eventually they parted but Berenice has no doubt that Lou was her soul mate during that period.

What should you look for in a soul mate? How can you know you've met yours? To avoid missing out on these relationships, you must let go of unrealistic expectations. Here's a summary of some fundamental qualities that define what a soul mate is and isn't. Though the intensity of these factors may vary in different phases of your lives, they form the basis of your bond.

HOW TO IDENTIFY YOUR SOUL MATE

WHAT A SOUL MATE RELATIONSHIP IS

- You feel a strong connection, comfort, and sense of familiarity.
- There's a physical attraction.
- You share mutual love, commitment, and support.
- You "get" each other; you're each other's biggest fans.
- You are emotional mirrors and teachers for each other.
- You're in synch, even telepathic.
- You're willing to work through conflicts, to compromise, and to surrender unhealthy patterns to improve the relationship.

WHAT A SOUL MATE RELATIONSHIP ISN'T

- All about you (or all about your partner).
- Lukewarm, boring, or noncommittal.
- Forced or merely a "good idea."
- Based on abuse, control, or rigidity.
- Only physical attraction or the sense of "lightning striking."
- The "answer to all your problems" or always conflict-free.
- Based on "settling," being together for convenience or out of a fear of being alone, breaking up, or change.

Whether or not a soul mate relationship lasts forever, these relationships are transformative and provide a gold mine of lessons. They bring you face-to-face with aspects of your masculine and feminine sides that you desire to integrate. Marriage, which is a civil agreement, doesn't require that you be with a soul mate. So if it happens that your spouse isn't one, or if you always stay single, numerous benefits and much love are still possible. I'm not saying it's necessarily better or worse to find a soul mate. The level of connection is just different. One thing I am sure of: each of our paths is uniquely perfect. Life presents us with what we need to grow. In this sense, a soul mate may not be appropriate or essential for everyone, as much as the heart may long for one.

Moreover, you can't force one to arrive or demand that the universe deliver one. I guarantee: that won't work. This is where surrender is key. It's a fine balance. You must clarify what qualities you desire in someone, then surrender expectations. Paradoxically, the "letting go" part is what most increases the likelihood of results. Being too hungry or fixated on finding a mate can backfire by acting as a death grip that stifles flow. To manifest a goal, you must always hold it lightly; don't inadvertently sabotage yourself by clamping down.

Naively, I used to think the role of my spiritual teacher was to bring me a soul mate. When he didn't I got angry and disappointed. With more maturity, I came to understand that the role of a spiritual teacher is simply to help me evolve spiritually, the most generous of gifts. The difficulty was that I'd been confusing him with a "good parent" who was supposed to meet all my needs. However, *being on a spiritual path isn't always about getting what you want.* It's getting what you're given and humbly learning from that. Even so, there are clear ways to hone your intuitive focus to make it more possible for your soul mate to materialize. Here is an exercise to do this.

INVITE YOUR SOUL MATE IN

Now you'll put surrender into action by setting the stage for a soul mate, then noticing signs that he or she has arrived.

1. *Make a wish list.* Spend some quiet time picturing the qualities you most desire in a mate. Ask yourself, "What would truly be good for me? What do I need?" Intelligence? Kindness? Support? Chem-

istry? Someone who wants children? Good communication skills? Someone who's spiritually connected? Who's successful? Do you prefer an extrovert, an introvert, or someone who's in between? When my father started dating long after my mother's death, he movingly told me, "I can't be with a woman who doesn't give to charity." Also make a list of traits that are unacceptable to you such as being self-absorbed or rigid. Everyone's needs are different.

2. *Release expectations.* Think of your list as a letter to spirit. You've put in your soul mate requests—there's no need to keep resending the letter. Now, let the list go. This means not obsessing about a soul mate, a time frame to meet the person (often the hardest part), or continually talking about the subject. Hold your desires lightly in your heart but don't push. Have faith that you've been heard.

3. *Listen to intuition.* Pay attention to intuitive signs that you've met someone of interest, even if he or she isn't obviously your "type." These include a sudden wave of chills, a gut feeling of attraction, or a flash of insight that this person may be right for you. One patient told me, "I heard a church bell chiming inside." Or, if he or she appears in a dream and then you meet in waking life, it's auspicious to pursue the connection. Also, stay aware of intuitions such as a sick feeling in your gut or a sense of distrust that warns, "Danger. Bad news. Stay away." These will protect you from unhealthy relationships.

4. *Be aware of synchronicities and déjà vu.* Synchronicities are moments of perfect timing when paths effortlessly interconnect. You sit next to someone in a movie who turns out to be your soul mate. Or, out of the blue, you have a chance to go to Paris where you meet the *one.* Pay special attention to these moments. Also, notice if you have a sense of déjà vu, as if you've known each other before. If this occurs with a stranger—say, in the market—act on the situation by smiling and making eye contact. Then strike up a conversation, maybe by asking for directions or simply by saying,

"You look so familiar. Have we met before?" Though I know this can feel awkward, the worst that can happen is nothing. But what if there is a connection?

Changing or Unclear Signs: Issues to Watch Out For

Sometimes your intuition will be clear. For instance, shortly after I'd first met a man, I dreamed he was silent while beating on a small round ancient drum with a deep haunting sound. Then, when he spoke, his words turned into a shower of flowers caressing me. This dream resonated through my being and connected us, presciently signaling our beautiful relationship to come. However, intuition and dreams may not always be clear-cut. A workshop participant once told our group, "In a dream, I was given my soul mate's name, the date he would arrive, and what he looked like. Just as predicted, three years later, I met this man, but he was an arrogant womanizer. That really put me off. And after waiting all this time! But should I have married him anyway?" *Good question.* My answer was practical: "Even when a voice from on high tells you to do something, always check in with your gut. If it doesn't feel right, don't do it." This goes for any kind of authority, including gurus. Wisely, this woman didn't marry the guy, but it took her a lot of soul-searching to make that decision given the dream's specificity. In your life, I urge you to keep checking in with your intuition about decisions. Never defer to opinions about whom you ought to love or be.

Also, your criteria for a soul mate may change with time. Mine did, partially from seeing what does and doesn't work. For decades, I went for rebel artists and poets, all of whom I considered soul mates. Creativity is a huge turn-on for me. My connection with each of these men was intense, sensual, always a major déjà vu experience. Plus, from the start, we could talk about everything, as if we'd just picked up an ongoing conversation. However, my ultimate deal breaker was that it seemed impossible to lead a calm, practical life with them. The artist's soul can have considerable angst, which fuels great creations but is awfully rough on domestic tranquility. Thus, these relationships, none of which I've regretted, typically lasted just a few years.

One boyfriend was a talented artist who supported my soul in many gratifying ways. He lived in a rambling gothic house that he boasted hadn't been redone since the sixties. There were spiderwebs on the ceilings. Plus, there was no heat. In the snowy winters, I had to bundle up and write in a room so cold I could actually see my breath! These quirks, which seemed almost charming in the blush of early love, became intolerable when reality settled in. After many months, my boyfriend reluctantly compromised a little by getting tiny space heaters for me (he was a well-insulated big bear, constantly hot). They didn't really warm me up enough, but I wanted to accommodate. The problem was that the space heaters kept blowing out the fuse box. The electricity cut off whenever I used them. And this short-circuited his personal fuses too. Exasperated, he abruptly announced, "I'm just not cut out to be in a relationship!" Though his panic lasted only through dinner and we did solve the electrical problem, in the end too many of his fuses kept getting blown out where intimacy was concerned.

While I worship creativity, I'm also exceedingly practical. I need a calm, lovely home in which I can live and create. Thus, my soul mate wish list has evolved to include this point. Now, my top five priorities include chemistry, mutual respect, creative conversation, doing good in the world, and compatibility on a practical level. Over the years, the feeling of "lightning striking" has become less essential.

So, in your search for a soul mate, practice defining what you want, then practice letting go of your attachments to those requirements, an excellent exercise in surrender. Set your intention, then release it—a tactic much different from obsessing or trying too hard to make something happen. You'll get the hang of intuitively knowing when to lean into the right relationships instead of trying to force people to be what they're not or having unrealistic expectations. Attaining such balance enhances the dance of intimacy.

WHAT PREVENTS US FROM SURRENDERING TO SOUL MATES

With my patients, I've observed some frequent obstacles to finding and keeping a soul mate. For instance, I've treated longtime couples who aren't soul mates but remain together out of loyalty, convenience, or inertia. It feels like a breach, "too much trouble," or "too scary" to change, disrupt their routine, or work on restoring passion. They may care about each other, have children and a social network, and have day-to-day lives that function well.

In addition, resisting change is often associated with the fear of being alone, of never finding a partner who's a better match. Or negative patterns such as abuse and low self-worth keep them hooked into destructive relationships. It's too big a leap to trust that the universe will bring them someone better, much less someone spectacular. My heart went out to one patient who was terrified of leaving his unhappy marriage. He told me, "The devil I know is better than the devil I don't know," a fear-based rationale for staying in an unfulfilling relationship. For many, it can seem easier to "settle" for what's familiar. I'm not saying settling is always a bad decision, nor am I suggesting that a soul mate is right for everyone. It depends on what you need to grow. *Healthy* non-soul-mate partnerships can have advantages such as stability, support, and companionship, despite lacking certain passions and a soul connection. My spiritual teacher tells us, "There are no wrong choices. Some just have different outcomes than others." Which type of relationship you choose must be the best fit for you.

Still, if you want to find a soul mate, I'll offer insight into how to overcome the following predictable, often confusing obstacles.

Obstacle 1: You're Attracted to Emotionally Unavailable People

I want to keep this simple. A soul mate must be willing and available to have a relationship with you. If he or she is unavailable, this is not your soul mate at the present time. So what is an available person?

Whether this is your spouse or a new love, he or she wants to know your feelings, your sensitivities, what scares you, what you adore, who your family and friends are. The person is single and open to commitment. There is no pattern of hiding, compartmentalizing, ongoing ambivalence, or sneaking around. This person's motives are straightforward. You don't have to go into a mind spin or try to decode with friends what he or she really means. He or she doesn't keep you hooked in with mixed messages or intermittent reinforcement of passion or caring—an addictive pattern that drives both sexes crazy in a bad way. He or she makes a plan with you and shows up, no cat-and-mouse games or habitual canceling. In all other cases, think twice about getting involved.

A confusing part of being attracted to unavailable, commitment-phobic people is that the emotional or sexual chemistry can feel so strong. You accept behavior that you'd never tolerate in friends. Why? The electricity can feel so incredible and rare, you mistake intensity for intimacy. You make compromises you wouldn't typically consider in order to give the relationship a chance. Still, connection or not, you must take a sober look to determine if someone is truly available for intimacy. Hear this: *Not everyone you feel a connection with, no matter how mind-blowing, is your soul mate. You can fall for someone who is totally wrong for you, as unfair and confounding as that reality can be.*

For a relationship to work, a soul connection must go both ways. Even if the intuitive bond you feel is authentic, it can remain unrealized. Just because someone might've been your soul mate in previous eras, it doesn't mean he or she is right for you today. Perhaps the person can't or won't reciprocate or is simply oblivious, a frustrating irony you must accept. Don't put your life on hold for unrequited longing. Love that is destined can never be stopped. Meanwhile, keep your options open. How do you avoid getting entangled in dead-end or delusional relationships where you see someone in terms of how you wish them to be, not who they are? To start, here are some red flags to watch for. Even one sign warns you to be careful. The greater the number present, the greater the danger.

SIGNS OF UNAVAILABLE PEOPLE

- They are married or in a relationship with someone else.

- They can't commit to you or have feared commitment in past relationships.

- They have one foot on the gas pedal, one foot on the brake.

- They are emotionally distant, shut down, or can't deal with conflict.

- They're mainly interested in sex, not relating emotionally or spiritually.

- They are practicing alcoholics, sex addicts, or substance abusers.

- They prefer long-distance relationships, emails, or texting, or they don't introduce you to their friends and family.

- They are elusive, sneaky, or frequently working or tired, and they may disappear for periods of time.

- They are seductive with you but make empty promises—their behavior and words don't match.

- They send mixed messages, flirt with others, or don't give a straight answer—you're always trying to decode what they really mean.

- They're narcissistic, considering only themselves, not your needs.

- They throw you emotional crumbs or enticing hints of their potential to be loving, then withdraw.

Some of these signs may be more obvious than others at first. It's tricky: we tend to show our best selves in the honeymoon stage of a romance. It can take time for a person's unavailability to emerge. One patient lamented, "I need a crystal ball. The first few months of a courtship, a man is so attentive, caring, passionate." Partially she's right, but it's also true that we tend to see what we want to see. That's why it's eye-opening to look at a partner's relationship history. Who he or she was previously with reveals volumes about his or her capacity for intimacy now. Beware of rationalizing, "I'm different. This person would never be that way with me."

I don't care how mightily someone blames an ex for a relationship's demise—this person played a role too. Being able to admit that or trying to understand the reasons for making such a terrible choice is a positive sign. Playing the victim is not.

Over the years I've worked with many perplexed, lonely patients to uncover why they keep holding a torch for unavailable, commitment-phobic partners and how to surrender this sabotaging pattern. Most of us aren't purposely drawn to these kinds of people—their mixed messages in combination with our particular susceptibilities, conscious or unconscious, can lure us in. Also, it helps to understand that unavailable people rarely choose to be this way. It's an unconscious defense against trauma or some emotional wound from the past. Research has shown that many are afraid of being clung to or smothered, which stems from having had a controlling, engulfing, or abusive parent. Commitment-phobic men, in particular, may just prefer sex without love. They are afraid of being controlled by feminine energy, though they don't know it or couldn't admit it. Rather, they see themselves as macho dudes who think women always need more than they can give. Thus they prefer to play in shallow water, not go deep. If being in a relationship with an unavailable person feels like love to you, I urge you to look closer. To bypass these relationships, I want you to see where you get snagged so that you don't repeat the same mistakes.

WHY ARE YOU ATTRACTED TO UNAVAILABLE PEOPLE?

Here are some common reasons.

- *Low self-esteem and feeling unworthy of love.* Think of the Groucho Marx syndrome, "I don't want to belong to any club that would have me as a member." If someone shows up who's capable of love, you push the prospect away or don't feel any chemistry.

- *Dysfunctional parenting.* You have inner radar for partners who mirror the unhealthy dynamics you had with a parent. In intimate relationships, you re-create the same dynamics in an attempt to receive what was lacking. For instance, if your father was emotionally unavailable you are drawn to similar men, hoping to finally win Daddy's love. This outcome is never going to happen because the men you choose aren't capable of true loving.

- *Codependency.* You believe your love can change or save someone so you take on unavailable people as projects, an approach that is doomed to failure.

- *The thrill of the chase.* You're addicted to forbidden fruit, the biological exhilaration of the hunt, the challenge of conquering the unattainable. (Interestingly, research reports that merely knowing people are spoken for makes them more appealing.) You want what someone else has instead of being grateful for your own blessings.

- *Fear of commitment or loss.* It's safer to keep a distance, especially if you've been hurt or betrayed, or if you've suffered a great loss. Also, you may resist commitment if you had an abusive, critical, or controlling parent who invaded your boundaries or smothered you. Or you may fear losing yourself in a relationship with a partner who would require too much attention without your own needs being met. The secondary gain of staying single is avoiding these fears. Therefore, you may unconsciously prefer unrequited love to the vulnerable, soul-stretching work of emotional intimacy.

- *You're willing to settle.* Perhaps you haven't been in a sexual relationship for some time. Then here comes this charismatic, hot Mr. or Ms. Right lavishing you with attention. You know it's all wrong but it feels so good. So you settle for sex or crumbs of affection which may seem better than nothing or celibacy.

- *You're seduced by the white-knight syndrome.* You want to be saved and someone swoops in to save you, emotionally, financially, or spiritually. Instead of owning your power, you surrender it to another. White knights are often on a power trip or end up resentful about assuming too much responsibility. Most aren't fully available for a loving, equal relationship.

- *You can't see through a charming facade.* Some people can look really good, say all the right things, and claim to be "spiritual" but they're just charming New Age narcissists or users. They have no intention of making a real commitment. You can get taken in by a facade if you don't check in with your gut and intuition.

If you want a soul mate but have a history of choosing unavailable people, identify which of the above dynamics rings true so you can begin to heal it. It's useful to journal about the causes and solutions to these going-nowhere attractions, then practice not acting on your impulses. For further insight, seek the help of a therapist or friends who've worked with this pattern in themselves. I'm also a big believer in surrogate parenting. If your parents didn't provide emotional or spiritual nurturing, look for other loving men and women as role models—people who can fulfill these needs in your life today. Seek out positive relationships. Philosopher José Ortega y Gasset says, "The type of human being which we prefer reveals the contours of our heart."

Once I fell hard for an emotionally unavailable younger man who'd just left a woman he couldn't commit to. It was an obvious red flag that I disregarded. Why? Mostly because I was attracted to him and craved physical and emotional contact. Like many women, I bonded quickly once we started making love. He, on the other hand, like many men, enjoyed the pleasure without bonding in the same way that I did. Finally, when we started getting too close and the relationship got too intense, he ran away from me.

So my surrender was to let go of him (as painful as that was) with no guarantees that I would feel like this about another man or ever find my soul mate. I'm not saying he was my soul mate; he was too unavailable and spiritually unconscious. But my feelings were real and hard to shake. Moreover, my surrender threw me into facing my fears of aging, of being alone, and of all the sorrows that losing a love can bring. It also involved what my shaman guide, Sandra Ingerman, refers to as "honorable closure." You don't reopen the door to a relationship that is hurtful. This means no communication: no emails, no letters, no calls. Therefore, my ongoing surrender was to keep moving on a day at a time, grateful for the blessings in my life, while searching for a faith that would sustain me until the day when my real soul mate arrived.

To find true love, ideally you want to avoid getting involved with anyone who can't reciprocate your affections. If you are in a toxic, abusive, or nonreciprocal relationship, withdraw even when your passion is strong and tells you to stay. It may feel excruciating to let go when you don't want to or if you're still hoping against hope that the person will change, but as my Daoist teacher once told me, "The heart knows when it's enough." You're sick of the pain and you are ready to surrender. The following exercise will show you how to let go, as it did for me.

SURRENDER YOUR ATTRACTION TO THE WRONG PEOPLE AND DELUSIONAL RELATIONSHIPS

Succeeding at this goal requires that you be a realist and surrender to your powers of logic, not the tugs of your heart or what you wish would be. The hard line you must take is to follow common sense and reason, not indulge in fantasy.

- *Declare your intention.* Inwardly tell yourself, "I am not powerless over my attraction to unavailable people. I am willing to do what's necessary to change and find my soul mate."

- *Surrender your fantasies of what could be.* Keep focusing on what *is* instead of what you hope for. If the person is committed to someone else, keep reminding yourself of that. Don't indulge in obsessing about how sexy or adorable the person is or how connected you feel. Don't fuel unlikely pipe dreams that Mr. or Mrs. Right will get a divorce to be with you. Instead, say no to tantalizing fantasies and yes to reality, even if it doesn't match your desires.

- *Get to know someone before having sex.* Bonding can occur more quickly for women than men during intercourse. Since men lack the same high levels of oxytocin, the bonding hormone, casual sex is possible for many. (A way for men to achieve faster and deeper bonding may be to take sublingual oxytocin.) Also beware of potential love partners who are unevolved spiritually or emotionally, or who are simply charming narcissists. If you choose to go ahead with one of them, all I can say is good luck! Be prepared for pain but learn from the lessons that come.

- *Let go of trying to "fix" partners or make them fulfill their potential.* It is inappropriate to try to fix anyone. People don't change just because you love, beg, or threaten them. They must want to fix themselves and fulfill their own potential. Even then, change takes dedication. Don't get seduced by the illusion of possibility. It's easy to misread someone's potential when the reality is quite different. You may be intuiting a very real side of a person, such as a desire for intimacy, but you can't actualize this for anyone else. Releasing the illusion will keep you from losing years in pursuit of improving someone. It's a sign of respect to allow people to be themselves. Seeing who your partner is, not just his or her "potential," liberates you to make healthy choices.

- *Test the situation—create a conflict.* To reveal someone's true colors early on, I suggest provoking a small conflict and observe the reaction. For instance, say, "It makes me feel unheard if you cut me off. I would love it if you'd let me finish my thought." If he or she can hear you and honor your wishes, that bodes well for intimacy. If the person gets defensive, critical, or withdraws, that's vital information too. I understand your reluctance to burst the blissful bubble of infatuation, but doing so, just a little, will help you determine how available your partner really is.

- *Break the unhealthy attachment.* Use this effective shamanic technique to sever bonds to toxic relationships. Go out in nature and find a thick branch or stick. Declare inwardly, "It is done," signifying that you are ready to let the person go. Then swiftly break the wood in half. Leave the two pieces in the wilderness or natural area. Then walk away without turning back.

- *Treasure yourself.* You deserve to be treasured by a partner. But first you must treasure yourself, the unique, sexy, and amazing person you are. Each day, treasure your joys, struggles, and shortcomings, but most of all your heart. Then you can attract someone who will be able to treasure you too.

Obstacle 2: You Confuse Lust with Love

Sexual attraction is notorious for obliterating common sense and intuition in the most sensible people—perhaps you can attest to this. Lust is a symptom of infatuation in which you are intensely turned on by someone and idealize him or her without seeing the real person. It usually takes off fast and burns out quickly. Lust is an altered state of consciousness programmed by the primal urge to procreate. Studies report that the brain in this phase is much like a brain on drugs. Functional MRI scans illustrate that the same area lights up when an addict gets a fix of cocaine as when a person is experiencing lust. Your brain is playing tricks on you that override logic. You get a huge surge of dopamine, which activates the pleasure centers in your brain. To sustain this high you may go to unhealthy extremes to keep the person in your life. Wrongly, you may interpret the dopamine surge as "I found my soul mate." One patient insightfully revealed a pattern she wants to break, "I have become attached to inconsistent men when lust is the main ingredient." However, dopamine requires novelty. It typically wears off when you get used to each other. At that point, your infatuation either ends or evolves into a real relationship based on love, passion, and reality or perhaps simply a nice friendship.

In the beginning of a relationship, when sex hormones are raging, lust is fueled by projection and idealized infatuation—you see what you want to see, you make someone into what you imagine him or her to be. You exaggerate the person's virtues and downplay flaws rather than scrutinizing whether the person is actually available. There's nothing wrong with the lust of infatuation: it can be beautiful and fun as long as you recognize it for what it is.

If you want a soul mate, not simply a hot affair, you would do well to memorize the difference between lust and love. Pure lust is based on physical attraction, dopamine intoxication, and fantasy—it often dissipates when the "real person" surfaces. It is conditional, triggered, for instance, by a person's appearance or status in the world. In contrast, true love requires time to get to know each other, though you can feel lust too during this important phase. You fall in love with someone's soul along with their body. True love is based on bonding, respect, and commitment. Infatuations are easily replaceable; true love isn't. Here are signs to differentiate lust from love so you don't blindly give your heart to unavailable people.

SIGNS OF LUST

- Your main focus is on a person's looks and body.

- You are primarily interested in sex.

- You would rather keep the relationship on a fantasy level, not discuss real feelings.

- You want to leave soon after sex rather than cuddling or eating breakfast together.

- Your gut may say, "Danger. Getting involved doesn't feel safe."

- You are lovers but not true friends.

SIGNS OF LOVE

- You want to spend quality time together other than just have sex.

- You get lost in conversations and forget about the hours passing.

- Your gut is comfortable, relaxed, affirming, "Go for it. Good things are ahead."

- You want to honestly listen to each other's feelings and make each other happy.

- He or she motivates you to be a better person.

- You want to be involved in each other's life.

The Allure of Bad Boys and Girls

The difficulty is that your gut and your heart aren't always lined up. The gut can scream, "Danger!" but your heart and hormones say, "Go for it." My patient Greg wanted a soul mate but was smitten with an unavailable "bad girl" who feared commitment. Barely knowing her, he leapt from lust to love, saying, "She's in my heart. I just can't stay away from her. I must surrender to my feelings." In the blink of an eye, Greg's common sense had evaporated. I've been there. I know how easily this can happen. But as I told Greg, "You always have a choice about playing with fire. You don't have to surrender to relationships that aren't smart or safe." Granted, the erotic draw to risky people can be intense. Your desires want what they want, healthy or not. But you don't have to act on them.

The appeal of bad boys and girls, if you're predisposed to it, is that they are elusive, seductive, unpredictable rule breakers, attuned to their primal instincts. They just don't care what other people think. And they have a knack for making you feel so right about being with them, even when your gut says it's wrong—that's part of their seduction. However, bad boys and girls aren't always the best prospects for a soul mate since they often aren't available for intimacy. Of course, I'm generalizing. Some also have the capacity for emotional maturity if they've developed other parts of themselves too. One patient told me, "My bad-boy soul mate finally stepped up to do the emotional work but it took being separated to motivate him." On the other hand, I've seen those who're overly identified with their elusive persona because it works for them. Thus, they may be unwilling or unable to be present enough for an authentic relationship. (Think James Dean in *Rebel Without a Cause*, a "too cool for school," sexy loner with a dark side.) Still, some packages are better left unopened. As the country song goes, "I know a heartache when I see one."

I've worked with many patients who are looking for long-term partners but are drawn to the excitement of bad boys and girls. Typically, they are nice, considerate, model citizens or spiritual seekers who haven't owned their dark sides. Thus, unconsciously attempting to become whole, they choose partners who act out a repressed part of themselves. My function is to help these patients contact and balance their dark and light sides. The process can begin by tapping into *their* own inner bad boy or girl. We all have at least a little of one in us, 'and it can be healthy, sexy, and fun to have it surface. It'll keep a sense of mischief alive in you. Once we've integrated this with the rest of our psyche, someone else doesn't have to play that role for us. Until we do, it's a tough pattern to break.

If you want a soul mate, my advice is to take a hard line: defer to your gut's warnings. The gut protects your heart. You don't have to follow all your chemical attractions. However, if you pursue a love interest despite your gut's warnings, at least go slowly and pay attention. With time, the truth will make itself known.

Obstacle 3: You're a Relationship Empath

In my practice and workshops I'm struck by how many sensitive people come to me wanting a long-term soul mate. Personally, I can relate to this. Yet, despite online dating services, expensive matchmakers, friend fix-ups, and blind dates, they still remain single. Or else they're in relationships but feel constantly fatigued and overwhelmed. The reason isn't simply that there aren't enough available people out there or that they're neurotic. Something more is going on.

In my life, I've discovered a vital piece to this puzzle: I am a relationship empath. Empaths are highly sensitive, intuitive, and caring, but they're also shock absorbers with an extremely permeable nervous system and hyperactive reflexes. They experience everything, pleasure and pain, sometimes to an extreme. They are super-responders: their sensory experience of a relationship is similar to holding something with fifty fingers instead of five. The amazing part of being so sensitive is that empaths are attuned to people (at times even telepathically) and to nature, and they can be exquisitely sensual, responsive lovers. The downside is that empaths are sponges for the world's angst. Without a membrane between themselves and the world, they unknowingly absorb other people's stress into their own bodies. Then they become overloaded, anxious, or exhausted. This differs from ordinary empathy such as when you sympathize with your partner's harrowing day at work. Relationship empathy goes much further. You merge with your partner and actually feel his or her joys and fears as if they were your own. Thus, romantic relationships, particularly live-in ones, can be challenging.

If you're an empath and haven't identified this dynamic, you may unknowingly avoid romantic partnerships because deep down you're afraid of getting engulfed. A part of you wants a soul mate; another part is frightened. This inner push-pull stops you from surrendering to a partner. The closer you are to someone, the more intense empathy gets. To feel safe enough to let go in a relationship, it's crucial for empaths to learn how to set healthy boundaries and assert their needs. Then intimacy becomes possible.

It's intriguing to examine ways our biology can contribute to fears of committing or getting engulfed. Take the sperm and the egg. During lovemaking, millions of sperm plunge into the vagina in a spectacular wave. They're all programmed for one thing: to find the egg and penetrate it within forty-eight hours, before they die. How astonishing—a massive army of sperm, tails whipping, urgently propelling themselves. The vagina's defense system attacks, protecting itself from invaders. Just a few sperm survive. Then the survivors spot it: the egg. Vastly larger than every one of them, a white luminous orb, so still, radiating. One tiny sperm reaches the egg's surface and is drawn inside, dissolving in her essence: the miracle of conception.

This demonstrates the stunning instinct men and women have to create together. But what holds us back? First, from a female perspective (hint—be the egg): fear of domination or invasion, or perceiving male energy as alien and therefore different from her own—feelings

I've heard women express often. Next, from a male perspective (be the sperm): fear of being engulfed. With intimacy, these unconscious dynamics get activated. One brave man in my workshop said, "I'm afraid if I surrender to a woman I'll lose my masculinity." For empaths and others, feminine energy is powerful and can threaten to overwhelm them. In fact, embryologically both men and women start as female until the sex hormones, testosterone and estrogen, differentiate the embryo. No one is just male. No one is just female. We each simply have a different ratio of these hormones. The key is balancing both aspects of ourselves.

To surrender to a soul mate, it's important to discuss with each other your fears of letting go. However, if you're an empath, you may not know what these are or that you're even resisting intimacy. Thus you can't convey your needs or set healthy boundaries. One patient admitted, "Before I found out I was an empath, I'd pine after unavailable men, keeping a safe distance to protect myself. I didn't realize I was afraid of being smothered or what the solution was." To determine whether you're a relationship empath, take the following quiz.

QUIZ: AM I A RELATIONSHIP EMPATH?

- Have I been labeled as overly sensitive?

- Am I afraid of getting engulfed or losing my identity in intimate relationships?

- Do I prefer taking my own car places so I can leave when I please?

- Do I get drained by too much togetherness and require time alone to refuel?

- Do I sometimes prefer sleeping alone?

- When my partner and I travel do I prefer adjoining rooms?

- Do I tend to take on my partner's stress or physical symptoms?

- Do I feel overwhelmed by noise, smells, crowds, or excessive talking?

If you answer yes to seven or more questions, you are a certified relationship empath. Four to six yeses indicate strong empathic tendencies with partners. One to three yeses indicate that you're at least part relationship empath. A score of zero indicates you are not a relationship empath.

Recognizing that you're a relationship empath is the first step to removing this obstacle to finding a soul mate. Next, you must redefine the traditional paradigm for coupling so you can find a comfortable way of being together. This means letting go of society's stereotypes about marriage or relationships and forging a new path for yourself. If you're an empath or if the ordinary expectations of coupledom don't work for you, practice the following tips.

SURRENDER OLD RELATIONSHIP RULES, CREATE NEW ONES

- *Evaluate a potential mate's compatibility.* As you're getting to know someone, share that you're sensitive, that you value having alone time. The right person will understand; the wrong person will put you down for being "overly sensitive." Also, notice how your energy responds to someone. Don't be with a partner who drains you, no matter how good he or she looks on paper.

- *Vibrations speak louder than words.* Notice how you relate to a potential mate's energy. Ask yourself whether the person's words match his or her energy. Or is something off? If you have any doubts about the person's authenticity, go slow. To avoid getting involved with someone who won't be good for you, keep tracking the person's energy with your empathic abilities to find out who he or she really is.

- *Allow quiet time at home to decompress.* Get in the habit of taking mini-breaks throughout the day. Tell your partner how important this is to you. Stretch. Breathe. Walk. Meditate. Listen to music. Then you won't be overwhelmed by the feeling of too much togetherness. This time alone will replenish you.

- *Limit your time socializing with others.* Tell your partner what your ideal time limit is to stay at parties or other social occasions before you burn out. If your comfort level is three hours max—even if you adore the people—make an agreement with your partner to take your own car if he or she prefers to stay longer. Then you won't dread going out or feel stuck somewhere. This will help you enjoy yourself.

- *Negotiate your square footage needs.* Breathing room is a must. Experiment with creative living conditions. Ask yourself, "What space arrangement is optimal?" Having a private area to retreat to? Separate bathrooms? Separate houses? Agree not to crowd each other. When traveling together, you may prefer getting adjoining rooms with your own bathroom (this works wonders for me). If sharing a room is the only option, hanging a sheet as a room divider will help. In terms of space, decide what is right for you and discuss this with your partner.

- *Get a sleep divorce.* Traditionally, partners sleep in the same bed. However, some empaths never get used to this, no matter how caring a mate they are. It's nothing personal: they just like sleeping in their own space. Feeling trapped in bed with someone and not getting a good night's sleep can seem like torture. So discuss options with your mate: separate beds, separate rooms, sleeping together a few nights a week. Because people who are not empaths can feel lonely sleeping alone, make compromises when possible.

In my medical practice, I've seen this creative approach to relationships save marriages and make ongoing intimacies safe for relationship empaths of all ages—even if they haven't had a long-term partner before. The secret is to keep emphasizing how much you love your mate, that he or she didn't do anything wrong, and how much it means to have your needs respected. These honest, loving conversations will help empaths and their partners feel more at ease embracing a new paradigm of intimacy.

Obstacle 4: Are You Having an Emotional Affair?

A soul mate relationship is based on trust, commitment, and a strong desire to be together. Still, despite this powerful bond, it's also true that your hearts will be stretched in countless ways. The danger, especially during challenging times, is that you may be vulnerable to having an emotional affair. This can damage trust and stop you from surrendering to the growth needed for your relationship.

What is an emotional affair? It's when you turn to a friend or co-worker for emotional (not physical) intimacy. The seduction is that this person gives you what you feel your mate doesn't: support, ego boosts, empathy, playfulness, an undercurrent of flirting or attraction. Initially, this can seem innocent but you may begin to share more with this "safe" person than with your mate. I understand how it can be easier to talk to someone sympathetic who's more peripheral. You're not wrestling with the same hot-button emotions such as anger or disappointment that can arise with a soul mate. Your dark sides aren't engaged which is what causes most impasses among couples. However, if you keep sharing with your special friend and not your spouse, your primary relationship will suffer. You'll become distant, less present, and therefore less able to resolve conflicts. Your partner will sense something is wrong. Basically, these affairs are a form of cheating, and like any infidelity, they can lead to deception and betrayal. In fact, research reports that about half of these "innocent" liaisons eventually turn into full-blown sexual affairs.

I am all for having platonic soul friends of the opposite sex. I treasure my male friends and the sharing and being there for each other in our lives. With my married male friends—I have a few good ones—I'm also either close to or at least friendly with their spouses too. If there's an attraction between him and me, we're up-front about it but agree not to act on it. We're not ambivalent or torn: we're just clear that this isn't who we are to each other in the here and now. With a true platonic soul friend, there's no deception or hidden sexual agenda, nor is anyone diverting your emotional energy from your primary relationship.

HOW DO YOU KNOW YOU'RE HAVING AN EMOTIONAL AFFAIR?

Watch for these signs:

- You withdraw from your spouse but confide in your friend.

- It's difficult to talk to your spouse about conflicts.

- You feel lonely and that your spouse doesn't appreciate you.

- You're frequently online with your friend, texting, or even sexting.

- You believe your friend understands you better than your spouse does.

- You keep your friendship a secret from your spouse or lie about how often you interact.

- When you're confronted with the emotional affair, you deny it.

If five to seven signs are present, it strongly suggests you're having an emotional affair. Three or four signs indicate that you're either primed to have one or already are involved. One or two signs suggest the possibility of an emotional affair. Zero indicates that you are not involved in one.

It takes honesty to admit you're having an emotional affair. The first step is to recognize what's happening. Then you have the choice to either continue the affair or decide to focus on your partner. The truth is, you can't do both. If you choose your partner, you must surrender to doing what it takes to heal the relationship. First, this means cutting off the emotional affair. In a respectful, clear way you must tell the other person, "I can't cyberchat, text, meet up with you, or talk on the phone anymore. It's not possible for us to be 'just friends.'"

Then openly talk to your partner about what's causing the distance. Is it his or her long hours at work? A lingering hurt? Lack of affection? Many therapists recommend confessing your emotional affair. In most cases I agree but how and whether you decide to do this depends on what will be most caring and helpful to your partner.

At the very least, I suggest that patients lovingly communicate something like, "I've been sharing my feelings more with a friend than I have with you. This doesn't feel right. I want us to be closer." Or you can acknowledge that you've crossed a line and how far you've crossed it. Use your intuition as a guide to how much you want to share. But be prepared for your partner's hurt and angry feelings. Listen without getting defensive. Then, with your partner or with a therapist, begin to address where you've grown apart or shut down. Despite great pain, soul mates have what it takes to withstand difficulty until things are resolved. It may take time, awareness, and love, but with bonds as strong as these, I know it's possible.

Being with a soul mate requires noticing where your heart closes, then being brave enough to reopen it again and again to each other. Trust between lovers is precious. Throughout your relationship, stay aware if you are drawn toward emotional affairs. Use this impulse as a cue to mindfully address issues in your relationship that require attention.

SURRENDER STRATEGIES FOR SOUL MATES

....

Inter nos perite amare volumus.
—LATIN FOR "WE AGREED TO LOVE EACH OTHER MADLY"

Once you've found a soul mate, let yourself surrender to being happy and grateful for the chance to love each other. Enjoy your relationship. It's rich. It's powerful. It's a portal to the mysteries of intimacy and spirit. Have fun together. Each day, allow yourself to open more and more to joy. Sure, there will be periods when you'll butt heads. And, as Buddhist teacher Stephen Levine says, sometimes the lesson of relationships is learning to "keep your heart open in hell." Still, stay clear about your priorities. You've met a trusted partner with whom you share a spiritual, passionate bond. How miraculous: despite the countless obstacles that could've kept you apart, you've found each other again! This person is the answer to your dreams, the one who was worth waiting for. Always remember that.

In the course of your relationship, I recommend some basic surrender strategies to keep in mind. They will help you soften rigidity and open your heart. Use them during ups and downs.

- *Be generous.* Give freely to your mate. Regularly express love, support, and positive feedback. Try not to be stingy or withholding. I adore one friend's view of marriage which he calls "a competition of generosity."

- *Laugh a lot.* Beware of becoming overly serious. Despite the emotional issues that arise in relationships, getting too intense aggravates the situation. Keep a sense of humor. Play and be silly. Be good company for each other. Surrendering to laughter breaks tension and is healing.

- *Stay flexible and patient.* Have a cooperative attitude. Being tight-fisted and impatient stops you from surrendering. Flow with conflict. If you notice you're getting overly controlling or pushy, take a break for at least a few minutes. Pause and breathe. Don't polarize into "I'm right, you're wrong." Instead, be willing to give a little and reach a middle ground without sacrificing your values.

- *Be able to live comfortably with unresolved problems.* Some problems take time to resolve. You can't reach a perfect solution right away—you must grow into it. In these situations, try to accept that there's no answer yet. In surrendered relationships, couples learn to flow with uncertainty. Have faith that both you and the universe will find the answer.

- *Go on inner dates.* When you're apart or are seeking to deepen your nonverbal spiritual connection with your partner, pick a time to meditate together for at least five minutes. Whether you're sitting across from each other or are in separate cities, simply close your eyes, breathe deeply, and silently attune to each other's essence, to each other's heart. This is a beautiful way of feeling close if you or your partner is away traveling or is simply stuck in the office working. These inner dates are a sacred form of intimacy, an infusion of love.

- *Love yourself and each other.* True love means first loving
  yourself, then extending that love outward. A soul mate can
  add to your happiness but he or she cannot make you happy.
  It's not the burden of your mate to heal your emotional issues,
  nor can you heal your mate's. One friend wisely said of her
  soul mate marriage, "The last thing we want to be is each
  other's therapist!" Love and healing start from within.

- *Be gentle with each other's imperfections.* No one is perfect. Not
  you. Not your mate. *Wabi-sabi* is the ancient Japanese practice
  of finding beauty in imperfection. With a soul mate this means
  appreciating his or her quirks, annoyances, and shortcomings.
  Even when someone wants to evolve and change, imperfections
  still remain. Surrender to the wonder of your soul mate,
  imperfections and all.

- *Accept your differences.* No matter how well you and your
  partner connect, there are differences between you. Accept
  these rather than insisting that you both see things the same
  way. That's never going to happen. Even when you have two
  versions of reality, try to empathize with where your partner
  is coming from. Seeing things through his or her eyes fosters
  understanding, even if you disagree. A soul mate relationship
  teaches you tolerance, even if some of your partner's qualities
  may never change.

- *Forgive.* When you or your partner inevitably hurt or
  disappoint each other, discuss how to remedy the situation.
  Whoever did the hurting must make amends and be willing
  to change the behavior. Whoever is injured must try not to
  harbor resentments. It's easy to cling to "justified" anger but
  that won't help you or the relationship. Forgiveness is the act
  of compassionately releasing the desire to forever condemn
  someone for an offense (though this doesn't mean staying in an
  abusive setting). Compassion opens a hidden door to a secret
  world that exists beyond anger or hurt.

Practicing these strategies creates openhearted communication rather than perpetuating friction or shutting down. The balance is always between when to assert yourself and when to let go. (Review Chapter 5 on communication.) Make it a policy to address conflicts quickly so that they don't sour joy. If you find you're hitting a wall, pushing too hard, or freaking out, it's wise to give the issue some breathing room and regroup. It's up to you to back off if your partner doesn't. My spiritual teacher says, "Frustration isn't the key to any door." Nor is fear. Always remember how exquisitely tender the heart is, how easily it withdraws when you're afraid. The strategies I've presented will let you and your partner rise higher than fear to trust the white light of love.

My philosophy of surrender applies to soul mates but also to other deep connections, though the set of challenges may vary. All intimate relationships will ask a lot of you. Continue tapping your inner warrior; this is the part of you that wouldn't hear of letting fear get the best of you. Stay open. Stay brave. Let yourself experience the ecstasy that comes from the devotion of loving.

SOUL FRIENDS AND ANIMAL COMPANIONS

Along with soul mates, I want to pay homage to the sacred bonds with our soul friends and animal companions. As with soul mates, you'll feel the same déjà vu connection, sense of familiarity, and flow. It's exciting: you'll recognize each other and begin again together.

I'm drawn to the Celtic notion of *anam cara*, Gaelic for "soul friend." Your *anam cara* is someone with whom you can share your deepest intimacies without hiding or feeling judged. Different from soul mates, these aren't lovers, but your tie is so close they may feel more like family than your biological relatives do. In Hebrew, these special friends are called *reyah*, lifelong companions. Author Kurt Vonnegut took this concept further in *Cat's Cradle* where he described a soul group called a "karass"—people who are bound together or work in unison for a great purpose. They're all born in the same era to support each other in their life's missions. Your friends are members of your soul group, as is your mate. Together you form a cluster of kindred spirits devoted to each other's well-being and evolution.

Take the famous soul friendship between the thirteenth-century Persian poet Rumi and the wandering dervish Shams of Tabriz. It is said that when they first met, they immediately fell into a deep, life-changing spiritual connection. One account describes Shams throwing Rumi's treasured books into a fountain, telling him to begin to live what until then he'd only been reading about. From that very first moment, Shams knew and loved Rumi's soul. This was the start of many conversations in which they awakened awareness, awe, and poetry in each other. After Shams's death, Rumi, stricken with grief, roamed the streets of Konya, Turkey. One day he heard the rhythmic beat of a goldsmith's hammer and, in his terrible sorrow, instinctively just started twirling. This was the origin of the whirling dervishes, the Sufi ecstatic dancers.

In my life, soul friends have been my salvation. I call them my tribe of other-worldlies; our real home is not this earth. They've become my family since both my parents have passed away and they are my consecrated community of support.

Soul friends share a steadfast devotion. My best friend, Berenice, and I have stuck together through thick and thin, though our relationship has sometimes been tumultuous. When Berenice turned eighty-five, I told her, "I adore you. Thank you for being my devoted friend for over twenty-five years." Berenice just beamed at me, teary with love, and said, "I know you will be with me in my final moments." I said yes without hesitation. When that moment comes, I will be honored to be with Berenice at her final passage.

In your life, be aware of soul friends. These connections are rare. Value them. I feel lucky if I meet one new soul friend each year. Put your intuitive antennae on alert. Even if you're not with a soul mate, you will never be alone. As in all soul relationships, these friends are teachers of love and surrender—mirrors for both your strengths and your insecurities. Thus, friendship becomes a vehicle for transformation, a chance to overcome resistance to intimacy.

I also include animal companions in the category of soul friends. Dogs, cats, horses, birds, or other animals teach us to be openhearted. In good times they stick by our side. When life gets too serious, they bring out our playful inner child. When we're down, they still love us unconditionally, not caring what other people think or what job we have or how much money we make. When the world is falling apart and all seems lost, they're curled up in our arms as consolers. Some days it may feel simpler to surrender to an animal's love than to a friend's or a soul mate's. It seems less problematic and so pure. How wonderful that our animal friends grant us such devotion. Let yourself take this love in. Surrender to it.

The souls of animals are just as real as our souls. I bow to all the animal rescuers of the world who fight to protect them from suffering. We are their guardians and companions, never their owners. We must protect the innocents of the earth, fight for the light of all sentient beings. I revere the Lakota tribal wisdom, *"Aho mitakuye oyasin.* All my relations, I honor you in the circle of life."* We are interconnected in harmony.

As a physician, I also greatly appreciate the benefits of animal-assisted therapy (usually dogs and horses) in clinical care, including with the elderly, psychiatric patients, and children with severe illnesses. Sigmund Freud had many dogs and often kept one nearby during psychoanalytic sessions to help patients relax. Research reports numerous therapeutic benefits that the animal-human bond can have for health and mood. It's been shown to lower blood pressure, lessen pain, and relieve anxiety and depression. Living with an animal can even increase longevity.

In the 1990s, I had terrible neck pain caused by a tiny cervical disc and the condition wasn't improving with conventional treatment. That's when I experienced the joy of dolphin therapy. At the Dolphin Research Institute, a marine park in the Florida Keys, I participated in a weeklong workshop with others who also had physical symptoms and sought healing. Every day, we swam with the dolphins in warm, womblike water. Initially I was afraid to let go, concerned they'd hurt me by jarring my neck. But, reassured by our workshop leader, I accepted that the healing was all about surrendering to trusting them.

If I kept my body tense, I might risk an injury. In our daily swims, I'd hold on to a dolphin's fin as this powerful but gentle creature pulled me in the water, never too hard or too fast. It was a gliding movement that seemed to adjust my neck in ways far beyond what even my skilled chiropractor had been able to do. The dolphins emitted an aura of sweetness and caring that infused us all. I felt even more of a kinship with them when I learned that they dream at night, just as we do, a state of awareness I so resonate with. These fellow dreamers became my healers. I felt privileged to be in their presence. When I left Florida, my pain had dramatically diminished. Soon after, it disappeared completely. Being with these dolphins jump-started my recovery.

What's also fascinating is that humans and animals can develop telepathic bonds. Consciousness researcher Rupert Sheldrake discusses the common phenomenon of how dogs can intuit when we are coming home, even at unpredictable times. They seem to sense our nearness minutes before we arrive. Once a dog has this precognition, it will wait patiently at the front door, eager to greet us.

One such telepathic bond created a miracle. A workshop participant of mine told this story about herself. Two years before, Simone longed to get pregnant but she had a rare kidney disease. Her doctor warned that pregnancy would overly stress her body, even endanger her life. Still, Simone's desire for a baby was so strong she decided to risk it. Fortuitously, she stayed healthy those nine months, which was practically unheard of for a pregnant woman with her disease. However, during that same period, her golden retriever puppy, her constant companion and "soul mate" with whom she was so attuned, was diagnosed with kidney failure. Soon after the birth of Simone's daughter, her loyal companion died, as if having held on just long enough to see her through. Selfless giving contains such mystery. How wondrous and far-reaching compassion can be among living beings.

Let all the animals of the earth be our teachers and healers. Both the ferocious lion and the sweet, sensitive "fainting goats" who keel over and faint when they get scared or overexcited are our brethren. We must forever surrender the notion that they are somehow inferior to us just because they aren't human or can't communicate with words. Such misguided arrogance of the mechanistic mind! We must persist in surrendering to humility, being able to admit we really don't know that much in the infinite scope of things. Still, what I do know is how powerful love is. When you view soul mates, soul friends, and animal companions with your heart, you can see their magnificence, their shining.

In this chapter, we've discussed different kinds of soul connections and how to surrender to them. For me, these relationships are ultimately about spiritual surrender, about barriers of fear dissolving into a more profound love. You embrace your beloveds but also have radical trust in spirit too. Spirit is the guiding force that oversees love in all its permutations. Spirit supports open hearts. Turn to it for guidance. If you're distressed that you haven't found a soul mate yet, ask for patience and clarity. If you feel hurt, confused, or tied in knots about the soul mate or friends you do have, inwardly ask, "How should I proceed? How can I reach them? How can they reach me?" Then intuitively listen for the answer. Keep surrendering your ego and expanding your heart. Keep looking into each other's eyes and don't stop, even during turmoil. Let soul relationships teach you about trust and faith and the ecstasy of love. These are the true secrets of the universe.

SURRENDER AFFIRMATION FOR SOUL RELATIONSHIPS

I embrace you.
I accept you.
I believe in you.
I am grateful for you.
I love and adore you.
I surrender to the flow of where our relationship takes us.

I sing the body electric . . .
That of the male is perfect, and that of the female is perfect.
—WALT WHITMAN

7

THE SEVENTH SURRENDER

EXPLORING THE DIVINITY OF YOUR BODY

AND SEXUALITY

DEVELOPING A SURRENDERED, LOVING RELATIONSHIP TO YOUR body and sexuality will transform your life.

Would you like to experience more pleasure and less stress? What if you could be happy with your body without reservations? Or make love without doubting yourself and holding back? Now nothing can stop you. Prepare to surrender to feeling this good.

I want you to enjoy your body's spectacular pleasures so that you can embrace passion fully and boost your sex appeal. As you do, you're going to feel more alive, aroused, and in touch with a mounting ecstasy that you can and deserve to experience. This is going to be the start of a lifelong sensual renaissance even if you currently feel out of touch with your physicality. The real sin is always being pleasure-deprived and stressed out. I'll show you ways to tap into countless sources of pleasure everywhere. The delight you get from savoring a juicy peach, breathing in fresh air, or making love depends on your connection to your body and your ability to surrender to pleasure.

Your body is so much more than you think it is. My definition of sexuality isn't the have-an-orgasm-and-it's-over mini-version that society touts. It's what happens when you surrender to the long, slow sensation of bliss within you which mercifully melts the tension of life's demands. Feeling this good is not complicated or out of reach. It just may be unfamiliar. I'll show you how to generate bliss on your own or with a partner. It starts with awakening your senses: sound, sight, touch, smell, taste, and the sixth sense, intuition. You'll become sensually aware of your entire body, then channel the pleasure you feel toward sexuality. This is where surrender is indispensible: you can't rush passion, control it, or analyze your way there. You must simply let go to the delight. I'll help you stop overthinking so you don't spoil pleasure. Surrendering to passion brings ongoing vibrance, renewal, and charisma at every age.

Too many people walk around as disembodied heads, forgetting they even have a body. Our world puts a premium on the ability to tough out adversity. We celebrate people who ignore their bodies' danger signals in order to achieve. One of my patients, a workaholic accountant, pushed himself so hard one tax season that he had a heart attack. Another patient stayed in a toxic marriage for twenty long years until she sank into such a major depression that she couldn't sleep, eat, or get out of bed. Only then did she seek counseling and gain the courage to leave her marriage. What enormous suffering we can put ourselves through before we listen to our bodies! But you don't want to do this. It's vital to retrain yourself to override mechanisms you've developed to push through fatigue or other warning signs like those my patients experienced. On a physical level, surrender means acting on your body's intuitive alerts, not fighting impulses that are meant to protect you. Listening to the following basic signals will radically improve the quality of your life.

PRACTICAL STRATEGIES TO SURRENDER TO YOUR BODY'S ALERTS

- If you're tired, rest.

- If you're hungry, eat a delicious meal.

- If you're sad, cry.

- If you're tense or upset, have some fun.

Your body is often wiser about your welfare than your mind is. Hippocrates wrote more than two thousand years ago, "There is a measure of conscious thought throughout the body." If you keep arguing with your body, refusing its attempts to protect you, it gets angry and rebels: you won't feel good or be healthy and symptoms will worsen. You'll also kill your capacity for passion and bliss. As I've seen in my medical practice, from overwhelmed parents to hard-charging executives, your schedule may be so jammed that you feel too tired to make love, are unable to have an orgasm, or lack any erotic desire at all. In most cases, this isn't from age, nor does it mean that you've lost your sexuality. It's that you're not respecting your body's needs by slowing down or reducing stress even a little bit—and *passion is the first thing to go*. The good news, however, is that when you start listening, your energy increases and passion returns.

No one would ever have accused me of being a quick learner about this. I know too well what it's like to push myself so hard I get drained or to get so frustrated in traffic on the way to yoga that it defeats the purpose of the class. I also know what it's like to wonder if I'm still a sexual being when I've been without a partner for a while. But I keep learning how to listen to my body to reduce stress and nurture my passion whether I'm single or not. (Actually, the sex life you have with yourself can be better than the sex lives of couples who are erotically out of touch.) I don't want to be so busy that I'm too spent to feel sexy. I refuse to sacrifice my passion to excessive work, to unavailable men, to draining people, or to anything my body rejects as not good for me. My ongoing surrender is revering my body, the intuitive wisdom she conveys, the sensual gifts she bestows. This may mean I have to cancel plans, say no to others, or make unpopular choices in terms of what others expect. Or I may spend a day in bed resting, retreating into the sweet respite of quiet time to listen to my body's needs.

Part of surrendering is also staying open to receiving pleasure, not halfway, but as completely as I can allow. (We'll discuss why we resist pleasure too.) Ironically, pleasure takes some getting used to. When I have too much to do, I may even forget to stop and feel that pleasure. But since surrendering to pleasure is how I want to live, I aim to listen to my body as my inner guru and intuitive guide.

In this chapter, I'll show you how to turn on and tune into your body. You'll discover how your physical self is intimately connected with spirit. We'll examine the physical and subtle energy aspects of the body, what holds us back from receiving pleasure, and how we can surrender to allowing it in. We're often afraid of what we can't control but you'll learn how to trust your sexuality enough to let go of fear. Everything about the body is divine, every organ, every cell. How you connect with all of it determines how alive you feel. *Ecstasy isn't just about orgasm, though it may be the only kind of ecstasy that most people know. It's how you sensually relate to the world.* Ecstasy is everywhere whether you're making love to your partner, to a sunset, or simply to the moment. I'm excited to help you wake up and find it. We'll also explore the following questions: What are the keys to a positive body image? How is surrender a beauty secret? In what ways can movement liberate you? Is sexual charisma always good? You'll pay attention to deeper levels of letting go so that you can keep surrendering to bliss.

SURRENDER TO YOUR BODY: TREAT IT LIKE A LOVER

Be a good animal, true to your animal instinct.
—D. H. LAWRENCE

How you inhabit your body shapes who you are during sex. The secret to feeling pleasure is to intimately connect with your body as you would with a lover, not just during sex but when walking, sitting, working, or even doing chores and mundane tasks. Try enjoying your sensuality as much as possible. You'll see how your body is responsive, a giving source of bliss. Sure, you can have purely physical sex with an orgasm—and it can be loving—but, as good as this may feel, it won't compare with the physical, emotional, and spiritual surrender during sex that I'll describe. The body gives pleasure when you know its likes and dislikes, and how it's made.

Problem is, we're conditioned to huddle in our brains, which won't increase bliss. Too many rules, too much regimentation prevents surrender. We're programmed to be overly proper and in control at all times, not earthy and free. We don't stroke or massage our bodies enough. We don't move. Don't stretch. Don't cry. Don't blush. We even get embarrassed when our stomachs rumble. We don't extend our arms out and twirl just because we feel like it, or spontaneously kneel in reverence. We're taught to criticize our "flaws," not revel in our lusciousness. As a result, we may feel so tight and constricted that it begins to hurt. Or we become so ashamed of our bodies that we avoid mirrors and don't want a lover to see our nakedness. This is the opposite of surrender. Don't worry if this describes you. *Life can be so much more!* Let me reorient your perspective so that you can surrender to the sensual miracle of your body.

A NEW KIND OF PHYSICAL EDUCATION: AWAKEN YOUR PHYSICAL AND SUBTLE BODY

Surrender to the Magic of Your Physical Body

One of the greatest gifts of my medical training was learning about the body. As a USC medical student scrubbing in on major surgeries, I had the awe-inspiring experience of watching a heart linked to a labyrinth of arteries beating in a patient's chest, and feeling the textures of a uterus, ovaries, and lungs—an initiation into what it means to be human. Imprinted in my memory is the energy of each organ, its smooth, moist surface, its warmth and glistening color. I was fascinated that the shape and size of our organs were slightly different in everyone. Now, when I intuitively tune in to patients, these diverse frequencies are easier to sense.

However, in medical school, I was taught only about the physical makeup of the body, never about its subtle energy. As you'll see, the two are interrelated and infused with divinity. From a strictly physical standpoint, what is the body? It's the basic structure of a human being consisting of a head, neck, torso, arms, hands, legs, and feet. Your body has one hundred trillion cells, the basics unit of life, which differentiate into organs, tissues, muscles, bones, and thousands of miles of blood vessels. It is composed of two-thirds salt water which bathes our joints and internal structures. The genetic material in cells (DNA) tells them what to become and what to do. The body is organized into thirteen major organ systems, each with a different function, such as the digestive, cardiovascular, and skeletal systems. In health, all systems work in harmony. When something is off, your body sends signals such as pain or fatigue. If you listen, you can determine the problem and take steps to heal. If you don't listen, you may develop a chronic state of "dis-ease." Your body wants to be happy and feel good. When it's cared for and pampered, it can experience well-being and ecstasy.

To feel more pleasure you must become acquainted with your body in 3-D so it doesn't seem like a foreign country. Most people walk around in denial about what lies beneath their skin. For their entire lives it remains a big blank, something they prefer to avoid. What a waste of resources not to celebrate this wonderfully alive aspect of our wholeness. Embracing our anatomy—the fact that we're made of muscles, bones, and organs—is shocking to many people because we're not used to seeing ourselves as we really are. We're just so fixated on what's above the skin that we've failed to acknowledge the gorgeousness of our inner workings too. I want you to be comfortable about how you're made. This will keep you humble and real rather than focusing only on the outside. Once you can lovingly visualize your inner territory, you can heighten your sensual and sexual responses.

How tragic that most of us aren't educated about our anatomy, that we often feel ashamed or repulsed by the sacred temple that houses our spirit. After all, we are spiritual beings having a human experience. Our bodies generously make that possible. Negative feelings about it stop us from adoring ourselves and can taint the ease we feel with our sexuality. Our internal anatomy can make us squeamish. Most people pay attention to it only when something goes wrong and they need to consult a doctor. We link the inside of our bodies to pathology, not vibrance and bliss. We see it as a scary, out-of-our-control place: bad things can grow there, our organs can experience disease and cause us pain, and we associate skeletons with death. We can't make our insides pretty like the outside. I can understand why you might think, "I'd rather not know about that." But don't give in to that reaction.

I am adamant when I say that our organs and internal structures are our friends: beautiful, intelligent, and full of passion. We want them to be happy, not stressed. They work nonstop on our behalf: our spine supports us, our liver detoxifies poisons, our gastrointestinal tract digests nutrients, our lungs breathe out toxic carbon dioxide and circulate oxygen through the blood. All of these are reasons for us to be grateful for our bodies. Other examples of biological surrenders that sustain us are bowel movements, urinating, tears, laughing, menses, and ejaculation. Blocking any of these isn't healthy. For instance, I've treated many overly controlling patients with terrible constipation and emotionally bottled-up depressives who can't cry. (In China, there are white-noise machines in bathrooms so that people don't hear others urinating or defecating—a cultural expression of modesty and shame, as well as an honoring of privacy.) I love the Hebrew benediction that honors our body's orifices: "Blessed is God who has formed the human body in wisdom and created many orifices . . . if one of them were to be opened or closed incorrectly, it would be impossible to survive." A friend in an Orthodox Jewish community told me that children are taught to say this prayer to revere their bodies after each visit to the restroom. These physical openings allow the perfect flow of fluids and the release of toxins. I marvel at this. Loving your body and appreciating the grace of its inner workings will help you surrender to the ecstasy there.

To learn about your body, I suggest that you get a copy of *Start Exploring Gray's Anatomy: A Fact-Filled Coloring Book*. This book is filled with simple color illustrations of your anatomy, from your tiniest bones to your largest muscles. For a more direct physical experience, you can take your own pulse or buy a stethoscope and listen to a friend's heart. Hearing and feeling your heartbeat connects you to your physical self in a palpable, primal way. Every inch of your body (not just the genitals) contains a secret bliss you can surrender to. Once you know your basic anatomy, you can tune in to the ecstasy of your whole body. Study the following diagram with this perspective in mind, envisioning every organ as life-giving and holy.

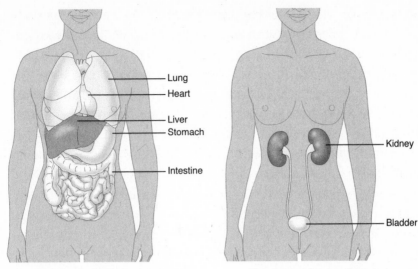

[Figure 2.] The Anatomy of   *[Figure 3.] Renal System*
Your Physical Body

Surrender to the Magic of Your Subtle Energy Body

The beauty of your body is that along with its physical structure it's also composed of subtle energy. Most people are primarily outer-focused and unaware of their subtle bodies, nor do they know that their physical and subtle bodies interact and share bliss with each other. They aren't separate entities: there's a constant fluid interplay between them that sustains health. I'll teach you strategies to awaken subtle energy. Most of us don't know how to do this. We need to be shown, something my Daoist teacher taught me. Moreover, sexual energy is one aspect of a larger energy in the body that we can tap to claim our full power. We don't realize that sexual charisma, the "vibe" we project, is more about energy than physical appearance. Understanding all this is crucial for you to exude charisma, attract the right people, and surrender to pleasure.

What is subtle energy? Think microscopic. Think tinier than microscopic. Picture another dimension of energy that completely penetrates your body and extends many feet beyond your skin. It's your inner and outer radiance, the essence of who you are, a light or "aura" penetrating the physical. Visualize this energy, especially when you're struggling with body image: your organs and your entire body are drenched in gorgeous light. To Hindu mystics this life force is called *shakti*. Chinese medical practitioners call it *chi*. To alchemists, it's the *prima materia*. In Western medicine an exciting new subspecialty has emerged: energy medicine. Drawing on ancient Hindu and Buddhist systems, it recognizes that our bodies and spirits are manifestations of this subtle energy which is composed of midline centers called chakras. As I'll describe later, you can activate these in order to heal (see Chapter 10) as well as to generate pleasure.

I'm drawn to the concept in alchemy of the "coarse" material world versus the more subtle worlds of energy and spirituality. Integrating both, surrendering to both, creates well-being and pleasure. Our bodies have depths and sensualities that can be discovered only through more subtle experiences. This has special relevance to aging as our hormones wane. You can keep passion alive but it's mediated more through subtle energy than through hormonal stimulation. Recently, I smiled as I read one seventy-year-old woman's lusty account of having orgasms in not one but four of her subtle bodies—emotional, sexual, intuitive, and spiritual—that her kundalini yoga practice describes. What a feat of human consciousness to have that much pleasure with all parts of the subtle body aligned! Regardless of age, never give up on passion. There are many more possibilities than you've been told.

Another wonder of subtle energy is that it permeates every aspect of nature from the vast oceans to the smallest flower. Since ancient times, a basic premise of indigenous healing traditions from all over the world is that our bodies are part of the larger living body of the cosmos. For instance, the twenty-four-hour circadian cycle of sleep and waking is set via our hypothalamus and pineal gland according to the rising sun. Thus, our bodies are elegantly shaped by the motion in the solar system. My friend, the performance artist Camille Maurine, talks about our erotic "galactic body," the cosmos we have within us. As she dances, she sensually feels the moon and the stars and the planets within her, an ecstatic experience. From an intuitive perspective, we're not "here" and other galaxies are "there," as the

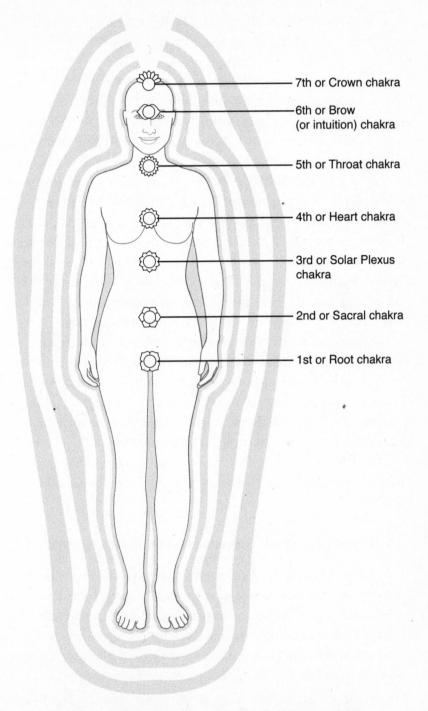

7th or Crown chakra

6th or Brow
(or intuition) chakra

5th or Throat chakra

4th or Heart chakra

3rd or Solar Plexus
chakra

2nd or Sacral chakra

1st or Root chakra

[Figure 4.] The Anatomy of Your Subtle Energy Body

linear mind dictates. It's all one. Our bodies are interconnected with nature, the cosmos, and all the rest of creation, a highly erotic experience when you can surrender to it.

I discovered nature's eroticism in the early 1980s while participating in a women's workshop on spirituality on Kauai's north shore. To begin a period of silence and fasting, I walked through a lush tropical grove to the ocean at sunset. Soft trade winds rippled through my thin cotton dress as I watched the gentle breeze in the palms. I was mesmerized by the fluttering of leaves in a nearby plumeria: their quivering was arousing me as I leaned against the tree trunk. I was astonished to feel it sending pulses of pleasure into me as the moist air caressed my skin. I glued my back to the trunk, afraid that any movement or critiquing of what was occurring would cause the escalating sensations to cease. Thank God my mind cooperated. There was no way I could have surrendered to this experience had logic been involved. Suddenly my whole body burst into orgasm.

That evening in Kauai I was introduced to nature's ecstasy. My analytic physician's mind said, "Impossible!" but my body intuitively testified to the reality of the bliss. Before this, I'd always depended on a man to trigger my erotic side. When I was single, I often felt less feminine. Realizing that sexuality originates in myself and in the subtle energy of nature has been transformative.

In praise of the body, I'd like you to practice the following stretching meditation to release tension and surrender to the sensual joy of your body.

STRETCH BY CANDLELIGHT: SURRENDER TENSION, AWAKEN PLEASURE

1. *Relax.* In a peaceful environment, get comfortable. To create tranquility, light a few candles and turn off electric lighting. This is a quick way to shift out of busy mode and calm mental chatter. You can do this exercise lying on your back, body fully extended on a yoga mat. You can also sit on the floor or in a chair or simply remain standing. Choose the position that feels the best for you.

2. *Breathe deeply.* In the candlelight, take a few deep breaths. Settle into your body: sense, don't think. You can close your eyes,

or not. Feel your belly rise up, then relax and soften. Appreciate the miracle of your breath. As you inhale, feel yourself taking oxygen into your lungs and into the body where each cell absorbs it. As you exhale, feel yourself releasing toxic carbon dioxide, purifying your system. Exhaling fully is the perfect physical surrender to release tension. Breathing shallowly is symptomatic of holding back, clenching, and guarding against sensual feelings. Let yourself enjoy the pleasure of each slow, deep breath. Sense your life force flowing.

3. *Stretch.* Focusing lightly on your breath, lift both arms above your head as high as they will go. Hold to a count of ten. Feel the lengthening of your spine and back muscles as the spaces between your vertebrae expand. Enjoy the pleasurable sensation of elongating your body, melting contractions. To enhance the experience, you can clasp your fingers together, palms up, and stretch your hands over your head. Really let go. Stretch long and slow, not resisting, reaching your body to the sky. Then let your arms fall relaxed to your side. Shake them out. Repeat this stretch as many times as you like.

4. *Meditate on pleasure in your body.* After the stretch, sit quietly for a few minutes feeling the pleasure this has created in your body. Visualize every part of your anatomy as a source of potential pleasure. See each structure as made of subtle energy, of divine light. Start with your spine. Its base is the seat of the kundalini life force energy that activates sexuality. For at least ten seconds, feel pleasure running up and down your spine. Then visualize your organs. For instance, your stomach and colon are emotional organs that respond much like the heart. When they get upset, they tighten. To soothe them, focus on feeling pleasure there. Do the same with your liver, your kidneys, and other organs as well as your genitals. Imagine pleasure in these areas. If you feel discomfort, breathe through it, relaxing into the sensation, not resisting it. Next, feel pleasure in your hands (palmistry says your palm lines tell your future) and your feet (which ground you and contain more than one hundred healing acupuncture points). Next, feel pleasure in

your head and ears (the outer ear has many acupuncture points too). Enjoy your body. Give thanks for its nurturing and support.

In this exercise, you'll know you've really surrendered when you don't think about what you're doing and forget about the clock. You won't be wondering if you're "doing it right" or if "time's up." Pleasure is timeless if you can let go. Your body loves meditation and gratitude. Together they nourish your organs and tissues, an antidote to the trauma of daily stress. As you practice, you're conditioning yourself to tap into your body's pleasure and hold the sensation of bliss for longer periods. You'll begin to experience this surrender first for seconds, then for minutes, and eventually for quite a bit more time.

THE SURRENDER OF MOVEMENT
....

My mother began walking five miles a day when she was sixty. Now she's ninety and we have no idea where she is.
—NASRUDDIN

Movement is a divine way of surrendering to your body and breaking loose of rigidity. Our bodies are meant to move. We're not built to spend our lives hunched over a computer, chained to our desks; this makes our bodies and spirits suffer. Studies have linked a sedentary lifestyle with more deaths even than smoking. It's a risk factor for back pain, obesity, osteoporosis, depression, and heart disease. Further, it reduces the spaces between the vertebrae so we shrink with age—not an attractive prospect! In contrast, movement has numerous health benefits. Research has shown that it reduces toxic stress hormones that increase your blood pressure, impair immunity, and decelerate aging. It enhances cardiovascular health, improves sleep, reduces depression, and even increases brain volume. Aside from these superb payoffs, the pleasure and tension release you can experience from exercise comes from a surge of endorphins, your body's natural painkillers. When I exercise, I can't wait to feel these "biochemicals of bliss" (also associated with a runner's high), so I move as much as I can. Along with my aerobic routine in the gym and daily yoga stretches, I do a lot of roaming on the beach and on the paths in the Santa Monica Mountains without a destination in mind, simply going where I'm drawn. Moving with no intention, just surrendering to new discoveries is freeing, spontaneous, primal fun. The goal of movement is not just to burn fat or to get skinny but to generate endorphins. It gets you out of your head so you can surrender to bliss and the body's sacred energy.

I am fascinated by my friend Katie Hendrix's story about how movement allowed her to go from being a C student to an A student in the fourth grade and later shaped her career. In class, sitting still in a chair, Katie struggled to concentrate but was fidgety and distracted. Her teacher, Mrs. Morgan, observed her restlessness and that Katie wasn't fulfilling her academic potential. Astutely, instead of telling her to "settle down and stop fidgeting," as most teachers in the 1950s would have done, Mrs. Morgan gave Katie permission to change her seat to the back of the room and move around. Katie said, "I was allowed to stand, stretch, walk, and swing my arms." She even took tests standing up. "Mrs. Morgan realized I was a kinesthetic learner, not verbal or auditory. To learn well, I needed to move around. After that I became a top student and later a movement therapist." Early on, Katie discovered how essential movement is for her well-being. I heartily concur when she says, "It opens blocks and heightens our internal sense of flow. Movement is about listening to our inner impulses."

I recommend that as part of physically surrendering to your body, you practice movement at least a few times a week, though daily is optimal. Remember that a little can go a long way. During busy periods, I've found that even one stretch a day can loosen up my body by getting me out of a clutching and pushing mode. Exercise is grounding and opens your sensuality. Whether you're lifting weights, playing tennis, or doing yoga, make exercise a sensual, mindful meditation. Sweating, breathing, stretching, and cultivating head-to-toe awareness can be a sensual feast. One of my fitness heroes, Phil Jackson, formerly coach of the champion Chicago Bulls and Los Angeles Lakers, has a philosophy called mindfulness basketball which is based on Buddhist precepts. He teaches players mindful awareness of their bodies and breath, and incorporates a sense of the sacred in each game. During your workout, mindfulness can also be very sensual as you strengthen your muscles and awaken your subtle body. While you stretch and move, try to gently go past old levels of resistance, stiffness, and holding back. During exercise, gradually stretch longer and deeper, breathe more fully and more sensually, and surrender to a loving force larger than yourself that can instill bliss.

To start, find an exercise that suits your needs. Ask your intuition: "Am I curious about an exercise or does it leave me flat? Does an exercise make my body happy or am I doing it because it's a fad? Does an exercise lift my spirit and energy or is it just a physical slog?" You're doing well if your gut answers yes to every question. If not, consider a change. Go slow. Be kind to yourself. Take baby steps, especially if you have an injury or physical limitations. Experiment with the following energy-enhancing exercises. Gradually allow yourself to let go more deeply to the enjoyment of moving your body.

SURRENDER TO THE PLEASURE OF EXERCISE

Stretching. This is a gentle way to begin to learn to surrender in exercise, especially if you've been away from it. Stretching centers you in your body, expels the stress clogged in joints, and gets energy moving. I adore stretching. It takes the creaks out of my being. Sometimes, after a virus, a round of toe touches returns me to the land of the living. Holding stretches, really melting into them, increases flexibility in your body, an asset that translates into all areas of your life. It trains you to go beyond rigidity and clutching to a more fluid way to be.

Aerobic exercise. The rhythm of aerobics calms an overactive mind. Just moving and breathing hard is pleasurable, primal—we often forget we are physical animals. Natural, spontaneous movements want to come through when we surrender control. Let go. Dance your spirit free as I often do before I write. Run like a wild mustang on the beach or around the track. Make that hoop with a guided hand. One of my patients, at fifty-two, does Brazilian dance which opens her sensuality by teaching her to "move like water." Surrendering during aerobic movement decreases stress and relieves daily frustrations.

Yoga. This practice (the word is Sanskrit for "union with spirit") originated in India five thousand years ago as a path to realization. It simulates the subtle life force energy through breathing, stretching, and postures. Many of my patients who previously avoided exercise have fallen in love with yoga. Just because yoga doesn't necessarily raise your pulse as much as aerobics doesn't mean you're not getting a good workout. I enjoy yoga. It gets me in touch with the tightenings in my body so I can use my breath to surrender them. My favorite practice is saying a prayer while doing the "child's pose" which is kneeling on the floor with both arms extended forward. Stretching in this pose amplifies my prayer and deepens my sense of reverence.

Tai chi chuan. This exercise involves graceful movements that help you find a balance point and inner stillness. Research has shown significant balance and coordination improvement in elders who practice tai chi. As I age, this has special relevance. Eventually my joints will appreciate an alternative to the pounding of aerobics. Whatever your age, this exercise strengthens your body and your subtle energy, and it feels divine.

Let movement give you a reason to love your body, not beat yourself up. When developing an exercise routine, you may encounter resistance that prevents surrender. Resistance comes from your mind, the part of you that fears change and newness so it talks you out of something before you give it a try. Resistance can also manifest as fear, anxiety, and shame about your body, or, if your live in your head, avoiding being in a body. Generally, unless you're too ill or fatigued to function, resistance is not an intuitive message to stop. Even if your fatigue or packed schedule is real, five minutes of exercise or stretching will provide a boost. In addition, when negative voices flare up, keep inwardly asking them to lift. Shift your focus by taking control of your mind. Don't let yourself obsess about the tiny body of the woman beside you twisted into a pretzel during yoga or the athlete with pumped-up pecs doing a zillion reps in the gym. Instead, keep your eyes lovingly on yourself. Take a breath and affirm how wonderful it is that you're working out, how fortunate you are to be able to do so. Be grateful for what you have, including health. Sometimes we forget the blessing of mobility. Appreciating this lets you revel in the glory of the body, distracts negativity, and allows you to relax enough to physically surrender during movement.

SURRENDER IS A BEAUTY SECRET: KEYS TO A POSITIVE BODY IMAGE AND WEIGHT

How can we be happy with our bodies? How can we surrender to the sensual creatures that we are in all sizes and shapes? Many patients come to me dissatisfied with their appearance, a perception aggravated by living in Los Angeles with its youth-obsessed, impossible Hollywood physical ideals. I've treated some patients who've loathed their bodies so much they can't look in a mirror or make love in the daylight without having a panic attack about how fat they think they are. I can empathize. For many of us, it's easy to get caught in these painful mind-sets. The *New York Times* recently reported that a whopping 75 percent of normal-weight American teens feel fat! Similarly, adults fear being either too fat or too thin, too short or too tall. Woman often obsess about wrinkles, sagging skin, cellulite, or a big belly and butt. Men most fear baldness, too much body hair, "beer bellies," and larger breasts as they age. Be aware: *your body hears everything you think.* No wonder it may not feel sexy! We'll address how not to succumb to the undertow of boorish, unevolved societal beliefs that contribute to a negative body image. I'll help you surrender to positive ways of viewing your body so you can appreciate yourself more.

What is body image? A key element to self-esteem, it's how you view the aesthetics and sexual attractiveness of your body. Body image is influenced by upbringing, temperament, media hype, and cultural values. I'll discuss how to free your mind from brainwashing so that you don't miss out on enjoying your physical form. I salute the Latin and African cultures that don't have the same stick-thin notion of beauty as Western cultures do. In fact, anorexia is mostly associated with Western cultures though exposure to global media is believed to be linked with increased cases internationally.

It's a misconception to think that you always have to change how you look in order to feel good about yourself. Much of body image involves perception. I've treated thin patients who think they're fat and voluptuous members of both sexes who feel attractive and have sexual voodoo you wouldn't believe. I've also observed that my plus-size patients who like themselves carry their weight lightly whereas others at the same size who despise their bodies look more obese. The attitude you have about yourself affects the energy you project and how others perceive you.

As a woman, I appreciate how vital it is to like how you look. But I also know how quickly my perceptions can change with my mood. Occasionally, after a hard day I look in the mirror and cringe. All I see are wrinkles, sags, and flaws—a totally unsexy, alarming experience akin to viewing my body under the punishing lights of department store dressing rooms. I think, "I'm over the hill. No man will ever be attracted to me again." I just want to put on some baggy pajamas, crawl into bed, and forget everything. On one such grueling night I dreamed that a snooty saleswoman in a chic clothing boutique told me, "Come back when you lose ten pounds," which made me feel horribly ashamed of my body. This dream was an unsparing reflection of my own tendencies toward self-criticism which I'm grateful I'm making steady progress in healing. Thank goodness, the morning after these bouts of criticism, my perspective typically improves. I look the same except for being more rested, but I like my appearance again. Just as two people observing the same event will see it differently, the same goes for how we see ourselves in different states of mind. Even though a good night's sleep is rejuvenating, I've also regained my positive attitude so I view my body through this lens. The lovingkindness with which we see ourselves dramatically impacts how sexy we feel.

Developing a Positive Body Image

To appreciate yourself in a larger, kinder, more intuitive way, focus on and keep surrendering to these three aspects of body image.

1. Your Physical Body Image

Each of us is born with a unique body and spirit. No matter your height, size, or shape, this is the gift we've been given. Your body is amazing simply because it's yours. Be grateful for your body, inside and out: every inch of you is spirit's masterpiece. We are perfect, imperfections and all. Your priority is to care for your body: eat nourishing food, sleep well, exercise, and stretch to stay flexible. It's harder to feel good about your body when you're run down. Also regularly pamper yourself—say, with a long shower, a luxurious bath, a massage, peaceful music, a new haircut, or just relaxing. In Costa Rica, I had a heavenly chocolate body scrub in a thatched hut overlooking the ocean, a special treat for me. On the other hand, a male friend told me, "My idea of pampering myself is not shaving on the weekend and watching football on TV." Though self-care can differ between men and women (men may consider "pampering" too fluffy and feminine), it's all replenishing. When you feel good, you look good. When you're tired and stressed, your appearance suffers.

If there's a physical trait you'd like to refine, set realistic goals. For instance, if you want to lose weight, increase your exercise routine without overdoing it and forgo sweets. When fear or other forms of resistance stop your progress, find a trainer to motivate you or a therapist or a book to help you conquer emotional blocks. With simpler issues, take specific action. For instance, when my hair was drying out like straw (not good for my body image), I began to condition it with excellent products. This improved its bounce and shine which then increased my sense of sexiness. Some solutions are faster than others but celebrate all your baby steps forward, especially in hard-to-change areas. Be gentle with your sweet self. Simply do your best. That's enough.

2. *Your Subtle Body Image*

Here are some tips to make the most of your subtle energy.

- Honor Your Emanations. When you picture your body, remember you are composed of dazzling light that emanates from you. Whether standing in a bank line or meditating, you are radiant. This radiance is the real source of beauty. You are not just your eyes, your hair, your clothes, your weight. We are sexy beings of light. Your ordinary eye may be unable to see the subtle body but your intuition can. Review this chapter's diagram and other pictures of the subtle body. Then you won't question your radiance again.

- Energy and Obesity. You can improve your body image by understanding the role subtle energy plays in overeating and food addiction. It goes beyond the psychology of emotions or calorie counts to explain why diets fail. Many of my sensitive patients overeat as a defense against absorbing the stress and negativity of others into their own bodies. Early twentieth-century faith healers often claimed they needed to be obese to protect themselves from taking on their patients' pain. True, added weight does buffer negativity and grounds you, though it's not healthy. If you think you are an energetic overeater, you must learn strategies that help you avoid absorbing all the stress in the world. To start, try putting a meditation cushion in front of your closed refrigerator, a reminder to pause and reflect before you eat something. For a few minutes, breathe, center, and meditate there before reaching for food. Also, set clear boundaries with difficult people or limit your exposure to them (see Chapter 5). Once you get better at this, you'll feel less compulsion to turn to food for armoring. Knowing about energetic overeating will clarify your relationship with food so you can more easily lose weight and be happier with your body.

- Radiate Sexual Charisma. Developing charisma involves activating sexual energy. Though charisma is usually linked with good looks and charm in both sexes, it's also an invisible energy you radiate that attracts people. The sexiest people, regardless of looks, know how to work this energy. The ancient priestesses considered it summoning the glamour, a form of erotic enchantment. Sexual charisma combined with self-esteem is a potent aphrodisiac. Some people seem to effortlessly ooze sexuality. But you can also consciously generate charisma. Here's how. First, tell yourself, "I am sexy." If negative voices arise, say, "Thank you for sharing," and keep moving. Next, focus on a sizzling erotic thought such as a lover stroking your body with a feather. Slowly feel the pleasure spread through your body. Then, in daily life, visualize projecting that erotic vibe. It starts with you, then becomes contagious. Others will sense it and respond. In addition, smiling and being friendly send the message that you're approachable.

3. Surrender to a Positive Mind-Set

Attractiveness is a tender topic. We must be kind to ourselves and make the most of our special type of sexiness. It's fine to want to improve your appearance but don't let that be an excuse to beat yourself up. If your parents conveyed negative messages about your looks, don't focus on those thoughts. (For instance, my mother tormented me about my hair, saying, "It's too wild and long.") Instead, practice the strategies for positive self-talk that I list below.

To counter negative conditioning, I urge you to commit to surrendering to a lifelong philosophy of loving your body and releasing shame. Here's how.

- Limit Exposure to Negative Media Images. This includes celebrity-oriented television shows and print publications as well as fashion magazines. Ironically, beauty magazines can make women feel ugly. When you're not overwhelmed by images of models and movie stars who had a team of makeup artists and stylists laboring for hours on them, you're less likely to brood about it.

- Let Go of Comparisons. When you start comparing yourself with anyone you think is more attractive than you, bring your eyes gently back to yourself and use the positive self-talk techniques below. Negative comparisons only fuel your insecurities. They are not helpful. Instead, train yourself to focus on your best traits. Review the tips I presented in Chapter 1 for surrendering comparisons. Developing self-compassion and learning from people who love their bodies can be antidotes to being mired in jealousy and feeling "less than."

- Practice Positive Self-Talk. Begin to talk to yourself differently. Concentrate on what you like about your appearance: your sparkling eyes, your soft skin, the shape of your arms or butt. Try this when negative parental or societal voices intrude or when you compare yourself to anyone. If you notice a bulge, a sag, or other "flaws," instead of telling your body, "I hate this. I hate myself," do not surrender to these tyrannical voices! Reframe the situation. Instead of seeing a bulge, see a sexy curve. Instead of equating gray hair with being over the hill, see it as luminous. Don't feed poisonous thoughts such as "I look terrible because I have a few wrinkles." Would you tolerate others judging you like this? I trust not. Even if you're not succeeding as you'd hoped with a goal such as losing weight, you have a choice. You can torture yourself with shame and criticism or you can treat yourself with kindness, meanwhile modifying your routine to be more effective. *Positive actions are more powerful than negative thoughts.*

Learning to surrender negativity and unrealistic expectations takes the pressure off. Invoke the Serenity Prayer to lovingly accept the things you cannot change so you don't cling to an impossible vision of your body. Sometimes surrender means accepting limitations. Do this by addressing yourself as you would the most precious child. Never show your body disrespect. Remember: it hears you! Allowing negative thoughts to control you betrays the body; it's similar to an autoimmune disease, in which the body attacks itself. Thus, when you look in the mirror, a fat, old, or unattractive person is all you will see. It's a pretty convincing hallucination—*but this is not the real you*. To see your true self, practice the daily affirmations below.

Surrendering to all aspects of life is the ultimate beauty secret. As you stop fighting the flow and relax more, you'll look and feel better. With patients, I've seen how chronic stress becomes etched on their faces with frown lines and a pursed, furrowed, tense look. Tension causes your facial muscles to contract which creates wrinkles. In contrast, surrender creates zero tension which makes your appearance more youthful, radiant, and attractive. When you surrender stress and negativity, you'll like what you see. As a result, your body image will improve along with your capacity to appreciate yourself and others through heartful eyes. Let the following affirmation be a mantra for befriending your body and your sexy self.

SURRENDER AFFIRMATIONS FOR A POSITIVE BODY IMAGE

I will focus on my positive points, not my flaws.
I will let go of criticizing my imperfections.
I will be grateful for my health and aliveness.
I will let go of the idea that to be attractive I must be thin.
I will let go of comparing my body to anyone else's.
I will appreciate my body as it is, even if it's hard to lose weight.
I am a sexy person.
I am uniquely myself.
I am enough.

Let me stand next to your fire.
—JIMI HENDRIX
. . . .

8

THE EIGHTH SURRENDER

IGNITING YOUR SEXUAL POWER

TO MANIFEST YOUR FULL SEXUAL POWER YOU HAVE TO SURREN-
der. There's no way around it. You must completely inhabit your body
and be in the moment. If not now, when? Holding back, fixating on
performance, or letting your mind drift is the end of passion. Don't
go there. I'll show you how to get out of your head and into your bliss.

What is true sexual power? I define it as proudly claiming your
erotic self and mindfully channeling sexual energy. You never use it
to hurt, manipulate, make conquests, or get addicted to the ego trip
of sensual pleasure at the expense of others. This is bad karma. Nor
do you allow others to harm or disrespect you. Sexual power is not
just who you are in bed, though that's an aspect of it. You also make
electric linkages to your body, to spirit, to a lover, to the universe. For
me, it's a turn-on when sexual power is blended with spiritual power.
Too many of us in this heady, frantic world lack the rich experience
of having a primal connection with someone. Sexuality can offer us
this, a satisfaction you can never get from your intellect alone. As you
open to both sex and spirit, whether you're single or part of a couple,
you'll be a vessel for erotic flow, enjoying pleasure without insecurities or inhibitions.

We'll discuss many fun approaches for letting go that you can integrate into your lifestyle. Don't worry if you can't succeed all of the time. Be happy with every bit of progress. Here are some general tips to keep in mind. The more you can practice them, for short or longer periods, the more sexually alive you'll be.

BASIC STRATEGIES OF SEXUAL SURRENDER

- Surrender your to-do list, making time for sensuality and lovemaking.

- Surrender your overactive, critical "monkey mind" that kills passion and stops you from being present in your body.

- Surrender to pleasure as completely as possible.

- Let yourself melt into the ecstasy of orgasm and become one with your partner.

Sexual power is something to revere and consciously cultivate. You can't just leave it to chance. When I get up in the morning, the first thing I do is meditate. I want to connect to myself, to every ounce of spiritual energy, heart energy, and erotic energy in me. I do this before any of life's demands interfere. Meditating in this way fortifies me and lets me be fully present. Being in touch with my sexual self is part of being present, along with being analytical or being kind or listening to the angels sing. Sexual power is not compartmentalized away from the rest of you. It is more present when you're whole. So, to begin the day, I offer thanks for every aspect of me, then proceed into the great unknown of the hours ahead.

In this chapter, we'll explore questions such as: How can you ignite sexuality and have more intense orgasms? What makes a good lover? What are the common killers of passion? Do you fear intimacy or do you fake orgasms? What is the difference between healthy bonding and overly attaching to a partner? Are you a sex addict? Do you lose your center around sexual energy or obsess about lovers? Do you resist pleasure?

I'll show you how to surrender if you have trouble letting go or are afraid of losing yourself in someone. Surrendering becomes easier when you trust your partner. Then you'll feel safer about letting down your guard and feeling pleasure without resistance or fear. There are no limits to where ecstasy can take you as you deeply connect to yourself and a partner.

CLAIM YOUR SEXUAL POWER

Sexual power has different aspects. In the most basic sense, it's about reproduction and survival. Nature has cleverly wired us to be rewarded with erotic excitement when we perpetuate the species. The bliss of orgasm is the catnip that motivates us to reproduce. Our choice of a partner is strongly influenced by our biological programming. Research has shown that both men and women are attracted to healthy, fertile mates with good genes. What physical signs indicate this? Science has identified several: a mate's thick hair, smell via hormones called pheromones, voice tone, facial symmetry, a man's muscular physique, and a woman's hourglass figure with a waist-to-hip ratio of 7:10 (which Marilyn Monroe had). Interestingly, when women ovulate, they produce copulins, a scent that attracts men causing their testosterone to rise. Our drive to procreate trumps most other human instincts. The power of this primal consciousness commands respect and awe.

Another aspect of sexual power is emotional intimacy, an instinctive desire to bond to a lover, to feel comfort, to be known. This makes the difference between pure physical sex and lovemaking. Emotional intimacy comes from affection, from sharing feelings, from being vulnerable. By caring, you reinforce each other's attractiveness and make each other feel special. As friends and lovers, you are fundamentally there for each other which creates trust. You see each other as real people, the good and the bad, not some idealized version. When conflict, anger, or hurt feelings arise you're committed to working through them. Bring your fears and insecurities to a partner in an undefended way. When you share all parts of yourself, even your secrets, you can truly surrender. Tantric sexuality teacher David Daida says to offer your emotions "from the deepest place of love's yearnings that you can occupy." With emotional intimacy, you're capable of exploring passion on every level. Without it, there's a limit to where you and your partner can go. In the short run it may seem like less trouble to avoid conflict but your erotic life pays a price. You can't tap your full sexual power if parts of you shut down. When you habitually hide your feelings, you waste time and opportunities for closeness. If you stay open, however, your emotional love will enhance your sensual love.

It's possible to have sexual intimacy without emotional intimacy but you will be using only a fraction of your power. Still, as I've observed with certain patients, many of whom had alcoholic or abusive parents, they may not feel deserving of love. One man told me, "I really wanted love but I settled for sex." Sometimes, though, sex is all people seek or can tolerate. Whether they're aware of it or not, they link emotional intimacy with psychic pain or being suffocated which kills their erotic arousal once they really get to know someone. When they get close to a partner they start feeling overwhelmed and turn off. "Women are always asking for more than I can give," one male commitment-phobe told me. Surrendering to love feels terrifying to him. Such people have never learned that communication can safely bring you closer to someone. Thus, so as not to stir up the beast, they must keep a safe distance from true intimacy which casual uncommitted sex allows.

Take my patient Roxie who came from an abusive home and grew up a hard-boiled Hollywood street punk. Strong and determined, she made a new life for herself and built a successful sexy lingerie company. At thirty-five, Roxie was an engaging mix of street-smart, hip, and funny. She had her own brand of sexiness which she seemed at ease with. During our first session she shared, "My boyfriend is an incredible lover. We keep it fun and light. Getting heavy ruins things." With this attitude, it's understandable that Roxie's relationships never lasted more than six months. Though Roxie wasn't worried about being single, she'd come to me because of an intense loneliness despite many romances.

During therapy Roxie began to grasp that when emotions get real, her sexuality shuts down. Before, she'd simply rationalize, "I'm just not attracted to that guy anymore." Intimacy was Roxie's particular blind spot (everybody has one). She didn't realize that because of her abusive upbringing, intimacy didn't feel safe. My role isn't to judge anyone or to push patients to change before they're ready. If people are happy with their lives, God bless them. But Roxie wasn't. Still, we had to tread gently. Long ago, I learned to work with where a patient is at, then go from there. Roxie wasn't yet ready to share her emotions with a lover. It was too threatening.

So, first, to ease her loneliness, I encouraged her to explore other forms of intimacy, such as friendships and getting a puppy—animals are master teachers of unconditional love. Then she could work her way toward intimacy with a lover. Roxie found that adoring her shih-tzu came more easily than sharing authentic emotions with humans. But gradually she started confiding in friends and letting down her "nothing bothers me" tough-girl facade to risk being vulnerable. I also helped her see how she'd armored herself as a child so that she wouldn't feel hurt by her spaced-out crack-addicted parents. Now, a year later, Roxie is testing out her new emotional skills with a caring, slightly uptight college English professor—her complete opposite, which lends the perfect balance. She loosens him up; he centers her. They've been together eight months and their sex life is good. I am optimistic. Roxie has started to heal the wounds that stopped her from surrendering to a partner.

If you want to discover all the dimensions of your sexual power, a relationship without emotional intimacy and trust won't be enough for you. Intimacy involves surrender, a desire to let go of fear. You and your partner will bravely explore the inner space of emotions together. *Sharing emotions—not excessively, but as they naturally come up—is part of the flow.* Lovemaking is about generosity and giving pleasure to each other. It's not just about you and your pleasure, important as that is. There's a playfulness that comes from trusting each other as friends and lovers, not holding back. In all these ways, emotional intimacy only makes sex better and is a balm that sustains couples.

If you desire more intimacy but resist it, I suggest journaling about your fears. Are you afraid of being hurt? Betrayed? Abandoned? Do you have painful memories of failed intimacies with parents, friends, or others as you grew up? Were you neglected, not "seen," rejected, or mistreated? Often abused children associate love and sex with pain and choose partners who will inflict pain. Identify what's stopping you from surrendering to intimacy. Our upbringing can shape us. For better or worse, we're born helpless, totally dependent on others. If your parents weren't nurturing and dependable, you may always be perpetually on guard against getting hurt in relationships—it's hard to surrender if you don't feel relaxed and secure. Nevertheless, being aware of your early conditioning will let you compassionately identify areas where you hold back from trust now. If you have a history of abuse, you can heal past and current relationship patterns with therapeutic help. Sometimes issues are too big to resolve alone. Old wounds must begin to mend before you're safe enough to let go to love. That's the beauty of reaching out for smart professional guidance to free you from the bondage of abuse or any other trauma.

When you feel ready, you can use these steps to free yourself. For instance, experiment with pushing your limits with intimacy. Then address any anxiety that arises to prevent you from surrendering. Here's where a good therapist can be invaluable. Like Roxie, tell yourself it's okay to go slowly. First start expressing emotions with friends where the stakes aren't as high as they are with a lover. Or you can get used to sharing love with animals: a dog, a cat, a bird, a hamster, whatever living being you're not afraid to care about. There's no rush. Embracing intimacy is a gentle process of desensitizing fear and getting rewarded by loving. As you gain more comfort and confidence, you can go on to a romantic partner.

However, even beyond the biological and emotional facets of intimacy, sexual power is larger than just your desires. It also involves tapping a higher power. There's a spiritual instinct that propels all of our body's primal drives. *Nothing about being human is ever just physical despite what our minds or genitals tell us.* Sexuality and spirit are intimately related. When you surrender sexually, you enter an open intuitive state, permitting the force of creation to flow through you, similar to how artists are moved. As a result, you may literally create a new infant life or you may be rebirthed yourself. During sex, ordi-

nary boundaries fall away and your consciousness is altered. You encounter the bliss of the transcendent. You can intuitively sense things
about each other. When you surrender, you are a conduit. I'll show
how to practice inviting spirit in which in turn triggers the body's
biochemical pleasure response. With age, spirituality and subtle energy keep sexual power alive. Passion of the body is kindled by the
passion of heaven. Knowing this is the beginning of knowing bliss.

What makes a good lover? There's an electric chemistry between
couples that is unique to them. Smell, voice, touch, and kissing style
all figure in. Technical skills and good hygiene are important as well.
But beyond these, here are some characteristics to look for.

TEN QUALITIES OF A GOOD LOVER

1. You're a willing learner.

2. You're playful and passionate.

3. You make your partner feel sexy.

4. You're confident, not afraid to be vulnerable.

5. You're adventurous and willing to experiment.

6. You communicate your needs and listen to your partner.

7. You make time and don't rush.

8. You enjoy giving pleasure as much as you enjoy receiving it.

9. You're supportive, not judgmental.

10. You're fully present in the moment with good eye contact and
    can let go.

What stops us from being good lovers? Frequently it's time constraints, self-centeredness, inhibitions, and lack of technique. Our
minds won't shut off which keeps us from being in the moment. Further, many of us resist surrendering to how sexy we really are. Why?
We haven't learned to see ourselves as sexy. We've been brainwashed
by the "skinny ideal." Also, sex is frequently viewed more as a performance feat than as a holy exchange. Growing up, most of us haven't

been given the right kind of education about what true sexiness is. If only we'd been taught that sexuality is a healthy, natural part of us that we must embody in a mindful, loving way—not something "dirty" or something to be ashamed of. Early on we learn that the words "vagina" and "penis" embarrass people. Except between lovers, they are rarely part of our vocabulary. We are a culture that embraces shame, only there is nothing to be ashamed of!

At sixteen, when I was about to make love with my boyfriend of two years for the first time, a life-altering rite of passage, I asked my mother about sex. Looking stricken, as if I'd just torn her heart out, she laid down the law: "Judith, it's far too soon. Let's talk about this when you're twenty-one." End of story. I guess Mother hoped that by refusing to discuss it she'd deter me. She couldn't have been more wrong. I felt equal parts guilty, mad, and rebellious, dead set on doing what I'd planned. I didn't want to hurt Mother, but as I saw it, this wasn't about her—it was about me. I knew she was concerned for my welfare but not addressing my sexuality wasn't helpful.

I wish parents and authority figures would finally grasp that when you tell teenagers that sex is forbidden, it beckons all the more. It then becomes dangerous, risky, more highly charged. Many sophisticated parents today understand this. They honestly discuss the pros and cons of teenage sex without shaming their children or cutting them off. Spirituality needs to be part of that discussion. Two souls sharing erotic passion is a way of celebrating spirit too. Knowing that a caring (not punishing) higher power is involved brings reverence, integrity, and responsibility to having sex for both teens and adults. It elevates the experience. Spirit is happy that we love each other. It has many sides, including sexiness. If only we were taught that sexuality complements spirituality by linking us with a greater force of love, that they're not at war with each other. How different our attitudes would be!

Just as baby chicks imprint on their mothers, we imprint on our parents. You were fortunate if your parents modeled a healthy sexuality and taught you to be proud of your body. My patients who've been raised like this are more comfortable in their own skin and with surrendering to their sexuality. Regrettably, for the rest of us, such self-esteem about our bodies is hard-earned. However, using this chapter's strategies, you can let go of negative programming. Seeing yourself as an erotic being and embracing your own allure are the rewards of awakening sexual power.

Sometimes, though, we resist our own sexiness or having sex at all because it mirrors our insecurities. Common ones include "Is my body attractive? Is my partner judging me? Am I a good lover? Will I disappoint my partner? Will I be rejected? Suffocated?" When these or other fears take over, even subconsciously, you may resist having sex. Resistance can manifest as legitimate excuses such as "I'm not in the mood," "I'm too tired or run down," "I'm preoccupied with work," "It's too much effort," "The kids will hear," or "I've got a headache." Still, if these excuses become habitual and your erotic life is suffering, it's essential to examine your resistance to sex.

There are practical steps you can take to overcome resistance. You have to want to be sexy and keep passion alive in a relationship. When you're tired or angry, or if communication with your partner breaks down, passion quickly disappears. Denial and apathy are the enemies of passion. So stay alert to the following deterrents to a good sex life. Then you can correct the situation.

COMMON KILLERS OF PASSION

- Exhaustion.

- Not communicating your needs.

- Losing interest.

- Rushing.

- Lack of creativity, boredom.

- Repressed anger and hostilities.

Sexual responsiveness is a sensitive barometer. Intimacy requires self-awareness and a willingness to remove obstacles. Taking action can help you achieve a loving, erotic relationship. On a daily basis, train yourself to be more mindful about getting rest and pacing yourself. It's not sexy to rush around and be constantly stressed out. Especially when you're busy, it's important to remember to breathe—a quick way to reconnect with your body. Though family, work, and other demands can intrude on making time for sexuality, being dedicated to self-care can help you prioritize it in your relationship. (Later in this chapter, I'll offer lovemaking techniques that factor in lifestyle demands.)

To cure self-doubts, you need to be solution-oriented. For instance, if you wonder, "Is my technique right?" honestly talk with your partner about how you can meet each other's needs. If you're bored with the same positions, playfully brainstorm together about exciting ways to experiment. Also, with respect, keep discussing the anger or hurt you may feel toward each other so that your resentments don't numb passion. For more complex issues such as fear of intimacy, reach out to a therapist or a friend for insight. While exploring your fears, be kind to yourself. Such sweetness allows you to mend wounds and reclaim your power.

SURRENDER TO THE ECSTASY OF ORGASMS: EXPLORE SACRED PLAY

Orgasm is the crown jewel of surrender. You tap into the primordial flow of life as well as release tension. The more surrendered you are, the more ecstatic the orgasm.

Sex and orgasms are an intrinsic part of being human. For me, these are the great rewards of having a body! The World Health Organization estimates that at least a hundred million acts of intercourse take place each day worldwide. (Imagine if even half of these were motivated by love—what ecstasy would surround the planet!) On average, American couples have sex two times per week. The average male orgasm lasts ten seconds and a female orgasm is twenty seconds or longer. I could hardly believe the national polls revealing that nearly 50 percent of women report having orgasms infrequently or not at all during intercourse. Moreover, numerous studies have found that women fake orgasms up to half the time to protect their partners' feelings. These statistics highlight a glaring reluctance many of us have to be honest with our partners about sex. We'll discuss how surrender, a basic knowledge of anatomy, and a little dexterity can improve communication and enhance orgasms for both sexes.

What is an orgasm? How could this miracle ever be just one thing? It involves physical, emotional, spiritual, and energetic surrenders. On a physical level, when you're sexually aroused, your orgasm discharges tension, resulting in rhythmic pelvic contractions and pleasure, even euphoria. In men, orgasm typically occurs from stimulating the penis; in women, from stimulating the clitoris or the sacred G-spot in the vagina. These parts of our body are marvelously sensitive due to a high density of nerve fibers. Caressing them activates pleasure centers in the brain. Your body shifts gears. You breathe harder. Your heart rate increases. Blood rushes to your genitals, making them swell. At climax, men and some women ejaculate. Endorphins, the natural "feel-good" hormones, flood your system. You experience waves of pleasure, stress evaporates, and a warm glow permeates your body. Oxytocin, the "love hormone," spikes, bathing couples in the warm and fuzzy "wash of love" feeling as you bond. Your biology wants you to relax into a blissful surrender.

Emotions play a different role in orgasm for men and women. I am reluctant to stereotype genders, but for women emotional intimacy and trust are often more necessary in order to feel safe enough to let go—though of course physical attraction is essential too. Orgasms are easier when we feel treasured. If we feel criticized, unappreciated, or rushed it can be difficult, if not impossible, to surrender during sex. In contrast, men are more biologically wired to prioritize orgasm over an emotional connection or even trust. Physical attraction may be all that it takes to climax. Thus, over the eons, men have been said to "think with their penises" when they're turned on, though women can also make terrible decisions based on sexual desire. Expressing feelings isn't always first on a man's mind, though the failure to do so may be a deal breaker for a woman. Nevertheless, there are also many loving, sexy men who are emotionally sensitive, responsive, and in no hurry at all.

The Erotic Ecstasy of Foreplay

Foreplay is an opportunity for couples to arouse and nurture each other though women seem to crave it more. It's a way to build erotic energy rather than simply releasing it. The average man can have an orgasm within a few minutes or less. Women may need up to twenty minutes of foreplay. Ideally, of course, neither partner hears a clock ticking. Many couples I treat are in paradise letting sexual tension mount before intercourse without any sense of time. Foreplay lets them feel close, explore, play, prolong the ecstatic pangs of arousal. I liken foreplay to tuning a musical instrument. You need to intuitively feel it, discover just the right touch, the right kiss, and sense how you and your partner's bodies respond. I smiled when I recently saw a man in a café whose T-shirt read, "I will work for sex." True, it may take more effort for a woman to orgasm but that's what being a good lover means: knowing how to please someone without rushing, getting pleasure from each other's pleasure. Then foreplay never just feels like work. In addition, here's a critical anatomic fact: nature didn't put the clitoris (unlike the penis) in the direct line of penetration. During foreplay it needs to be manually or orally stimulated unless the angle of your bodies happens to be just right, which is less likely. Most women can't have an orgasm with intercourse alone. Couples must know this so they can mutually pleasure each other.

If a man wants to win a woman's heart, the time and the tenderness he puts into foreplay help her surrender during sex. She can't be rushed. A common problem I've seen with couples in my practice is that if a man is spent, he may want to have intercourse without much foreplay, then just fall asleep since ejaculating makes him tired. I'm not saying a woman can't enjoy a quickie at times but in general this practice doesn't support a passionate relationship. I encourage couples to openly discuss the dilemma of balancing all of life's demands, to agree to try not to lapse into the rut of quickies. Then they can plan erotic interludes to leisurely enjoy each other and the pleasures their bodies have to offer.

To enhance foreplay, try the next exercise to awaken your senses and let go to pleasure.

SURRENDER TO YOUR SENSUAL SELF

Set aside uninterrupted time to playfully experiment. Begin to relax by breathing deep and slow. We habitually breathe shallowly to temper sexual and other feelings. I want you to sense, not think, to be fully in your body.

- *Awaken touch.* Take a fresh flower or a feather and gently stroke each other's bodies. (For me, it's a rose in full bloom with petals about to fall.) Start with the face, neck, chest, breasts, and the heart area, gradually making your way down to the genitals. Repeat delicate, circular motions over these areas. They respond to a light touch. It'll feel lovely and exciting. Let go. Revel in the sensations.

- *Awaken taste.* Select a few foods, herbs, or spices that have zing. Arrange them on a plate. My favorites are papaya, peppermint, and honey. I have a patient, an engineer with a nonstop mind, who perks up her sensuality by savoring a succulent piece of watermelon. To heighten your sense of taste, I suggest wearing an eye mask or a loose blindfold, perhaps made from a silk scarf. Then, with eyes covered, have your partner offer you each selection one by one. The tongue is a sensual miracle of sensations. Let the pleasure of taste spread throughout your body. Allow it to arouse every pore.

- *Awaken smell.* Now, explore smell. It is an intimate and important part of sexuality, one that can turn you off or on. Let a blindfold accentuate your exploration of this sense. One patient, a full-time mom, gets a sensual lift from a few whiffs of lavender or gardenia oil during the day, and she keeps them handy in her desk and car. Test out various scents. See how your body responds to the aromas of different herbs, oils, or perfumes. Use them as a sensual refresher.

- *Play with movement and rocking.* Experiment with moving your bodies together to build sensuality. Rocking your bodies while holding each other can be extremely sensual. Also, when you first see each other after being apart, a long, silent embrace or hug combined with rocking is arousing. Dancing or spontaneous free-form movements are beautiful too.

- *Explore sacred slapping.* Sometimes slapping each other on, say, the buttocks awakens you erotically. Get feedback from your partner about the intensity of the slap that feels right. Do this in the spirit of love and play, never anger. Though this technique doesn't appeal to everyone, it can jolt some people into a new level of openness and sensual participation.

- *Tune in to nature.* Draw on nature's passion to heighten your sensuality. Thunderstorms, mist, rainbows, wind in the woods—enjoy whatever moods of nature excite you. Let them arouse your body. Be aware of colors, textures, sounds. Absorb them all. For instance, I'll twirl on my balcony to the sensual tone of a distant foghorn, becoming one with it and the ocean nearby. Sensuality can be transmitted from nature to you, a spontaneous osmosis if you allow it to happen.

This exercise intensifies your own sensuality and the erotic relationship between you and your partner. Exploring each other is never just a one-time event. Keep discovering the nuances of each other's sensitivity and aesthetics. Experiment with what gives you both goose bumps, tingles, or surges of warmth. Notice how your body feels, all of it, especially your belly, genitals, breasts. Share what arouses you. This lets you both experience more pleasure and intimacy.

The Problem with Faking Orgasms: How It Hinders Surrender

Since most couples would agree that communicating with each other is important, why do so many women (and men) fake orgasms? Research suggests there's a massive amount of pretending going on in the bedroom that no one wants to talk about. The reports are strikingly consistent: about half the women surveyed admit to regularly faking orgasms, mostly during intercourse. And from 10 to 20 percent of men admit to occasionally faking them too. If you want to claim your sexual power and surrender freely, this is a vital issue to address.

What are the top reasons for faking? Women say they don't want to hurt their partner's feelings or not meet their partner's expectations. They also don't want to appear "unsexy" or "inadequate" or to be "taking too long." They fake to "get sex over with" because it's unsatisfying or they're not in the mood. Typically, men say they fake when orgasm is unlikely. Faking might seem like the most caring, innocent, polite way to address not having an orgasm—and can buy time until you relax enough to let go—but in the grand scheme it hinders surrendering to intimacy.

As a psychiatrist and a woman, I understand why we fake and the crazy expectations associated with orgasms. The Hollywood version is that two young, attractive people meet and immediately have hot sex with simultaneous orgasms. Talk about unrealistic! Seriously, who ever really has synchronized orgasms without learning about each other's bodies? Maybe some lucky few or those anointed with genius technical skills, but not the rest of us. The expectation that we're supposed to know everything about how to turn a lover on without him or her educating us is absurd. Given the improbable Hollywood model that we measure ourselves against, is it any wonder that women might fake, especially the first time they have intercourse with someone, no matter how exciting lovemaking can feel?

The solution to faking is honest conversation. Ideally you'll start this when you begin a sexual relationship. Then, as you get used to sharing your likes and dislikes, it will become natural. Or if you've already been with someone for years, you can gently start expressing your needs now, never wronging your partner or making him or her feel incompetent. Just as you wouldn't keep your taste in food a secret from your partner, it's important to share your preferences about sex. It's never too late. If you're both open, you can always surrender to a deeper intimacy.

Find a way to connect that is more authentic and honors sexuality without having to pretend, the antithesis of surrender. No one can meet your every need without your uttering a word. Yes, we can be empathic and sexy and free, following intuition to attune to our partner's body. But it is also necessary to receive guidance from each other. You haven't failed if you need your partner to describe how to help him or her have an orgasm. It's a beautiful discovery process. After all, anatomist Matteo Realdo Colombo didn't "scientifically" discover the clitoris until 1559!

Consider your exploration of orgasms sacred play. Surrender to trying new techniques, even if you initially feel awkward. For a woman, squeezing her pubococcygeal (vaginal) muscles in the pelvic floor, then bearing down for a count of five to prepare for pleasure, increases orgasms. You can also experiment with a vibrator or other sex toys. (Physicians actually invented the vibrator because they were getting hand pain from masturbating women patients to orgasm! This technique of "vulvar massage" was used in the Victorian era to treat "female hysteria.") Today you can use vibrators for your own pleasure, a creative way to have an orgasm that can deter faking.

How can faking prevent surrender? First, it too easily becomes a habit. Instead of telling your partner, "I adore you. You turn me on. I just don't feel like having sex tonight," you fake it. Maybe you are too tired or not in the mood or maybe you would rather just lie beside your partner who's pleasuring him or herself. That's all fine. There are no "shoulds" in lovemaking. Instead it has rhythms: sometimes the earth moves, sometimes it's a more mellow pleasure. Listen to your intuition about what feels right in the moment. Stay true to your body and to yourself. Then you won't betray your instincts or pretend because you're afraid of being real. This may be a new kind of dialogue to engage in. It may feel uncomfortable at times, but the effort will help you claim your true sexual power.

There Is No Such Thing as Casual Sex

From an intuitive perspective, your orgasm is never just your own during lovemaking. Energy gets transmitted to your partner, affecting his or her well-being. Your energy fields overlap, conveying both joy and despair (even during brief hookups). From that perspective, there is no such thing as casual sex. In fact, my sensitive patient Pete prefers not to make love with his wife if she's angry about work. Reasonably enough! He's happy to listen to her vent when she comes home but if she's still clinging to the anger when they have sex, it gets transmitted even without speaking it. This doesn't feel good to Pete and drains him. Such energy transfer between couples frequently happens, though most aren't aware of it. I want you to be. During orgasm ordinary boundaries blur. You're vulnerable. Your heart opens. In the best of situations, orgasm is an exchange of energy that blesses both partners. The French call it *le petit mort* or "the little death," a total surrender that catapults you and your lover into the ecstatic arms of the divine.

Tantra is a potent Hindu system that teaches the art of erotic love by combining sex and spirit. Westerners often see sex as linear, the goal being orgasm, but tantra views sexual love as a sacrament and an energy exchange. According to tantra, orgasm isn't simply a physical release. Using specific positions, you move erotic energy upward from the genitals to nourish and purify your whole being.

I've had a series of tantric sessions that have helped open my sensuality and sexuality. My teacher always keeps his eyes steady on me, conveying appreciation and sexiness. In tantra, women are treated as the "goddess" and the feminine energy is revered. This feels incredible! In a session, you touch, do breathing exercises, and share energy with a partner. Sometimes "sacred spot massage" (G-spot) occurs which offers a direct experience of a vaginal orgasm. This is a joy every woman can have with the right instruction and a skill that every couple can learn. In tantra, intercourse, which is called "sacred union," isn't always necessary to feel fulfilled and isn't typically part of the tantric session.

It's fun to be aware of energy during lovemaking. Energy is emitted through the eyes: the sensual way you look at someone can arouse him or her. Eye contact is a way to stay connected to your partner. Also during orgasm, when energy rises, you may liberate uncomfortable emotions. I've had numerous (mostly male) patients say, "My partner sometimes cries when we make love. Have I done something wrong?" I explain, "In both men and women, crying and laughing are emotional releases, signs of passion, not anything that needs fixing." Tantric educator Barbara Carrellas calls spontaneous laughing during sex "giggleasms." Check out these reactions with your partner. Unless he or she says differently, there's nothing you need to do except rejoice in how free your partner feels to emotionally surrender with you.

To experience how knowing about energy can improve your sex life, try the following exercise alone or with a partner. It takes orgasm beyond the short version of "it feels so good and it's over" to a level of extended meditative bliss.

SURRENDER TO AN ORGASMIC MEDITATION

- *Relax and unwind.* Set aside some time to be sensual. Turn off the phone. Put a Do Not Disturb sign on your door. It's important not to be rushed. To unwind, take a few deep breaths. Feel your belly rise with each in-breath, become softer with each out-breath. Focus on the sensuality of your body.

- *Have an orgasm.* Stroke yourself. Indulge in a sexy thought. Arouse each other with foreplay if you're with a partner. In whatever way you like, whether you're self-pleasuring or making love, bring yourself to orgasm. Feel the orgasm rise, then peak, then explode. Let yourself melt into it. Surrender to the pleasure.

- *Meditate.* A wonderful way to feel sexual energy move is to meditate immediately after an orgasm. A minute or so following climax, sit in an upright position. It's much easier to meditate when you're relaxed. Close your eyes: this intensifies any experience. Inhale and exhale slowly. Focus lightly on the lingering bliss of orgasm. Let it spread throughout your body. Don't force anything. Sexual energy moves through you naturally. Surrender to the sensations as they heighten. Savor the warmth, tingles, or rush. Eyes still closed, you may slip into a state of intuitive awareness. You may see colors, vibrate from head to toe, or even feel God. Spontaneous intuitions about people, work, or health may flash through. Later, be sure to write these down and act on them. There is no time limit for this meditation. Continue as long as you like. Let the orgasmic energy transport you to higher states of consciousness, visions, and pleasure.

Overcoming Your Fear of Letting Go

If you want to let go during sex but something is holding you back, it's essential to examine and heal fears that can undercut your pleasure. See if the following fears are stopping you.

COMMON FEARS OF LETTING GO

- Fear of losing control.
- Fear of not performing.
- Fear of taking too long to have an orgasm.
- Fear of speaking your needs.
- Fear of pain, abandonment, or emotional harm.
- Fear of losing yourself in a lover.
- Fear of getting obsessed or overly attached to a lover.

To surrender these fears, envision a new paradigm of sexual success. Dispense with old ideas and embrace truer ones. The first switch is to permanently retire the notion that good sex is equated only with performance. The belief that "I'm not a real man or woman if I don't perform on command with an erection or an orgasm" is obsolete and spiritually ignorant. It's grim when sex is reduced to a contest to keep proving yourself by how you perform—motivations that also apply, sad to say, to succeeding in corporate America. This leads to performance anxiety, which only prevents good sex and orgasms.

Just as trying to fall asleep doesn't work, trying to perform is doomed. Do you think basketball pro LeBron James is worrying about his performance when he's going for a slam dunk? Or Aretha Franklin when she's belting out a song? Or Steve Jobs when he was inventing the iPad? I kinda doubt it. The same goes for sex. Attention should be focused on giving and receiving pleasure, not on expectations of erections and orgasms. I urge couples to be more candid, more innovative, more willing to question and blast apart notions that are anti-passion and anti-love.

Emotional wounds can also stop you from letting go. Lovemaking may trigger old hurts, fear of abandonment, or trauma. When this happens to my patients, their first instinct is often to shut down. In psychoanalyst Alice Miller's eye-opening book *The Body Never Lies*, she describes the long-term consequences of child abuse in the body such as chronic pain, numbness, and impotence. Trauma lodges in our muscles and tissues until it's allowed to be released. One of my patients who struggled with low self-esteem spent a decade in an abusive marriage. She told me, "My husband was into having sex during commercial breaks when we watched TV. He'd be finished by the time *Monday Night Football* came back on. I didn't want to make him mad, so I faked orgasms." On those occasions, my patient hated her husband, herself, and the sex. No wonder she suffered from chronic pelvic pain. She loved her husband, but he was hurting her with his abusive treatment and definitely not treasuring her the way she deserved to be treasured. My beaten-down patient had reached that point of surrender. Finally she was ready to let go. During our therapy, she gained the courage to leave the marriage and eventually her pelvic pain disappeared.

Techniques that benefited my patient and will help others heal trauma include psychotherapy, bodywork—such as energy healing and massage—and spiritual work focusing on self-compassion and the complicated subject of forgiveness. If you have a history of trauma that prevents you from letting go, I recommend reaching out to a therapist or guide to help you release it. As healing occurs—and it will—letting go during lovemaking will feel safer and more plea-surable.

Perhaps you hold back from surrendering during sex because you're afraid of losing yourself in a partner or sacrificing your power. Like some patients I've worked with, you may find it difficult to stay centered around sexual energy. You may resist the merging that hap-pens during orgasm because it makes you feel invisible or consumed. Paradoxically, you must be confident in who you are in order to enjoy such profound letting go. Otherwise the ecstatic dissolution of the ego during lovemaking may seem threatening. One college student told me about her conflicted emotions: "It feels like I give my power away when I let go. My boyfriend makes me feel so amazing, I'm afraid he'll possess a part of me that I'll never get back. But I'd do anything to keep him." This speaks to how easy it is to get seduced by bliss, what people are tempted to give up for it. Since Adam and Eve, erotic pleasure has made even the most sensible people forsake their priorities.

A related aspect is when one member of a couple too greatly sub-ordinates his or her identity while caring for a spouse or children. What's been useful for my patients in this predicament is to create a daily life with more individual meaning and also to set clearer bound-aries. Maybe that means returning to school, doing charity work, or insisting on private time to meditate and pursue spirituality. If this sounds familiar to you, as you minister to your own needs you'll feel more centered. Then it will be safer to enjoy the freedom of surren-dering, both during sex and in your relationship.

The Difference Between Bonding and Overly Attaching to a Partner: Liberate Your Love

Bonding with a partner is a natural part of getting to know someone and of falling in love. But getting overly attached goes beyond healthy bonding and is disempowering. When you truly love someone, you're not interested in possessing the person or keeping him or her in your clutches because you're afraid of losing the relationship. Instead, you respect your partner's autonomy and spirit. You're not too entangled;

rather you're standing together side by side. True intimacy is always a balance between bonding and letting go so the relationship can breathe.

Take the following quiz to determine your bonding patterns.

QUIZ: ARE YOU OVERLY ATTACHED TO A PARTNER?

- Do you cling to your partner?

- Do you want to possess him or her?

- Are you often afraid of being abandoned or betrayed?

- Do you get anxious when you don't hear from him or her every day if you're dating?

- Do you constantly think about the person?

- Do you start obsessing about a partner after you have sex?

- Does your partner feel you are trying to control or suffocate him or her?

- Do you feel you can't live without the person?

If you answered yes to six to eight questions, you are extremely overly attached. Three to five yeses indicate that you are moderately overly attached. One to three yeses indicate that you have a tendency to overly attach. A score of zero indicates that you have healthy bonding with your partner.

An aspect of myself that I've made progress in healing is my tendency to get overly attached to men. During sex I bond quickly and fuse with a man, but I can't unfuse with him later. I start yearning for him and thinking about him constantly. Some of this is organic and beautiful but becoming overly attached crosses a line. I can become obsessed and intensely hungry for contact, particularly if I've been single for a while. I am a sexual being so if I haven't had sex for a while, I can become needy. Being in this position makes me (and many women) vulnerable to getting overly attached. For instance, if I don't hear from the man for a few days, I can get anxious and afraid of losing him or of being abandoned. It's not good for me, and moreover, most men don't appreciate this kind of response. So in my tantric sexuality sessions and in therapy, I discovered how to enjoy passion from a more grounded place. Here's how:

- I learned that over-merging with a sexual partner can decrease sexual charge. It actually can be more erotic to go in and out of intense connection with a partner rather than sustaining it. This gives both lovers their space and more breathing room.

- I don't "root" in a man. I root primarily in myself and the earth. One way I do this before and after lovemaking is to visualize my body developing roots into the soil like a tree. I'm still surrendered to and immersed in pleasure, but I also keep a fuller sense of myself intact. I'm able to separate from him and more comfortably see us as separate beings.

- After lovemaking, I find it useful to meditate with my partner and then say to each other, "I adore you. I honor you. I release you." This is a healthy way to bond and produces a beautiful equilibrium of loving.

The solution to becoming overly attached is to focus on strengthening your self-esteem while addressing and releasing fears, including the fear of abandonment, which can cause the need to cling. Working with a skilled relationship therapist or coach can be productive. Also, you can practice the tantric techniques I described above. These will help you develop autonomy and grounding. Being willing to surrender the tendency to get overly attached in favor of a healthier bond will allow you to have more joyous and pleasurable relationships without the pain of obsession.

The Lure of Sex Addiction: Are You Addicted to Ecstasy?

An extreme example of being seduced by bliss is sex addiction. Sex addicts become hooked on sex like a drug—they constantly crave it, have multiple partners, even put themselves in dangerous situations and risk health, marriages, and jobs to experience pleasure. They look to sex to fill an emotional and spiritual emptiness that can't be filled in this way or through other addictions. But their cravings drive them on. Just as studies have proven that rats will do anything for pleasure, including starve themselves, people in this predicament are addicted to ecstasy. Nothing else matters.

What's the solution? Along with psychotherapy to heal compulsive behavior, I refer my patients to Sex Addicts Anonymous, a twelve-step program that focuses on connecting with a higher power and developing self-esteem. Although relapse is common, as is true with any addiction, I've still observed significant progress in my patients. For sex addicts or those afraid of giving their power to sexual partners, finding one's center is key. Once they surrender the notion that anything external, including sex, can fix them or make them whole, they become more centered. Sexual energy is seductive but we must not surrender to it at the expense of our body and soul. As with all things, balance is the foundation of inner peace.

SURRENDER TO BLISS

The goal of sexual surrender is to keep letting go in healthy, positive ways, at your own pace, in your own time. Lovemaking is an ongoing surrender to bliss. What is bliss? The dictionary defines it as extreme happiness, ecstasy, and the joy of heaven. As I see it, it's also the bliss of connecting to the body, to a partner, and to God. For me, this is the place where great rivers converge, the intersection of human life and heaven. Bliss isn't as distant as you might think. It's always right in front of us, in this moment, when we can open to it.

Philosopher Alan Watts wrote, "When you are in love with someone, you do indeed see them as a divine being." This "aha" moment can raise lovemaking from the physical to the transcendent. Remember: that divine being you are making love with is the same person who forgot to pay the rent last month and who sometimes doesn't do the dishes. Seeing the divinity in your partner while making love, and always, is acknowledging the miraculous in the ordinary. That's the secret to bliss.

Human bliss is only a sliver of what divine bliss can be. During sex, you want to touch the eternal. A relationship is never just about two people. Each of you has a direct line to the divine that you can bring to each other. Learning to invite spirit into sex keeps passion high. During lovemaking, your mutual spiritual, heart, and erotic energies blend together as they permeate your body. Your lusty, heartful, and heavenly parts fuse in utter bliss.

If you've never had the experience of bringing the divine into lovemaking, you have a lot to look forward to. Here's an exercise to practice.

THE ECSTASY OF BLENDING SEX AND SPIRIT

- *Create a sacred space.* To set the mood, create an environment that's sensually and spiritually uplifting: a vase of tulips, some sandalwood incense, candles, perhaps oils to rub on each other. Turn your phones off so there are no disturbances or reasons to hurry.

- *Hold each other; make eye contact.* Spend as long as you like in each other's arms before you go further. Gaze lovingly into each other's eyes, a way of exchanging energy. For a few minutes, breathe together, synchronizing in-breath and out-breath, becoming intuitively attuned. Feel your energy and warmth blending. Soak up the joy of intimacy.

- *Allow spirit to flow through you.* When you're ready, go on to intercourse. Inwardly ask, "May the divine flow through me." Then stay open. Once you invite spirit in, bliss will come through. Bliss is a way of the divine saying, "I'm here. I love you. Let go." Trust the gift. Let your genitals reach for bliss. Let your heart

surrender too. Feel bliss as it glides up your spine and out the top
of your head and back to the heavens.

- *Relax together.* Linger in the moment. Don't rush out of bed. If it
  feels right to be silent, fine. If you want to talk with each other,
  do. Cherish this sacred union.

Igniting your sexual power lets you surrender more completely to
bliss, no holding back, no resisting. From the caress of sunlight on
your shoulders to a lover's sensual touch, take in the bliss, nice and
slow. Don't go on to the next thing too fast. I want to convey how
mysterious and sanctified bliss can be, how it's always been within
you to summon. Immerse yourself in the bliss of everyday life and of
sexual passion: they are wedded to each other, not separate. Realizing
this changes everything.

Across many spiritual traditions, erotic poetry celebrates the sacred wedding of body and spirit. Mystics see all love songs as about
God. The body, a form of the Formless, is a manifestation of divine
love. In Judaism, the Song of Songs, an epic love poem, exalts sensual
pleasure and God. Similarly, the Christian mystics Teresa of Avila
and Hildegard of Bingen, both virgins of course, wrote rapturous,
erotic love poetry to God and used imagery from the Song of Songs.
In Hinduism, the world is believed to have been created through a
sexual act. Thus, the Indian poet Mirabai praises the erotic through
sex and creation. The great Sufi mystic poets Hafez and Rumi revere
the union with God through a surrender to erotic love, divine love,
and the love of friendship. I get chills from the depth of the surrender
that Rumi writes about: "I merged so completely with love / and was
so fused, that I became love / And love became me." I suggest reading
such erotic poetry with your partner to honor the sensual sacrament
of your relationship.

One winter I had the privilege of visiting Konya, Turkey, the
place of Rumi's death. The day he died, December 17, is affection-
ately called his "wedding day," Rumi's reunion with the divine. Each
year, thousands of people make the pilgrimage to Konya on this date

to honor the poet of love. That evening I saw a performance of the whirling dervishes, an ecstatic surrender to spontaneous movement, to passion, to grief, and the divine. Their dance isn't just for entertainment. The dervishes, dressed in simple white robes, spun in reverence to the unseen, in trance. Watching their radiant faces and the effortless fluidity of their spinning, I was transported into bliss too. I left feeling happy and in love with everything again.

When gazing into the eyes of your beloved, you are always looking into the eyes of God. Keep surrendering to the ecstasy of lovemaking. View it as practice for making love with the entire universe. Sexual passion connects you to the joy of heaven, earth, and realms beyond. You'll be illuminated. Trust the many incarnations of bliss. Once you get just a glimpse of them, there is no turning back.

SURRENDER AFFIRMATION FOR SEXUAL POWER

I am a vibrant sexual being. I will use this power with respect and care. I will allow myself to fully let go to pleasure. I will delight in the bliss of my sensuality. I will surrender to giving and receiving love.

If you surrenderred to the air, you could ride it.
—TONI MORRISON

9

THE NINTH SURRENDER

DISCOVERING THE SENSUAL ESSENCE OF THE NATURAL WORLD

FROM MY EARLIEST MEMORY, THE NATURAL WORLD HAS enlivened me. The trees, the stars, and the secret oceans I frequent have been my lovers and companions. As you will see, nature and all her creatures are givers of a special kind of ecstasy when you can receive and surrender to it.

Imagine a condor with nine-foot wings soaring the thermals over a deep aquamarine ocean. Imagine lush rolling fields of golden wildflowers. A shooting star. Or the sweet fragrance of jasmine on a warm summer's night. Nature transports us to a realm of beauty that replaces our worries and stress with awe for something larger. There's also a palpable enchantment infusing every petal, every ribbon of rain, every cloud. I'd like you to be aware of this and go further than merely observing scenery so that you can open yourself to the sensual magical powers of nature.

Nature has held the answers all along. She is a profound teacher of surrender. Nature brings you back to the present moment. When you're in the moment you are surrendered just by putting one foot in front of the other. Nature doesn't constrain herself or hold back. She fully and ecstatically lets go. By example, nature models solutions to everyday human problems. Watch, learn, imitate. Nature shows us how to flow past obstacles we encounter, then release rigidity. Does the stream fight the boulder obstructing its path? No, water is a shape-shifter and just moves around it. Do branches get rigid during storms? No, they bend. Nature also instructs us about perfect timing and patience. Seeds don't try to sprout in winter when they're meant to bloom in spring. They wait and gestate, not forcing change when the time is wrong. Even more, nature exudes joy. The flowers revel in sunlight, mist, and rain. They are never too busy or bothered to be joyful—and they want us to be part of their joy. In my workshops I always have a bouquet of flowers beside me and a garland of flowers adorns my front door year round. I also make potpourri from rose petals in my garden. This gives me so much pleasure, I'm sure I could've been an herbalist in the forest in previous eras. (In fact, my friend, author Caroline Myss, has nicknamed me "Petal.") Flowers make me happy and sometimes they whisper secrets to me too! Before a talk or when I'm feeling overwhelmed, I recite a prayer to St. Thérèse: "Little Flower, in this hour, show your power." This is the kind of joyous, playful flower power I want to have. In all of nature, there are rhythms and cycles that create perfect balance. When we attune and surrender to these, our bodies and souls will flourish; a hunger will be satisfied. As is written in Ecclesiastes: there is "a time to every purpose under heaven."

No living being is separate from nature or can function well, let alone ecstatically, without being in harmony with her. Human nature and the natural world are one. Each flows organically from the other.

Take our circadian rhythms, the biological shifts our bodies go through each day. Our brain's neuroendocrine (hormonal) clock is reset every twenty-four hours to earth time by the rising sun via the pineal gland. This gland is ruled by the motion of the solar system. Thus, the cycles of day and night dictate your sleep and waking patterns. When these are disrupted your physical and mental health suffer. We all know how even one bad night's sleep or a case of jet lag can throw us off!

Similarly, the moon's cycles can affect well-being. As a psychiatric resident working in emergency rooms, I saw how extra crazy and packed the ERs were on nights when there was a full moon. In fact, the term "lunacy" is associated with full-moon madness. Further, the moon's gravitational pull regulates the ebb and flow of tides (new and full moon have highest tides) and is linked to women's menstrual cycles, timing of ovulation, and labor. You can see what sophisticated interconnectivity our bodies have with the natural world, even though many people aren't trained to appreciate this miracle.

In addition, weather stunningly expresses the changing moods of nature and the earth's atmosphere. Since I was a young girl, I've been mesmerized by weather. I used to climb on our roof just to look at the clouds and feel the wind. Even today, I can't stop watching weather, sneaking peaks out the window wherever I am. If I'm up in the middle of the night, I always check out the sky and the alignment of the stars to see what's happening. I consider sunshine, rain, storms, wind, fog, and clouds to be friends. They're mystical and alive. They keep saying what I need to hear. I can lose myself in weather and then find myself over and over again. Weather is also inside us. Our emotional weather is as real as outer atmospheric conditions. Everything in nature that is light and dark, hot and cold, calm and stormy, we are too.

Nature is complex—sometimes gentle, sometimes fierce. It can also be destructive as when tsunamis, wildfires, hurricanes, or earthquakes obliterate entire communities. You don't want to upset nature's balance and make her angry. She is our host and benefactor, while we are just visitors—an important distinction. Nature demands respect. The more you can live in harmony with her and sensually relate to the weather, the more ecstasy you'll feel. Nature's stillness will impart tranquility and her wild side will fuel your tribal, instinctual wildness, a secret to passion.

What moves me about Daoism is the teaching that human life is part of the larger process of nature and that the only actions that make sense are those in accord with it. Daoists believe in the doctrine of *wu-wei* or nonaction. This doesn't mean doing nothing; rather, it means doing nothing unnatural to obstruct nature's flow. That's part of surrender, taking time to intuit the flow of things and go with it. In my Daoist practice, it means embracing what's spontaneous and simple, always listening to the signals of the natural world and receiving its radiance.

In this chapter, I'll show you how to cultivate a reverence for nature and experience the ecstasy that comes from surrendering to it. To help you do this, I'll focus on each of the four elements: earth, water, air, and fire. These elemental forces bestow enormous power and passion on us. You may resonate more with one than another—I'm such a water person—but I'd like you to explore them all. Tribal cultures believe that each of us contains all the elements, though we have a greater affinity for one than the others. The element we most strongly relate to is the one that best represents our life essence and genius. Increasing your awareness of the elements in daily life will make you more sensual, more vibrant, attuned to larger instinctual voices and less at the mercy of your mental chatter. Along with this, silence and solitude can heighten your ability to connect to nature, the divine, and intuition. With your mind quieter, you're more receptive to healing visions which can get obscured by the numbing noise of civilization. Just as Native Americans go on vision quests in nature to listen more acutely to their spirit guides and power animals, you'll learn to access these too.

During this phase of your journey to surrender, keep putting yourself in the presence of green growing things. Notice how all of life moves and breathes. Begin to rest in the grace of the natural world. To get started, you can honor nature's cycles by taking these simple daily vows.

SURRENDER AFFIRMATIONS TO NIGHT AND DAY

May I surrender to the dawn.
May I surrender to the sun at noon.
May I surrender to the trees and all the wild things in the late day.
May I surrender to the twilight.
May I surrender to the night and the moon.

SURRENDER TO THE EARTH

....

Very little grows on jagged rock.
Be ground. Be crumbled, so wildflowers will come up where you are.
You've been stony for too many years. Try something different. Surrender.

—RUMI

The earth has no problem loving. Just give her a seed and soon a plant will blossom. We harvest the earth for our food. We drink her fresh water. She gives us oxygen, fire, and wood to build shelter. Surrendering to the earth means loving and being responsive to nature and our environment. The trees, rivers, and oceans are an expression of the earth's body and also an extension of our own. We must look at the natural world not as "other" but as a cherished part of ourselves with which we are constantly interacting.

To get a clear perspective on the earth, it's important to realize that it hasn't always existed. Scientists believe our earth and solar system were formed about four and a half billion years ago from a massive cloud of interstellar dust and gas. (The Big Bang is thought to have created the universe thirteen billion years ago.) Initially, the earth was largely molten and red-hot from volcanoes and collisions with cosmic bodies. One large collision is believed to have tilted the earth at an angle and formed the moon—a mind-blowing event I meditate on to spark my imagination. Comets and asteroids brought water here where it condensed into clouds and eventually formed our oceans. Our earliest life-forms enriched the atmosphere with oxygen. About 580 million years ago, multicellular life began and then rapidly diversified. Interestingly, *Homo sapiens* (modern humans) have been around only a mere 200,000 years. Therefore, in the grand scheme of the universe, neither the earth nor human life has been here all that long, nor is our future guaranteed given the flux of the cosmos. The gift we have been given is a special opportunity to live and learn and love on this gorgeous planet. Never take that for granted. Let our reverence for nature be a daily expression of our gratitude

Enter the Sanctuary of Silence

To sense the earth and all the elements, it's vital to learn to slow down and embrace silence so that you can really see and hear. Silence is a period of time without speech or noise. You're not on your cell phone, checking messages, or making plans. Silence also means quieting your mind's chatter so that you can fully partake in nature's sensuality. For me, talking is highly overrated. It's such a relief to stop talking and thinking for a while, to just be still in the natural world with a friend (it's wonderful to agree to be silent in nature with others) or in solitude. There's beauty there, and also holiness. On a recent speaking tour when I was all talked out, the man I'm seeing would call me and we'd simply be silent on the phone together. Silence is the secret key to the secret door that lets holiness in.

Our spirit thrives on quiet where it has vast spaces to breathe. Unobscured by noise, you can return to your center. Excessive thinking and noise jam our circuits. Silence dissipates brain fog and keeps your inner space clear. It flushes out layers of stress and resistance so that you can surrender to the sounds and signals of the natural world. You want to savor the ecstatic colors of the sky, the invigorating rush of a waterfall, or the sweet scurrying of birds in the brush. You don't want to distract or stop yourself. The earth's sounds and sights will revive you, inspire you, and trigger intuitions so that you can hear the voice of your soul and know the mystery. You don't have to leave the earth to experience other realms. When you're silent, all you have to do is go inside!

As a psychiatrist, I understand our aversion to silence. At first, being so still can feel odd, anxious, or lonely. Your mind keeps nagging, "What's the point of just sitting here? I'm wasting time. I have too much to do" or "Who am I when I'm not talking to people in my life?" Or you may encounter fear or worry. Thus, like some of my patients, you may resist being silent. (Once they acclimate, however, a few even request that we begin each session with quiet meditation.) Accordingly, I suggest that you ease into the practice of silence slowly. Start with a few minutes a day when walking outdoors. Gradually increase the silence in different beautiful settings. Most of us aren't taught the power of silence; it takes some getting used to. But experiencing the replenishment of silence in nature will itself be reinforcing.

Sense the Ecstasy of Trees, Flowers, and Green Wild Things

You deserve an escape from responsibility and stress, a time to tune out the world. When you need to be recharged or if you feel you are up against a wall with no apparent way out, don't keep pushing. Instead, take refuge in the presence of green wild things. They'll help you release burdens as they welcome you into the earth's arms. I love that Daoism and native cultures honor the spirits in plants, flowers, and trees. They view these spirits as an actual part of the forests, canyons, vegetation, and streams, just as I do. Spirits inhabit nature. Have you ever noticed how holy it feels to be under a canopy of leaves or to be held in the embrace of a wildflower meadow? As Ralph Waldo Emerson wrote, "Earth laughs in flowers." Recently I had a beautiful dream on the night before my birthday in which I was told to "activate flowers." I awoke excited and interpreted this as a joyful imperative to activate all the flowers I can in myself, in others, and in every living thing—a mission I wholeheartedly embrace!

Plan regular breaks to commune with nature, though even a short walk works wonders. Give your figuring-out mind permission to rest. Be in the moment. Whether you're walking in a tree-lined neighborhood or through acres of fertile wilderness, inhale the freshness. Absorb the peace. Let yourself surrender to all that is green and flowing. The earth will impart vitality and clarity. Then you'll return to your life ready for whatever awaits you.

Green isn't just beautiful. We are indebted to green growing things for our survival. They give us shade and cool the earth. Chlorophyll, the pigment that makes plants green, captures energy from sunlight, which triggers photosynthesis. In this brilliantly designed process, leaves take in toxic carbon dioxide from the atmosphere and from humans (we expel it with each exhalation). Then the plant processes the carbon for its own use—storing much of it as tree trunks, roots, and branches—and releases oxygen for us to breathe. This is a miracle that most of us don't think about. In school, we learn only about the technical aspects of photosynthesis and we miss the real point.

Plants are intelligent. Their wisdom is evident in the elegant biology of how they communicate. *Science Daily* reports that plants can send danger signals to genetically identical cuttings growing nearby. One study found that sagebrush bushes alerted others of their kind to avoid being devoured by grasshoppers. Scientists suspect that plants warn their own kind of impending danger by secreting chemicals that deter herbivores or make the plant less attractive to anything that might eat it.

Plants also have healing powers. Since ancient times, herbalists have been thought to be in touch with the secrets of nature. Medicinal plants such as aloe soothe burns and chamomile quells anxiety. Shamans use hallucinogenic mushrooms for spiritual purposes to part the doors of perception and experience other realities. In homeopathy, the essence of the plant is distilled to "make it more itself." These homeopathic remedies treat diverse maladies from depression to exhaustion and ward off viruses when you travel. So when you encounter different species of shrubs, know that they are multidimensional, even healing.

I hope you can view all the earth's physical processes, including photosynthesis and plant medicine, as consecrated. Everything, *everything* is the hand of spirit. Shamans believe material reality is simply a "consensus dream." Just because the majority agrees on "what's real" doesn't mean it's true. Useful as it is, the linear mind sometimes can't see further than its own nose. Spirit is hidden but can be discovered through portals: the heart is one, nature is another. I invite you to "see" nature as shamans do: with your heart, not with your ego. Self-importance keeps the heart closed. Humbly appreciating the sanctity of the earth helps you see with your heart. In this way, when we seek guidance in nature, when we are willing to surrender to other forms of knowing, nature responds by giving us messages, something we all can intuitively receive when we are open.

Each day, practice surrendering more to the abundant natural world. In the presence of a flower or a blade of grass, sense, don't think. Listen. Smell. Absorb. Hug a tree! Be alert for visions the earth offers. Nature contains more mysteries than the intellect can hope to comprehend. When we can see the earth and all verdant life as companions and bearers of sustenance and grounding, we can start to partake of nature's ecstasy. Cities just can't do that for us. Whenever you can, leave them behind. As one patient told me, "Everything I love is at the end of a dirt road."

Meet Your Power Animals and Messengers

The instincts are a far better protection than all the intellectual wisdom in the world.
—CARL JUNG

Animals are in synch with the earth. They don't question nature, as we do. Poet Robert Hass writes that animals are "at home in the world in a way that human beings are not." Just watch a stallion gallop or an eagle take flight. They're in their bodies, in the moment, instinctual. I'll never forget the dramatic photos of elephants fleeing to higher ground hours before the 2004 tsunami devastated parts of Asia. Animals are extremely sensitive and attuned to the earth so perhaps they sensed the vibration of a distant flood. Though two hundred thousand human lives were lost in this disaster, only a small number of animal deaths were recorded because many animals were able to flee and escape the flood. Animals have a sixth sense for danger.

The ancients honored animals, depicting them in cave paintings, on jewelry, and through totem carvings. Native Americans attribute distinct powers to different animals. For instance, the raven is a trickster whose power, both positive and destructive, must be tamed for the good, what's known as "raven knowledge." Bears convey healing and courage. Owls are associated with wisdom and death. The white buffalo—a creature so rare, it appears in only about one in ten million births—is considered holy, and according to Lakota legend, the birth of one signals new hope and awakening for our planet. People come from all over the world to visit it and pray.

Shamans say that each of us is born with a power animal, a guardian (similar to an angel) that provides protection and guidance.

You've always been watched over, hard as it may be for the linear mind to accept. Teddy bears are a miniature version of this. Children and some adults (my eighty-year-old male friend is crazy about his) hug theirs for security all night long. I hug my white seal every night! Don't hold yourself back or be too "grown-up" if you want to do this too. It nurtures your inner child but more, each power animal has attributes that complement our emotional makeup. A lion is not necessarily more powerful than a mouse. For one patient, a testosterone-overcharged hockey player, it's a deer to teach him gentleness. Another corporate attorney who lives in the fast lane has a turtle which embodies patience and the value of moving slowly. By connecting to your animal, say, a jaguar, you are aligning with the spirit of all jaguars—mind-blowing archetypal energy as Carl Jung called it.

How do you identify your power animal? First, notice which animals you are drawn to or which are drawn to you. Think back to your childhood. Was there one animal who was protective or consoled you? In your life now, spend time with a friend's dog, cat, horse, or rabbit. See how you relate. Or walk in nature—observe butterflies, hummingbirds, egrets, lizards, whatever happens to cross your path. Also, look at photos and videos of domestic and wild animals. Does one pique your curiosity or make you happy? Do you feel a kinship with, say, a whale, a coyote, or an iguana? Which creatures do you love for absolutely no reason at all? In addition, you can request your power animal to appear during meditation or in a dream. No forcing, no expectations—simply see what arrives and welcome it. Keep learning from your animal and surrendering to its power. This will ignite your wilder, instinctive side, fortifying your life force.

My patient Jill has an affinity for red-tailed hawks. When she hikes in the canyons there is often one nearby. Recently, while she was cruising down the Pacific Coast Highway in Malibu, a large hawk swooped down past her car window and stared at her with piercing black eyes for several intense seconds. When Jill is confused, harried, or down, she meditates in the canyon and asks the hawk for wisdom (either inwardly or, if she spots one, aloud). For instance, during a painful period, she asked, "How can I save my marriage?" Then she waits, tuning in to the hawk, whose power is her touchstone. While she communes, answers come to her, such as actually seeing the face of a therapist whom Jill then reached out to and who helped her. In the silence, her friend the hawk imparts guidance to solve problems and remove obstacles.

In finding your power animal, you connect to the earth by bonding with her creatures. Keep learning from this animal's traits, whether crafty or fierce, scavenger or hunter. Tapping and surrendering to its power will strengthen and balance you.

My power animal manifests as a flock of white birds which portend auspicious changes for me. I can be walking on the busiest city street and they may suddenly appear winging past buildings and traffic, signaling bounty ahead. Or they can arrive in a dream or meditations. To me, birds feel like the most surrendered of all creatures because they can fly. On Christmas Day I gather a flock of gulls around me on the beach with an offering of bread crumbs. I am graced as they sit quietly in a circle, a delicate strand of gleaming white pearls. I stay very still. I can't get too close without making them disperse into the sky, so I sit there as long as they will, surf pounding, receiving the sacrament of these peaceful beings. Even as flocks of white birds have, at different times, guided my life I suspect they will also escort me on my final passage to distant places of unknown light.

Explore Stones, Caves, and Mystical Travel

I marvel at stones and rocks and boulders: the grounding of the earth, conveying the strength of resolve and reliable shelter. I come alive around the red rocks of Sedona and Utah. I was awed by the crystal-clear rover photos of red rocks populating the surface of Mars. I relish having a stone in my hand when I walk in the hills, feeling it solid in my palm. I find it comforting in different ways than the fluidity of water. I can hold on to a stone, put it in my pocket, and find it again. When my book *Emotional Freedom* was first released, I wrote the title on a piece of paper and placed it beneath a stone for safekeeping in Topanga Canyon, a perfect launch into the natural world before I toured the world of cities.

I also feel a strong attraction to caves. I recommend that everyone find one of his or her own to retreat to. A cave is a natural passage under or into the earth with an opening to the surface. It is a womb of stillness and echoes, of reclusiveness, of subdued light and sound. You silently hibernate and heal there, get yourself together, intuitively tune in to confusing issues in your life and surrender to visions.

I was captivated watching the 3-D film *Cave of Forgotten Dreams* about the magnificent Chauvet Cave in France. In this cavernous, darkened space amid glowing stalactites are the world's oldest recorded cave paintings. Depicting nature and all her creatures, these paintings were created over thirty thousand years ago. Cave art is primal and reverent. I too long to paint on cave walls—to mix pigments of earthen color in praise of the life-forms that bless twenty-first-century earth.

Throughout time, spiritual masters have lived in far-off caves located in a mystical geography, findable not through ordinary maps but only through the compass of the heart. What these people of power do there is mysterious, unspoken, a different way to be that's based on quietude. In our own way, we can emulate this in daily life.

When I'm writing a book, I go into cave mode much of the week, cocooned by solitude and a safe, airy, still environment where I can stare into space, hear inner voices, and create. My home office, where I write, is my cave, though I meditate in a favorite cave in Topanga Canyon too. I also look forward someday to experiencing the glistening crystal caves of Pennsylvania and Arkansas. Especially when I feel overwhelmed, hurt, or in need of healing, I make my bedroom into a cavelike space, perfectly dark and soundless or I retreat under the covers beneath a tent of blankets and sheets, hidden from everything.

I urge you to find one or many cave hideaways for yourself. It may be in nature but it can also be a place in your home or even in your own mind. If you're stuck, overwhelmed, in need of healing, or otherwise stressed out, simply taking a few moments to visualize a cool, restful cave can transport you to a place of peace and power. It makes me happy that Ovid's quote about caves is carved on a bench by the

Los Angeles Central Library: "My palace, in the living rock, is made by Nature's hand; a spacious pleasing shade, which neither heat can pierce, nor cold invade." Caves provide primordial havens to leave worldly concerns behind and surrender to your most ancient self.

If you wish to search for a cave or explore earth's other sacred sites, I strongly advocate traveling. If you want to expand your mind and visionary capacity, it is a must to take periodic breaks from your routine, including bills, repairs, and other demands.

My friend Michael Crichton, the late author, wrote a marvelous book, *Travels*, in which he describes how he uses travel as therapy to cure creative blocks, depression, and small ways of thinking. In one chapter, Michael recounts our experiences in the 1980s at a retreat in a remote California desert with Brugh Joy, a physician turned spiritual teacher. At Sky High Ranch, with no phones or no contact with the outside world, Michael and I learned about energy fields and experienced ecstatic, loving states of consciousness that forever raised the bar for who I wanted to be as a woman and physician. This was my initiation into the possibilities of healing beyond conventional medicine. Afterward, Michael and I shared the continuing adventure of how to sustain these revelations at home in Los Angeles.

In my recent travels, I visited the stone formations of Avebury and Stonehenge in southern England one summer. Following an intuition workshop I gave at St. James Church in London, a friend and I drove through the gleaming golden countryside to Avebury, a small town on a winding fairy-tale road. We picnicked on a blanket encircled by massive Neolithic stones believed to have been set in place four thousand years ago for ceremonial purposes. Unlike Stonehenge, which was breathtaking but cordoned off and filled with tourists, Avebury—the oldest stone ring shrine in existence—was uncrowded and intimate. As I stood barefoot in the grass by these forty-ton stones, the seer in me rose up to touch their noble, ancient presences: to remember myself, to reclaim a time when nature informed my movements, my breath, my heart. Resonating through my palm, I felt the thunder and rain of the ages, perhaps even as the stones do themselves. Mother, Father, God, my body, my spirit, and the earth are one—nothing less than this integrated self will fulfill me.

Stones are patient and enduring. They contain the wisdom of time. Let yourself intuitively feel it. In our hectic world, we're often unaware of the holiness we've lost. We've sacrificed too much at the altar of technology and the linear brain. As William Wordsworth put it, civilization can be "too much with us." Stones can remind us of who we once were and what we can be if we stay close to nature's pulse.

Mystical travel helps you surrender, makes you whole in ways psychotherapy alone never can. The land itself conveys messages and healing when you can surrender to its intuitive transmissions. I encourage you to be aware of places that are drawing you and to travel there. Then discover the meaning that awaits you. A location's history is fascinating, but go further than recorded facts in order to experience what that piece of earth has to convey. The land downloads memories, prayers, emotions—all that has taken place there, past and present. I'm asking you to expand how you see things. Be mindful of intuitions, dreams, and parts of yourself that suddenly make sense and come together.

For example, I was pulled to travel to the sacred mountaintop site of Delphi in Greece just so I could dream there. Dreaming in different parts of the world can convey different kinds of wisdom. You may have an idea of what you'll find but you actually must make the trip to fully experience it. More than three thousand years ago, the oracles' prophecies guided kings and communities. My own dreams at Delphi tapped into that visionary motherlode. They revealed new depths of self-awareness and crystallized past connections to an epoch when intuition played a central role in culture. Dreaming in Los Angeles and dreaming in Delphi have their distinct qualities mediated by the legacy of the land and its past.

The earth is not an inert mass. She has energy, lessons, and mysteries to impart to everyone. The earth feels at one with each of us even if our minds are too distracted to pick up on it or reciprocate that communion.

CENTER YOURSELF WITH THE EARTH

Cars, noise, and telephone cables matting the sky can divorce us from what is natural. When you're overwhelmed or tired, or when you crave more contact with the earth, try these strategies. Give in and enjoy them.

- *Go barefoot.* Touching the earth with your feet is literally and energetically grounding. Go barefoot at home or in your garden, dance barefoot, massage your feet with oil, warm them on rocks. Personally, I don't much like wearing shoes. High heels have always seemed beyond me, wobbly and too hard to walk in though they can look sexy. I'm often barefoot at home, drive barefoot, take my shoes off under the table in restaurants, and adore foot massage and pedicures. Our feet are earthy parts of us that give pleasure.

- *Practice being a tree in meditation.* Sitting in meditation is a lifeline to your center and to the earth. Close your eyes. Focus on your breath. Visualize yourself as a tree with roots extending below ground. Then gently reach your awareness downward through soil, rock, and minerals. From the base of your spine begin to feel a continuity with the earth. Whether you meditate for five minutes or an hour, allow this rootedness to stabilize you.

SURRENDER TO WATER

Mine, O thou lord of life,
send my roots rain.
—GERARD MANLEY HOPKINS

The element of water epitomizes surrender. Water is impressive because it can take any shape. It is yielding, reaches its goal by flowing, fills up every depression, and is able to erode what's rigid. It's cleansing and also puts out fires and prevents drought. Daoists say that superior men and women follow its example in life. My daily mantra, one I suggest to patients, is "flow like water." I strive not to resist or argue with what is, even if a situation isn't ideal. I don't want to fight my emotions, people's toxic personalities, or negative forces that could pummel me. When a monster wave is about to crash on you, it's wise to slide under the surface beneath the foamy turbulence. Remember this as an example of how to relax with life's intensities. If you struggle, you risk being harmed. Thus, I am devoted to learning to flow with suffering and adversity so I don't exacerbate them by constricting—and to flow with bliss so I can relish it.

The ocean is one of my primary relationships. When I'm writing, I often spend more time with the water than I do with people. The roar of the surf is the sound of surrender to me, a roar our primordial ancestors also heard. I listen to the waves breaking as they release themselves to the shoreline over and over again, never holding back, centuries of waves marking time's passage with certitude. I often walk to the far end of the Venice Beach pier by my home to watch the surfers. It juts out thirteen hundred feet from the shore. My perspective is beyond the waves which allows me to look back at dozens of surfers from behind. It's sublime: the water swells, their bodies push off, then, in complete balance, they go with the wave. Surfers know the ocean is more powerful than they are. They don't dominate the wave but make love to it. Waves are energy moving through the water. My surfer friends say that when they surf, they blend with a force greater than themselves, never forgetting that the ocean could destroy them if they aren't surrendered enough. For me, surfing is spirit in motion—that's what makes it hypnotic and ecstatic to watch and to do.

Water teaches us how to surf life's rapids without tensing up. When you can trust this and stay fluid, you'll always be taken where you need to go. Of course, you use all your brainpower to make the right choices. However, along with logic, be mindful to choose what's in the flow so you don't go against nature and suffer. Value people and situations that organically come to you without forcing them to fit. When something flows, it's a good indicator of what's meant to be. For instance, choose the appealing romantic prospect who's on your doorstep smiling, not the unavailable mystery person you're trying to make fall in love with you. Or accept the nice job you're offered rather than spinning your wheels fixating on the "better" one that's unattainable for the moment, despite all your efforts. We often misjudge what is "better" for us when our egos obsessively attach to a desire rather than soberly intuiting what is right.

Enjoy the Physicality of Water

The ways of water are so relevant to us since water constitutes two-thirds of our bodies, bathes our cells, and covers more than 70 percent of the earth's surface. Water is made of two hydrogen atoms and one oxygen atom, a basic configuration for life. It manifests as liquid, solid, or gas—drinking water, a snowflake, an icicle, a fog bank, sweet rain, a dewdrop, a tear. Sweating allows us to stay cool and break fevers. When I was growing up, my mother had me inhale steam to clear congestion if I had a cold, an effective old-fashioned remedy. Today, steam showers and saunas are known to help respiratory infections and give us clearer skin as well as being a sensual delight. Water hydrates, heals, lubricates, and protects our organs so our bodies can be healthy.

We humans and most organic life evolved from the sea, our original home. Our bodies never forget this, no matter how "advanced" we become. In fact, our blood contains minerals similar to those in ocean water. We spend our first nine months after conception developing in amniotic fluid until we can survive independently. (Interestingly, many midwives consider water births to be the most natural, least traumatic transition from the womb to the world.) Further evidence of our watery nature is that fluids in the brain and spinal cord, or "tidal body," ebb and flow. Stress accelerates these rhythms; meditation slows them.

The link between water and home is hardwired into our biology. For some creatures, the instinct to return to the sea is compelling. I bore witness to this while watching the breathtaking sight of hundreds of tiny baby turtles hatching in synchrony on a pristine Costa Rican beach. (Their mothers leave after laying the eggs.) In the first moments of life, they fiercely struggle to break out of the shell. Then, as if guided by radar, the turtles instinctively start crawling en masse toward the turquoise ocean hundreds of feet away—a Sisyphean trek for these quarter-inch newborns, and one that took about a half hour. A group of us volunteered to protect them by throwing rocks at swarms of vultures poised in the air ready to swoop down and eat them. We each shepherded several turtles at a time to the water's edge, a job the locals usually perform with great affection. Once the turtles reached the ocean, they sailed away on the currents which lovingly drew them in. So we said our goodbyes and watched them disappear out to sea.

Not only is water present on earth but it has been prevalent throughout almost all of the universe's existence. We all know that NASA has been searching for water as a sign of life on Mars. Did you also know that scientists recently discovered a gigantic cloud of water vapor around a quasar twelve billion light-years away? It contains over one hundred trillion times more water than all of our oceans combined. Try to let the marvel of that sink in. Water is a common element that unites interstellar life.

Discover the Spiritual and Intuitive Nature of Water

Water's physical assets are complemented by its spiritual and intuitive properties. The ancient Egyptians and Christians linked water to spirituality and consciousness. Both used baptism to wash away impurities and as preparation to open to spirit. Similarly, in the Jewish tradition, ritual immersion in water is called a *mikva*. It is thought to purify a bride before her wedding. The Druids of Europe and the Shintos of Japan believed that bodies of water were consecrated openings to inner worlds and they performed holy ceremonies there. Seers from many cultures have gazed into watery reflections, whether in a pond or in a teacup, to glimpse the future and, some say, contact the dead. Since childhood I've instinctually gazed into water for answers, not always knowing what I'm asking, but insights do come. I also get great pleasure seeing the night sky reflected on rivers, the sea, or even puddles in the street: having water, the moon, and the stars merge is my version of paradise. Numerous healing traditions consider water to be sacred. Christians bless themselves with holy water. Native peoples use water to purify themselves. In my Daoist practice, twice a month I bless a glass of water with prayer and lovingkindness, then drink it for renewal, a lovely ritual I have been practicing for over twenty-five years. I do this on the nights of new and full moons, auspicious times for spiritual development that mark the beginning and completion of cycles.

Water can also provide protection. When you are stressed or dealing with draining people, mindfully drink water (don't just gulp it down) and take a bath or shower to cleanse negativity from your system. Plus, you can visualize placing a body of water between you and someone toxic, such as an anger addict. This creates a buffer that prevents his or her anger from cutting into you. For daily purification and rejuvenation, I recommend immersing yourself in water whether in a tub, in a Jacuzzi, or, when possible, in the ocean or mineral springs.

In addition, water is a perfect conduit for intuition. I call my shower my "psychic phone booth." As one patient says about her shower, "This is where I see the lights." When I stand under a stream of warm water, completely letting go in those luxurious moments, it has consistently sparked potent intuitions and creative breakthroughs over the years. Surrendering feels more natural to me in water than in any other place. My mental chatter recedes into a dreamlike state. It's much harder to worry in a shower! Water just isn't conducive to obsessive thinking. Rather, it quiets our thoughts, lets the intuitive forces in us emerge, and washes stress away. One friend says that when she feels emotionally stuck, taking a shower allows her to cry and release pent-up feelings. Water is soothing to our muscles and minds so we can see in more expanded ways.

In my travels, a heavenly location I visited is the public water temple in Glastonbury, England (the goddess's Isle of Avalon in Celtic lore). Mercifully, only silence was allowed. The instant I stepped into this candlelit, cavernous gray stone building and heard the rushing water echoing everywhere, I felt more fully myself. Though the structure itself (previously a reservoir station) was on street level, I felt like I'd entered an underground portal. Spring water streamed down the walls, surging in free fall onto parts of the stone floor, silken moisture in the near-darkness. Beatific-looking young men with ponytails quietly tended the many altars of flowers recessed in stone. Swept into this sensual otherworldliness, I remained in a suspended state of wonder for who knows how long. That day, I surrendered to the liquid stillness and the deep solace of home.

Let water inspire you to flow with larger forces than your ego or linear mind. Just as all rivers flow into the ocean, make your life about gravitating toward a higher consciousness. A single dewdrop on a petal can carry you there. Pay attention to water. Abandon yourself to how it flows. Savor the smell of rain, the whispers of fog, the calm of a glowing lake. Taking in these ecstasies of nature will make your inner light brighter.

In the following exercise I'd like you to apply the wisdom of water to your daily life. Let water teach you about surrender and how to face adversity and uncertainty with ease.

PRACTICE FLOWING LIKE WATER

When you encounter a block or lack clear direction about the future, use these strategies. They'll help you release tension, remain flexible, and find an answer.

- *Observe water.* Spend time sitting by a stream, a waterfall, the ocean, a fountain, or any other body of water. If one isn't nearby, watch a video of water. Observe the naturalness of how currents glide around obstacles, the rhythmic ebb and flow of tides. Also, notice how still water can become. This is the kind of ease with which to approach a dilemma.

- *Solve a problem.* Ask yourself, "How can I flow with a situation the way that water flows? For example, "Can I be less rigid and compromise more with my spouse? Can I step back and let a project develop momentum instead of forcing progress? Can I say yes more often to good opportunities that organically come to me?" Instead of tying yourself into knots or trying to overcontrol an outcome, keep practicing flow.

- *Surrender to not knowing.* In periods of change, uncertainty, or chaos—say, during a divorce or a health crisis—flow is essential. Accept uncertainty; don't fight it. Resistance only causes suffering. Anxiety constricts flow. Faith enhances it. This surrender involves trusting that a solution will be revealed. For now, focus on what you do know, such as "I need to be there for the children" or "I must consult a pain specialist." Also observe options that come spontaneously or evolve from your efforts to reach out. Keep assessing which ones feel good in your gut. Go with these. When you relax, pieces of the puzzle come together as the future makes itself known. Then surrendering to "not knowing" can be fun.

SURRENDER TO AIR

....

I was reaching for the sky just to surrender.
—LEONARD COHEN

As a baby lying in my crib, I recall being drawn upward into the air, to look at the sky, moon, and stars outside my window. There was a force above that I understood and which understood me. What lay horizontal, what was right before my eyes, including the world of people and the parents I loved, didn't have the same instinctive fascination or sense of safety for me. I've always felt more a daughter of the stars than of this sphere.

What is air? Though it physically refers to our atmosphere which mostly consists of nitrogen and oxygen, precious gases we breathe, I extend its scope to outer space and the infinity deep within you. Our atoms (and all atoms) are more than 99.9 percent empty space, and scientists postulate that we may be made of stardust too. Amazing! Just as the universe is constantly expanding at the speed of light, we too have the impulse to expand our consciousness beyond known horizons. Air gives us enough room and time to become who we yearn to be. It provides an openness around everything so we don't feel claustrophobic. Especially during periods of disappointment or when you're down on yourself, it creates a spaciousness in you that is pregnant with possibility.

Surrendering to air takes different forms. First, it means allowing yourself to experience the vastness of your spirit. In Sanskrit, *akasha* is the space or "ether" from which both mortals and immortals arise, the spiritual substance of creation. Focusing on air links you to this and the boundless space and love around you, a truth that's easy to forget with life's demands. Here's how to train yourself to remember. Each day, make it a point to look up at the sky, the clouds, and the heavens. Say hello to Brother Sun and Sister Moon, as St. Francis called them. This reminds you that you're more than the material world and that "more" is incredibly beautiful. Sometimes I remember this by dancing to the Beatles song "Across the Universe," moving and twirling to the cosmic rhythm. My friend and colleague Edgar Mitchell, the Apollo 14 astronaut, stunningly describes his spiritual awakening on his journey home from the moon. Watching the earth rise from space, he experienced *samadhi*, an ecstatic sense of oneness with all existence which forever transformed his perspective on life. Similarly, as we surrender to the awe of witnessing the cosmos, we can know that exhilarating sense of oneness too.

Exploring your inner cosmos also expands your consciousness. One way I enjoy doing this, and which I suggest to you, is regularly letting the mind wander to the invisible, airy spaces between things. For minutes or more, I unfocus my eyes and just stare into space. In this surrendered state, you're not thinking or logically solving problems, just drifting somewhere powerful if you can forget about yourself long enough to go with it. Such "spacing out" or daydreaming transports you to a limitless inner realm, sparks your intuition, and provides entrée to parallel universes of imagination.

How to Levitate Above Problems and Fears

Another benefit of surrendering to air is that it imparts a lightness of being, the antidote to getting overly serious, intense, or heavy. A conflict can't always be solved at its own level. To rise about the plane of problems, you must know how to become light like air, a practical tool I teach patients and use myself. To get the hang of this, observe balloons, bubbles, or clouds floating in the sky. Notice how effortlessly they move, never hurrying or erratic; this is a state we can learn from. (In that spirit, I love what my friend Ann, a Zen romantic, says about the lightness of our friendship: "It's like two beautiful balloons hanging out together.")

Though it's easier to feel light when you're happy, this is a wise strategy to use during tense times too. When you catch yourself bearing down, wanting something or someone too much, that's your cue to mimic air. Instead of continuing to press your nose against the glass of a door that hasn't opened yet, try levitating a little. Picture yourself twenty feet or more off the ground. Then observe the situation as if you were a bird—or an angel—from a higher, more surrendered viewpoint.

From a spiritual orientation, nothing is ever just about a career or a person or a goal. What's paramount is how we interface with a force larger than ourselves to coalesce the positive in our lives. Evoking and surrendering to air lets you rise higher to get a reality check on any situation. You're never as limited or alone as it may seem. With a wider skyscape, you can see the possibilities and protection that have always been there.

The Magic of Cloud Interpretation

Watching clouds can show you how to become lighter. Clouds are made of water droplets and ice crystals sailing in the sky. Feathery cirrus clouds are the highest. Cumulus clouds cruise in the middle and look like giant cotton balls. Low-lying stratus clouds resemble bedsheets. When they touch the ground they become fog. I'm an avid cloud watcher and belong to the Cloud Appreciation Society (trust me, it's a real club). Clouds are graceful, ever changing, always surrendering to different forms.

I am a proponent of cloud interpretation, the art of finding wisdom in their shapes and movements. Clouds can appear as the thinnest of sensual veils, or as dragons, angels, or whimsical creatures of yore. Similar to a Rorschach test in which our interpretations of inkblots reveal aspects of our psychology, clouds can reveal our deepest longings, fears, and motivations. Sometimes I ask patients to share what they see in clouds for me to interpret. One architect who was phobic of swimming saw horrible sea monsters in storm clouds. In therapy, knowing this helped him uncover and heal a childhood trauma—an accident in which he nearly drowned. Another patient who was uptight about starting a demanding job with long hours saw a giant golden chariot cloud. Envisioning herself riding in it made her feel free at work. In the same way, notice what you see and feel when you look at clouds. Let yourself play. Whatever you discover, evaluate what the meaning is for you. Cloud formations reflect the dark and light of your emotions and soul. They're both a part of you as much as all of nature is.

To achieve a lightness of being, imitate the movements of clouds. Here's what I mean. When you experience worry, fear, or anxiety, picture them drifting across the sky like clouds, not attaching to the feeling. Do the same with all difficult emotions. Keep breathing slowly and deeply. Let the air of your breath move them along. Practice letting emotions pass in the sky, light as feathers, formed, then formlessly disappearing. Buddhists talk about the coming and going of all things. Thus, try to approach life's fluctuations with a light touch. When you don't hold on too tight but remain cloudlike, surrendering to whatever comes will be easier.

Let the Wind Purify You and Help You Fly

The wind is air in motion, a current blowing in a particular direction. Global wind patterns are elegantly governed by a combination of solar radiation, ocean currents, landmasses, and the earth's rotation. The interconnectivity of the natural world is secured by a sensual balance of elemental forces.

Wind can be purifying, clearing debris from the land, streets, and the atmosphere. It provides circulation for our inner and outer environments. After a windstorm at the beach, it's spectacular to see pristine white sand without a single footprint, untouched by humans or gulls, a clean slate to begin again. The wind can also be destructive as during hurricanes, tornados, and the warm Santa Ana or "devil winds" that bring wildfires to the dry Chumash canyons in Malibu. Since I was a girl, I've been drawn to roam around during the Santa Anas. I become alive watching them whip through eucalyptus trees, blowing tumbleweeds down deserted city streets. These winds are seductive, unsettling, conveying an edge of danger.

Surrendering to the wind means letting its power rush through and purify you. Environmentalist John Muir climbed to the top of a fir tree in Yosemite in midwinter just to experience what the wind felt like. A naturalist and mystic, he was connecting with the energies of nature.

In your life, you can call on the energy of the wind to clear blocks from your system. Be aware of the soft breeze caressing your face and allow that gentleness in. Also go outdoors during gusty winds without resisting them. Let the surge of air rush through you and muss up your hair. Feel yourself getting lighter, more youthful, carefree. Imagine your fears and troubles being purged, no longer a burden. The wind can help you let go if you are ready. Consciously surrender your struggles to the wind in gratitude.

The wind and flying are connected. I was a child when I first dreamed I could fly. It was pure bliss. Each time, at the onset, my little feet would start running down a wide-open plain until a gust of wind would lift me up barely an inch from the ground—but just enough to provide the momentum to thrust me skyward. After that boost from the wind, my own capacity for flight would take over. The weight of gravity was gone. I'd take off and soar high over hills and valleys, as free in the air as I could possibly be. Often all we need is a jump start to do what we've always had a natural affinity for such as flying, whether it's in your internal sky or in your everyday life. Now you try it. Let the wind help you fly and realize the fullness of your spirit.

LET GO: EXPERIENCE YOURSELF FLYING

Take a few quiet minutes to meditate. Close your eyes. Breathe deeply. Relax your body. Picture yourself walking slowly in an open natural space such as a meadow, then moving faster until you start running. Then feel yourself gently lift off into the air and take flight. It's exhilarating. Savor the pleasure of fresh air gently brushing against your face and hair. Feel your body rise higher at a comfortable speed. Arms outstretched, you glide over oceans, mountaintops, and cities, even into space. Nothing can stop you. You are light. The heavy load has disappeared. Your burdens are gone. Allow yourself to surrender to this ecstasy.

SURRENDER TO FIRE

I want burning.

—RUMI

Fire can help you to surrender to your passion, heat, and aliveness. It inspires you to be on fire about your life, not lukewarm, boring, or disconnected. Surrendering to the fire within conveys to your life force that you honor it. I well understand how life's stresses and demands can make you lose track of your fire. I also know how other people's opinions about how you "should" behave can inhibit you from being your most fiery, wild self. As is true of many patients who begin psychotherapy with me, you may feel "old," "tired," or "without energy"—very real experiences that I've had at various periods too. Still, don't conclude that these states are irreversible. Hear this: no matter your age or the struggles you've endured, your flame is always there, eagerly waiting for you to rekindle it.

What is fire? On a physical level, fire provides warmth and light. It allows us to cook food, a luxury that we may take for granted (evidence of cooked food dates back only 1.9 million years). Burning happens when a combustible fuel such as wood, a candle wick, or coal

is heated up to its "flash point"—such as by the friction of striking
a match—and mixes with oxygen. It's dazzling: when the right elements come together with enough heat, you create fire. Remember
this principle in every area of your life, including team building in
business or when you're launching a project into the world. Don't
hold back. Heat yourself up to your flash point and burn. Be on fire
about your passions.

Our primary source of energy and light is the sun, the life-giving
star at the center of our solar system. Imagine: the earth has been
revolving around it every single day for five billion years. The sun is
on fire but since there's no oxygen, its core burns at fifteen million
degrees from a nuclear reaction, a kind of hydrogen bomb! What boggles my mind is that most of us don't remember to be grateful for the
sun even though our well-being depends on it. In fact, some scientists
believe that when the sun's activity erupts—for instance, with solar
storms—it disrupts the earth's magnetic field. This makes us humans
antsy and jams electronics. Such sun phases have been associated
with political revolutions, epidemics, major technological snafus, and
increased anxiety and restlessness on a global scale.

The ancients had a profound respect for the sun, making offerings
to the sun god and constructing sundials to track the seasons. Solar
eclipses were seen as events with incredible spiritual power, cause
for reverence and meditation. Many cultures made tributes in ceremonial tombs to the summer and winter solstices (the longest and
shortest days of the year, the sun's highest and lowest points above
the horizon). In Ireland, I visited the cavernous tomb of New Grange.
It was built to view the first rays of the winter solstice sunrise
through a thin aperture in a small pitch-black stone chamber. (We
saw a simulated version since I was there in May.) At the moment the
solstice begins, light peeks through, then floods the room, an achingly
beautiful turn from night to brightness, a new year's omen of hope.
What's exquisite about the solstices is that they strike a perfect balance of planetary light. When one of my workshop participants who
lives in South Africa emailed to wish me a happy winter solstice, she
reminded me that it was the lightest day of the year in the Southern
Hemisphere. Everything is in harmony.

The sun offers us direct experiences of light and power that we must not overlook. To appreciate these, contemplate the grandeur of the sun and our solar system. Though this miracle may be too huge for any of our minds to fully assimilate, your intuition can begin to grasp it when you feel, not think. As with all miracles, the spark of ecstasy is there. Tune in to it. Open yourself. Let yourself experience it. On an intuitive level, no separation exists between you and the universe. Sensing this oneness—the fire in me, the fire in you, the fire in all things—for even a few seconds is the big bang that can break the trance of lethargy. If we don't keep surrendering to the natural world, we risk becoming bland, stagnant, estranged from our own fire. If we do surrender, we'll find passion.

In spiritual terms, fire has profound meaning. For Native Americans, fire represents clearing. Smoke is used to cleanse sacred items such as drums and pipes before ceremonies. Sweat lodges are rites of purification in which a wikiup made of willow boughs faces east to honor both the rising sun and the sacred fire pit where fire keepers heat up the rocks. During the sweat lodge, water is thrown on these hot rocks to create steam, which induces sweat. The purpose is to pray and to contact the spirit realms. Native Americans also believe that fire offers renewal. Just as the mythological phoenix burst into flames, then rose anew from its ashes, out of ashes comes the potential for new growth and ideas. From this perspective, even when your house burns down and you're forced to surrender all your possessions—a literal trial by fire and test of courage—there's always opportunity for rebirth and a better life. I saw this attitude applied firsthand with my close friend Ann who lost her home in the devastating Malibu fire of 1993.

Historically, visionary women have not always had an easy time with the element of fire. In bygone eras pagan priestesses openly celebrated fire festivals and Judaic women have always lit Sabbath candles to welcome the light of God. However, during the Inquisition more than two hundred thousand alleged "witches" (mostly female) were burned at the stake. This nightmarish misuse of fire was aimed at eradicating witches and "cleansing their souls," a desperate attempt to squelch intuitive power by a patriarchal society that was petrified of it. For me and many contemporary women healers, this haunting cellular memory lies subconsciously within us. It's crucial that we identify it as arising from the past. Then we won't let such fear, or people with a "witch-hunting" mentality (I've run into my share of them), stifle our strong voices now.

In many Eastern mystical traditions, our vital life force or kundalini energy is called the "serpentine fire." When you activate this through yoga or meditation, it can feel like a surge of heat that starts at the base of your spine and rapidly rises in a winding snakelike motion up the back and to the head. One patient described it as like "being plugged into a socket and getting lit up like a Christmas tree." To spark your kundalini energy while sitting quietly, meditating, or during yoga, visualize a fire building in your lower spine and moving upward. It's a potent coming alive, a signal to dormant energy in your core to wake up. Whatever you feel—hot, cold, tingly, or electrified— try to let it happen without constricting. Surrendering to these sensations ensures that all your systems are ready to rekindle passion.

Getting in touch with your fire also involves igniting your sexuality, your erotic self, which is wired into the elemental forces. After all, the term "new flame" refers to new love, an evocative expression equating love and fire. There's also the burning of passionate love and loss, including the lingering slow burn of "I haven't gotten over you yet" after a painful, unwanted breakup. However, as I emphasized in Chapter 8, even if you don't have a sexual partner, you can still keep the erotic fire burning brightly simply by staying connected to your own vibrance and to nature. This won't happen if you're constantly in your head or worrying. That's why I'm conveying the passion I feel about connecting with fire and its three sister elements: earth, water, and air. Your linear mind always thinks it has so much to do. But the fire in you yearns to flare and pulse if you permit it. You are spiritual and sexual. You are alive and burning.

Creativity and passion are related. The sun is a creative powerhouse, constantly providing light for new endeavors. When I was blocked in my writing, my Daoist teacher advised, "Look to the sun for inspiration and to the moon for feeling." Wildly in love with both,

I protested, "I always watch them." He said, "Yes, but you're not taking in their power." It was true. I was admiring them from afar but not absorbing their creative oomph. To surrender to creativity, we must be permeable and receptive to imaginative flashes so they can gestate in us. It sensually engages our bodies, not just the eyes. Creativity smiles at our willingness to surrender to that fire. It responds with inspiration and visions, lets the sun rise in us when it seems nowhere to be found.

To explore the element of fire, spend time gazing into the flames of candles and fireplaces, watching lightning, and standing near bonfires. One of my great pleasures is soaking in a bath surrounded by a circle of flickering candles. Also be aware of the power of the sun. Enjoy its variations of light from the brilliant pink of dawn to the violet hues of twilight. Realize, though, that the sun isn't just out there. Visualize it in your belly—a bright, warm, luminous orb. Get into the glow. I see it. I feel your fire. I want you to experience that heat too.

Surrendering to fire means claiming our own radiance. We give off flames just as fire does. Others feel it as the quality of our presence. You must be the flame for yourself and those you encounter. Kindling others' torches feels good. If the whole world turned dark, there would still be no reason to panic because when you can light your own flame, we will see you and each other. One flame is enough to illuminate the world and combat the forces of darkness.

I suggest that you explore what fire means to you. In service to surrender, kneel in reverence to the sun, to fire, to all things red-hot and vibrant. Absorb the heat; emulate it. We all have that radiance in us, a reason to be happy!

IGNITE THE FIRE WITHIN YOU: PRACTICE THE SUN SALUTATION

This series of simple yoga poses will help you surrender to the fire of the sun. In ancient Vedic tradition, the sun was revered as the source of all life. The sun salutation is an act of thanks to the sun and nature. As you gently practice these poses, picture the sun rising before you. Feel the warmth of its rays. Embrace the sustenance of fire.

[Figure 5.] Sun Salutation Yoga Pose

May this chapter be the start of your ongoing love affair with the four elements: earth, water, air, and fire. Let them seduce you into experiencing the sensual essence of existence. Surrendering to the natural world makes you more intimately physical as well as more transcendent. It will further all your goals, including finances, love, health, and success by aligning you with your life force's fire. The skills we've discussed—how to flow like water, ground yourself in the midst of chaos, rise like air above your fears, and ignite your own flame—will give you a tremendous advantage in your career and personal life. People will be more attracted to you. You'll make smarter moves and experience the growing sense of ecstasy that comes from letting go.

I challenge you to test out the techniques I suggest so that you can learn from nature. Become partners with your life instead of making it an exhausting wrestling match. Have a momentary lapse of logic: stop protesting the hand you've been dealt, even if it's painful and unfair. Of course you have the right to complain, but if you stay in that place where will it lead? I challenge you to stop trying to tightly control situations and people whether or not things go your way. All storms pass, as do sunny days. Thus, dance with everything, be flexible, lean into the rhythms of the moment to know how to proceed. Befriending nature is one of the biggest wins you'll ever have. Why not start now? No matter where the cycles of life take you, mortal and beyond, you'll have the grace to flow with change.

SURRENDER AFFIRMATION FOR CONNECTING WITH NATURE

Today I will look up at the sky and the stars. I will watch a cloud pass and enjoy the sunlight. I will slow down and observe the beaming beauty of nature. I won't keep it at a distance. I will take pleasure in the sights, smells, and sounds of the natural world. I will appreciate every moment in gratitude.

Part Four

MORTALITY AND IMMORTALITY: CYCLES OF LIGHT

Each body is a lion of courage, and something precious to the earth.
—MARY OLIVER

10

THE TENTH SURRENDER

HARMONIZING WITH ILLNESS AND PAIN

BECAUSE I'M A PHYSICIAN, PEOPLE OFTEN ASK ME, "WHAT'S THE most important factor in health and recovering from illness?" To their surprise, my answer is always surrender. They are expecting recommendations that are more conventionally proactive such as diet, the proper medications, or reducing stress—all of potential benefit to wellness. However, surrender must be the engine that drives all choices about healing. Why? Inevitably, your life goes through cycles, some celebratory and some painful, some healthy and some not. Still, the way you flow with them, including illness, can make the difference between serenity and suffering. Surrender doesn't mean giving in or giving up. It's accepting a course of action and not constantly second-guessing yourself or obsessing over what you're "doing wrong." Illness is a call to courage and steadfast self-compassion so you can rise higher than fear. Surrender is your chance to triumph over suffering. Instead of checking out of your body during periods of "dis-ease" and leaving it to someone else to "cure," you can live in every molecule of your being and be forever changed in the most incredible ways.

Illness can wake you up physically, emotionally, and spiritually. But it may be a crucible for awakenings you didn't ask for and would've preferred to avoid. That's what happened with my patient Ginger, who at twenty-five was a mover and shaker in the fashion industry. An extroverted party girl, she hobnobbed at chic catwalk events wearing the latest sexy-edgy outfits. She was, understandably, more focused on career, guys, and nightlife than spiritual development. Illness wasn't even on her radar.

One evening, on her way to a club, a drunk driver crashed into her two-seater convertible. Ginger told me, "The next thing I remember was waking up from surgery with a new lower back made of titanium plates and screws. My right leg was paralyzed. I needed a wheelchair." Though the doctors thought Ginger would eventually regain the use of her leg, she plunged into a dark depression, convinced that her life was over. Her devastation was heartrending to me. Ginger was young and had her whole life ahead of her. Now, in an instant, her mortality and scary physical limitations were right in her face—a shocking turnabout for a golden girl. Suddenly Ginger was forced to cope with an unthinkable reality.

Our work with surrender was a turning point. Without it, Ginger was traveling at warp speed into a vortex of despair. After a few weeks of therapy, she recognized that the first step toward surrender was to return to the moment. "Instead of raging against my situation and being a victim, I had to learn to walk again. Once I surrendered to that, I literally took one step at a time. Talk about starting at the beginning!" In that same period, we focused on Ginger surrendering her worst-case scenarios—she was driving herself crazy with fear of becoming an invalid, of losing her job and friends. Fear is the enemy of hope and healing, but it's not insurmountable. Letting go of fear was a huge undertaking for her, as it would be for any of us in that position, but she also knew it was the only good answer she had.

Ginger's recovery taxed her body, her emotions, and her spirit. But it also awakened her faith in herself and a new depth of gratitude. And, for the first time, she called on a spiritual guiding force for strength. All these tools of surrender helped her celebrate each small step she took, rather than ruminating on potential catastrophes. I'm pleased to report that a year later Ginger had achieved a complete recovery. As was true for her, we can either resist illness, rail against it and torment ourselves, or we can surrender to the opportunities for growth and love that are also there. That's our great challenge.

WHAT IS ILLNESS?

Whether you get the flu or require heart surgery, there are always body-mind-spirit components. Physically, illness is an imbalance in your body, a state of "dis-ease" that impairs healthy functioning such as infection, cancer, diabetes, or hypertension. It also results from trauma—say, if you break a bone or get a concussion. With fibromyalgia or arthritis you may suffer pain, a signal transmitted to the brain by sensory neurons indicating something is "off" in a part of your body. On an emotional level, dis-ease might manifest as depression, panic attacks, or other psychiatric diagnoses (though these can affect you physically too). With patients I've learned that it's futile to neatly separate the physical from the emotional. They're closely intertwined in every dis-ease.

To heal more speedily, strive to surrender fear. As we'll discuss, pain is especially tricky. Even minor discomfort can trigger dormant memories that require healing. One of my patients simply twisted his ankle but was suddenly flooded with anguish about his wife divorcing him ten years earlier. His ankle was a satellite for another constellation of pain and loss that also needed tending to. Recovering from his injury also involved addressing his unresolved grief about the marriage. Spiritually, illness is a call for your soul to grow. Rugged as this process can be, remember: every illness is an opportunity for compassionate revelations.

As we explore how surrender can accelerate healing, I also want you to be clear about what illness *isn't*. This will help you maintain a positive attitude and stop you from sabotaging your progress. Illness isn't:

- A punishment.

- A sign you're a bad person or not spiritual enough.

- An excuse to torture or hate yourself.

- A cause for shame.

- A reason to give up or close your heart.

- Proof there is no God.

Fundamentally, the basis for healing is compassion. You might not always get there, but moving toward it is what counts. Keep trying. As the saying goes, "God helps those who help themselves." Even if you've never taken good care of your health, illness is your chance to surrender old habits and start anew—to eat well, to stop smoking or abusing alcohol, to exercise, to meditate, to listen to your body's signals, to live in the moment. I believe that the purpose of being human is to heal ourselves whether or not we've been diagnosed with an illness. When you're sick, it's natural to feel afraid, lonely, or despondent but surrender is an ongoing compassionate practice of not letting negative emotions control you.

Illness asks you to love yourself and your body more than you ever thought possible. If an organ gets a disease, treat it like a wounded friend, not like an enemy who's betrayed you. During dialysis a patient said, "I'm focusing less on 'fighting' kidney failure and more on loving the 'soft animal' that is my body," referring to a poem by Mary Oliver. Another patient who had a hysterectomy asked, "What if my uterus is removed?" My response: "Love the space that is there."

If you require medications, try to mercifully accept this instead of fighting it or feeling you're weak or that you've failed spiritually. Remember that God is in the laboratory with the scientists who discovered the medications that are helping you, just as God is everywhere else. Of course, you want to be discriminating about medications and careful not to overuse them, but the compassion you have about your choices can determine your serenity.

During a health challenge or if pain remains no matter what you do, loving your body can seem impossible. But that conclusion isn't accurate. Truly, we're never given more than we can handle. I want to fully acknowledge that this may be a hard concept to accept, let alone to surrender to. You will keep grasping the truth of it more deeply in the longer term as you build faith and see proof of your capacity to cope and grow. Still, it may not appear this way in the beginning, when life feels like more than you can bear. This sense of hopelessness, of being worn down and fragile, worsens if you're attempting to go it alone without reaching out to friends for support or if the treatments you've tried aren't working. Your reaction is human and understandable. That's why it's crucial to get the right kind of spiritual and medical guidance, particularly if chronic pain has beaten you into submission or you're depressed.

Over the years, I've been privileged to rescue many patients from the edge by holding the hope for them when they've lost it. Still, I appreciate how our limited egos, our "small selves," can resist owning our strengths in the face of illness. The ego's negative dialogue about illness and pain adds a layer of judgment that causes suffering on top of the discomfort that's already there. Since the ego alone is often no match for a daunting illness, it's understandable to feel "I'm overwhelmed and angry. It's unfair. I've been suffering for too long." Justifiable as this reaction is, it's not going to help you much. To deal with illness effectively, you have to gain a wider perspective. How? By surrendering the ego and drawing courage and healing from a deeper source. I'll show you ways to activate your "large self," which has a direct line to spirit, a therapeutic alliance that changes everything. Then your power will surge and you'll have more resources to draw on. Over the years, there's been so much that I thought I couldn't handle, but in retrospect, when I expanded into my larger self, I saw that I could, and was better for the experience.

Sometimes the only way to surrender to illness or pain is one moment at a time. Surrender means knowing *you are not just your diagnosis, your genes, your pain, your addiction, or even your body*. You are a radiant soul becoming more radiant from the compassion you develop. The surrender I'm suggesting is to harmonize with illness and pain, not to resist them, a Daoist practice you'll learn that facilitates healing. *Resistance can amplify suffering whereas flowing with symptoms diminishes them.* This will allow you to stay close to your radiance and view illness as a passage to greater heart and light.

I'm clear about what conventional medicine knows as well as what it doesn't know. If you have a heart attack, a broken hip, or appendicitis, you need to be under the care of a conventional physician. Science has made many stunning advances—such as cancer diagnosis and treatment, arthroscopic surgery that spares you the stress of general anesthesia, and laser therapies to preserve sight. It would be foolish to ignore them. However, as we'll discuss, there is so much that conventional medicine doesn't understand including intuitive and energy healing along with other valuable complementary therapies such as acupuncture, yoga for flexibility, meditation, and chiropractic adjustments. Illness is an opportunity to access an infinite matrix of healing energy via both conventional and complementary modalities.

In this chapter, we'll explore the role of surrender in health and recovery from illness. When do you surrender to illness? When do you refuse to succumb to symptoms? How can intuition and spirituality help you heal? What's the difference between pain and suffering? What is resistance and how can you overcome it? Are you a hypochondriac or an empath who absorbs other people's symptoms? Are you addicted to doctors? How can you tap in to your own self-curative powers? While we'll focus on physical illness, we'll also address the emotional elements of healing—for example, tears are a healthy way to surrender. As you learn to harmonize with disease, you can heal faster with less effort.

Healing is all about flow and courage. It's about believing in yourself and the regenerative capacity of your body. As the Chinese ideogram suggests, crisis is an opportunity. I hope you take this opportunity to find the true power in yourself that you didn't know you had. And if a loved one is ill, you can help that person find his or her own power too. Let illness *refine* your heart, not *define* you. Let illness help you surrender fear. My spiritual teacher says, "If it is true gold, you need not fear the furnace."

PREPARING TO HEAL:
THREE STRATEGIES TO REMOVE EMOTIONAL AND
PHYSICAL CLUTTER

Setting a clear intention to heal prepares you for many surrenders along the way that can hasten your recovery. As part of this process, it's essential to examine your attitude, the people around you, and the quality of your physical space. Once you start to remove emotional and physical clutter, you'll more readily tap in to the mighty healing forces awaiting your call.

Strategy 1. Unclutter Your Mind: Open to Spirit, Surrender Fear

The mind has the power to think positively or negatively. The direction you choose can shape your healing. *All thoughts aren't created equally. Some are more aggressive than others and take up more space in your psyche.* Thus, if you indulge fear, a master seducer that preys on your doubts, there will be less room for hope, faith, and love. It's hell to be trapped in the snarled confines of a fearful mind. Summon all of your resolve not to stay there. Even when you think you can't do it, even when the dark is all you see, you *can* and you *must*. While legitimate fears warn you of danger so that you can avert it—say, if a hurricane is headed your way—more often unproductive, worry-based fears about illness defeat your healing instinct.

It can be useful to think about the word *fear* as an acronym for "false evidence appearing real," a grand illusion of the linear mind. I will train you to call its bluff. Fear is so seductive because the future appears real even though it hasn't happened yet. Do your best to resist it using this chapter's techniques. The unfortunate snowball effect is that fear triggers your body's biological stress response, flooding your system with cortisol and adrenaline, which increase anxiety and decrease your immunity—not what you want to have happen when you're recovering from an illness or trauma. Worry, a form of fear, is just the mind's attempt to control the future. Surrender is the antidote to worry since it keeps you in the moment rather than obsessing about hair-raising scenarios that could happen.

Uncluttering your mind requires a daily commitment to surrendering fear by letting it pass over' and through you as you increasingly open to spirit. One astute patient told me, "Being raised by an out-of-control alcoholic dad was a boot camp for surrender. A child in my situation either curls up in a ball and stays angry at the world or, like me, decides that there is a greater power at work and everything happens exactly as it is supposed to. I have spent my life holding on to this truth and living it." Similarly, spirit can help you rise above intense physical and emotional trials too. The more you practice the next exercise, the faster you will heal.

SURRENDER TO THE HEALING POWER OF SPIRIT

When fear or discomfort arises, you need to make a spiritual connection. First, take a few deep breaths to relax. Close your eyes and repeat this mantra: "I am not just my fear or pain. I am larger." Then also connect with a loving force greater than your fear or pain. Your heart is about to expand beyond your discomfort as you merge with infinite love. No longer must you do everything by yourself. Help is here. Surrender to the warmth, to the light, to protection. Let this well-being infuse you with the courage to be positive. The spiritual world contains healing that goes beyond the linear mind. Let it lift you above your fear and sorrow. Stand in the place where the light is strong. Let yourself be saturated. The light can reverse the stranglehold of fear and create miracles. Return to it again and again on your healing journey.

Strategy 2. Unclutter Your Relationships: Surround Yourself with Positive People, Eliminate Energy Vampires

People are medicine, good and bad. To heal, you must be surrounded by those who are loving. When you're ill, you're at your most vulnerable. You deserve to be encircled by people who support you, not those who suck the life force out of you with their fear, anger, criticism, narcissism, or neediness. When my friend Stephan's wife was undergoing treatment for colon cancer he told me, "My job is to create a positive bubble around her and prevent anything negative from intruding." This included people who were draining, complaining, or rude, violent newscasts, and anyone who was cynical about the miraculous role of love and spirit in the healing path of recovery.

His attitude isn't based on any form of denial. Quite the opposite: it's simply an effective intervention to generate positive energy when it's needed most. Similarly, we must create a positive bubble around *ourselves* when *we* are healing.

A key factor in getting well is surrendering to the love of friends and family. As your angels, they emit an intense glow that has the power to make you feel good and soften pain. The more you absorb these vibes, the better you will be. However, if you're not up to socializing or can't field many phone calls and emails, join websites such as www.mylifeline.org (meant for those with cancer) or www.carepages.com to share love at your own pace. My patients have felt supported by reading the caring responses to the posts they or their families have written. Also, they have benefited from offers of help when it was most needed. Love is potent medicine. My Daoist teacher says, "When you live in people's hearts don't be afraid to go through difficult times."

The Option of Surrogate Parenting

Creating a positive bubble around yourself can be sensitive where your parents are concerned. If you haven't received the nurturing you deserve, the situation isn't likely to change when you're ill. Perhaps your parents are alcoholic, abusive, hypercritical, or self-involved, or maybe they just lack the emotional skills to love you unconditionally. Expecting them to suddenly be different sets you up for disappointment. True, some parents are exceptions. However, mostly I've observed that my patients deplete the precious energy they need to recover by hoping their parents will be supportive, then get crushed when they are not. As painful as it may be to surrender to this imperfect reality, it is necessary for your healing. To help you do this, keep repeating this wonderful version of the Serenity Prayer: "God grant me the serenity to accept the parents I cannot change."

Still, the good news is that you can find loving surrogate parents—other mother and father figures who can be there for you no matter what you're going through. For the past two decades, I've been blessed with three surrogate mothers, all supersmart free spirits who accept me as I am, including my intuitive side. Though it's preferable to find a surrogate parent when you are well, if you are ill, it's not too late. There are many unconditionally loving people who will embrace a parenting role. Start to be aware of potential prospects. They could be parents or grandparents of friends, mentors from work, even the supermarket checker with a heart as big as the world. Listen to your intuition. Look for people with open hearts and life wisdom who enjoy being nurturing. Begin to share your feelings and life with them.

Surrender the Energy Vampires

When you're ill, identify energy vampires in your life so they don't steal your vitality and peace of mind. These include guilt trippers, narcissists, and anger addicts (see Chapter 5). If these people are peripheral in your life, such as a hairdresser or handyman, simply stop using them. If you're dealing with a negative friend or family member, try to set clear limits with them by saying in a kind, firm tone, "I need you to be positive around me while I am healing." However, if you depend on these people for help and they aren't likely to change, visualize a capsule of radiant white light around you for protection. This will keep their negativity out so you don't absorb it. Communicate to loved ones that you need them to be supportive and loving. If they can't adhere to these boundaries, you can limit the time you spend together.

Strategy 3. Prepare Your Space: Surrender to
Quiet and Beauty

Your physical environment affects your healing. No matter the square footage, a serene, light-filled, uncluttered home provides the open space you need to get well. A dark, stuffy, noisy, chaotic environment can slow your recovery because you'll be spending energy fighting off unpleasant distractions and stagnant clutter. You won't be able to relax or surrender in peace to the healing forces.

Ancient physicians were much smarter about the aesthetics of health than most of us physicians today. In the fifth century BCE, Hippocrates, the father of medicine, created a healing oasis on the Grecian isle of Cos. The sick recovered there in a quiet, natural setting with soft sea breezes, lulled by the rhythms of the surf. Physicians of that era understood that healing came from the sky, the moonlight, the water. They knew to avoid caustic noise and harshly lit rooms. We all need to learn from this and create peacefulness around those who are sick—or ask for that to be done for us.

The Toxicity of Noise

Intrusive noise is toxic to healing. Research has shown how it can harm your health by increasing stress, insomnia, agitation, hypertension, heart disease, and even birth defects as well as impairing immunity. Thus, you need serenity when you are healing. One workshop participant told me, "We endured two years of horrific renovation in our New York apartment. It made my husband and me exhausted and sick. Plus, to cope with stress, I'd binge on carbs so I was getting fat. And, tragically, an elderly woman died of a heart attack when workmen jackhammered the ceiling below her bedroom."

Though this is an off-the-charts example of toxic noise—there are many lesser kinds, including traffic, sirens, barking dogs, loud televisions, and partying neighbors—I understood her dilemma. While I was writing this book, my condominium complex underwent endless construction. In accordance with my Daoist practice, for a few months I really tried to flow with the jackhammers and the throngs of workmen outside my windows. But it became impossible to write, meditate, or even think. I'm thankful that I wasn't recovering from an illness but I was getting irritable and had started the wretched habit of swearing like a truck driver about the racket. After a while, my empathic system was getting so overwhelmed that I made the painful decision to sell the sanctuary where I'd written all my books.

Of course, it was no coincidence that I was writing a book on surrender. Truly, we teach what we need to learn. My challenge with the move and later was to keep letting go and trusting, even at low points when I questioned, "Did I do the right thing?" Still, I've pledged in my life to trust intuition above all else and not let fear drag me down. This is always the greater spiritual purpose of adversity, loss, and change. The noise started me on a fantastic surrender into the unknown that is still unfolding.

In your life, when you need physical or emotional healing, uncluttering your environment can help. Prepare your living space so that it is as free of toxic noise as possible. When you're in pain or ill, you deserve to at least suffer in peace! One patient recovering from Lyme disease told me, "Noise makes my brain hurt." Another patient with an autistic, epileptic son says, "Too much noise causes him to have a seizure." If you're in a hospital room or receiving outpatient treatments, ask the staff for quiet in your vicinity. One of my patients who was getting a chemotherapy IV drip (which took a few hours) told me, "A man in the clinic, also receiving chemo, was on his cell phone doing business the entire time." This upset her but she felt too ill and awkward to speak up. Certainly the man was entitled to his way of coping—continuing business as usual could've been his lifeline to normalcy. Still, if it were up to me, I would ban cell phones in places where healing occurs—or at least have phone-free areas—so that intrusive chatter doesn't interfere with another patient's right to tranquility. However, I also suggested to my patient that she listen to the mystical chants she loved on her iPod with headphones which improved the situation.

At home, if it isn't always quiet and if moving is impossible, there are solutions. You can get sound-blocking machines that use the sounds of the ocean or rain or other sublime moods of nature to block other annoying noises. To add beauty and comfort, enjoy bouquets of flowers around your space, lovely scents such as gardenia or sandalwood, and soft comforters and sheets. You can also gain strength from talismans such as Native American healing bears or crystals or by burning sage to remove negativity, a ritual used by many indigenous cultures. In my home, I always have a Quan Yin statue with a bowl of fruit and candles. Also, begin to eliminate clutter by clearing off visible surfaces such as kitchen counters or dressers. What you see, smell, breathe in, hear, and touch can improve your well-being.

Surrender to Beauty and Peacefulness

Find a serene place in your home where you can rest and relax. Settle into the stillness as you surrender to the peace and beauty. No rushing. No pressure. Take your time in the space. Breathe in the sweet smells; admire the quality of light, the joyous flowers, the lusciousness of a bowl of fruit. Enjoy soothing music that inspires your healing. Feel reverence for your sacred statues—Quan Yin, Buddha, Jesus, or whomever you resonate with. Meditate. Feel their power and compassion. Absorb the goodness, healing, and rejuvenation that your environment exudes.

PRACTICE THE ART OF SURRENDER IN ILLNESS AND HEALING

Healing
is not a science,
but the intuitive art
of wooing Nature.
—W. H. AUDEN

Healing literally means "to make whole." It is our body's miraculous capacity to regenerate itself when it is wounded, compromised, or in pain. Take a moment to consider the wonder of healing. If you have an infection, armies of white blood cells and the entire immune system rush to the rescue to kill viruses and bacteria. If you cut yourself, platelets rally to form clots and stop bleeding; cells divide to protect injured tissue by covering it and forming scars. If you're in pain, endorphins, opiate-like natural painkillers, kick in to lessen your suffering. We get sick when our bodies are out of balance. This can be from stress or toxins such as nicotine and excessive alcohol, or from factors beyond our control including genetic disorders, cancer, or organ dysfunction (i.e., the pancreas producing insufficient insulin to reduce blood sugar, as in diabetes).

Surrender quickens the healing of disease. It means compassionately accepting the need to tend to imbalances or discomfort in your body instead of resisting, fighting, or denying them. As a physician, I've seen the battering that happens when patients don't surrender during an illness. One man, a type-A fashion photographer I knew, got on a plane to Paris for a *Vogue* shoot right after a chemotherapy treatment for metastatic cancer. He didn't even need the money but he was in serious denial about how ill he was. Not surprisingly, he got worse on the shoot and had to be hospitalized. Sad to say, soon after that he died. Denying illness and not surrendering to the need for self-care make difficult health situations more difficult. You become tense, anxious, and out of touch with lifesaving impulses. You can't relax, breathe, or flow around constrictions in your body so that you can heal.

As counterintuitive as it may seem, softening around discomfort reduces suffering. A basic principle of surrender is that what you resist persists. Harmonizing with (not succumbing to) pain and fear gets you to the other side of them faster. Doing so is saying to these symptoms, "I'll come to you. We'll ride the currents of the painful sensations together." Ironically, becoming one with discomfort is the first step to neutralizing it.

There is a sacred energetic flow to healing. I'll describe how to align with this and how not to be afraid of or disdain blockages that test your health. On a subtle energy level we all have blockages that may not have manifested yet as symptoms but still limit our capacity for radiance. The nature of being human is to be blocked in certain ways. But wellness is predicated on our hunger to heal so we can dissolve blockages and begin to sense the ecstasy that results from the body's energy moving freely. Recovering from illness offers you an opportunity to experience this release, perhaps for the first time.

Visualize the Body as a Plant, Not a Machine

Our ideas about the body need to evolve. Modern medicine has become so technologized and fast-paced that physicians tend to view the body simply as a machine that needs to be fixed. Medicine can make marvelous interventions that aid healing by, say, splinting a broken wrist or using antibiotics to treat stubborn infections but let's be clear: nature does the bulk of the healing and we just offer assistance. That's why I resonate with the work of Hildegard of Bingen, a twelfth-century nun, mystic, and healer who likened the body to a plant that grows, blossoms, and repairs itself. Hildegard called this instinct to self-heal in plants and humans *veriditas* or "greening power." So when Hildegard treated a patient, she focused on what was draining this power and how she could boost it, not on what was broken. Calmly taking small steps, she fortified a patient's inner and outer environment with specific prescriptions for diet, exercise, sleep, medications, and quiet. Then she waited to see what would happen.

Similarly, Dr. Victoria Sweet, a physician whose work is based on that of Hildegard of Bingen, practices what she calls "slow medicine," where doctors write chart notes longhand, pay attention to detail, and revel in a patient's small but daily progress. Dr. Sweet talks about illness as a pilgrimage to learn about spirit and the self. She waits, watches, and intuitively listens to her patients in a free inpatient facility for indigent "castaways" of the world who are suffering from chronic illness—a transcendent journey Dr. Sweet describes in her book *God's Hotel*.

My soul is moved by both of these women from different centuries who urgently help us reclaim the essence of medicine that has been lost in our overzealous quest to quantify the body's functions without honoring the mystery. We must surrender to how much we don't know and to what we can learn from nature. We physicians are but servants to the mystery and to nature. Our sacred duty is to tend to the body and souls of our patients. It is here that the greatest healings arise.

Honor These Natural Surrenders in Your Body

During an illness and always, it's vital to let go to the natural healing forces in the body which I'll outline below. The body wants to mend itself if we can let it do its job. What stops us from surrendering to our innate instincts to heal? Several things: society's uptight, misguided attitudes about what it means to be stoic and strong, our worried overactive minds, our fears of getting lost in pain, and our inhibitions about letting joy in. I want to help you get past these so that your restorative impulses can take over.

Let Go to the Healing of Tears

Tears are your body's release valve for stress, sadness, grief, anxiety, and pain. You also have tears of joy such as when a child is born or tears of relief, as when a difficulty has passed. I am grateful when I can cry. I wish I could do it more. It feels cleansing to purge pent-up emotions so they don't lodge in my body as stress symptoms such as fatigue or pain. To stay healthy and release stress, I encourage my patients to cry. For both men and women, tears are a sign of courage, strength, and authenticity.

Research has shown that tears have many health benefits. Like the ocean, tears are salt water. They lubricate your eyes, remove irritants, and reduce stress hormones and they contain antibodies that fight infection. Our bodies produce three kinds of tears: reflex, continuous, and emotional. Each kind has different healing functions. For instance, reflex tears remove noxious particles from your eyes when they're irritated. The second kind, continuous tears, keep your eyes and nose lubricated. The third kind, emotional tears, stimulate the production of endorphins, our body's natural painkillers which help us recover from trauma. Crying also helps the body excrete stress hormones. Interestingly, humans are the only creatures known to shed emotional tears though elephants and gorillas may do so too.

Crying makes us feel better, even when a problem persists. Along with physical detoxification, emotional tears heal a broken heart. You don't want to hold tears back. Patients sometimes say, "Please excuse me for crying. I was trying not to because it makes me feel weak." I know where that sentiment comes from: parents who were uneasy around tears, a society that tells us we're weak for crying, and in particular that "real men don't cry." Also, we may feel that it's too painful to cry, that floodgates of anguish might open that can't be closed. I reject these notions. The new enlightened paradigm of what constitutes a powerful man or woman is someone who has the strength and self-awareness to cry—and if necessary the willingness to seek support to deal with overwhelming feelings. These are the people who impress me, not those who put up some macho front of faux bravado.

Try to let go of clichéd conceptions about crying. Crying is necessary to work through grief. When waves of tears come over us after we experience a loss, they are helping us process the loss so that we can keep living with open hearts. Otherwise, we are leaving ourselves open to depression, bitterness, or physical symptoms (emotional pain can morph into disease in our bodies) if we suppress these potent feelings. *The point isn't to get consumed by emotional pain but to resolve it.* When a friend apologized for curling up in the fetal position on my floor and weeping over a failing romance, I told her, "Your tears blessed my floor. There is nothing to apologize for." Thank God our bodies can cry. I hope you too can surrender to your tears. Let them purify suffering and negativity.

Let Go to the Healing of Sleep and Dreams

When you're ill you require a lot of sleep. Try not to fight it. Sleep is a natural healing mechanism in your body, and your body knows what it's doing. Surrender to its graces. Listen to how much your body wants to sleep, nap, and dream. If you have insomnia or a head full of worry that keeps you from surrendering to sleep, practice deep breathing and refocus on a soothing image such as the ocean, a daisy, the glowing moon, or butterflies flitting from flower to flower. You can also pray, "May my worries lift," as you turn your problems over to a higher power. This conscious mental refocusing can help you let go. During an illness, do not push through fatigue or force yourself to be "on" when your body needs to hibernate. Your sleep requirements may change on a daily basis. Your body will tell you what you need if you listen closely.

Since childhood, I've felt that during sleep, loving healing forces, in all their tenderness, recognize how vulnerable, tired, or in pain we are. Surrendering to sleep, we let down our guard and are more receptive to the kind of healing that can occur only when the mind and its worldly concerns recede.

Physically, sleep heals you in many ways. It increases immune cell production, protecting you from infection. It recharges the part of your brain that controls emotions, increasing your emotional stamina while awake. In addition, every night you get "beauty sleep"— skin cells regenerate and damage from stress, aging, and ultraviolet radiation is repaired. When you look better, you feel better.

Along with these advantages, sleep is also an opportunity to dream. Train yourself to remember your dreams (a technique I discuss later in this chapter). They provide guidance about health issues or offer healing themselves. I've had patients receive information about which health practitioner to choose, guidance about which types of therapies to explore, and even consoling information to relieve their fears about illness. Emotional solace mercifully comes in dreams. Once, when I felt terribly hurt by a lover, I dreamed that a shawl of forgiving grace was placed over my shoulders. Feeling this profound sense of comfort helped me relax and soften so that he and I could resolve the conflict from a more loving position. Whether dreams are offered spontaneously or you specifically request answers, dreams are committed to supporting your well-being.

Let Go to the Healing of Laughter

Laughter is therapeutic, a balm for body and soul. Being constantly serious during an illness, no matter how challenging the diagnosis, adds heaviness to an already difficult situation. One thing I love about Buddhists is that they laugh and giggle at everything—illness, death, pain, heartbreak—not disrespectfully but with innocence and cosmic lightness about the very real, sometimes excruciating trials of the human predicament. My eightysomething best friend, Berenice (her patients call her a psychotherapist who's really a shaman), was laughing on the phone with me the other day even though she was enduring a grueling health challenge. I asked her, "Why are you laughing?" Unfazed, even cheerful, she answered, "Why not?" Yes, Berenice has courage. But even more, she has lightness in the face of pain, a degree of spiritual attainment I am aiming for in my lifetime, though I still have a way to go.

Laughter is profoundly healing on many levels. Physically, muscular tension loosens, energy increases, fatigue lessens. Emotionally, laughter lifts your mood and softens rigid defenses and worries that keep you uptight and unsurrendered. Studies have shown that laughter elevates our immune response and endorphins, our natural painkillers. It takes the edge off stress, anxiety, and depression, and prevents heart disease. Journalist Norman Cousins, beloved father of laugh therapy, treated his own pain from a life-threatening joint disease with a daily ten-minute dose of laughter.

I routinely prescribe laughter to my patients. It's a surrender to hilarity, a way to get out of your head and into your heart. You're pressing the pause button on problems so you can be silly and carefree. The worried mind can have difficulty allowing you to laugh when there may seem to be no good reason to do so. However, I urge you not to indulge your inner worrier. Its tendency to stay miserable seems logical but it is really off base. My consistent message of surrender is to fight to find the cracks of light in everything—not to succumb to misery even when circumstances are grim. One friend says it well: "I was born with cerebral palsy. I have had many aches and pains. Still, I always found a way to joke about it and not have a pity party. When your desire to live fully is stronger than any pain you experience, laughter pushes you forward." Like my friend, keep surrendering to laughter. Try to respond to illness differently. Let laughter reveal the light that exists in even the darkest places.

MANIFEST THE POWER OF INTUITIVE HEALING

Have you ever known that your health was in danger but ignored the signs your body was sending? Have you ever known a relationship would be abusive but entered into it anyway? If so, you are not alone. Most of us haven't been trained to listen to our intuition and have suffered enormously both physically and emotionally as a result. If you want radiant health or if you're ill, your intuition is the best friend you will ever have. It's there to protect you and further your happiness. At times your life may even depend on it. Healing energy isn't static. It has an undulating movement, flowing into your body's main channels and tributaries, depending on your needs. Intuition lets you surrender to where the healing force wants to go. It's an unerring internal compass.

What is intuitive healing? It is listening to your body's signals—your inner voice, your gut instincts, your energy level, your spiritual connection. By sensing warning signs, you can act sooner to restore immunity. During an illness, intuition reveals innovative ways to accelerate healing, regenerate, and repair, even when science lacks solutions. Intuitive healing is integrative. It means respecting your analytical mind and also calling on a deeper wisdom to guide you. As a physician, I've seen how frequently my patients were told by well-meaning doctors, "Your disease is chronic. You'll just have to live with it," or "The only way to feel better is to take a pill." Such advice can be dangerous and untrue, a kind of hex. You can't get it out of your head. Realize that there are always options. To find them, you must become a kind of revolutionary. Listen to your intuition and other answers will become clear.

Let illness impel you to surrender to a more compassionate, intuitively nuanced understanding of healing. *A basic premise of Western medicine to reconsider is that the only kind of healing involves a cure.* In truth, there is healing to be found in even the most stressful phases of your life if you can perceive it. In some cases, healing may mean being disease-free but I'd like you to let go of the notion that it must always be associated with a cure. Healing can also come from experiencing depression, living with chronic pain, or surviving cancer. Is illness a failure? Definitely not. When we try to control the terms of our healing, we eclipse a greater wisdom that can intercede in our lives. Though none of us would choose to be sick, it is still true that it would be wise to surrender to healing which can occur in unsuspected ways.

Let me tell you about my friend Jill Bolte Taylor. She was a Harvard-trained, hardcore neuroscientist but also always intuitive. At thirty-seven she suffered a massive stroke in the left (logical) hemisphere of her brain. Suddenly she could not walk, talk, read, or write. Jill's loving, distraught mother described her as "just a breathing body in the bed." Lying there, this master scientist had to come to grips with the reality that she might never get her left-brain function back. Still, a miracle was occurring: Jill's intuitive brain opened and she felt a sense of peace, euphoria, and connection to something greater. For the first time in her life, she was experiencing *everything* as energy; all sense of separation had disappeared. She had to depend on the intuitive side of her brain. This entailed a radical consciousness shift that forced her to surrender her linear perceptions of the world. She describes this metamorphosis in her world-famous book *My Stroke of Insight.*

Jill considers her stroke a revelation that spurred her to have a more intuitive, spiritually awake, and joyful life. Eight years later, Jill now celebrates both her natal birthday and the day of her stroke—what she calls her "rebirth day." Her message is that anyone, including those with brain injury, can find inner peace, that intuition and logic are complementary. Jill said, "My scientific training didn't teach me anything about the human spirit." She advocates that physicians, scientists, and patients can all excel by using both the logical and the intuitive parts of the brain. Like Jill, we can be enlightened by surrendering to the initiation of illness and all that it might teach us.

SURRENDER TO INTUITION:
FIVE WAYS TO HEAL YOURSELF

If you are ill, here are some steps to access intuition that I suggest to patients and describe further in my *Guide to Intuitive Healing*. Use these along with information your doctor offers about various treatment options.

If you don't know what to do about a health issue, if you're afraid or depressed or frozen in inertia, intuitively tune in for a direction. Keep tuning in until the answers come. Be patient. Don't do anything unless it feels right.

Notice Your Beliefs

Your beliefs set the tone for health and healing. Positive attitudes such as focusing on a healthy brain or healthy breasts instead of on just preventing Alzheimer's or cancer is good for the body. So is the belief "I trust my inner wisdom." Negative attitudes impede recovery and create self-fulfilling prophecies. Part of surrendering means releasing attitudes such as "I will never heal" or "This illness is my fault." No organ system stands apart from your thoughts. Your beliefs program your neurochemicals.

Listen to Your Body

Your body is a sensitive intuitive receiver. However, many of us in the West are conditioned to live in our heads, ignoring the rest of our bodies. Instead, pay attention to the natural surrenders that your body asks of you. Let yourself cry. Let yourself laugh. Let yourself sleep when you require healing. Track you gut instincts. Ask yourself, "Does this treatment or this doctor's suggestions feel right or do they feel off? Does my body feel toxic? Tired? In pain? Or relaxed and comfortable? Then take steps to remedy the situation. Become attuned to early warning signs your body sends.

Sense Your Body's Subtle Energy

We are made of flesh and blood but also of subtle energy, what Chinese medicine calls *chi*. (See Chapter 7.) Subtle energy affects your health. Thus, it is important that you learn to sense this energy, recognize when you're drained, and correct the imbalance. To begin, notice which situations or people raise or lower your energy. Be aware of your energy fluctuations so that you can quickly rejuvenate yourself and surround yourself with what is positive.

Ask for Inner Guidance

For answers about your health, learn to find inner stillness through meditation or quiet contemplation. Spend a few minutes daily listening to your intuition. Inwardly pose a question such as "How can I have more energy?" or "Is back surgery the right choice?" or "Shall I take medication?" Then remain quiet and listen. Intuition may appear as a gut feeling, a hunch, an image, a memory, or an instant knowing like a lightbulb suddenly switching on. Then apply the answer to your situation. The more you do this, the more you will trust the results.

Listen to Your Dreams

Intuition is the language of dreams. Every ninety minutes during the REM stage of sleep, you dream. Dreams provide answers about your health. The secret is to remember them. Keep a dream journal by your bed. Before sleep, ask a question—for instance, "Is this relationship good for me or should I move on?" The next morning, record any dreams immediately before getting out of bed. Try repeating the question every night until an answer comes.

Practice these approaches in all aspects of your health. You might want to experiment with one at a time until you get the hang of it.

Then you can go on to another. Some of these approaches may resonate more than others, which is fine. Stick to those that feel the most
doable and relevant. Test each one and notice if following the advice
makes you feel better. No intuition is insignificant. For instance, if
you get a specific flash to eat more cantaloupe, as one of my patients
did who was chronically fatigued, simply follow it. Then see if you
benefit, as she did. Get in the habit of tuning in, then applying this
information to remedy health issues. This will develop your capacity
for intuitive healing.

EMPATHIC ILLNESSES: DO YOU ABSORB OTHER PEOPLE'S SYMPTOMS?

Empathic illnesses are those in which you manifest symptoms that
are not your own. Many patients have come to me with panic disorders, chronic depression, fatigue, pain, or mysterious ailments that
respond only partially to medications or psychotherapy. Some were
nearly housebound or had been ill for years. What they had in common was that they all said, "I dread being in crowds. Other people's
anger and stress drain me and I need lots of alone time to refuel my
energy." When I took a close history of all these patients, I found
that they were what I call physical empaths: people whose bodies are
so porous they absorb the symptoms of others. I relate because I am
one. Physical empaths do not have the defenses that others have to
screen things out. Knowing this significantly changed how I treated
these patients. My job became teaching them to center and protect
themselves, set healthy boundaries, and manage how they processed
energy.

If you tend to absorb others' stress, you may be a physical empath. See if you relate to some of my patients. One mother awoke in a
sweat, feeling ill. She instinctually raced to her infant's room to find
him feverish. Once she realized it was the baby who was sick and got
him treatment, her own symptoms resolved. Another of my clients
was a nurse who became depressed whenever she treated depressed
patients. And then there was the legal assistant who started experi-

encing extreme exhaustion at work, even though lab tests showed nothing. However, he noticed that when the new coworker in the next cubicle went on vacation, he felt fine. To test whether this was physical empathy, I advised him to move to another desk. His exhaustion disappeared. It turned out the coworker had chronic fatigue syndrome. My patient was so empathetic he felt her depletion.

Since I am a physical empath, I want to help my patients develop this capacity and be comfortable with it. Similar to the special needs of relationship empaths (discussed in Chapter 6), if you are a physical empath you need to be fierce about self-care practices. Otherwise the intense physical and emotional suffering you may take on can obliterate your own health. It's vital to know how to avoid absorbing an individual's stress or the free-floating anxiety found in crowds. With my patients, I've seen how shouldering another's discomfort can trigger anxiety or depression; food, sex, and drug binges; and a plethora of physical symptoms that defy traditional diagnosis. The Centers for Disease Control and Prevention report that more than two million Americans suffer from chronic fatigue. It's likely that many of them are physical empaths who need to recognize their capacities and develop better coping skills.

The illnesses, fatigue, and other emotional symptoms you experience may not always be your own. You can "catch" them from others—a notion that conventional medicine is beginning to acknowledge although many doctors don't define it in terms of subtle energy.

To determine if you are a physical empath, take the following quiz.

QUIZ: AM I A PHYSICAL EMPATH?

- Have I been labeled as overly sensitive or a hypochondriac?

- Have I ever sat next to someone who seemed nice but suddenly my eyelids got heavy and I felt like taking a nap?

- Do I feel uneasy, tired, or sick in crowds and avoid them?

- Do I feel someone else's anxiety or physical pain in my body?

- Do I feel exhausted by angry or hostile people?

- Do I run from doctor to doctor for medical tests but am told "You're fine"?

- Am I chronically tired or do I have many unexplained symptoms?

- Do I frequently feel overwhelmed by the world and want to stay home?

Eight yeses indicate that you are a full-blown physical empath. Six or seven yeses indicate that you have a high degree of empathy. Four or five yeses indicate that you have a moderate degree of empathy. One to three yeses indicate that you are at least part empath. A score of zero indicates you are not a physical empath.

Discovering that you are an empath can be a revelation. Rest assured that you are not crazy. You are not a malingerer. You are not imagining things though your doctor might treat you like a nuisance. You are a sensitive person with a gift that you must develop and successfully manage.

Often empaths are confused with hypochondriacs since there is no obvious medical cause for their symptoms. Plus, both tend to be driven to find the answer by running to doctors, healers, and psychics. If these practitioners reassure them that nothing is wrong, they don't believe it. Empaths know something is off. Worse, they pay for costly but futile medical workups or go on expensive holistic wild-goose chases that do not resolve their problem.

The massive amount of medical information on the Internet and relentless television ads from pharmaceutical companies can turn even the most sensible people into hypochondriacs (in much the same way that medical students become susceptible to this syndrome). A stomachache can mean internal bleeding. A minor cough can be lung cancer. A natural feeling of sadness can mean you need medication for depression. Though both empaths and hypochondriacs can live in terror of having a terrible disease, these conditions are not the same. Here are some tips to help you tell them apart.

HOW TO TELL THE DIFFERENCE BETWEEN AN EMPATH AND A HYPOCHONDRIAC

- An empath's body absorbs the emotions (positive and negative) and physical symptoms of others. True hypochondriacs do not absorb people's emotions or symptoms but are simply preoccupied with their own discomfort or fears.

- An empath's illnesses and anxiety respond to the energy-based interventions I recommend such as meditation and boundary setting (see next exercise); a true hypochondriac's ailments do not.

- A hypochondriac's preoccupation with poor health is more emotion-based than body-based. It's responsive to insight-oriented psychotherapy which addresses early fears, as well as cognitive behavioral therapy, which shifts attention away from symptoms to reassuring thoughts. Antidepressants have also been used to relieve obsessive fears. None of these therapies will significantly improve an empath's symptoms.

Strategies to Combat Toxic Energy

Physical empathy doesn't have to overwhelm you. Now that I can center myself and refrain from taking on other people's pain, empathy has made my life more compassionate, insightful, and richer. Here are some secrets I've learned so that being a physical empath doesn't take a toll on my health.

When I'm tired, sick, upset, or off-center, my tendency to absorb other people's symptoms increases. At these times, I must surrender to the immediate necessity for self-care. I stop, regroup, and don't try to push through this precariously raw state—trust me, that won't work. Personally, self-care means that I withdraw from the world for an hour, a day, or longer and revive myself. Sometimes this means being at home, in nature, and especially beside bodies of water. This allows me to go inward to the spaces between the worlds, free and clear: no talking, no difficult people to contend with, nothing else that disrupts my inner flow. I partake of the eternal spring within and rejuvenate. Only then do I feel ready to return to what Buddhists

term *mara*, the material realm of emotions, desire, suffering, and ecstasy.

For us empaths, periodic retreats are necessary to maintain stamina and clarity. Even if you can't take time off, decompress by planning mini-breaks, five-minute periods throughout the day when you
take a walk, breathe in fresh air, or meditate. Even these moments
of inner peace go a long way toward beginning the replenishment
process.

Also, I've found that if I'm injured, I'm more prone to absorbing
energy. This is because (1) pain weakens our energy field, (2) the fear
we carry from being traumatized attracts more fear to us, compliments of the law of attraction, and (3) after an injury the world seems
to conspire to reinjure the part that's been hurt—a common phenomenon. For instance, after I broke my toe, people and dogs were more
apt to step on it, stuff was suddenly falling on or near it, doors would
almost slam into it, and wheelchairs seemed to be looking for an opportunity to run over it. Similarly, a patient told me that after she
had a tetanus shot that left her arm hot, swollen, and sore, a playful
relative who didn't know about the injection punched her right there!
Whether this happens because of Murphy's law—anything that can
go wrong will go wrong—or because an injured part of your body is
more vulnerable to mishaps, be especially protective and loving with
the painful area. Also keep surrendering any fears related to the injury so that you don't attract unwanted chaos. This will allow you to
heal in peace.

If you are to be happy and energized as an empath, your mantra
must become: "It's not my job to take on the pain of others or the
world." We're trained that as caring people, it's admirable to want
to ease another's discomfort. But many of us don't stop there; we become drained or sick. This loss of center does not serve us (unless of
course you want to explore the martyr archetype, which some people
do). Moreover, it's none of our business to deprive others of their life
experiences, whether difficult or uplifting. Sometimes suffering has
its own cycle that must be respected, hard as that may be to witness.

I've come to know the value of being a catalyst for people's growth
without compromising my health. This was a lesson I had to learn as

a young physician—patients have taught me that I can't do the work for them. Compassion and the desire to console are human. However, there's a fine line between supporting someone and taking on his or her issues. No matter how well intentioned you are, doing too much is not an act of love but of sabotage. You can be caring and honest with people, yet still let them be. Don't equate honoring their growth process with abandoning them. It's essential to strike a balance between learning to preserve your energy and serving others.

The strategies I discuss below will help you manage empathy more effectively and stay centered without absorbing the issues of others.

A SURVIVAL GUIDE FOR EMPATHS: STRATEGIES TO STOP ABSORBING OTHER PEOPLE'S ILLNESS AND PAIN

- *Evaluate.* First, ask yourself: "Is this symptom or emotion mine or someone else's?" It could be both. If the emotion such as fear or anger is yours, gently confront what's causing it, whether on your own or with professional help. If it's not yours, try to pinpoint the obvious generator. For instance, if you've just watched a comedy, yet you came home from the movie theater feeling depressed or with lower back pain, you may have incorporated the ailments of the people sitting beside you. The same can happen when you're at the mall or airport. Energy fields overlap when people are in close proximity.

- *Move away.* When possible, distance yourself by at least twenty feet from the suspected source. See if you feel relief. Don't err on the side of not wanting to offend strangers. In a public place, don't hesitate to change seats if you feel a sense of dis-ease imposing on you.

- *Know your vulnerable points.* Each of us has a body part that is more vulnerable to absorbing others' stress. Mine is my gut. Scan your body to determine yours. Is it your neck? Do you get sore throats? Headaches? Bladder infections? At the onset of symptoms in these areas, place your palm there and keep sending lovingkindness to that area to soothe discomfort. For long-standing depression or pain, use this method daily to strengthen yourself. It's comforting and builds a sense of safety and optimism.

- *Surrender to your breath.* If you suspect you are picking up on someone else's symptoms, concentrate on your breath for a few minutes. This is centering and connects you to your power. In contrast, holding your breath keeps negativity lodged in your body. To purify fear and pain, exhale stress and inhale calm. Picture pain as a gray fog lifting from your body, and wellness as a clear light entering it. This can produce quick results.

- *Practice guerilla meditation.* To counter emotional or physical distress, act fast and meditate for a few minutes. You can do this at home, at work, at parties, or at conferences. When necessary, take refuge in the bathroom. If it's public, close the stall door. Meditate there. Calm yourself. Focus on positivity and love. This has saved me many times in busy airports or at social functions where I feel depleted by others.

- *Set healthy limits and boundaries.* Control how much time you spend listening to stressful people and learn to say no. Remember, "no" is a complete sentence.

- *Visualize protection around you.* Research has shown that visualization is a healing mind-body technique. A practical form of protection many people use, including health care practitioners, involves visualizing an envelope of white light around your entire body. Or if you must interact with extremely toxic people, visualize a fierce black jaguar patrolling your energy field to keep out intruders.

- *Develop X-ray vision.* The spaces between the vertebrae in your lower back, the lumbar spine, are especially conducive to eliminating pain from the body. It's helpful to learn to actively expel stress from this area. On the Internet or in an anatomy book find an X-ray of the lumbar spine. Study it to learn its basic anatomy. Then visualize pain leaving your body through these spaces. Say goodbye to it as it blends with the giant energy matrix of life!

- *Take a bath or shower.* A quick way to dissolve stress is to immerse yourself in water. My bath is my sanctuary after a busy day. It washes away everything from bus exhaust to long hours of air travel to pesky symptoms I have taken on from others. Also, soaking in natural mineral springs divinely purifies you of all that ails you.

Keep practicing these strategies. By protecting yourself and your space, you can create a magical safe bubble around you while simultaneously driving negative people away so that you'll have less absorbed distress to deal with. Don't panic if you occasionally pick up pain or some other nasty symptom. It happens. With strategies at hand to help you cope, you can have quicker, more positive responses to stressful situations. This will make you feel safer, healthier, and your sensitivities can blossom.

HOW TO SURRENDER WHEN YOU ARE IN PAIN

Not much suffering compares to being a soul crazed by pain. I'm aware that it's all too easy for someone who isn't in pain to recommend that you surrender to your pain. Platitudes abound in this area. However, I also want to say that fighting or resisting pain is not the most effective way of relieving it. Healing pain requires a fine balance of harmonizing even with what feels excruciating while also not letting yourself be brought down by the intensity of this misery. Sometimes healing means flowing with discomfort; sometimes it means rising above it. It may be a tricky juggling act but it's not impossible. I want to show you how to maximize your chances of being pain-free or at least accepting ongoing symptoms more serenely.

Never believe anyone who announces, "You will always be in chronic pain." Though many excellent medical advances have been made in pain management, the nature of pain is fundamentally complex and mysterious. Multiple factors enter into experiencing pain from the physical and emotional to the spiritual and karmic. I've seen many patients who have every reason to experience chronic pain but don't. Their MRIs reveal alarming problems—bulging spinal discs, arthritis, collapsed this and that—yet they feel mostly okay. On the other hand, some people have minimal evidence of why they are in pain yet they are miserable and sometimes bedridden. Let's discuss the factors that make the difference.

What causes pain? On a biological level, nerve impulses alert the brain about physical damage that either still exists, even minimally, or no longer exists. Sometimes an injury or disease can heighten your sensitivity to pain—you have a lower threshold for it and feel it more. Social and psychological factors influence pain too. Loving support helps you be more resilient to it and having your life unravel does the opposite. Stressful emotions such as anxiety and loss can aggravate discomfort of all kinds. Studies have shown that if you fixate on pain and keep telling yourself scary stories such as "I'll never feel well," you'll be more debilitated; if you downplay the symptoms and have a lighter, more positive attitude, you'll cope with it better. Interestingly, people with chronic pain from a work-related injury heal faster if they like their jobs compared to those who do not.

No one wants to be in pain. However, it presents a profound spiritual challenge if you can figure out the compassionate lesson that the pain offers you. Here's the perspective I advise. Pain, as teacher, asks you to cope and survive in ways you never thought possible: taking risks, finding new skills even when you think you can't. Buddhists say some surrenders are about "learning to ride the ox backward." The ox is lost and untamed—akin to our overactive minds or our pain. We must tame it, then let it carry us home. To survive pain, you must become versatile, stretching past your resistance to change. It pounds the ego which can reinforce humility and build self-compassion. It exposes your blind spots, those areas where you clench, hold back, or are afraid. Pain lets you see that you can't overcome it alone. It drives you to reach out to something stronger within and larger without. If you don't collapse into it, pain makes you grow vaster. When you're in pain, you have a choice: either you can tense up or you can surrender to the path of recovery. Spirituality means breath, inspiration, reaching upward, and indeed it's all that—but pain also teaches you more. No one can tell you the right way to handle it. Moment to moment, you must keep trusting your intuition about what feels right, what comforts you, and how to progress.

The pain of addiction is often the spiritual prompt for substance abusers to surrender to change. My brave patients in recovery had to reach bottom with pain before they could get clean and sober. Many push addiction to the point of liver failure, destroyed marriages, bankruptcy, or suicide attempts until the surrender finally happens. Trouble kept following them because they continued running from their addiction, refusing to address the pain. Once they faced it they could begin to heal and make reparations, finally leaving trouble behind.

From the perspective of a twelve-step program, the surrender of having reached bottom is the spiritual experience of awakening, the gift of a new path. Then, for those in recovery, surrender becomes a lifestyle, the solution to loosening the agonizing obsession to drink, use, or otherwise give in to the dark undertow of addiction, a day at a time. The potent surrender mantras of the twelve steps include "I am powerless over my addiction and my life has become unmanageable" and "I turn my life and will over to a power greater than myself." This daily assertion of spiritual power and the relinquishment of ego helps those who would otherwise be "hopeless" addicts lead more loving, joyous lives that aren't dictated by cravings and pain.

Practitioners of mindfulness meditation talk about the importance of not being thrown off center by pain or other distractions. Their beautiful spiritual practice is to keep centering yourself no matter what's happening within or without. Pain qualifies as a distraction worthy of conquering. So do the toxic side effects of medications that you sometimes must take to heal.

I like reminding myself of the instructive story of Valmiki who goes to a guru for enlightenment and to learn detachment. The guru tells him to sit on an anthill and center himself so that he is not distracted. With faith in his teacher, Valmiki sits for hours, then days, which evolves into hundreds, maybe thousands of years. You can imagine Valmiki's terrible discomfort, those tiny ants biting and crawling all over him. But with time he learns to coexist harmoniously with the anthill. Seeing this, the guru declares him a sage of the highest order. Tears of joy well up in Valmiki's eyes. He then sets off to establish his famous ashram of fruit and flowers on the Ganges.

Each of us has his or her own anthills. Whatever yours may be, do your best to coexist harmoniously with such disturbances instead of waging war with what is. Yes, I'm advocating a rigorous spiritual stance to deal with discomfort. I'm asking you to view even horrendous pain as a teacher, to use it as a springboard to overcome distractions as best you can, to fight for self-compassion again and again. Still, as a doctor I know what a harsh mistress pain can be. That's why you need to counter it with everything you've got and overcome any resistance that prevents healing.

THE POSITIVE AND NEGATIVE SIDES OF RESISTING ILLNESS AND PAIN

Resistance can both help and hinder healing. What is resistance? It's when you refuse to comply with a situation and exert an oppositional force that tends to retard motion and growth. It's defending against someone or something. For instance, you resist dieting or letting yourself fall in love. You may not know why but something stops you. Resistance is the opposite of surrender. It's the energy you put forth, either consciously or unconsciously, to stop flow.

How can positive resistance serve your health? Consider your immune system's natural capacity to withstand disease. Developing resistance lets you form antibodies to viruses, bacteria, and toxins. Also, resisting acute pain in dangerous situations—say, moving your hand away from a fire—is protective. In terms of emotions, positive resistance lets you reject the option of caving in to pain or despair. Positive resistance also gives you the wherewithal to turn away from the dark places inside where you can get lost. I was impressed by the story a correctional officer told me: "I work in the federal prison that housed McVeigh and Nichols after the Oklahoma City bombing, the most destructive act of terrorism by American citizens on American soil. Some of the older guards became bitter from all the crimes, all the violence, all the innocents hurt by the many inmates who had no remorse. I was nearing that point. But I didn't allow myself to surrender to this bitterness. Instead, I chose a more hopeful outlook."

Similarly, positive resistance to negativity lets you change course to avert emotional disaster. Therefore, resistance to what is unwholesome and unhealthy—whether it's microbes, emotions, or toxic people—can save your body and soul. On the other hand, negative resistance exacerbates stress and pain which can impair immunity. Physically, resistance clenches your muscles and jaw, makes you hold your breath, aggravates constipation and irritable bowel, and keeps you rigid—not exactly the fluid state that accelerates wellness. Emotionally, resistance inhibits you from expressing difficult emotions or joy, and stops you from crying as a therapeutic release. Negative emotional resistance is often a stubborn defense against being hurt, an inner fortress of fear you erect to guard against heartbreak, disappointment, and pain of any kind. Sad to say, this also mutes your ability to love and heal. So you may shut down, get depressed, hold on to resentments, or become frozen in physical and emotional pain, thereby giving yourself no room to maneuver. Spiritually, it can stop you from opening to a healing force greater than yourself. No wonder negative resistance is notoriously portrayed as the enemy of creativity: the dreaded block that prevents you from writing, painting, surrendering to intimacy, or tapping the healing forces. It fuels procrastination and distraction so you're doing everything *but* art or healing yourself.

Thus, negative resistance is the part of you that doesn't feel safe to flow, to be experimental, to surrender to what it takes to recover from pain or live with it, even when the path feels scary and unclear. Resistance may be conscious, as when you dig in your heels and say, "I refuse to face being sick. It's too painful." So you go into denial or futilely rail against what is, rather than accepting it and somehow, some way, learning to live with an imperfect reality. When you resist what is, you're struggling with what you can't control at the moment, and that's a formula for misery. It's natural to wonder, "What did I do to deserve this?" and go through all the other versions of "Woe is me." But to consciously cling to these out of anger or fear or frustration is like battling with Behemoth, the unconquerable chaos monster poor Job encountered when he questioned God. You can't win.

Mostly, though, resistance isn't conscious. It inhabits you as repressed fears and traumas. You can unearth them through journaling, meditation, psychotherapy, or spiritual guidance. Once they surface, they can be healed. Also, unconscious resistance can be a defense against uncomfortable feelings that allows you to avoid taking certain actions. For instance, one patient, a terrible procrastinator, told me, "I procrastinate because I don't want to feel the anxiety of paying my medical bills or getting potentially scary lab results from my physician." When unconscious resistance is unaddressed, you may be clueless about how much it controls you or stops you from healing pain in all areas of your life.

EASING YOUR PAIN: THE DIFFERENCE BETWEEN PAIN AND SUFFERING

To use the principle of surrender to relieve disease and pain, it's important to know the difference between pain and suffering. On the most basic level, pain consists of the uncomfortable physiological sensations themselves. Or, as in Chinese medicine, it's a blockage of *chi*, your vital life force. Suffering, in contrast, is your response to pain— your thoughts and emotional reactions to the sensations.

My approach to lessen suffering involves using positive resistance to respond to pain with as much optimism as you can muster and saying no to fear and what-ifs. *Suffering is amplified by the scary stories you tell yourself about pain.* I'll provide you with a meditation that can help you cease doing this. Also, I want to help you melt negative resistance to pain by harmonizing with it. This means getting on the same frequency as pain rather than bracing against it. When you brace yourself—say, for an arduous medical procedure, before taking medications with unpleasant side effects, or for a charged conversation with your spouse—you're already tense and anxious before anything even happens. This anticipation makes suffering worse. In comparison, when you harmonize with discomfort, you're not amplifying it by clenching or meeting it with fear. You're letting pain pass in, then out, not attaching to it with your frightened mind. I want to reassure you that I'm not advising you to do anything unsafe or overwhelming. If the pain gets too intense, you can always withdraw and regroup. Harmonizing with pain or unpleasant sensations is a gradual desensitization process through which you dissipate fear and aversion to discomfort.

Practice the following meditation to learn to surrender to pain and disease. Be happy with baby steps of progress. The idea is to let go, let Spirit intervene, and become one with the discomfort so that you relax with pain instead of inflaming it with fear and tension.

A SURRENDER MEDITATION TO HARMONIZE WITH PAIN AND ILLNESS

- *Relax into the discomfort.* Don't try to change it or rid yourself of it. Don't brace yourself for pain or discomfort; that makes it worse. Simply let the discomfort be. Gently breathe through any tightening, fear, or resistance. Loosen your grip. Get to know the geography of your pain or discomfort. Map it out. Become familiar with it.

- *Intuitively tune in to the discomfort.* Does it have color? Texture? Emotion? Is it hot? Cold? Does it move or stay in one place? Do you notice images? Sounds? Scents? Memories? Ask the discomfort: "What can I learn from you? How can I ease my pain?"

- *Focus lightly on the discomfort.* Feel it completely but do not fixate on any sensation. As you inhale, breathe in all your pain. Visualize it as a cloud of dark smoke. Let it flow throughout your body right to the core of your compassion. Now picture every last bit of the black smoke dissolving, purified by love. As you exhale, picture this love as clear white light and then send it back to your area of discomfort. Breathe in pain. Breathe out compassion. Breathe in pain. Fill the pain with the healing breath of compassion.

- *Center yourself with a mantra.* Using a mantra, a positive phrase, can help you drag your mind away from being obsessed with pain or discomfort. Use your mantra as many times as necessary. When the discomfort gets too intense or you start feeling overwhelmed or hopeless, repeat your first and last name three times. This will help you reconnect with your own power. Another surrender mantra I love is "This too shall pass," a reminder that all things ebb and flow, including pain; no state of mind is permanent.

- *Rise above the pain.* At any point, feel free to back off from the discomfort. Change directions. Concentrate on a part of your body that is pain-free; feel those sensations. Also, you can affirm, "This pain is terrible. But I'm not going to let it bring me down. I will take control of my thoughts and focus on something positive." Shift your awareness to an image or thought that makes you happy such as a sunrise or a waterfall. Remember, your higher power is always there. Be sure to keep asking, "Please lift my pain so I can be at ease and happy." Then do your best to attend to what is right in front of you such as work, chores, or family. Be fully in the present moment.

Note: During this meditation, if painful memories arise such as clashes with an abusive parent or childhood loneliness, it's important to work these through later, on your own or with a guide, to relieve any unsuspected blocks to healing.

By actively engaging discomfort you can transmute it. This is a form of mystical alchemy that must never be misconstrued as succumbing to weakness or admitting defeat. You'll be in a position of power rather than running scared from disturbances that throw you off. All the while, practice compassion and more compassion. Pain is a bear but the heart is stronger. Keep stretching toward the heart. Keep countering pain with love and miracles can occur.

Over the years—in hospitals, homes, and clinics, even with someone hurt on the street—I've sat with patients, friends, family members, and strangers who were in pain. The simple act of sitting with someone, the power of a loving presence, can make the difference between a nightmare for someone and a warm, protective cocoon. One barely verbal patient who'd been hospitalized for depression after losing her child told me in a rare utterance, "You make alone not seem so alone." Also, just because you don't know someone doesn't mean you can't help that person when a situation presents itself. Recently, in a ladies' room at Starbucks, a teenage girl in the stall beside mine was weeping her eyes out (that kind of crying is usually about a guy). Though I never actually saw her, I said calmly, "Whatever happened will work its way out. I promise." In a tiny voice she said simply, "I know. Thank you." Then there are times when you can't do anything for those you care for but sit there anyway. Consider sitting with someone a sacred vigil. You're keeping watch over him or her. Don't underestimate the impact your loyal presence has on someone who is ailing or lost or broken. We are all those things, you know, in some way. With people in severe pain, it's just more obvious.

So, with an open heart, address your pain and the pain of others. Especially if it's chronic or agonizing, pain doesn't always make sense. At these confusing times, try to accept not knowing and enlist your wait-and-see mind—while also doing everything possible to get the best treatments. I realize patience is hard to come by when you're in pain. Still, attempt to let solutions play out and flow with the forward motion of your life, despite your understandable need for relief now.

When healing pain, you must surrender to all your powerlessness and all your power, depending on what's needed. This may change every day. It's an ongoing passionate interplay of when to "do" and when to let go. Faithfully check in with your intuition for which direction to take even when everything in sight looks like it needs saving. Be grateful for the pearls about pain you discover. Surrender to the tender spiritual teaching of it all.

In this chapter, we've discussed various aspects of how to surrender to pain and illness. I hope your mind has opened a little bit more. I hope your curiosity has been sparked about how to address discomfort differently. The warrior path of healing is to get knocked down, then, when you've recouped, to begin again, always again. Keep your eyes on the light. Yes, it's a strenuous endeavor that can make you feel defeated. It asks everything of you. But don't succumb. Moving toward the light—even if you're just crawling—is your soul's great achievement. I want to impart to you how central this is for your evolution and how your courage makes it easier for the rest of us.

There is heavy-duty pain on earth. When you are the one feeling it, when it is your task to confront misery in your body or soul, you are doing a service to us all. On the deepest, most primal human level, your pain resonates through the human family, and the steps each of us takes to overcome pain individually and together better everyone. With every twinge of pain, I want you to feel me loving you, feel us loving each other. Love is our most enduring incantation. Realizing our intuitive interconnectivity and forming nets of love is crucial to surmounting what seems unconquerable. Doing this requires faith and letting go to a higher grace that you may not even fully believe in. Still—and this is the miracle—you do it anyway. Faith in the midst of disbelief has massive power. It can comfort your body and the entire world.

SURRENDER AFFIRMATION FOR HEALING YOURSELF

I pledge to honor and love my body in sickness and in health. I pledge to keep surrendering negative thoughts and behaviors that sabotage my healing. During a health challenge I will keep surrendering pain and embrace gentleness, patience, and faith in the power of love.

If you want to see what your body will look like tomorrow,
look at your thoughts today.

—NAVAJO SAYING

....

11

THE ELEVENTH SURRENDER

EXPERIENCING RADIANT AGING: THE SECRET

OF SLOWING DOWN TIME

~~~

WHAT IF AGING COULD FEEL NATURAL, NOT JUST BE A STRUGGLE or high drama? What if you weren't obsessed with fear about surrendering to the process? What if you felt comfortable handling the changes that are inevitable? With each year, imagine the possibility of increasingly feeling more connected and more yourself instead of dreading each birthday. You're not fighting the cycles of years passing or denying them, but instead surrendering deeply to your own power and light during both tough passages and periods of grace. This is the path to radiant aging.

Our society has an aging phobia. If you buy into this—and it's all too easy to do—your optimism about aging may be no match for the onslaught of fear-based stereotypes dictating that you can't do this or look like that. Truth is, worrying about aging only makes you age faster. If you see yourself as old, then you will be. In fact, research has linked negative perceptions of aging to people with a life span that's seven years shorter! I remember that even at forty, people began to use annoying phrases with me such as "at your age," then make presumptuous predictions like "soon you'll lose your sexual energy" or "you're almost over the hill." (Reality check: maybe *they've* always been over the hill but you don't have to be!) The older you get, the more you're bombarded by these hexes that try to derail intuitive, passionate living. In defense of intuition and passion, I want to reexamine the prevalent Western thinking about aging and blow apart assumptions that make no sense or are mistakenly portrayed as inevitable.

Radiant aging is a game changer and intimately related to surrender. I'm defining it as a life cycle process connected to the rhythms of nature, divinity, and universal flow. Radiant aging is about letting go, being fluid, and not tensing up, whatever happens. *It means viewing all your body's creative expressions of change through lenses of light.* Each day, moment to moment, you'll be tapping your physical, emotional, spiritual, and energetic well-being to boost health and lessen negativity. To age radiantly, you must embrace all these elements, even though conventional medicine focuses mostly on physical aging. Each element enhances you in different ways, creating an intricate mosaic of life forces.

Radiant aging begins the moment we are born. Think of it as an ingenious unfolding of your essence. You can hone your vibrancy at every age despite the common biological contractions of getting older such as wear and tear on joints or a decline in muscle mass. What you need to focus on are energetic and spiritual expansions. Chronological age is less important than how you wear the years, how you glow energetically and spiritually. True, earlier in life your hormones and biology go through acceleration phases such as getting taller, puberty, and preparing for childbearing, then decelerate later. Your priorities can shift at different stages but these aren't always as predictable as some "experts" claim. Aging, the process of time passing during a human experience on earth, must be intuitively informed. Thus there's no use generalizing about aging or expecting that we all do it the same way. Maybe you get married at twenty, or sixty, or never! Maybe at ninety you're finally ready to address issues about your mother. No fault. No judgment. Just be grateful you're ready at all and go for it. What matters is that you must trust your gut.

Life is wondrous, every single instant—if you can only view it that way. The point of radiant aging is not to loathe the years that pass or the changes that come even if you suffer illness and limitations. Surrendering to aging involves letting go of your attachment to previous years or decades, bittersweet or unsettling as that may be. The great poet Rumi wrote that the stream you stepped into yesterday is not the same stream you step into today. It is the same place but the water that rushes by your feet is new.

Personally, I'm inventing aging as I go along. We contain within us the joy, sorrow, and wisdom of every year we've experienced. Just because you pass one age doesn't mean those states of mind are gone. They've been downloaded into your being. You can access all your experiences without attaching to them. The fourteen-year-old in me is just as alive as the forty-year-old. If you're fifty or sixty or seventy, you don't have to always "act your age," whatever that means. The calculated mischief of aging is that you can act however young or old you choose to be. Tapping different ages in yourself changes your appearance and how others relate to you. It's a choice of consciousness.

AGING IS NOT FOR SISSIES

Though the experience of aging differs for everyone, it is a journey of courage that asks you to surrender in ways you may feel incapable of—but you are capable. Aging is determined by numerous variables including genetics, attitude, lifestyle, and karma. However, the spirit with which you approach the changes and accept your mortality will determine the quality of your passage.

Mostly, I find Western culture's attitudes about aging to be misleading and ageist. In Asian cultures, it's a privilege to be in the company of an enlightened elder. We must create a new vocabulary to describe the process of time passing that pays homage to the mystery. What defined our parents may no longer fit us. Many of us will not be joining a senior center for activities or bus rides to the casinos, though this option may be perfect for some.

In this chapter, we'll discuss the science of aging, including what ages you from the shortening of a cell's telomeres to free radicals to stress and resentments—and we'll also explore what keeps you robust. How can you surrender your fears of aging and mortality? How do you slow down time and appreciate your life? We'll discuss the four types of aging—physical, emotional, energetic, and spiritual—and describe strategies to optimize each for greater fitness. Though growing older may present you with the poignant surrenders of loss or disease, the practice of radiant aging involves striving to surrender to all the changes, growth, and miracles that come.

What typically makes aging a struggle? When we try to control it, deny it, fight it, or rigidly define the process. Truth is, to our egos, the idea of change is scary. It makes us feel out of control of our lives and the universe. Our children are leaving home, our bodies may be getting slower, we see friends dying. Spiritual teacher Ram Dass says, "Sure, certain doors will close to us but the changes will offer us opportunities. Behind all the drama and clinging to the past is a place of soul."

Aging is an embodiment of an unraveling mystery. Our surrender is to go along for the ride, to flow with both joys and impediments while doing what we can to stay healthy and happy. Some people lose hope and become resigned but this is not the same as surrender. The point isn't to forsake passion or your wild spirit. Rather, surrender is a mindful way to slow down time, to be *present in this moment*—not the moment ahead or behind, but the eternal now. Don't try to predict your future. Instead, savor the moments. Being willing to surrender to the mystery of it all will make aging feel more adventurous.

Here, we'll focus on how surrender can liberate the four types of aging: physical, emotional, energetic, and spiritual. Tales of the Fountain of Youth, a legendary spring that imparts vigor to all who drink from it, have been recounted in various cultures for millennia. It is told that Alexander the Great and his servant crossed the Land of Darkness in search of this restorative spring. But I believe this fountain isn't just a mythic, symbolic place. It's close to home, our sacred life force that can be tapped. It bathes our bodies but is also replenished by our soul's light. I'll show you how to access this Fountain of Youth in body, mind, and spirit.

THE ART OF SURRENDER IN PHYSICAL AGING

You may need to brace yourself for conventional medicine's brutally empirical, nonspiritual definition of aging. Simply view it as a starting point to expand your consciousness about this topic. *Aging is not a disease.* It is an organic evolution that we can honor and augment once we learn to tap our vital energies and surrender fears.

Science defines aging as the progressive deterioration of physiological function associated with our body's lagging ability to respond to stress. Signs of physical aging can include:

- Lowering of immunity.

- Sluggish digestion, increased constipation.

- Loss of muscle strength, mobility, and balance (increasing risk of falling).

- Gray hair.

- Decreasing height—between the ages of forty and eighty men can lose an inch and women two inches due to muscle and bone shrinkage and flattening of spinal discs.

- Less saliva and lubricating fluid in joints.

- Reduced hearing, vision, taste, and smell.

- Forgetfulness (especially people's names, where your keys are, or why you entered a room).

- Severe memory impairment such as Alzheimer's disease or other forms of dementia.

- Less production of collagen, elastin, and oils in the skin causing dryness, wrinkles, or sagging, which are worsened by ultraviolet radiation, smoking, air pollution, and the downward pull of gravity.

- Weight gain, particularly hard-to-lose belly fat associated with insulin resistance, the body's reduced ability to break down glucose and carbs.

- Decrease in stem cells from which all body tissues develop.

- In women, cessation of fertility, leading to a reduction in sex hormones, vaginal lubrication, and sometimes libido, plus weakening of bones.

- In men, decreased testosterone and erectile function, and fewer viable sperm.

- An added risk of age-related diseases including high blood pressure, degenerative arthritis, type 2 diabetes, cancer, cataracts, and heart disease.

- Death (though "old age" is not a scientifically recognized cause of death—specific diseases such as stroke are).

Okay, this is a daunting list! But now I want to disprove the notion that all these troubling changes are inevitable. They'd frighten the bejesus out of any sensible person. It's one thing to gracefully accept the rhythms of aging and address issues as they occur—if they occur—and another to be tormented by catastrophic thinking about what might happen. Thus, it's important to keep surrendering your fears of aging by not presuming that something bad will happen to you. Keep in mind that aging includes a range of experiences from being healthy (or healthier than ever) to having minor to moderate limitations or enduring a debilitating illness such as a stroke. Extreme suffering, which can be experienced at any time in our lives including in our early years, is simply at the far end of the spectrum. Since thoughts affect your health, instead of giving in to fearing the worst, alter your focus and surrender to solutions.

How you age is more in your control than you might think. Research has shown that poor health isn't a necessary consequence of aging. If you practice healthy behaviors, take advantage of preventive services, and engage with family and friends, you are more likely to remain fit and have fewer medical issues. Though about 80 percent of people over sixty-five have one chronic condition and 50 percent have at least two, keys to staying vital include preventing chronic diseases and actively maintaining wellness. It's essential to surrender the notion that you are too old or too sick to create positive change in your body. Below I will describe six aging factors to consider. Even if you've neglected your health before, practicing the anti-aging strategies I'll describe can help you improve chronic symptoms and increase well-being.

Aging Factor 1: Genetics

About 30 percent of the changes associated with aging are strongly influenced by genetics. For example, genes control cholesterol metabolism which impacts cardiovascular health. They regulate cytokines which influence inflammation and immunity. Hereditary illnesses include early-onset Alzheimer's disease, diabetes, Parkinson's, and heart disease. Being aware of family history makes you mindful of risk factors so you can take steps toward the right diet, exercise, and other forms of prevention.

Though there's still much that science doesn't know about the link between genetics and disease, longevity does seem to run in families. Centenarians, those over one hundred, share some genetic traits including mutations that may prolong life. Many are tall and lean. Few are obese. Most show no signs of cognitive impairment or dementia prior to ninety and haven't suffered typical age-related illnesses such as diabetes or heart disease. They also tend to have a profound belief in spirituality and an innate ability to cope with stress. Many reside in nonindustrial, unpolluted areas. Common to all these groups are a plant-based diet, relatively low caloric intake, little or no smoking, moderate exercise, making family a priority, and a supportive social community.

Studies indicate that children of centenarians are more likely to reach one hundred and are less likely to suffer life-threatening illnesses. An American Heart Association study concluded that children of centenarian parents have a markedly lower incidence of heart disease and stroke when they reach old age than those whose parents died in their seventies. So if your parents lived long, you have added protection in your genes.

OPTIMIZE YOUR GENETICS BY SURRENDERING BAD HABITS: MIMIC THE DIET, EXERCISE, AND SLEEP HABITS OF CENTENARIANS

- *Caloric restriction.* Research has shown that reducing caloric intake by 40 percent extends the life span of mice by nearly a third. It also reduces blood glucose and insulin levels, and decreases rates of tumors in tumor-prone rats. In Okinawa, home to many centenarians, there is a saying: *hara hachi bu*, "stop eating when you are no longer hungry." In contrast, Americans tend to stuff themselves far past the point where their hunger is satiated. Reducing calorie intake along with eating a fresher, plant-based, whole-grain diet while avoiding processed foods prevents accelerating aging with unhealthy habits. In addition, it's important to stay hydrated. Drinking five glasses of water daily flushes out toxins, carries nutrients to cells, and decreases hunger cravings.

- *Exercise.* Find a physical activity you enjoy and do it regularly. It may be going to the gym, doing aerobics, hiking, stretching, or gardening. The secret is to keep your body flexible and mobile. Studies indicate that the risk of heart disease decreases by as much as 50 percent in people who engage in consistent moderate exercise of twenty to thirty minutes a day. Our world is overly linear so make curvy movements to bring a luscious flexibility to your body. This counters the rigid linear motions used in, say, weight training. Hula hoops are amazing ways to do this by moving your hips in circles to engage your core.

- *Sleep.* Centenarians report sleeping soundly and uninterrupted for at least seven hours a night and some for up to nine hours. Sleep rejuvenates the body and enhances hormone balance and immunity.

Aging Factor 2: Telomere Shortening

Cutting-edge science is investigating telomeres as a secret to anti-aging. A telomere is a region at the end of a chromosome that protects it from deteriorating or fusing with another chromosome. Over the years, with each cell division, the telomeres become shorter which limits cells to a fixed number of divisions in a lifetime. This determines aging and sets a limit on how long you can live. (There is a blood test to measure telomere length.) Consequently, the number of times a cell has replicated may be more important than chronological age. The American Heart Association published a report linking telomere shortening to heart attacks and premature death. Some scientists postulate that preventing telomeres from breaking can extend our cells' lives and slow down aging. Genetic researchers were awarded the Nobel Prize for discovering an enzyme called telomerase that can reverse aging. This enzyme appears to guard against shortening, thereby protecting our DNA.

I find it interesting that most cancers are the result of "immortal cells" whose telomeres don't degenerate. These cells have infinite reproductive potential. Though we don't want the immortal cells that create cancer, we do want those that perpetuate health and life. Having more telomerase as we age could potentially offer this by protecting the genes of normal cells from degenerating. In contrast, children with progeria, a rare genetic disease in which they are born old, lack telomerase and have short telomeres. They age prematurely and die at about thirteen.

It's exciting that telomere biologists are researching practical breakthroughs for anti-aging and health. Possibilities include telomerase inhibitors for cancer and activators for progeria. Scientists postulate that if they can find a way to turn on the telomerase gene in all our cells, people can live longer. ·

SURRENDER A CLOSED MIND: KEEP INFORMED ABOUT TELOMERE ADVANCES

Though scientific consensus is not definitive, it's possible that supplements such as vitamin D, fish oil, multivitamins, TA-65 (a telomerase activator from the astragalus plant), carnosine (an amino acid/antioxidant), and a healthy lifestyle can enhance the resilience of telomeres. What science does know is that certain factors such as obesity, lack of exercise, excessive alcohol, and free radical production accelerate telomere degradation. You can make lifestyle changes to avoid these risks. This exciting field holds promise. I intend to closely follow telomere research and suggest you do too.

Aging Factor 3: Free Radicals and Oxidative Stress

Studies suggest that we age, in part, because free radicals (molecules with unpaired electrons) accumulate and injure other cells besides telomeres. Free radical damage to your DNA increases with age and is implicated in age-related diseases from cancer to Alzheimer's, along with wrinkles and other signs of aging skin. Though some free radicals are necessary for normal cell function and energy metabolism, with aging our bodies have a harder time keeping them in check or clearing them. These unstable molecules are a by-product of oxidative stress—the process that makes a banana turn brown or pipes rust. Oxidative stress can harm the body and is accelerated by toxins, infections, trauma, a sedentary lifestyle, and consuming fats heated to high temperatures (oxidation occurs more readily in fats than in carbs or protein). To retard aging, it is important to reduce free radicals and oxidative stress.

REDUCE FREE RADICALS AND WRINKLES WITH ANTIOXIDANTS

Antioxidants help to slow aging by preventing free radicals from damaging cells. It's smart to expand your diet to include antioxidants found in brightly colored fresh fruits (blueberries, acai berries, pomegranates), vegetables, sprouted grains, and green tea. You also might consider supplements such as vitamin A (beta-carotene), vitamin C, vitamin E (alpha-tocopherol), L-carnosine, and reservatrol. These antioxidants improve brain function and reduce signs of aging in your body and skin. To reduce wrinkles you can use antioxidant creams and moisturizers (or rub berries on your skin!) along with using sunscreen, eliminating nicotine, wearing sunglasses to prevent squinting, sleeping on your back to prevent sleep lines, and remaining hydrated by drinking plenty of water.

Aging Factor 4: Chronic Inflammation

Research indicates that chronic inflammation is a major contributor to age-related deterioration. Acute inflammation is your body's first response to injury, allergy, and disease. Your immune system goes on hyperalert and attacks unwanted invaders—tissues become red and swollen as with a sore throat. Chronic inflammation, however, is unhealthy and can degrade tissues when unchecked. Some studies suggest that it may be the cause of all degenerative diseases associated with aging. It results from an overactive immune system—think ongoing allergies, rheumatoid arthritis, or other autoimmune diseases. With chronic inflammation, the body thinks it is under attack. In response, cytokines are released that kill cells in the brain, artery walls, and elsewhere with toxic oxidative chemicals. Heart attack, stroke, increased cholesterol deposits in the heart and blood vessels, cancer, and Alzheimer's have all been linked to this. Some inflammatory triggers include infections, allergens (including food), toxins (including air pollution and secondhand smoke), obesity, a poor diet, lack of exercise, high LDL ("bad" cholesterol), and elevated blood sugar and insulin in diabetes. It follows that if your body is chronically inflamed, it will break down and age faster.

The great news is that you can make specific lifestyle changes to treat inflammation and slow down aging. Begin practicing the following strategies right away.

SURRENDER YOUR RESISTANCE TO CHANGE: ENLIST THESE STRATEGIES TO REDUCE INFLAMMATION

- *Get tested.* The most commonly used blood test to detect inflammation in your body and blood vessels is called the high-sensitivity C-reactive protein test. Your physician can easily order this routine lab test (though the results may yield false positives if you have a cold or other temporary conditions that raise inflammation levels).

- *Eat a whole-food diet.* Get enough fiber and eat lots of fresh foods, particularly vegetables. Also, alkaline foods such as watermelon, leafy greens, root vegetables, lemons, garlic, and melon can limit acidic stress on your body. Avoid sugars, starches, and processed and junk foods, refined flour, and trans and saturated fats. These cause your body to store fat rather than burn it as energy.

- *Decrease belly fat with exercise.* Excess belly fat releases cytokines (inflammatory substances). Regular exercise will help you lose weight and belly fat and improve your immune system and cardiovascular wellness.

- *Eat healthful fats.* You can get omega-3 fats from cold-water fish such as wild salmon, mackerel, and sardines, or from olive oil, nuts, avocados, or a daily fish oil supplement. Omega-3 eggs from hens fed a special diet are also available.

- *Avoid allergens.* Two common food allergies are to gluten and dairy. You can try eliminating these from your diet to see if you feel more energetic and less achy and fatigued. Identify and remove allergens in your environment and diet. Allergy testing may be helpful.

- *Maintain a healthy gut.* Taking probiotics helps to reduce inflammation and eliminate bad bacteria.

Aging Factor 5: Insulin Resistance/Glycation

Insulin resistance occurs as part of aging. It's when your cells become less responsive to the sugar and carb-processing hormone insulin. How does this affect you? When you're young, fit, and healthy, you utilize carbs and sugar for energy—only a minimum of them are converted to fats. With insulin resistance, you develop higher glucose and insulin levels and tend to put on weight, especially belly fat. It also makes you more prone to type 2 diabetes which occurs with obesity or later in life. Insulin resistance can cause you to age prematurely by damaging your kidneys, eyes, nerves, and blood vessels. In addition, the extra unprocessed glucose binds to your DNA, proteins, and lipids in a process called glycation. This inhibits their function and results in disease and aging.

PRESCRIPTIONS TO DECREASE INSULIN RESISTANCE, GLYCATION, AND WEIGHT

- *Exercise.* Vigorous aerobic exercise decreases insulin resistance. Start any new exercise routine slowly and aim to increase to thirty to forty-five minutes daily.

- *Get adequate sleep.* Sleep deprivation is associated with insulin resistance. You will need at least six to eight hours of sleep.

- *Eat small, frequent meals.* This can help keep blood sugar levels stable throughout the day which will prevent spikes in insulin.

- *Reduce carbs and sugar.* Stick to high-fiber, low glycemic foods— carbs that create a smaller insulin spike, such as whole grains, beans, fruit, and green veggies. Cut back on high-glycemic foods that create a big insulin spike such as mashed potatoes, pasta, white rice, white bread, cookies, candy, chips, and sugar.

- *Increase lean protein.* Lean protein is great for avoiding insulin resistance. Not only is it filling but it also forces your body to burn its fat reserves as energy. Include lean protein such as skinless free range chicken breast, wild-caught salmon, nonfat yogurt, tofu, beans, or organic lean meat with each meal.

- *Use supplements.* Chromium is a mineral that can help the body utilize glucose and burn fat. In addition, alpha-lipoic acid, vitamin B_6, and co-enzyme Q_{10} have been shown to lessen insulin resistance.

Aging Factor 6: Hormone Imbalance

Aging creates hormone imbalances that can impair the quality of your life. These imbalances contribute to depression, inflammation, and sluggish metabolism with subsequent weight gain, osteoporosis, coronary artery blockage, and loss of sex drive. For many (but not all) menopausal women, declining estrogen, progesterone, testosterone, and DHEA can wreak havoc with mood, energy, memory, sleep cycles, vaginal lubrication, and sex drive. In addition, low thyroid hormones can cause fatigue, brittle hair, weak nails, dry skin, and depression. Similarly, with age, a man's testosterone can wane as estrogen builds. This means he may experience decreasing muscle mass, more belly fat, memory problems, and limited ability to sustain erections. If you want to explore the option of hormone replacement, the first step is to have your physician order blood tests to determine your levels. Then discuss whether this choice is right for you.

REPLACE HORMONES WITH BIOIDENTICALS

Bioidentical hormones are thought to have the same chemical structure as your own naturally produced hormones, compared with the older, previously prescribed, synthetic versions. However, there is no one-size-fits-all prescription. Through careful monitoring of your blood tests and your body's response to the hormones, you and your physician can find the right dosage. For both women and men, hormone replacement is a calculated decision to be made with a physician's advice. It has many potential benefits including a drastically improved quality of life, health, sex drive, and appearance (shinier hair and softer skin). But the risks, including increased incidence of cancers, are still unclear. More research is required to offer definitive conclusions. Your family history, medical condition, and current lifestyle may be factors as well.

Why is surrender critical to easing physical aging? It helps you overcome a sense of powerlessness about your body and lets you explore options that can keep you vital. If you have physical limitations, be kind to yourself. Say you need reading glasses to see small print— get cute or funky ones (or contacts) and start loving the new accessory instead of loathing the glasses and yourself. Or if your stamina isn't quite what it used to be, allow yourself breaks to replenish. Don't let anyone tell you that a more enlightened way to age is impossible. Try the anti-aging techniques I've presented here. If you feel better, there is your proof. Keep listening to your intuition and how your body responds to your new habits. Stick with strategies that work. Age your own way. Discover what's true for you. Give yourself permission to live outside the box.

THE ART OF SURRENDER IN EMOTIONAL AGING:
THE DIFFERENCE BETWEEN AGING AND
FEELING OLD

What is emotional aging? On the positive side, it is the wisdom and radiance you gain over time from being committed to compassion, love, and an open heart. It's a lightness of being you keep aiming for, a dedication to surrendering fear and negativity so they don't steal the soul from your eyes. It's living a life of intuitive guidance, of bending with the wind rather than trying to control everything with your will. The point is to loosen up and get happier with time.

On the negative side, emotional aging can manifest as rigidity, bitterness, and resentments, all etched on your face and spirit. You feel a heaviness of being, a numbness, a closing off that comes from clinging to hurts and resentments, the tightness of not surrendering year after year. I know how life sometimes appears to want to rob us of our optimism and faith. Still, you cannot afford to let that tragedy of emotional shutting down occur. Along with making you feel old, from the perspective of pure vanity, it doesn't look attractive. Your facial muscles move in certain ways with each emotion—for instance, worry furrows your brow, patience relaxes it. Therefore, to age well, feel energized, and look good, you want your emotional balance to tip toward the positive.

Let's recognize that there's a huge difference between aging and feeling old. Aging is natural but what we project onto the process determines whether we feel tormented or tranquil. Buddhists talk about the first and second arrows. The first arrow is what happens on the outside—you lose your job, you become ill, your body ages. The second arrow is what you do to yourself in terms of negative thoughts. Pay attention to the second arrow so you don't harm yourself. Make peace with getting older.

As I try to do, dedicate yourself to surrendering bad ideas about aging that keep you feeling old. For instance, avoid thoughts such as "Who would want me now?" "I'm too fat," "I'm all saggy and wrinkled," or "The best part of my life is over." Though I understand the tendency to put yourself under a microscope, obsessing about flaws, disappointments, and shame is akin to cursing yourself. Even worse, it's self-fulfilling. The more you repeat these ideas, the more stressed—and old—you become. (News flash: most people are too self-absorbed to scrutinize you as closely as you might suppose.) Especially in Western culture, many of us end up staring terrified into that black hole of self-criticism about our bodies. Don't get drawn in by it. To reverse course, turn practicing surrender into an intellectual discipline. This means you need to intentionally drag your mind away from negativity and point it toward the positive.

The way you perceive your body and spirit is crucial. One patient at fifty-six would look at her lovely self and see nothing besides a drooping neck, "old" hands, and cellulite. The surrender I focused on with her and suggest to you is letting go of the need to obsess about signs of aging. Rather, adjust your perspective. Make your mind a shelter, a safe place to go. Your body hears all your thoughts. You can make it feel younger when you say nice things about it and older when you don't. (See Chapter 7.) On the truest level, when you strip away all the ego distortions and cultural fears about aging, you are perfect, beautiful, and capable of renewal. In support of this, concentrate on what feels most alive such as your sparkling eyes, radiant smile, or arousing touch. Define yourself by your passions such as walking in nature, creative work, sensuality, or serving the world, not by your insecurities, hurts, or physical infirmities. Yes, ideally you want to love and accept every part of your body including the wrinkles, but if you're not quite there yet, you can begin by appreciating your attributes.

I'm frequently asked how I feel about plastic surgery. Though common sense dictates that it's healthier to avoid surgery and injecting foreign substances such as Botox (botulism toxin) or fillers into your body, the decision is personal. There is no right or wrong answer. You have to weigh the aesthetic benefits of looking younger against the risks of surgery such as infection, bruising, bleeding, numbness, an extended recovery period, and bad results. With fillers and Botox, you need to consider risks such as allergies, lumps, sagging muscles, and the lack of facial expression known as "the corpse look" (a result of paralyzed nerves). I've known many people who are pleased with their cosmetic interventions. They've told me, "My appearance is refreshed and that makes me feel better about myself." However, I've watched others get addicted to plastic surgery and abuse it. Sad to say, they never feel beautiful or perfect enough, no matter how many procedures they get. Be clear: plastic surgery can't make you a happy person if you weren't happy before. One attractive forty-year-old patient with breast implants dreamed that at her funeral, the only part of her body that people were admiring in the casket were her large breasts. Our work in therapy was to help her build self-esteem and emotional strengths in important ways that went way beyond breast size. Plastic surgery or other cosmetic changes are not miracle cures if you loathe yourself or your body.

Ageism is rampant. Consider the doddering blue-haired old people on TV commercials for dementia medications and the perky young couples advertising real estate loans for new homes. As hard as it may be to rise above such exploitation of stereotypes, you must in order to maintain a more balanced approach to aging. I've treated many over-forty actresses who suffer from Hollywood's ageism. They don't receive the attention they used to from their beauty and can barely land roles as mothers or grandmothers. Along the same lines, my eightysomething friend Berenice was looking to buy a car but angrily left one dealership when, as she put it, "a salesman treated me like I was senile."

I must admit I wasn't pleased myself when I was at dinner with some younger yoga friends and a snippy woman I hadn't met before asked me if I was the mother of one of the attractive men there. I'd walked in feeling sexy but as soon as she said that, I felt old. Don't get the wrong idea—I think mothers are goddesses but given my insecurities about aging at that time, compounded with never having had much of a maternal instinct, the comment made me feel as though I wasn't being seen. Certainly I strive to be more mature and secure. However, aging is a sensitive subject and the assumptions and putdowns of ageism can hurt. We each have our own emotional triggers that make us feel old. Still, let's try to use them as prompts to reject ageism and gain confidence in our allure.

The last thing most people want as they grow older is to be treated as if they *are* old or infirm. The greatest compliment you can give anyone at any age, in any state of health, is to recognize that person's wild spirit and beauty. When my seventy-five-year-old friend's ten-year-old granddaughter said, "Wow, Grandma, you're old!" my friend replied, "Honey, it's true that I've accumulated a lot of numbers but I'm really only thirty-five inside." So when you are thinking about yourself and others, be sure to respond to the light and the marvel that reside within us all. Treat everyone as gorgeous.

The mind-body connection is intimately linked to aging. How could it not be? A revelation of twentieth-century medicine is that anxiety and anger aren't just feelings. Nor are love and joy. All emotions trigger biological reactions. How you respond to any situation is a choice—and those cumulative choices shape your health and how you age.

Numerous studies have linked chronic emotional stress to premature aging, decreased mental acuity, and feeling old. Research shows that loneliness and social isolation increase the risk of heart disease. Also, women who've suffered years of grinding stress from caring for a sick child had shortened telomeres as well as a higher level of oxidative stress and free radicals. Of course, our stress hormones, adrenaline and cortisol, rescue us in emergencies but when they're on a perpetual slow burn we age faster and our health suffers. It makes sense. Adrenaline accelerates heart rate, constricts blood vessels, tenses muscles, generally puts your system on overdrive without time to refuel. Cortisol elevates blood pressure and blood sugar, weakens your immune system, makes you fat, and hardens arteries. It's no wonder that when we're under chronic stress, our bodies show visible and internal signs of aging.

Still, despite our best intentions, life happens. Stress can be unavoidable. Your relationship breaks up. You experience loss. You get depressed. To love ourselves and others with a maximum of grace, we must have a plan so we don't get overwhelmed. Though stress itself doesn't condemn you to aging poorly, how you cope with it is critical. Remember: *Unchecked stress is the enemy. Calm is your friend.*

Being calm is an emotionally stressed-out person's salvation, a break from turmoil when you're centered and at ease. A state of biological calm floods your body with the bliss of endorphins, our body's natural painkillers, which make stress hormones recede. Levels of serotonin, a natural antidepressant, increase so daily hurdles feel more manageable. Dr. Herbert Benson calls this the "relaxation response," a balm for tension. The answer to aging well, in spite of stress, is learning how to find calm in the storm.

In summary, stress ages you and makes you feel old whereas calm slows aging and makes you feel younger. There's also evidence that reducing stress by instituting lifestyle changes such as exercise, rest, diet, and learning new intellectual skills, along with the tips I offer below, can enhance your brain's neuroplasticity, the ability to regenerate cells even into old age.

TIPS TO SURRENDER STRESS, INCREASE YOUR BRAIN'S NEUROPLASTICITY, AND FEEL YOUNGER

- *Don't sweat the small stuff.* Get in the habit of letting minor annoyances and concerns go. This reduces your stress hormones and slows aging.

- *Cultivate gratitude and positive thinking.* Be grateful for every breath, every moment. Cultivating an "attitude of gratitude" has been linked to better health, sounder sleep, less anxiety and depression, being kinder to others, and a higher long-term satisfaction with life. For instance, instead of dreading a birthday, be grateful you've been gifted with another year to live.

- *Be playful.* Regularly take time out from responsibilities or worries and have fun. Play increases endorphins, happiness, and longevity. Play with your children, your grandchildren, your friends. Shoot hoops, do a crossword puzzle, skip down the sidewalk, see movies, go on outings, tell jokes, be silly. Incorporate play into your life every day.

- *Embrace humor.* Laughter increases longevity. Being overly serious and intense decreases life span due to chronic stress. Instead, laugh about things. As Bob Hope did, keep a sense of humor about aging. He said, "I don't feel old. I don't feel anything till noon. That's when it's time for my nap."

- *Get a pet.* Studies have shown that pets increase longevity and health by providing companionship and unconditional love. They also reduce stress and blood pressure, improve the appetites of Alzheimer's patients, and increase the life span of heart attack survivors. Let yourself enjoy the unconditional love!

- *Practice forgiveness.* Harboring grudges is linked to high blood pressure, which can lead to stroke, kidney or heart failure or even death. Anger has been proven to shorten your life. Forgiveness is a decision to let go of anger, resentments, and thoughts of revenge. Choose to forgive. Muster all your strength to let go of an offense so that you can move on, be happier, and live longer.

- *Meditate.* Regular meditation keeps you calmer, less anxious, and younger by enhancing your brain's neuroplasticity. Research has shown that daily meditators live longer and have higher levels of telomerase, the enzyme that prevents cells from aging. By reducing stress hormones, meditation counteracts the battering fight-or-flight mode of emotional coping. Start with ten minutes daily and increase the duration as you become more comfortable with meditating.

THE ART OF SURRENDER IN ENERGETIC AGING: AWAKEN THE FIRE WITHIN

Having abundant energy is a precious gift. It's associated with youth though I've had plenty of twentysomething- and thirtysomething patients who are chronically exhausted from pushing themselves too hard and vibrant seventysomething patients who've told me, "I've never felt better."

Nevertheless, many older people often say, "I don't have the energy I used to," a shift my friend Berenice didn't experience until eighty. The experience is real and honoring the changing rhythms of your body is essential—but simply surrendering or succumbing to fatigue is not the answer. The Harvard School of Medicine reports the following contributors to age-related low energy. Some solutions are traditional but others challenge you to awaken your subtle energies (discussed in Chapter 7) and the fire within.

Factors Associated with Decreased Energy with Age

- *Your circadian rhythms shift.* With age, you tend to go to sleep earlier and wake up earlier. By sixty-five, you spend about 5 percent of the night in deep sleep compared to 20 percent when you were twenty. Insomnia increases, as do frequent awakenings so you don't feel as rested in the morning. What helps explain these shifts is that melatonin, the hormone that makes you feel tired at night, declines with passing years and significantly decreases with old age. **Solution:** Respect this change in your circadian rhythms by adjusting your sleep habits along with taking a melatonin supplement. Yoga and meditation also can increase melatonin.

- *Menopause and other hormonal changes.* As estrogen levels dip, many women have hot flashes, insomnia, and disturbed sleep, resulting in fatigue. **Solution:** Awaken and balance your body's subtle energies using techniques such as Chinese medicine, herbs, energy medicine, and *chi*-building meditation. You can use these along with bioidentical hormone replacement.

- *Sedentary lifestyle.* By seventy you can lose 30 percent of the muscle mass you had at twenty. Your metabolic rate decreases so you tend to gain weight. Your ligaments and joints stiffen so you move more slowly. All these variables limit your strength and aggravate fatigue. The paradox is that exercise boosts your energy but you want to exercise less when your energy is low.

Solution: Regularly practice a form of activity, no matter how gentle, that you feel comfortable with. Go slow, take baby steps, but move in some way. Weight training, walking, aerobics, gentle yoga, and stretching can counteract the physical wear and tear or low energy that may accompany aging.

- *Illness.* Age-related diseases can deplete your energy and interfere with sleep. Fatigue is a symptom of hypothyroidism, anemia, diabetes, heart disease, depression, cancer, and other illnesses. Also, side effects from prescription and over-the-counter drugs can cause fatigue and insomnia. **Solution:** Seek out medical treatment if you're ill and make positive lifestyle changes such as a healthy diet, adequate rest, and meditation to speed up healing. Also, stay informed about a medication's side effects so that you're not complicating the drain of illness with toxic drug reactions. Augmenting conventional medicine with subtle energy techniques including acupuncture and energy work will accelerate healing and boost your vitality.

To counteract the energy decline associated with age, you must realize that there's a fire within us that most people don't know about. It's called the kundalini energy, the coiled serpent power at the base of your spine. If you want to function at your peak, age radiantly, and live longer, it's crucial to awaken this force. Then it can rise up your spine like an electric current to your crown, nourishing your cells and life force—an experience my patients have called "exhilarating," "invigorating," even "orgasmic." In Hindu mysticism, the kundalini is seen as the goddess Shakti who surges up to unite with her beloved, Lord Shiva, the Supreme One. In your body, the result is bliss. What a waste that in most people, especially us overintellectualized Westerners, the kundalini stays dormant. Once you learn to ignite and tend to it as you would a fire, you'll exude a spark that keeps you timeless and bright.

Here's a diagram to visualize where the kundalini is located in your body. Using the practices I suggest, you can feel this energy ascend from your lower body to the head.

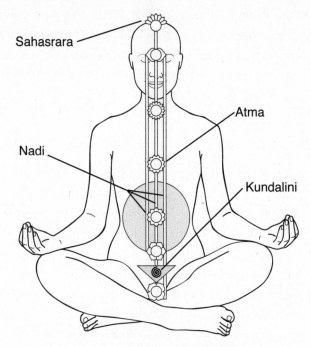

[Figure 6.] Kundalini Energy Diagram

Surrender is key to awakening your inner fire. You can't think your way there. For instance, during yoga or a massage (both of which awaken your energies) you need to yield, to open, to let go and flow with the sensations, emotions, healing, and ecstasy that come. If your mind is chattering or you hold back, you reduce the benefits. What blocks your kundalini? Overthinking, overwork, forcing, pushing, disease, waning hormones, unchecked stress, fear, and even benign neglect. Many of us age prematurely because we simply don't know how to nurture this energy.

I invite you to explore the following practices to keep your fire bright. See which ones you enjoy. Their purpose is to awaken your kundalini and subtle energy system in various ways. Though it's preferable to begin these practices when you're young, with patients I've seen that the kundalini can open at any age if you are receptive. Sometimes your mind will be blown immediately by a sense of blissfulness and rejuvenation. However, even if you don't feel anything initially, give your sensitivities time to attune to the subtleties of these interventions. During sessions, keep surrendering and relaxing, deeper and longer. Over a few weeks, the benefits of greater clarity, balance, and well-being will sneak up on you.

Six Practices to Awaken Your Kundalini

1. *Surrender to Yoga*

Yoga practitioners are the youngest-looking people I know. Yoga originated in India five thousand years ago as a holy path to realization (the word yoga is Sanskrit for "union with spirit"). It stimulates the life energy called *prana* through breath and postures. Many of my patients who've avoided exercise adore yoga. Scientists have found that yoga helps straighten the hunched-over back called kyphosis that can come with age; it also reduces back pain. Regular exercise can maintain muscle strength, tone, bone density, joint flexibility, balance, and mobility. Your posture improves, which stops you from slouching. In most yoga disciplines, there are specific classes for the elderly and those with physical limitations.

Though all forms of yoga raise your vital energy, kundalini yoga goes beyond physical poses to also include meditating on your *chakras* (the body's midline energy centers) to blend the emotional, sexual, and the divine. A kundalini class begins with a short chant followed by a warm-up to stretch the spine and improve flexibility. The focus of the class is called a *kriya*, a sequence of poses, alternate-nostril breathing, *mudras* (hand positions), and *chakra* activation to raise the energy up your spine and light your fire!

2. *Surrender to the Kundalini Golden Flower Meditation*

- *Sit cross-legged in a meditative position.* Get comfortable. If you can't cross your legs, it's fine to keep them straight or sit in a chair. Close your eyes. Center yourself by gently focusing on the tip of your nose. Don't think too much about your center. Just intuitively feel it.

- *Block out the Ten Thousand Things.* It doesn't work to attempt to quiet the mind directly. Rather, you must distract the mind by assigning it a task such as counting your breaths or simply by focusing on your breath. You can inhale to a count of four and exhale to a count of four to keep the mind occupied so it doesn't focus on the Ten Thousand Things.

- *Redirect the breath with the backward-flowing method.* Get in the habit of belly breathing—expanding your belly when you breathe rather then just your chest. Feel your breath hover in your pelvis, in your genitals, and at the base of your spine. With each inhalation feel your belly expand, depositing the breath's *prana* in these areas. Breathe in and out five times; feel the *prana* pool there. Then, men: lightly put your attention on the sperm in your testicles. Women: focus on your cervical fluids. Next, use the breath to raise the life energy from the testicles or through the cervical opening and up the spine to the top of the head. The purpose of this backward-flowing method is to divert the energy of the seminal or cervical fluids via the breath to the brain, an anti-aging secret for continuing vibrancy. Visualize and feel this energy moving. You're commanding the breath to change directions, then drawing it upward. Practice this meditation daily to nurture your kundalini force.

3. *Surrender to the Delight of Body Work*

A good massage calms the mind, defuses tension, eases disease, and transports you to a surrendered, altered state. The purpose is to un-knot your body and get energy flowing through your subtle system. Massage smoothes all the spots where you hold, clench, or have remnants of past injuries, kneading out stress so it doesn't age you. If you don't have body work, where do you think the stress goes? Your body will just get tighter, more rigid, and more contracted each year—not a pretty or healthy way to age. Instead, why not become more fluid and flexible?

Muscles and tissues also house emotions and memories. For

instance, massaging your shoulders can stimulate an emotional catharsis and emergence of past memories lodged there. You want these to surface and to be released. Physical manipulation is often necessary to achieve this. During a massage, if you are moved to cry or laugh, let it flow. If other emotions such as anger or joy surface, surrender to these too. Don't inhibit yourself. It keeps you young to clear out negativity and stress that otherwise sap your energy. For decades I've had regular massages, ideally once a week, and advise my patients to do so too. Techniques range from the gentle Swedish variety to Rolfing (deep tissue work) to shiatsu (pressure on specific points).

4. *Surrender to the Healing of Acupuncture*

Traditional Chinese medicine includes a range of therapies such as acupuncture and herbs as well as qi gong and tai chi (subtle energy-building movements). While health is considered a harmonious balance of *chi* (vital energy) in the body, diseases, including those associated with aging, reflect a disharmony of *chi*. Acupuncture works by using needles to stimulate energy meridians from head to toe to reinstitute harmony. The World Health Organization has recognized disorders for which acupuncture is effective including pain, arthritis, migraines, nausea, hypertension, and fatigue. Acupuncture is therapeutic in age-related illnesses by decreasing pain in your back and joints, increasing mobility, and alleviating stress and trauma. Cosmetic acupuncture, known as "acupuncture face-lifts," entails inserting needles into frown lines or wrinkles; this purportedly stimulates blood flow and new collagen formation. One patient reported, "It gives a *chi* rush to my face and makes me glow." Another didn't have noticeable results. My Chinese medicine practitioner says it works for some people but not all. Though acupuncture facials are said to help your own body create a more youthful appearance, no scientific studies have substantiated this yet.

As you get older, acupuncture and other traditional Chinese medicine practices are extremely helpful. They can balance your energy and reduce the wear and tear of aging. If you have surgery (especially with anesthesia), an illness, or an injury, acupuncture can accelerate your recovery and lessen discomfort and toxicity. Acupuncture is one of the best things you can do for your body to keep it happy. Since conventional medicine doesn't typically address balancing your subtle energies, acupuncture is integral to healing and wellness. I also recommend monthly acupuncture tune-ups even if you aren't ill. It rejuvenates your body to keep you more radiant at any age. And tai chi and qi gong make the elderly more stable and agile.

5. *Surrender to the Renewal of Energy Medicine*

Energy medicine is a branch of complementary medicine in which you tap your body's kundalini and other subtle energies for health and longevity. I feel privileged to be part of a renaissance that is sweeping modern health care in which doctors, nurses, and other practitioners are incorporating energy medicine into conventional methods of treating patients. Take Dr. Mehmet Oz, for example. He's a gutsy cardiothoracic surgeon who brings energy healers into the operating room during open-heart surgery. These healers send vital energy to patients through their hands, a technique shown to accelerate post-op recovery. "Energy fields definitely impact our lives," Oz says. "Understanding what energy is gives us a new grasp on how the body functions."

What I appreciate about energy medicine is that, similar to acupuncture, it balances your subtle energy system, which in turn enhances your aliveness. It is also a gentle alternative to relieve all sorts of symptoms, from aches and pains to illness-related malaise, in highly sensitive bodies like my own. The different techniques include reiki and therapeutic touch. A practitioner channels energy into a recipient to provide an extra boost to jump-start the person's own innate healing mechanisms. In my office, with the patient lying face-up on a couch, I place my hands a few inches above his or her body and sense where healing is needed. Then I lightly touch the body and transmit energy as it comes through me. Most important, I send energy from my heart to awaken a patient's heart, which is the center of healing and youthfulness. I am simply a vessel for this energy. I don't "try" to do anything, nor is my ego involved. Sometimes the results are immediate—panic melts, eyes sparkle, fatigue lessens. More often, though, there is a gradual brightening that comes with balance.

Recently I gave a friend an energy healing session in his hospital room after he'd been diagnosed with abdominal pain from food poisoning. My friend loves to sing but stops himself from doing it around anyone, afraid that his voice isn't good enough. As I put my hands on his body, sending him energy, he closed his eyes and sang a beautiful Italian song. This tender moment together felt replenishing to him, and to me as well.

Energy medicine also specializes in helping psychosomatic symptoms and pain. My patient Peg, an office manager who'd seen numerous doctors for fibromyalgia (extreme pain in muscles and joints), improved with energy healing. Her pain cycle was broken and she could reduce her dependence on anti-inflammatory drugs. And when she felt better her joy of living returned. As a consequence, she looked, felt, and acted younger.

I recommend energy medicine as an anti-aging practice as well as to supplement conventional medical treatments. It can speed healing and rekindle your fire after surgery or during an illness.

6. *Surrender to Ecstatic Dance*

Dancer Gabrielle Roth pioneered modern ecstatic dance, a form of meditative spontaneous movement that unleashes the body's kundalini in a free-form blissful surrender to spirit and the universe. It stems from the ancient shamanic rite of journeying inward through movement to receive guidance and joy in the whirling dervish Sufi tradition. Roth's ecstatic dance focuses on five basic rhythms: flowing, staccato, chaos, lyrical, and stillness. There is a no-talking rule which allows you to move out of your head and into your body. Some dances are specifically solo; others are interactive. You don't watch people— just close your eyes and feel the music or drumming. Dancers let loose and surrender to their bodies' rhythms to revive their zest and clarity. Ecstatic dance classes from the Gabrielle Roth tradition and others are offered internationally with schedules available on the Internet.

Awakening your kundalini fire is enhanced by the above techniques for radiant aging but also goes beyond any technique. It's an organic moment-to-moment *darshan*, an energy transmission of wisdom that brings passion to everything. Feeling your fire is about how surrendered you are in your body as you walk down the street. It's the ecstasy in your eyes as you take in the wonder of a tiny rosebud. It's laughing and loving; being genuine, playful, and wild. My friend Rabbi Don Singer says, "A reward of cultivating the aliveness of subtle energy as we age is being able to see things vibrate." Great joy and satisfaction come from this multidimensional reverie of radiance. Awakening your kundalini lets your life force commune with the universal life force. I can't imagine having greater fun than dancing with that mystery. When you're in touch with the awe of it all, you'll have a lightness of being at any age.

THE ART OF SURRENDER IN SPIRITUAL AGING: THE POWER OF YOUR SOUL'S LONGEVITY

When you view aging from a spiritual perspective, everything changes. Spiritual aging allows you to see that there is more to your life experiences than the material world or ego. The soul has a life of its own, free of the time-space continuum. As Einstein knew, time is just an illusion. The soul goes through cycles of light, here and beyond. If you believe this, it frames how you view getting older and what comes next in terms of the everlasting. If you don't believe this, you'll frame aging and mortality in terms of the bleak standpoint of the material world and of mere decay.

At high school reunions I've been intrigued by how differently people have aged. Take the stunning homecoming queen whose beauty has eroded from years of chronic depression. Or the class nerd who has practiced yoga for decades and looks radiant and youthful. Or the scowling class bully who has become a timelessly beautiful Buddhist monk. Clearly, former classmates who had been on spiritual paths looked younger and less rigid, giggled more, and didn't play the victim or seem downtrodden by life's hurdles.

Numerous studies have found a strong link among spirituality, longevity, and physical and emotional health. Spirituality has many advantages, including greater optimism, less stress and loneliness, and more of a sense of belonging to a community. Believing in a higher power has been shown to impart strength during tough situations such as grappling with serious illnesses and loss. When you're at peace and stress hormones aren't ravaging your system, you'll age less and live longer.

Spirituality makes you more powerful and attractive with age. There is no downside to cultivating it. Here, time is your friend; youth isn't typically a plus in this case. Even if life has dealt you a bitter hand, developing a spiritual connection can improve your outlook and help you attain peace. Over the years you just keep surrendering to light, compassion, and a force greater than yourself. You increasingly feel the ecstasy that comes from this, not succumbing to fear. You have a truer perspective on the eternality of your spirit and aren't terrified by the prospect of death. Plus, if you meditate and develop your heart, you'll emanate an irresistibly loving charisma, with immortal eyes and a depth of soul that get only more arresting.

Still, gratifying as the gains of spiritual aging are, the surrenders demanded of us, such as letting go of ego attachments to younger versions of our bodies, are not for the weak of heart. Change terrifies the ego. That's why it clings to what we think we know or what we wish would be. Healthy and sexy as we may feel at any age, we must accept that our physical selves and priorities are changing and not fixate on past ideals. We must fight the good fight to surrender our egos. We must see ourselves as souls, not just bodies. I'm moved by how spiritual teacher Ram Dass, at eighty-three, articulates this in "Aging Body, Ageless Soul":

> *The whole journey of aging is something designed to lead us from thinking of ourselves as egos to knowing ourselves as souls. We're given opportunity after opportunity to practice letting go and to shift our perspective from ego to soul-view. However if aging doesn't do it for*

*us, then the next stage, dying, certainly will. Because at death the ego
ceases; the soul, on the other hand, goes on. The soul doesn't age the
way the body ages, so aging and dying are trips of the ego and of the.
physical manifestation.*

Like it or not, you can't hold on to time. The time it took for you to
read this sentence is already gone. When surrendering to aging, you
want to move forward fluidly in mind, body, and spirit, not get bogged
down in the good or bad of the past. I admit that when I feel nostalgic
or sad, I occasionally zone out by losing myself in memories. I get
pleasure from looking at the piece of driftwood on which my artist
boyfriend painted nineteen candles in a sunlit field for my birthday.
And I am happy thinking about the sexy strapless dress I wore when
I was twenty-five and had a perfect body. I remember loving people
and losing people and walking my beloved dog under the old amuse-
ment park pier in Venice Beach a long time ago. I even enjoy recalling
the time I cut out my photo in the high school yearbook because I
didn't like the way I looked. That insecure girl is endearing to me. I
revisit these memories but try not to dwell there.

Our journeys—mine and yours—are toward the future, toward
aging, change, and destiny—a movement archetypally conjured by
the Chariot card of the Tarot. And with age, spirit grows enticingly
larger and closer, as does the light on the other side. Surrendering
to these mysteries while still never being completely certain of what
will happen is the fun of it for me. There is so much about aging that
exceeds our frail manipulative powers. Sure, you can try to fight the
flow of time and all the other forces you can't control, but what's the
point?

Why People Want to Live Forever:
The Trouble with Immortality

It boggles my mind that many people surveyed in Western culture say
they want to live forever, or at least for hundreds of years, if they can
stay healthy. In fact, a group known as "immortalists" are freezing
their bodies with an unproven technique known as cryonics in the

hope that future advances can "cure aging" and their illnesses as well as resuscitate their memories and personalities!

What motivates the desire for immortality? For some of my patients, it's linked to a primal terror of death, of bidding a final goodbye to their physical form. Our reptilian brain, wired for survival, is inconsolably attached to keeping us alive. It just can't fathom the merits of surrendering the body or that the spirit lives on. (More on the afterlife in Chapter 12.) I want to show these patients ways to gain a visceral sense of spirituality and their eternal selves through meditation, contemplation, and prayer. Theoretical notions of spirit are useless here. They're just in the head, not a deep enough knowing to sustain us through the radical initiations of aging and the surrenders it asks of us. I want to help my patients experience the immortality of their spirits in their whole beings.

The work I do with patients, along with the spiritual exercises in this book, awakens their intuitive, noncerebral awareness of a larger, loving intelligence. We have been and always will be a part of this. It's our home, a realization that lessens the fear of aging and death. For as many sessions as it takes, I sit with my patients to help them intuitively feel their spirit nonverbally in the stillness. I teach them to close their eyes, meditate, and sense who they really are. I show them how to breathe their mental chatter away so they can know they are so much more than linear thought. This process of awakening to their larger selves is beautiful. First my patients may sense a flicker of inner light. Then a flash of ecstasy. Then an inkling of peace. They're discovering themselves and their awakening just keeps unfolding. Once they catch a glimpse of this larger perspective, prolonging our stay here doesn't seem nearly as appealing.

Honestly, as much as I love this wondrous planet, I'm not interested in returning here. I confess, even at this age, I often feel like an ET, longing for my true home. Still, I'm grateful that my Daoist training has instilled in me a confidence in the soul's longevity after we pass on. As my teacher says, "The soul work continues."

I'm not trying to dictate how long it is best for anyone to live. Still, I urge you to have realistic expectations. Even if you make it to a thousand in good health, you still need to deal with fears, obsessions, pain, anxiety attacks, and endless trials in the material realm, known for its intense level of suffering. The numerous scientific advances in longevity on the forefront will offer you more choices. I hope you can assess them from the point of view of spirituality as well as life extension.

From a past-life/future-life perspective, the issue of longevity takes on new dimensions. I smiled when one patient said of herself, "I'm forty going on four thousand." Buddhists believe in reincarnation—that our soul keeps returning in different bodies to clear out bad karma (emotional wrongs and other debts we've accrued in past lives) and to create good karma through spiritual evolvement and acts of service and love. I resonate with this. One life couldn't possibly be enough for us to sort through all of our spiritual lessons. In this sense, you are given all the time you need to complete your soul's work. They say there are young souls (the less experienced person with only a few incarnations) and old souls (those who've gained wisdom from countless lives). Whether we're young or old souls, we are all works in progress gradually heading toward enlightenment and learning to transcend our attachments to people, things, and desires. At that point of liberation, your job is done. There's no longer any need to remain on the physical plane. You will proceed to other, more elevated, blissful forms of existence. This is the view of the traditions that believe in reincarnation.

Fundamentally, people want to live forever because they don't trust there's anything else but here, nor do they believe in the soul's longevity. So they attempt to defy or deny the aging process, wanting to be immortal. Don't get me wrong—I understand how hard it is to surrender to the inexorable changes of passing time. Mother, father, lover: we want the security of these relationships. I'm as attached as anyone to people I treasure and to my other appetites. But my overriding goal is to keep loosening my grasp even on what I love most without compromising the giving of my heart—a paradox of surrendering to love in a dominion of impermanence. Still, a time will come when even this will be in the past and the only reality ahead of us is radiance. Our only choice will be to surrender.

Consequently, I'm adamant about practicing the art of spiritual surrender as part of aging. Grasping that you are more than your body frees you from fear so you can relax and enjoy your life. Spiritual aging celebrates the luxury of going inward, a chapter of satisfaction that has nothing to do with outer achievement. Surrender becomes easier if you don't have something to prove. In one ancient Daoist tradition, it's accepted that at sixty, elders are rewarded for having been good providers by being allowed to surrender all their worldly obligations. They literally leave everything behind including their families and work, to live in the forest and go deeper. A great gift they're given is to have their distractions removed. Finally they have time and space for undisturbed spiritual expansion. Though most of us won't have the freedom or desire to leave loved ones and our professions in service to the unseen, such shifting of priorities with age is worthy of emulating.

Keep Your Spiritual Connection Current

What may be disconcerting about making a connection with the divine is that it keeps changing. Every day, in meditation, I stay open to rediscovering what my connection is, making sure it matches the person I am at the age I happen to be. Nothing, including this bond, is static. I don't assume anything about spirit. I tune in to it over and over again, reigniting our love affair. As old layers of myself melt away, I reach out to my higher power in new ways. Occasionally I even lose the connection. It crushes me every time, bringing me to my knees. Still, these lost periods happen. This is when I become patient or at least I try to be. I grope in the dark, feeling my way little by little toward even the slightest divine spark. Intuition is in charge of saving me. Over the years, surrendering to it lets me find my way as my communion with spirit evolves.

Aging brings change. That's inevitable. It's not about staying the same. Ram Dass correctly says, "When it comes to getting older, we have a choice: cling to the past (and suffer), or let go and enjoy the spiritual journey." My goal is to be reverent in the face of the ripeness that comes with age, to surrender to the expansions and sacrifices of my body-mind-spirit metamorphosis. It is said that your reverence

pleases the Lord. Reverence also softens your fears of aging and se-
cures your divine bond to the universe. To help you flow with age, I
suggest practicing this surrender chant, either speaking or singing it
to whatever melody you choose.

SPIRITUAL SURRENDER CHANT

I surrender to aging and change and to all the cycles of light that
I am privileged to encounter. With each new year, I will make the
great leap into the arms of spirit with increasing passion. I will
have great faith that these arms will catch and embrace me. I will
not hold back. I will surrender to the mysteries of time, life, and
eternity.

In this chapter we've discussed how to maximize the four components of aging—physical, emotional, energetic, and spiritual—to slow
down time. I hope my perspective has helped free you from being
held hostage by your fear-based ego. Age can't be defined by just a
number. It's the person that counts. From the standpoint of surrender, aging is about *growing* old and evolving, not remaining emotionally or spiritually stunted. You both accumulate radiance and release
attachments to the past. You gain so much—and you let so much go.
Aging is the quintessential mindfulness exercise, a continuing stretch
toward the heart, accepting the body's impermanence and forgiving
it for not lasting forever. Surrender comes from understanding this
and embracing all the cycles of light you pass through.

At a recent concert, one reviewer observed that master performer
Leonard Cohen, a Buddhist at seventy-nine, "skipped off the stage
like a schoolboy in love," the spring in his step suggesting "a giddy
adolescent," "a Zen romantic." That's who I want to be. Never give up
on hope or creativity or passion. Keep falling in love with the world.
Once in a while, kiss the ground. Your life is an offering from spirit.
Your body is the altar within which your soul grows. Something good
has begun. It's been coming for some time. Shining on you as you age.
Shining on you, always.

SURRENDER AFFIRMATION FOR RADIANT AGING

I am a beautiful, sensual, spiritual person at all ages. I am grateful for every breath. Each morning has the promise of a new day. I will keep surrendering my fear of getting older. I will keep surrendering criticism of my body. I will surrender to my radiance, my joy, and the sacredness of my life's journey.

Oh wow. Oh wow.
—FINAL WORDS OF STEVE JOBS, FOUNDER OF APPLE COMPUTER

12

THE TWELFTH SURRENDER

MAKING PEACE WITH DEATH AND

THE AFTERLIFE

DEATH IS THE ULTIMATE SURRENDER. EACH ONE OF US, INCLUDING members of the medical profession, knows that this is an appointment we all must keep. But from my intuitive perspective, it's also a daring expansion of ourselves that we are destined for—the biggest spiritual happening of our lives. I want to quell any fears that you might have and show you that there is nothing to be afraid of. You're not losing power; you're gaining it. Death has gotten a bad rap in Western medicine and culture. The transition itself is endowed with an aura of unnecessarily high drama. When the Dalai Lama was asked about his own death he shrugged and laughed, calling it just a "change of clothing." Imagine feeling so relaxed about death! That's the peace and drama-free acceptance you too can know when you surrender.

Everything in this book has led up to the final letting go. Practicing surrender in various aspects of your life, from finances to sex to aging, prepares you for the leap of surrendering to the beyond. Whether you're forty or ninety, accepting death is necessary for your serenity now and helps you live more fully. Research indicates that the top regrets of dying people include "I wish I hadn't worked so hard," "I wish I'd had the courage to be true to myself, not just do what others expected of me," and "I wish I'd let myself be happier." Why not set those priorities now and lead a truly meaningful life? Making peace with death allows you to live more fully and to achieve a mindful closure with your life when the time comes to go.

With this intention, we'll explore: What does surrendering to death mean to you? What can you gain? Do you stop existing? What does death really feel like? Is the afterlife real? How can we heal our collective death phobia? It's natural to feel afraid or confused about death. Truth is, the passage itself requires both improvisation and trust. It's the mother of all exercises in humility in which you must surrender your ego and let go of control. Even so, from this, our current world, I'll describe how you can get a reassuring intuitive sense of what happens next, how safe and insanely beautiful it is.

From the standpoint of surrender, what is death? First, you surrender physically. We do not possess our bodies. They're simply on loan to us for a short while. Science defines physical death as cessation of our biological functions, including blood circulation via the heart and breathing (cardiac death) and brain activity (brain death). At the onset of death, we lose consciousness in a few seconds. Our brain waves flatline on the EEG in about forty seconds though the brainstem may still register impulses for a few minutes. Like many of my patients, you might understandably wonder, "Is death painful?" Don't worry. As a physician, I can assure you: the answer is no. Since the brain mediates pain and the brain has stopped functioning, you are free of any discomfort.

Second, at death, you spiritually surrender to a force larger than yourself. There's no bad news here, only an opening and freedom from constriction. You don't have to "do" anything, just relax and let go. What this larger force actually is will become evident as you pass over. Anticipate all you like, but you can't completely know what lies beyond: it's a big surprise party just for you. The *Tibetan Book of the Dead* calls the revelation of death "seeing the primary clear light." The brain is a filter that dumbs down consciousness. When you die your consciousness is liberated to a higher level. You are unfettered by the confines of your body and suffering lifts in ways you can't even imagine. During my medical training at the UCLA/Wadsworth

Veterans' Hospital hospice, I had the great good fortune to be at many deathbeds observing the beauty of this final release, especially when patients had endured terrible illnesses. Immediately prior to death, as a patient's body wound down and could no longer contain the person, there was no pain. Then an extraordinary letting go occurred, followed by a sense of peace, even ecstasy. It's often difficult for us on this busy, pain-intense planet to imagine that surrendering to such ecstasy is our spirit's legacy, the place where we came from and to which we'll eventually return. But it is.

Death is not the enemy, nor is it alien or sinister. Instead, I'd like you to consider it a teacher and healer. Here's why. Fundamentally, death is a creative energy that impels both destructive and constructive change. Throughout life we experience this energy: the death of a relationship allows us to find something better; we outgrow a negative part of ourselves and become freer; the loss of a loved one or animal companion sparks both grief and growth. In French, an orgasm is called *le petit mort* or "the little death," a surrender that gives you bliss. Sleep is similar to death: we temporarily surrender the linear mind and ego until we awaken the next day. And there's nature's seasonal death/rebirth cycles for us to contemplate: the wonder of autumn, winter, spring, and summer. But to me, death's most impressive creative show is catalyzing our transition from matter to spirit. Death is energy in motion. It is not tame. You can't control it. Turning back is not an option. You can't pull away from this edge. You must go over it. Let me help you overcome fear so you'll surrender more comfortably to this transition and not worry so much about it.

DEATH AS TEACHER AND HEALER: SURRENDER YOUR FEARS AND DEATH PHOBIA

. . . .

I'm not afraid of dying, I just don't want to be there when it happens.
—WOODY ALLEN

Why is the subject of death so charged, our fears so vast? How can we console ourselves and heal our collective death phobia? I laughed out loud when reading surveys citing that the only thing people fear more than death is public speaking! I can understand death's number two ranking. In front of an audience, you're figuratively naked and suddenly, inescapably up against worries such as "Can I speak? What will others think of me? Who am I really? What do I stand for?" Death demands the same self-scrutiny though from a day-to-day perspective it seems more remote.

During my medical training it was sadly evident how strong the death phobia was among physicians and other health care professionals. Death was coldly referred to as "crashing," "coding," or "expiring": no light or sacredness in those words. Terminal patients were often left alone, abandoned in hospital rooms at the end of long dismal hallways with few visits from medical personnel except for angel nursing staff checking vital signs. Or else the dying were spoken to in such technical, sterile language that it was horribly depersonalizing and downright insulting to them. Can you imagine being addressed in this sort of intellectual psychobabble—simply a distancing defense against fear—at this most critical moment? Thank God for loving relatives and friends who sit with their transitioning beloveds, not forsaking them in harrowing circumstances, though hurting and grieving themselves.

Frequently, doctors view death as a failure rather than seeing their jobs as showering light and joy on the dying during their sacred passage. Instead, valiant hospice workers guide patients and their families through this complicated period. To the detriment of patients, physicians frequently haven't made peace with their own deaths, nor do they see themselves as shepherds for a patient's final surrender in a spiritual journey. So they project their fears onto the terminally ill who need love and support more than anyone else as they prepare to transition. I don't think I'm being too harsh when I say this is an unwitting form of abuse of the dying.

What about death most terrifies us? What is it that makes us shrink into our smallest unsurrendered selves? Since you can't control it or know exactly what will happen, this alarms the part of us that fears change, legitimately craves reassurance, and wants bulletproof answers. This unknown can turn death into the perfect tabula rasa on which to project our fears of the boogieman. But surrendering to death necessitates rolling with some uncertainty.

At a recent intuition workshop I conducted at the UCLA Mindfulness Research Center, a woman asked me with fierce immediacy, "Are *you* afraid of death?" I had to pause. The best answer I could give, the only one that felt authentic to offer was, "Not at the moment." At this point, I still don't think I'll be afraid when the time comes because of how magnificent the other side has felt in my intuitions and dreams since childhood. I have encountered the eternal and I don't fear it. Still, you never know. I could very well cling to my last moments and last breath as tenaciously as others have. In fact, I watched my mother, herself a physician, who had cancer and was clearly in her final days, drag my father to the Armani store in Beverly Hills to buy yet another designer outfit for her wardrobe. Mother was stubborn and was making it clear that she didn't want to have anything to do with dying. I understand how painful it was for her, as it is for many of us, to let go. But, to make peace with death, it behooves us to address and surrender fear.

In order to leave the fear zone, you must examine honestly and compassionately what you're so afraid of. There's no point denying fears. They don't go anywhere. Fears just lurk within, handicapping your heart, your intuition, and your ability to feel safe letting go in all areas. What are your worst fears? Let's get down to it. Here are some common ones.

Physical pain	Loneliness
Loss of power and control	Being alone and lost
Lack of choice	Abandonment
Unfinished business	Depression
Missed opportunities	Disorientation
Hell	Estrangement from people we love
The devil	
Purgatory	There's no God
Being stuck in limbo	Separation from the earth
Annihilation of everything about yourself	Being judged
	Punishment

One fear that I had a difficult time surrendering was what would happen to my body after I died. I felt extremely attached to my body, this particular package of self I've been given in this particular lifetime. It felt so sad to let go of my books, my writing, the ocean, the trees, my friends, my loves, my struggles, my joys. And the thought of degenerating in some coffin with worms eating me or being cremated felt horrifying. Not to mention the waste: all of those facials, the endless hours in the gym, the time spent with hair stylists, the chiropractic adjustments—all my efforts to stay healthy, beautiful, and fit ended in this! Clearly, I was working myself into quite a state. So I called my friend Rabbi Don Singer who is also a Zen *roshi*. He just laughed and said he thought the intensity with which I was grappling with this dilemma was fabulous. He told me, "The body knows what to do when the time comes. Just trust it." This felt so intuitively right, I immediately relaxed.

Processing the fears of my body's post-death fate let me freshly appreciate how much I adore this body and the rest of me right now. As long as I'm "me" in this form, I intend to enjoy every moment of my physicality. Plus, I realized that after I'm dead, I won't care about physically degenerating. I'll be on to new endeavors. My Daoist teacher says about the other side, "The work continues." All this helped me surrender the fear.

For me, releasing my fear of death, or anything else, is a process. It's not as simple as changing my thinking, though that's part of it. Sometimes I'm a hard case to convince. "Experts" offer a multitude of good solutions for releasing fear which for me are impossible to execute without intuitive confirmation. To know a solution is valid, I must feel waves of goose bumps propelling chills from head to toe, my gut saying yes, my inner guidance relaying, "You've found a secret! Trust it." In your life, train yourself to be mindful of your intuitions too. Personally, these are the stars I choose to follow, and so may you.

How can you surrender your fears of death and realize that we are all eternal beings? First, examine the attitudes you were raised with. Were your parents afraid or in denial? Did they impart that to you consciously or unconsciously? As a child, I remember a series of sweet goldfish ominously floating belly up at the top of the tank. My well-intentioned mother, without a hint of a eulogy, would abruptly flush them down the toilet (which to me was shocking, considering what else went down those pipes). She'd sympathetically say, "Don't be sad. We'll get you another one." Actually, I was *really* sad—each time—and never felt that goldfish or any other creatures were so easily replaceable. I wish Mother would've taught me more about how natural death and the sadness of loss are. But, like many caring parents, she just wanted me to be happy and to spare me upset. Plus, as I've conveyed, she wasn't that keen on facing death herself. So I was left hanging, never fully able to process the loss or to resolve, "What really happened to my goldfish? Where is it? Did it go to heaven or somewhere else?" For all of us, it's useful to track our early reactions to death. What was your first exposure to it? Did a relative die? An animal companion? Did you see a gull decaying on the beach? Did you witness someone killed in a car accident? Do you remember your emotions? Were you alarmed? Revolted? Confused? Shocked? Inconsolable? Did you share your feelings and get a satisfying explanation? Or did you hold your feelings in or fail to get a useful response? Identifying the source of fears and misconceptions makes it easier to substitute the positive attitudes I'll share.

ARE THERE FATES WORSE THAN DEATH? REPROGRAM YOUR FEARS

I've seen even the coolest people lose their cool around the subject of death. Keeping a balanced perspective helps you stay centered and out of nervous drama. I agree with Father Greg Boyle, fearless leader of Homeboy Industries, a rehabilitation program for Los Angeles gang members, who advises kids, "There are fates worse than death. For instance, being unloved or having your head jammed in the toilet by your violent psychotic mother." When I had the honor of visiting Homeboy Industries in the barrio, Father Greg told me, "During gang wars, many kids don't fear death. They fear the horrors of their lives.

Death would be a sign of honor." Consider: are there fates worse than death for you? Looking at things this way will lend a more realistic perspective when you are conquering your fears.

To reprogram fear, a key intellectual surrender is for you to open your mind to the notion that *consciousness isn't limited to time and space*. We are not simply brain-based beings. Think larger. Our consciousness is so much more resilient and multifaceted than the limitations your linear mind can invent. This applies to your deceased aunt Pearl, your cat Cupcake, and all life forms that have passed over. Consciousness is energy; it survives. In this chapter, I'll offer research on near-death experiences (NDEs) revealing that consciousness is "nonlocal," existing outside the brain and body, continuing past death into exciting phases of soul growth. Also you can start reprogramming your fears by considering the following concepts.

Concept 1. The Spiritual Revelation of Observing a Dead Body

Witnessing the absence of the soul can accentuate what your soul is. The soul animates the body making it luminous and engaged. When the soul is gone, the body looks vacant and lightless. Witnessing this striking difference lets you grasp that you're more than your physical self. That's why I suggest to patients and to you that you view a dead body. I realize the mere mention of one triggers fear and loathing. We're not supposed to look. We're not supposed to touch. It's creepy and disgusting. When you can change this perspective, surprising insights will confirm the enduring brilliance of your spirit. Therefore, if you are present to witness someone's death and also have time to stay with the body, consider not looking away or leaving. Be specific. Notice the skin, the eyes, the face. How do your impressions compare with when the person was living? Does the person look odd? Cold? Distorted? Rubbery? Inert? Remote? Peaceful? More beautiful? In what way? Try to remain intuitively unguarded. It's natural to be put off. But see if you can go further. What else can you sense? Notice any intuitive flashes, images, or knowings you may have. Place the palm of your hand a few inches over the body. Can you sense its energy? Or is it gone? Touch the skin. What do you feel? There's wisdom in the experience. Alternatives include visiting museum exhibits on human anatomy such as *Bodies: The Exhibition* (which is also on the Internet), going to a wax museum (which has a less authentic but similar effect), and looking at anatomy books.

Concept 2. Cultivating Faith

To overcome fear, our world's diverse spiritual traditions offer much-needed solace. For instance, Buddhists believe in the liberation of reaching nirvana as you heal past the realm of karma and your spirit evolves. I smiled when one Buddhist friend cheerfully said, "Since we've probably had thousands of incarnations, we already know how to die, so we can relax!" Daoists believe that all paths lead to one divinity, the Tao. Then there are the differing Christian and Islamic conceptions of heaven. In the Sufi tradition, the mystical poet Rumi's death day is described as his "marriage day" when he ecstatically joined with the divine. Faith in the hereafter is a potent tool to overcome fear. However, faith is intensely personal. When you're up at three in the morning with a head full of fear, just staring at the ceiling, faith must be authentic, not just some theory or politically correct idea.

Concept 3. Death Is a Parallel Universe: Leaving the Fear Zone

What matters more than anything I can say to comfort you about death is your own experience of what lies beyond. I can tell you that all fears are merely projections of your insecurities. I can assure you that there's nothing to be afraid of. Still, this won't suffice if you're not intuitively convinced yourself. It's important to understand: *Death is simply a parallel universe that exists simultaneously with our lives. It is not the end.* The membrane between us and the other side is thinner than you think. You can access death through intuition. With that in mind, I offer the following meditation journey for you to experience death and the afterlife firsthand.

A MEDITATION JOURNEY INTO DEATH

The shamanic tradition uses the potent inner process of journeying to explore different levels of consciousness and obtain insights that will help us better understand ourselves and the universe. Here we'll use it to explore death.

1. *Relax and let go.* Sit upright in a comfortable position. Take a few slow, deep breaths. Feel the warmth of your breath as air passes through your lungs and out your mouth. Be completely present. For a few minutes, inhale and then exhale. Go slow. Soften your shoulders, chest, belly, and legs. No guarding or holding back. Then focus on what you love the most. It could be a person, an animal, a deep blue lake, or the divine. Whatever you select, let beauty and love surround you. Allow your heart to open until you feel centered and secure.

2. *Invite death in.* When you're at ease, get ready to silently invite death in. If old ideas or fears intrude, let them pass by like clouds in the sky. Visualize death as a presence, a force. At a safe pace, ask death to come closer. Go as slow as you like while exploring this realm of energy, sounds, visions, and sensations. First visualize death as being ten feet away from you. What do you sense? Colors? Fragrances? Sounds? Do tears come? Do you feel relief? Let yourself surrender to it all. Then, gradually shorten the distance. Five feet . . . three feet . . . two feet . . . a foot. No hurry. At each stage, ease into it. How do your perceptions change? What else are you learning? Notice any spontaneous visions or insights but don't cling to them. Concentrate on your breath. Rely on your intuition to signal when to proceed.

3. *Surrender to death.* Gently, slowly, allow yourself to merge with death. Become one with it. Dissolve into spirit as awareness of your body slips away. Pure energy. All heaviness recedes. You grow lighter and lighter. Take a moment to orient yourself. How do you feel? Calm? At peace? Confused? Exhilarated? What are you observing? Is there silence? Music? Light? Does anyone or anything look familiar? Do you feel relief? Welcomed home? Notice it all.

Cling to nothing. Breathe into the sweetness, unbound by physical constraints. Breathe out all pain and concerns. Breathe in the ecstasy of spirit. Breathe in the boundlessness of love. No separation. No holding. Let death carry you. You are rising. You are glowing. You are floating like a feather in a never-ending sky! Stay with the experience until it feels complete. Remember what happened. In the future, you can come here again.

4. *Return to your body.* Gradually prepare yourself to return to your body. Clearly picture your physical self: your clothes, hair color and style, jewelry, makeup—the more details the better. Let gravity draw you back to your body, toward earth and the material world. Inwardly express gratitude for what you've been shown. Then solidly reconnect with your feet, legs, arms, hands, abdomen, chest, neck, and head, fully grounding yourself. Take as long as you need making the adjustment.

If you feel scared or hesitant during this meditation, it's fine to stop. Let what you've learned sink in. Later, when it feels right, go further. Some people prefer to practice this surrender meditation in stages. Check in with yourself. Honor your own pace.

Journeying into death is possible and safe. Many people fear that if you try to explore death, you'll die. Wrong. My Daoist teacher says, "When you can accept death, the path gets longer." Your lifeline truly extends into eternity and becomes richer in the now. Sometimes after an exhausting workday, I purposely meditate on death to replenish myself. I also do this if I'm creatively blocked. It feels like I'm reattuning to an ancient, eternal drumbeat. Bursts of new ideas can break through. Death is a muse that inspires. Thus, it makes sense that we'd benefit from the same creative boost when we finally transition out of the body. There is no harm involved at all.

I offer this meditation to patients, terminal or not, to defuse fear. Often when one nears death, there's an urgency to glimpse what's next. In such cases, I integrate this meditation into psychotherapy. As a physician, I want to support patients through this transition. Even

if someone is in perfect health, experiencing death through meditation can be life-changing. It's not only a look forward but a portal
through time to a holy place where we partake of divinity. Afterward, we resume our lives refreshed.

SPIRITUALLY SURRENDER TO DEATH AND GRIEF: AN EXERCISE IN HUMILITY AND FREEDOM

Ultimately, the ecstasy of spiritual surrender means letting go to
grief, death, and the beyond. It requires humility and the renuncia-
tion of control. This applies whether we are losing a loved one or are
ready to pass over ourselves. Many patients have asked, "Judith, what
happens when we die?" My response, which took years to have the
courage to stand behind with my whole being, is, "We don't die." As
a physician I've spent decades with the troubled, the tormented, the
very ill, and the dying. All this is at the heart of my medical practice
and what I've learned about our lives. I've also devoted decades to
spiritual growth and intuition, including studying Daoism. So what I
tell patients about dying is based on a profound commitment to what
I've worked so hard to recognize and make sense of. Therefore my
conviction is: Yes, you surrender the transient temple of the body but
your soul, which is way larger than your ego, endures.

Still, your soul's journey requires change: change of location,
change of characters, change of form. As is said in Ecclesiastes, "To
everything there is a season, and a time for every purpose under
heaven." Though naturally you grieve the loss of your current life
and loves, change is definite. My Daoist teacher also says, "Heaven is
not a dead-end road. Work is longer than life."

Nothing lasts forever. Eventually our time will run out. Spiritually surrendering to death means risking total annihilation in service
of integration. But don't worry: the point of shedding your physical
identity is for your soul to grow, not to destroy you. You awaken
again and again in different forms, an infinite process of becoming

more whole. The life-death cycles are designed to help you evolve into the most beguiling light you can imagine.

A compelling reason I—and I hope you—avidly practice this book's surrender techniques is to be as prepared as possible for the spiritual surrender of death. Do you realize how hugely important that is? When you pass over, you want to transition smoothly, not be drawn back by lingering earthly attachments. The Tibetan Buddhists believe that there are different *bardos*, intermediate states between life and death. Ideally you see the pure light and ascend to higher levels of consciousness. Problems occur when unresolved desires, obsessions, and resentments about money, possessions, or people (including your ex-spouse or ex-boss who may seem to lack any redeeming qualities) prevent you from moving on. These nasty attachments have an intense magnetism that can keep your soul stranded in *bardo* states of suffering. For some, the earth itself is considered a *bardo* of obsession with the hellish emotional pain that comes from clinging to whatever preoccupations you're gripped with. We're attached (in Sanskrit, *samudhaya*) and so we suffer (*duhkha*). This is the Tibetan Buddhist view. As a physician, working with so many people who have suffered in so many different ways, I know all too well the cost of obsessions, the power they have to pull you into a personal hell.

Surrendering Your Obsessions: Beware of Hungry Ghosts

The Buddhist Wheel of Life, depicting the Six Realms of Existence, includes the hungry ghosts or *pretans* located between the nonhuman animal kingdom and what is called the hell realms of fire and ice. Buddhists warn us about hungry ghosts: insatiable, withered creatures suffering the torments of greed, abuse of power, and other unwholesome obsessions. Their hunger can never be fulfilled, no matter how much they consume.

Hungry ghosts aren't just in other realms. They're in us and in other people too. Since I'm no stranger to experiencing the hell of obsessions, I am dedicated to freeing myself from this emotional trap, a humbling endeavor that has brought me to my knees more than once. How can we heal the hungry ghost within? First, with humility. The starving parts of us can have incredible power. They command respect. Second we must honestly, compassionately begin to soothe these places in ourselves. Compassion for our own emptiness feeds our starvation and supports spiritual fulfillment by opening our hearts.

Buddhist scholar Robert Thurman told me about a scene he translated from a sutra, a sacred verse. He said, "A bodhisattva of compassion goes to hell and floods it with tears from his thousand eyes to put out the red-hot broiling fires. His compassion beams those suffering beings out of hell." Our compassion can save us and others too. Spiritual surrender means accepting that obsessive desires are bottomless pits of need that can't bring lasting happiness. Whether you're a crack addict or are hooked on pleasure or money (I love Charles Dickens's image of Scrooge's ghost chained to his money box), the ongoing spiritual practice of surrendering these attachments can free you now and in the hereafter.

A MANTRA TO SPIRITUALLY SURRENDER YOUR OBSESSIONS

To release yourself and all hungry ghosts from the suffering of obsessive desires, recite this compassion prayer: "Om mani padme hum." Use this mantra as many times as needed. In addition, those who are dying can repeat it to gain a sense of peace as they go. In the Buddhist tradition, it is said that one syllable from each word has the power to send nourishing light rays to whatever hell you're in and draw you out of it.

The Spiritual Surrender of Grief

Grief is spiritual surrender in action, a deep sorrow and suffering catalyzed by loss and death. You courageously let go of attachments when someone or something you love—a relationship, a job, your health—has been taken away, or when physical death occurs.

Love is a high-stakes surrender. When you love profoundly you risk everything, including the pain of loss and grief. No half measures would ever dignify the heart. As one patient with a dedicated spiritual practice told me, "I've heard all the theories and the how-tos about death, but there is still a deep sadness about having to let go. That's the price of love."

While grieving, I urge you to stay open and brave. No way around it: grieving is rough. I know how brutally unfair losing someone can feel. I understand why some of my patients want to shut down and guard themselves against the searing agony of loss instead of opening to it in service of their healing. Still, squashing the potent energy of grief leads to only depression, physical pain, and other symptoms, plus an eerie dissociation from yourself and the rest of life. Unlike the slogging inertia of depression, grief has a healing trajectory that seeks to resolve itself. I tell my patients and you: to heal, you must surrender to grief since it ultimately carries you forward with a more open heart.

Flowing with Waves of Grief: Mourning and Surviving Loss

I'm attracted to the depth in people. Grief is a reaction to loss that can deepen you. It is strangely yet wondrously liberating if you can hang in there during the intensity. To me, *grief is a form of passion.* Try to flow with it rather than attempting to change it, resist it, or get it over with. As I've learned from experiencing the death of both my beloved parents, grief comes in waves. You're suffering, then you're better, then a wave of sorrow rises up and overcomes you again. You can't control or hurry grief. The pain lessens with time but it can well up over the years spontaneously, especially on anniversaries of deaths. Whenever grief arises, it is vital to allow yourself to cry. Surrendering to the tears of grief, not holding them back, cleanses your soul and hastens healing.

In psychiatrist Elisabeth Kübler-Ross's classic book *On Death and Dying*, she presents common stages of grief. Denial: "This can't be happening." Anger: "I'm furious about the loss." Bargaining: "I promise I'll be kinder if you just bring him or her back." Depression:

"How can I go on? Why try? Life is just unfair." Acceptance: "I'm crushed but I'm coming to terms with the loss." We all have a different time frame for these stages. And they may occur in different order. You surrender when you allow your emotions to flow spontaneously as you mourn fully.

Mourning is a healthy expression of grief. The rituals of mourning you prefer are shaped by your culture, religion, and beliefs. Specifically, how can you mourn? Visiting the gravesite of a loved one on special dates may be comforting. Or keeping a photo album to remember the person lets you celebrate him or her. In Judaism, family and friends sit shiva for about a week. They gather in prayer, bring food, and reminisce to provide survivors loving support. Mourners know they are not alone during this difficult transition. The Irish wake is a time of rejoicing in a person's life, exchanging stories about the loved one, singing traditional songs and laments, drinking and sharing meals. In other cultures, there are varied and sometimes dramatic expressions of mourning, including tearing at one's clothes. Do what is most comforting. How you mourn is personal. There is no "correct" way to do it.

Like many of us, you might find that a heartwrenching aspect of grieving is releasing your attachment to a loved one's physical form—how the person looked, smelled, sounded, or felt in your arms. Even when you have strong spiritual faith, this can be a difficult, lonely journey. The harsh fact is, the person can no longer relate to you in ways you've depended on. You can't talk to him or her on the phone, give or get a hug, or make love with this person—all of which is inconceivably sad to confront. Still, to achieve closure, you must accept this new reality and treasure your memories. As you adjust more to letting the physical version of the person go, your spiritual surrender then becomes opening your mind to different ways of contacting your loved one through intuition, meditation, and dreams. In the next section, I'll show you how to feel your loved ones nearby during quiet moments.

Seeking loving support will help you heal and surrender your pain. Even if your grief feels private, being stoic or isolating yourself can make you depressed. Talk to supportive friends, family, a therapist, or a spiritual guide. Journal about your feelings. Don't censor them. Rail at the universe. Get angry at God. Do whatever you need to do. Bereavement support is a great benefit that hospice care offers survivors. The period after losing someone can be a roller coaster of emotions, a trying adjustment that includes financial pressures and helping children cope. Bereavement counseling provides tender loving care and guidance to help you acclimate to this new reality.

Spiritually surrendering to grief and releasing your physical attachment to others is eased by cultivating humility for the elegance of the birth-death cycle. Even in the midst of terrible melancholy, it's possible to find awe in the alchemy of change—an emotional paradox I experienced when my mother was in a coma and nearing death in the hospital. Sitting at a mother's deathbed is about as pure as pure gets. Staying there for endless hours, I became entranced by the beauty of her body, her lovely hands, her soft pink belly rising and falling with each labored breath. Looking at her, I saw the horizontal caesarian section scar above her womb and saw myself as a newborn being raised out of her into the world. Circles get completed. Parent-child roles become reversed. Just as Mother had ushered me into this life, I had the honor of ushering her out. There could be no consolation for losing her, but the roles we fulfilled for each other in our time together felt satisfying, rich, and complete.

Nature never promises us that anything in the material world will last forever. The big wheel keeps on turning. What nature does give us is the blessings of cycles, growth, and the mystery of change. Certainly, losing a loved one who's ninety and has led a full life can feel more organic than grieving for a younger person or child who dies suddenly from an accident, violence, or a virulent cancer. But as much as you are torn apart by loss, the grieving process is necessary if you want to heal. Offering no resistance, even during the harrowing surrender of loss, can impart unsuspected ecstasy in ways that may surprise you and broaden your experience of the world.

The Sacred Deathbed: Honor Love's Final Moments

Grieving isn't just for survivors. It's also a spiritually important sur-render for those who are dying. When working with terminal pa-tients, I support them in gently letting go of their bodies, this life, and everything they have known and loved. I help them see that they are shedding an old identity in favor of another luminous one. Granted, this is a tall order, but it can be mindfully accomplished if the transi-tioning person is open. How? I guide patients to find faith in a higher power. I meditate with them so they can glimpse the light on the other side. I hold their hand as they grieve or as they are transition-ing, sending energy, hope, and faith so they can be peaceful, even smiling when they go. As patients get closer to death, their interest in life often slips away as if preparing their attention for what comes next. When the dying can grieve well during the very final losses they face, less baggage drags them down as they start to fly.

Still, not everyone who's dying wants to address these emotions or any of the surrenders to grief I mentioned. Some patients aren't afraid to go so a lot of words aren't necessary to prepare them. Once when I worked in a hospice there was a Holocaust survivor who had lung cancer. Right before she died she sat up in bed, said the *shema* (a sacred prayer pledging her love to God) in Hebrew, lay back down, closed her eyes, and passed over. She knew her moment had come and she made a stunningly graceful exit.

I am aware that people experience grief and death differently, some more quietly than others. You don't want to badger your father or mother to express his or her emotions or to "find God" if it's not his or her style. One of my patients, a sports fanatic, just wanted to watch a Lakers game in his final moments and his wife respected his wishes. However, I've watched some well-meaning, caring people impose ridiculous expectations on their dying relatives. This isn't useful! Though spiritual awareness can greatly enhance the ease of transitioning—and I always discuss this with a terminal patient—how or if people find a higher power is their business. Soon enough they will find out.

Be clear: If someone is dying, this is their moment. It's his or her deathbed. Not yours. You must defer to the person's every need and wish. Your job is to help your loved one be happy and leave in peace. As Aldous Huxley wrote, "Lightly, my darling, lightly. Even when it comes to dying. Nothing ponderous, or portentous . . . Just the fact of dying and the fact of the Clear Light." Despite how people choose to cope outwardly, remember that grief is built into the dying process. In the end, we all know we have to let go. Giving people some credit is a sign of respect.

Also realize that the timing of when you or a loved one dies naturally is out of your control. Years ago, when my soul mate Labrador retriever Pipe was dying (she waited until I graduated from medical school), I called my mother from the animal hospital. She rushed across town to meet me. Arriving, she saw me sitting in the kennel crying, Pipe in my arms. "You must say goodbye and leave," she tenderly advised. "Pipe will fight to stay alive if you stay." I knew Mother was right. My love was holding Pipe here. Agonizing as it was, my mother and I went home. My sweet dog died soon afterward.

At a deathbed, try to surrender expectations about when a passage will occur. My Daoist teacher believes the time of our death is predestined. He says, "You can run from death but if you're meant to go, even if you travel to the ends of the earth, an airplane will still fall on you there." The same sense of fatedness is true of who is present when we die. I've heard of a few psychotherapists who've died suddenly in mid-session with a patient—quite a challenge for the patient to process i am sure! Or perhaps you wanted to be with your sister at her passing and you were there, adoring her completely. What you desired was meant to be. But sometimes spirit has another plan and this is not possible. Frequently I've seen how spouses leave the deathbed for just a few minutes—to grab a cup of coffee, to go to the bathroom—and suddenly their beloved passes over. If this happens to you, you didn't do anything wrong! You must trust the organic timing of someone's passage. Showing up for a person in such a profound way is a holy testament to the strength of your heart and devotion.

A sacred deathbed is a highly intimate experience. It must be cocooned in a bubble of loving protection for the transitioning person and for attending friends and family. Regrettably, not everyone honors its sanctity. Recently, I was shocked to receive a call from a reality TV show producer asking, "Can you recommend dying patients who would allow us to film their last moments in order to educate millions of viewers about death?" Whether the producer's motives were altruistic or he was simply exploiting the dying for ratings, his claim that "the cameras won't be intrusive" showed an audacious disrespect for the privacy of the deathbed. A camera crew that's not intrusive? Come on. With as much tolerance as I could muster, I declined to participate in the show. I also explained the absurdity of a psychiatrist risking a terminal patient's trust and the confidentiality of therapy by inquiring, "Would you like to be filmed as you die?" Though my response probably made little impact on the producer, I'm pleased to say I never heard of that reality show materializing on air.

To make leaving this world feel a little safer and less haphazard, it's freeing (not morbid) to visualize your perfect death and clarify your goals for the passage. Setting your intention brings clarity to the experience. For instance, shaman Hank Wesselman told me he wants "a clean getaway." Dannion Brinkley, tireless advocate of dying veterans, said, "I want a death where I don't come back!" I agree with both of these men about preferring (if the choice were mine) to move on from this suffering planet without incarnating here again. As much as I am crazy about being alive, I am eager to experience places of even higher love. I'm also moved by the following responses from a mini-survey I took among other friends and patients when I asked them about their wishes about passing on (see page 367).

One friend told me a charming account of her grandmother's death. She said, "Grandma announced to everyone at ninety-five that she was having her hair done because she would be leaving overnight. My father called her the next morning and Grandma answered the phone, saying "Shit! I'm still here." She died the next night after a full life with her sense of humor intact.

WHAT IS YOUR PERFECT DEATH?

---

1. Knowing I haven't left a big mess.
2. Quick and painless.
3. Watching the sun rise with my beloveds.
4. Dying in my sleep at the end of a three-hour massage (but not so great for the massage therapist!).
5. When I am old and fast asleep.
6. Having an orgasm.
7. Death by chocolate.
8. Quickly in the wee hours of the morn without anyone watching.
9. Fast—no lingering, dementia, pain, or drugs.
10. Holding my partner's hand or him holding me.
11. Being utterly alive in an ecstatic moment of bliss.
12. In a magnificent fireball.

As of today, my perfect death would be writing during the day, soaking in a hot bath, making love to my partner, then passing away in a dream—all the while staying right in there enjoying my last tastes of sensuality in everything. Natalie Goldberg, Buddhist teacher and writing guru, talks about "writing as a practice" in life and how one can also use writing as a practice into death. One last time, I'd like to write like a wild woman. Then I'd let my physical self go! When the time comes, we'll see what actually transpires. But for now, my vision of death sounds to me like nirvana.

To prepare for this surrender, contemplate your own priorities. See which scenario of death appeals to you. Addressing death with a lightness of being rather than dread is liberating. It also clarifies your place in the universe with a loving sense of realism. I encourage you to start this conversation about passing over with yourself and others in order to lessen your grief about departing someday. The next exercise will help you accept death as another part of life and allow you to spiritually surrender to the journey onward.

Ask yourself, "How would I like to pass over? Where would I be? Whom would or wouldn't I want to be with? Or would I like to be alone? What is the ideal environment? Would I be awake and aware? Asleep? Would I like music? What scents would I prefer? What about the lighting? Would I want to go fast or more slowly?"

Picture the details of what would be most perfect and comforting for you. Write these down in a journal so you document them. Be sure to inform loved ones of your wishes so they can be carried out.

SURRENDER TO THE MYSTERY OF THE AFTERLIFE

After you die, where do you go? Are there other dimensions? Does your identity survive? Can you be certain of the lights of eternity? How can you stop worrying and know that you'll be fine? I'll offer scientific and intuitive evidence that your consciousness survives in nonlocal realities beyond our local physical world.

Since the word *death* has been ruined by too many scary connotations, I propose removing it from our vocabulary. It's more useful to view death as simply a natural extension of nonlocal consciousness into more timeless realms. Our being isn't forever limited to living in California, Kansas, or Paris or even in this body or on this planet. Think of it this way: at death, we are liberated from a small container to adventure in an infinite sky far beyond the world we know. Whether this is a new direction or simply a break before you reincarnate here to continue your soul work in a different body (as Buddhists and Kabbalists believe), feel the wonder and possibilities of it all. Don't overthink it. Surrendering to the mystery of an afterlife comes down to trusting your mind, heart, and intuition.

Scientific Evidence of the Survival of Consciousness:
Near-Death Experience (NDE) Research

With extraordinary new advances in cardiopulmonary resuscitation, which can revive patients after cardiac arrest (clinical death is reversible for up to a few hours), numerous survivors worldwide have given accounts of near-death experiences. In fact, a whopping 4.2 percent of Americans—more than thirteen million people—have reported having had an NDE! Who has them? Survivors of life-threatening crises such as a cardiac arrest on the operating table, stroke, shock from blood loss, and near-fatal drownings or car crashes.

What is a near-death experience? This is when people who've crossed over the threshold of death have come back to report what they found. Their descriptions are compellingly similar. Often people see a beautiful white light, a tunnel, and deceased relatives and friends who meet them. They feel enormous love, even euphoria, safety, and a sense of coming home. They sometimes report feeling a strong draw to continue moving into the light. There's often a sense of hyperreality: colors are crisper, sounds more resonant, emotions and memories more intense. Some are sent back to life, having been told, "It is not your time yet." While having an NDE, people remember every detail of their lives; there is no amnesia.

Additionally, many survivors report having dramatic out-of-body experiences where they peacefully hover over themselves, looking down from above. This is the common scenario. A patient goes into cardiac arrest and "codes" during surgery. The medical team rushes to give CPR. Meanwhile, the patient calmly surveys all this from many feet in the air, observing everything, overhearing conversations (later documented as accurate when the patient regains consciousness). Near-death researcher and physician Pim Von Lommel told me, "I recall one man who the ER nurse said was cyanotic [blue from lack of oxygen] but when revived remembered the nurse who had taken off his glasses and put them on the crash cart while he was 'dead' and floating outside his body. Apparently the nurse almost went into cardiac arrest herself upon hearing this!" Simultaneously, during an NDE, people experience a state of grace and insight. Often they go through what researchers call a "life review" where they see all they've experienced—things they regret and would've done differently and what they did with goodness and love. Afterward, some people develop newfound healing and intuitive abilities.

The NDE is usually transformational, providing profound insights into survivors' lives and priorities (such as expressing more love). Survivors see that love is the force that holds the world together and also connects us to the beyond. And, like Dannion Brinkley, who had an NDE when he was struck by lightning, they realize that there's nothing to be afraid of. No wonder Dannion told me that he doesn't want to reincarnate here again after his life is over. Since NDE survivors have seen that they clearly still exist outside of their bodies, their fear of death disappears. That is so liberating.

My friend Kheller had an NDE after a near-fatal motorcycle crash when he was living in Bali. He experienced the brilliant light and the feeling that he was being cocooned in love. He told me, "When I regained consciousness in a small primitive hospital, I felt content and complete. I thought I was dying but I wasn't afraid. A small circle of loving friends who had been living in Bali too surrounded my bed and I thought about them: 'You are my final moments. This is a perfect way to go.' Though I am thankful I survived, the NDE changed me. I had gazed in amazement at what Einstein called 'the moving beauty of the eternal.'"

In a groundbreaking article published in the prestigious medical journal the *Lancet*, Pim Van Lommel argues that the NDE phenomenon is authentic—that it can't be reduced to imagination, fear of death, hallucination, psychosis, drug effects, or oxygen deficiency, as some scientists contend. Most patients are permanently, positively changed by an NDE. Thus the current conventional medical view regarding consciousness and the brain must be expanded to more accurately understand what happens to these patients.

As a physician, I'm interested in the commonalities of NDEs. During my intuition workshops, I experiment with replicating these findings. However, to avoid cueing the group, I don't initially reveal my intention. Here's what I do. In an exercise, I train the participants to intuitively read others simply by tuning in to a first name. I select the name and repeat it aloud. I then ask the group to tune in to whatever images, flashes, or gut feelings they sense from the name. Afterward, I provide feedback about the accuracy of their intuitions.

I'm consistently fascinated by what happens when I repeat "Margaret," a friend's name. Each time people begin sharing impressions such as "I see bright white light," "It feels like heaven," "I am overwhelmed with love," "I have a sense of weightlessness and euphoria," and "Margaret was ill but she's not sick anymore." Some people even say, "I think she's passed over." In fact, my friend Margaret died years earlier at age eighty from a debilitating lung disease. You can imagine how powerful it is when the group discovers this—that, most likely, they were picking up intuitions from the other side, perhaps even heaven! My group's descriptions are stunningly consistent with common NDEs. Tuning in like this—focusing on the name of someone who has passed over, then noting what you intuitively pick up—lets you make contact and get a sense of their well-being.

What all of this suggests is that our consciousness, the thing that makes us who we are, doesn't die just because we are pronounced dead. Max Planck, father of quantum mechanics, said, "I regard matter as derivative from consciousness. . . ." If he's right—that matter (you and me) originally came from consciousness—it makes sense that when our bodies (matter) are gone, we will become pure consciousness again. I hope this helps to reassure you that you were fine before you came here and that you will be fine afterward. You're just going through a metamorphosis that occurs with all sentient life.

As part of your surrender to the possibility of an afterlife, I'd like you to contemplate that your consciousness is quite skilled at existing in nonlocal ways, independent of space and time. Let yourself absorb and contemplate this. Understanding the enormity of your spirit's scope and the versatility of your consciousness will let you approach death less apprehensively.

Communication After Death: Mediums, Ouija Boards, Visitations, and Dreams

In the recent *Time* magazine cover story "Rethinking Heaven," a Gallup poll revealed that 85 percent of all Americans believe in heaven. What is heaven? Is it real? Can we find it? In our discussion of afterlife communication, my desire isn't to convince you of anything. Rather, I want to present information. Then you can intuitively decide for yourself.

By now, you know I have a profound belief in spirit and in the sweetness of eternity that lies ahead for all of us. But truly, accepting this yourself is a very personal matter and depends, at least in part, on how much you're willing to trust what you sense. It's fine if you can't totally surrender to the idea of an afterlife. It's fine if you want to hold back a little or a lot on committing to conclusions. With this particular topic, the linear brain can go crazy trying to defend its limited material version of reality. Don't force anything but be curious. Yes, there have been frauds and charlatans involved in afterlife communication who cause people to be wary but there is truth out there too. When you can let your mind open just a crack without cynicism or defensiveness then you're inviting the mystery to work with you, to be a partner in your own awakening.

From the beginning of history, humans have tried to contact the dead. It's a primal urge to want to know what happens to loved ones and to ourselves when our time here is over, particularly as the passage nears. In Native American traditions, shamans fulfill this role as messengers between realms. In ancient Greece, people from all walks of life, including kings, consulted the oracle of Delphi, a trusted seer who provided guidance about everything from love to strategies of war. In the Old Testament, the Witch of Endor was said to have raised the prophet Samuel's deceased spirit so that the Hebrew king Saul could consult his former mentor about a battle plan. And of course, Jesus had the gift of love strong enough to raise the dead, a depth of love I pray for.

However, the practice of mediumship with séances didn't become popular in the United States and Europe until the advent of spiritualism in the mid-nineteenth century. Mediums such as Helena Bla-vatsky and mediumship supporters such as Arthur Conan Doyle, author of the Sherlock Holmes stories, helped give spiritualism cred-ibility. Séances were even held in the White House and at royal pal-aces. Currently in the United Kingdom, mediums are plentiful and continue the spiritualism tradition.

What is the medium's role? Believers feel they are a clear chan-nel conveying messages from the other side, a go-between who con-nects a departed individual's spirit with those of us who are still here. In terms of nonlocal consciousness, mediums are thought to extend their awareness beyond linear time to access additional lev-els of information. Whether a medium is simply picking up intuitive data about loved ones or is actually communicating with them is an ongoing debate among consciousness researchers. However, from a therapeutic standpoint, the great potential value of mediums is that they can convey that the deceased loved one is fine and that there is nothing to worry about. This is a useful contribution to the grieving process that can help mourners find comfort and peaceful closure. Also, maybe for the first time, grasping that an afterlife is possible can feel incredibly reassuring to survivors. But is the medium sim-ply telling you what you want to hear? Are these messages merely "wish fulfillments" as strict Freudians would claim? That's where your intuition is key. In this area, no one else's opinion matters. Most important, you must gauge the authenticity of the medium's message by trusting your gut feelings, your deepest instincts, and how the ex-perience resonates in your core.

Over the years, I've had several productive sessions with medi-ums. In the United Kingdom, I saw a wonderfully prim and proper woman in her late sixties who relayed important truths about a late colleague whom I was conflicted about, as well as provided insight into current relationships that needed clarity. She also made me laugh when she told me, "You have more friends on the other side than you do here!" I knew exactly what she meant. I am blessed to have treasured friends but I've always sensed that I have an even larger cheering section out there. How did I know she wasn't just fabricating something? If a person—a friend, a medium, anyone—

says something to me, I can feel what intuitively rings true. Musician Quincy Jones told me about his own intuition: "I listen for the goose bumps!" I do too. I've reached the point where I trust my intuition. I surrender to it. Doing so has served me well for a long time.

Because I have tremendous respect for the power of nonlocal communication with the other side, I urge you to be discerning in this area. I've seen some people get into trouble by "playing" with Ouija boards. This is not just a game. When two people put their hands on the pointer (which spells out the message) and call in spirits to give them messages, they have no idea who will answer, nor the quality of the advice they will get. I've had some patients get terrified by horribly wrong declarations the Ouija board has spelled out, such as "Your wife is betraying you" or "You will soon be very ill." That's why I advise staying away from Ouija boards and relying on your own intuition or a trusted intuitive advisor instead.

Opening to Visitations and Dreams

Have you ever had a dream about a departed loved one? An intriguing aspect of surrendering to nonlocal awareness and the possibility of an afterlife is being receptive to our loved ones reaching out to us in visitations and dreams. Just because our intimates aren't communicating to us in the conventional fashion doesn't mean they can't do so in other ways. Again, your linear brain may find this outlandish but to your intuition there's nothing supernatural about it. Once you get used to the concept, such communication can feel perfectly natural and even exciting.

What is a visitation? It's a sighting from the other side. Think of it as a visit from a friend like any other but the visitor is not quite like you or me. He or she is the same person you knew, only the pure-energy version. Practically speaking, for the purposes of interacting, it doesn't matter whether these visitors are in their bodies or not. You are still able to connect in a tender though more limited way. A visitation can occur as a waking apparition or vision; as feeling a person's presence; as a scent, a touch, a voice, a song; or in a dream.

Though most of us aren't accustomed to such intense overlaps with other realities, you don't have to be afraid. Over my years of medical practice, many patients have shared comforting visitations they've had from deceased family, friends, and animal companions. Interestingly, these visitations happened whether or not my patients had previously believed in such things.

Typically, in a visitation, loved ones appear in their prime. They're not suffering any longer. Commonly, those who've passed on want to reassure you that they are all right. After the recent death of one patient's husband, a proud former Marine Corps officer, she told me, "While I was washing dishes, Joe suddenly appeared out of the corner of my eye. He was in uniform and saluted me, smiling and glowing with health. It was very healing for me to see that he looked so marvelous."

Often visitations happen at the exact time of someone's death. These can range from gentle and touching to highly dramatic. Here are some examples. At the moment a patient's brother died, she was sitting in her living room and heard her brother's guitar, which was leaning against the wall, suddenly strum a few chords from his favorite Willie Nelson song, "On the Road." She was startled, naturally, but later when she learned the time of his death, she had to smile—the song was a perfect preamble to his path on the big road ahead. Another patient's grandfather clock, a family heirloom, stopped at the very minute her grandfather died. Another smelled the scent of her best friend's perfume. One patient was checking on her five-year-old daughter, who told her, "Grandma is here tickling me!" My patient asked, "Where, honey?" Her daughter pointed and then kept insisting she was right there by the bed. Yet another patient actually had lightning strike his home the instant his rambunctious mother-in-law died! When my aunt passed away, I felt her stroke my cheek as I was falling asleep. When an ex-boyfriend died, I felt him sweetly come to hold my hand.

Similarly, over the centuries, numerous people on the edge of death—astronauts, polar explorers, pilots, divers—have seen loving presences that guided them to safety. This kind of visitation is called the "third-man factor." For instance, Charles Lindbergh, in his historic transatlantic flight, described presences who were reassuring him and offering details about how to navigate to avoid danger. Then there is the striking account of a 9/11 survivor, a financier, who lay nearly unconscious in a smoke-filled stairwell, heard an invisible presence say, "Get up. You can do this," and then felt the presence literally lift him so he could get out of danger. T. S. Eliot wrote in *The Waste Land*, "Who is the third who walks always beside you? / When I count, there are only you and I together. / But when I look ahead up the white road / There is always another one walking beside you."

It's been postulated that the experience of being close to death can trigger an "angel switch" in the brain that puts us in a mystical state during an emergency. If only a few people had experienced the third-man factor, it might be dismissed as a stress-induced hallucination. But aided by these visitations, all have escaped traumatic events and were led out of harm's way to tell strikingly similar stories.

Sometimes visitations can happen in dreams. Dreaming seems to be an easier place for the departed to make contact. People worldwide have told me about loved ones who have appeared in dreams. A high school student said, "I dreamed I was called to serve as a chaplain for my best friend's funeral. The next day we learned that she had been killed in an auto accident." Similarly, loved ones have appeared in my patients' and my own dreams telling those who remain here that they are okay and that they love us, or imparting specific messages ranging from the practical to the cosmic. For instance, a patient's deceased sister came to her in a dream communicating, "Always take care of Philip," their brother who had schizophrenia. And when I dreamed of my mother soon after she died, she instructed, "Be grateful that your life has so much passion." I heard Mother's wisdom and rarely take for granted the blessing of my passion. Reaching out to loved ones who've transitioned isn't just something mediums can do. Your love is strong enough to cross those bounds, to be heard by companions who aren't as far away as you think. To experience this, practice the following exercise every day for a week until it feels comfortable. Record your impressions in a journal.

SURRENDER TO ETERNAL LOVE: SENSE YOUR BELOVEDS ON THE OTHER SIDE

During quiet moments, close your eyes. In a relaxed state, focus your love on the one who has transitioned. Erase the idea that there's a "here" and a "there." Don't worry about whether communicating is possible or not. Just sit and be present in love, faith, and happiness about your bond with each other. Inwardly invite the person to come closer. With a pure heart, ask to feel, hear, or see him or her. Stay open without pretense or expectation. Then note any intuitions you receive now, later, or in dreams. Do you feel a wisp of movement or breeze? Do you sense the person nearby? Do you have a vivid image or a long-forgotten memory or do you hear a voice? Are you feeling an emotion? Let the tears, laughter, or other feelings flow. That will help you receive the person's messages, subtle or direct. Don't ask others to confirm if these are real. Simply know what you know in appreciation of the link that invisibly connects us all. Accept any signs of communication as a token of goodness that comes from humbly surrendering to the mystery.

THE GRACE OF CLOSURE

Surrendering to the mystery of an afterlife using the above exercise and other strategies I've presented can help you find healthy closure after a loss. Closure means recognizing that an ending has occurred, an acceptance of "so be it"—as painful as it is to begin releasing your physical attachment to someone. Closure gives you a sense of completion or at least a sense of knowing that the relationship had gone as far as it was meant to. You benefit from closure by gaining more peace. Those who've crossed over benefit since there's no pull of unfinished business so they can move on. To honor their journey, and your own, reflect on this Japanese prayer of solace and surrender:

> *Like the day of my birth,*
> *Like the day of my death*
> *Is this day: I begin to travel.*

Closure signals the end of an era for the relationship but not the end of love. Whether you meet again in some other place or time is yet to be seen. For now, though, closure lets you surrender to living fully embodied in the present instead of getting derailed by the past or what you've lost. As poet John O'Donohue wrote, "When you've gone as far as you can go, quietly await your next beginning." Closure allows you to surrender to your future with faith and an open heart.

There are enchanted, compassionate forces operating in the universe if you can allow yourself to open to them. There are invisible hands at work—you can call them angels if you like—that are watching over each one of us. When your loved ones pass over, they may become one of the angels who watch over you. Michelangelo once said, "I saw the angel in the marble and carved until I set it free." Of course, there's no ironclad method to prove or disprove the particulars of the other side. However, the great power that you possess is the crystal-clear knowing of your intuition. My wish is that you can increasingly honor intuition and cherish the bursts of revelation about the mysteries that it offers. Over and over again, your surrender will entail deepening your commitment to what you want to trust, live by, and gain solace from.

The tremendous challenge and promise of this book, from accepting death to succeeding in business to falling in love, is letting yourself be catapulted beyond the ordinary to view all of existence in extraordinary terms. The cycles of light—mortality and immortality—are part of the astonishing adventure of surrender. This path of awakening to wholeness is open to anyone who desires it. Every experience you go through—good, bad, or indifferent—can offer a teaching that enriches the sacred practice of letting go. The artfulness of life, the clumsiness, the grace, the messiness, the faltering, and the clarity are integral to this dance. Breathe deeply with it all. Keep surrendering through the pleasure and the pain. Keep releasing what constrains you as you immerse your body and soul in the cosmic rhythms.

Life is permeable and ever-changing. You can't do it all right. You can't do it all wrong. Relax: imperfection is part of the beauty you're after. Let go to the passionate perfection and imperfection of every-thing. You have just one imperative: live each moment with the most open, generous heart you can have, with the most magic and faith you can summon. Then wildly spread these heart-altering blessings around.

What a relief when you can realize that we're dying all the time and being rebirthed again and again into our own lives, into the heav-ens and hells that constitute our exquisite human experience. Flow-ing with the diverse, sometimes contradictory aspects of yourself is enticing and impressive. Don't run from your changes. Ride them out. Meet power with power. Constantly, in nature, synchronicities of birth and death are paired: your grandmother dies, your daughter is born; a relationship is lost, a love is found; night and day merge into each other with the setting and rising of the sun.

May surrender be your prayer for wholeness that comforts you on your never-ending path of discovery. What I'm certain of is that if you yearn to surrender, if you yearn to be free, everything in the universe will conspire to assist you. Then you'll become more alive, more experimental, more interesting. You are laughing. You are cry-ing. You are old. You are young. You are innocent. You are experi-enced. You are chanting the songs of the eternals. You are falling upward ecstatically into the sky.

I am full of optimism for us all. Your time has come. Our time has come. When surrender is a priority, you are ready to savor an abundant, more fearless life. What you've learned in this book about letting go of fear and embracing an ever-growing ecstasy will keep you attuned to the pulse of your life and your vitality. Lean into your heart, always. Hold back no goodness or passion. Treasure yourself and each other. Our hope, the hope of this planet and human evolu-tion, comes from our dedication to surrendering to the oneness and radiant life force of love.

SURRENDER AFFIRMATION TO PRAISE THE MYSTERY

I am one with my body. I am one with the earth. I am one with the heavens. I am not just my body. I am not just this earth. I surrender to the vastness of spirit, to the infinity of love, to the ecstasy of the unexpected, and to the bounty of happiness I deserve. I surrender to the love of all things in our time and beyond.

Part Five

EMBRACING ECSTASY

'Tis so much joy!
—EMILY DICKINSON
....

THE FINAL SURRENDER

CELEBRATING

THE BLESSING OF JOY

SURRENDER IS THE UNEXPECTED AND UNCOMMON DENOMINATOR that permits you to feel the blessing of joy. Joy comes from letting go of fear, then allowing yourself to experience the everyday miracle of being happy. You will come to find that joy is a habit as much as a gift. It becomes more and more accessible once you realize you are the keeper of your own bliss. Outside events can spark it—the music of your child's laughter, your success taking off, a scarlet blush of sky, your beloved kneeling at your feet with affection. Still, beautiful as these may be, joy is an offering you must ultimately accept or reject. You alone decide how fully you want to surrender to it. You are the only one who can allow joy in and let it heal you.

Being joyful is a courageous choice which makes your path of surrender vital and thrilling. Then your adventurous spirit will guide you to the promised land of love. Along the way, you'll hear tons of "convincing" arguments to perpetuate fear-based, unloving approaches to the world. Use your intuition and common sense to see through them. Only surrender to principles, emotions, and actions that intuitively feel good and right. By consciously embracing joy—which can become lusciously addictive—you're declaring, "This is the person I want to be and can be." What an incredibly savvy referendum against fear this is. Joy is not naive. By opting to be happy, aware, and free, you are powerful.

Of course, life is fluid: no one is joyful every single second. But the more you get used to the feeling, the more joyful you will be. As for those people you'll encounter who want to dampen your joy because it threatens their fragile sense of self, just smile at them, pray for their happiness if you can, but let their ill will go. Stay grateful for every instant of joy you're blessed with.

Surrendering to joy will help you actualize your dreams. For instance, I tell patients that an effective way to attract a creative job or a devoted partner is to actually let yourself experience the joy of having achieved this. Picture this future as an absolute reality. Feel yourself happy doing the work you desire or in the arms of someone you're passionate about. By experiencing that outcome as already yours, you are manifesting a goal and marshaling the power of joy.

Surrender is urgently necessary for awakening not just on a personal level but also on a global scale. Revolutions will stick only if the inner work is done by the revolutionaries. Heroes need healing too. For all of us, the way to surrender to joy is to surrender your fear. The way to surrender fear is to embrace your heart. The way to surrender war is to address all the painful, shameful, warring aspects of yourself to find peace. Consider this: what if there was no enemy left to conquer? What if all we had were one another and the need to get along, to join the circle, and surrender to the joy of our global community? Social activist Howard Zinn said, "You can't be neutral on a moving train." Therefore, take a stand. How wrong is it to rape our forests and pollute our oceans? How wrong is it to forget our oneness with mother earth? This is great sacrilege, a dishonoring of nature and of life. Don't look to leaders to liberate you. Liberate yourself with your attitudes and choices, over and over again.

Collective change occurs when a critical mass of people alter their consciousness about how they want to live. I advise you to choose joy, not hatred; to choose collaboration and tolerance, not alienation or prejudice. I believe compassion is so powerful it can even mend broken social systems and impel us to heal our earth. When we're in service to love we cannot go wrong. The Dalai Lama said, "If we wish to save the world, we must have a plan, but unless we meditate, no plan will work." I understand this to mean that change isn't just about lip service or altruistic intentions. Our inner life must authentically reflect the change we want to see. Beyond the good advice, beyond the rhetoric and ideas about how to better the world, a critical mass of people must surrender to our capacity for compassion and dedicated action. There's boundless joy in that and a meticulous allegiance to the inherent goodness of humanity.

To that end, I offer this prayer of love for the planet:

Bless all of the earth's creatures, light, dark, or struggling. Bless all the twinkling beings in and around us. Love is large enough to hold us all. Joy is expansive without limit, leaving no one out. May our surrender, our bliss, come from loving ourselves, each other, and the earth.

As you complete this book, let yourself bask in the afterglow of what you've learned about surrender. Revisit what has most resonated within you. As your life unfolds, keep referring to those topics that have more meaning. Slowly absorb the benefits of practicing the art of surrender. It has been said of champions in all fields, "They take their time." Surrender is the epitome of coolness. It's about taking the time to intelligently and intuitively scope out any situation. It's about absorbing joy, not just sporadically but for longer and longer periods while you pursue what's been undiscovered and unexplored. Each day, surrender to the ecstasy of tiny things—a juicy apricot, a tender kiss, a kind word. This cultivates the sacred practice of your happiness, your serenity, the ongoing miracle of feeling so good.

I'm both excited about this book coming to an end and reluctant to let it go out into the world from its home with me in the Venice Canals, California. When I began this holy journey four years ago, I longed to experience surrender more than anything else. Now, as my writing concludes, I see how generous this book has been to me, how much I've softened and learned to let go. I am in the midst of radical change—a great blossoming for which I am profoundly grateful. And yet I yearn to surrender even more as I continue this spiritual path. No doubt life will gladly provide me with that opportunity.

Our joyful duty is to live well, to be positive models for the best that is possible even if we think we'll fall short. Sometimes I feel so young, playing in wonder with whatever is in front of me. Let yourself play in the wonder too. Celebrate your joy, your courage, and all your surrenders as they are presented. You'll grow stronger every day. Believe in yourself as much as I believe in you. Then, together, let's blow the world away with hope. Let's dare to surrender anything that stands between ourselves and our joy.

Selected Reading

Brother Lawrence. *The Practice of the Presence of God and Spiritual Maxims*. Dover Press, 2005.

Csikszentmihalyi, Mihaly. *Flow: The Psychology of Optimal Experience*. Harper Perennial Modern Classics, 2008.

Dalai Lama. *The Art of Happiness: A Handbook for Living*. Riverhead Books, 1999.

Dass. Ram. *Be Here Now*. Crown Publishing, 1971.

———. *Still Here: Embracing Aging, Changing, and Dying*. Riverhead Books, 2001.

Geiger, John. *The Third Man Factor: Surviving the Impossible*. Weinstein Books, 2009.

Greene, Robert. *The 48 Laws of Power*. Penguin Books, 2000.

Ingerman, Sandra and Wesselman, Hank. *Awakening to the Spirit World: The Shamanic Path of Direct Revelation*. Sounds True, 2010.

Kabat-Zinn, Jon. *Mindfulness for Beginners: Reclaiming the Present Moment and Your Life*. Sounds True, 2011.

Muir, Charles and Caroline. *Tantra: The Art of Conscious Loving*. Baby Book, 1989.

Roche, Lorin. *The Radiance Sutras: 112 Getaways to the Yoga of Wonder and Delight*. Sounds True, 2014.

Rosenberg, Marshall. *Nonviolent Communications: A Language of Life*. Puddle Dance Press, 2003.

Somers, Suzanne. *Bombshell: Explosive Medical Secrets That Will Redefine Aging*. Crown Archetype, 2012.

Todeschi, Kevin. *Edgar Cayce on Soul Mates: Unlocking the Dynamics of Soul Attraction*. A.R.E. Press, 1999.

Tolle, Eckhart. *The Power of Now*. New World Library, 1999.

Acknowledgments

I'm grateful to the many people who have generously supported my writing and my spirit:

Richard Pine, literary agent and champion of my work; Shaye Areheart, my soul mate editor with whom I joyously edited chapters at a picnic table by a lighthouse in upstate New York; Gary Jansen, my soul mate in-house editor who has endless patience and devotion and who reminds me to dance on the full moon; Susan Golant and Thomas Farber, word magicians who helped me define the book; Berenice Glass, my best friend who has been with me through thick and thin; and Rhonda Bryant, my angel assistant who is my shaman, sounding board, and friend.

My profound gratitude to the spectacular team at Harmony books: Tina Constable, Mauro DiPreta, Meredith McGinnis, Tammy Blake, Lauren Cook, Linda Kaplan, Karin Schulze, Amanda O'Connor, Jessica Morphew, Cindy Berman, and Wade Lucas.

I also bow in appreciation to friends and family, my precious anam cara: Ron Alexander, Barbara Baird, Barbara Biziou, Dannion Brinkley, Rev. Laurie Sue Brockway, Ann Buck, Roma Downey, Lily Dulan, Felice Dunas, Corey Folsom, Stephen Gaghan, Michael and Stephanie Garcia, Sandra Ingerman, Amy Iverson-Adams, Pamela Kaplan, Cathy Lewis, Camille Maurine and Lorin Roche, Mignon McCarthy, Meg McLaughlin, Richard Metzner, Liz Olson, Dean Orloff, Charlotte Reznick, Robert Rosen, Al Saenz, Stephan Schwartz, Rabbi Don Singer, Leong Tan, Josh Touber, Roy Tuckman, Mary

Williams, and, finally, my parents, Maxine Ostrum-Orloff and Theodore Orloff, still with me, though now on the other side.

In addition, I am indebted to my patients and workshop participants who continue to be my teachers. I have disguised their names and identifying characteristics to protect their privacy.

Index